SAGE was founded in 1965 by Sara Miller McCune to support the dissemination of usable knowledge by publishing innovative and high-quality research and teaching content. Today, we publish over 900 journals, including those of more than 400 learned societies, more than 800 new books per year, and a growing range of library products including archives, data, case studies, reports, and video. SAGE remains majority-owned by our founder, and after Sara's lifetime will become owned by a charitable trust that secures our continued independence.

Los Angeles | London | New Delhi | Singapore | Washington DC | Melbourne

Public Sector Enterprises

in India

Thank you for choosing a SAGE product!
If you have any comment, observation or feedback,
I would like to personally hear from you.

Please write to me at **contactceo@sagepub.in**

Vivek Mehra, Managing Director and CEO, SAGE India.

Public Sector Enterprises

in **India**

Evolution, Privatisation & Reforms

Govind Bhattacharjee

Los Angeles | London | New Delhi
Singapore | Washington DC | Melbourne

First published in 2020 by

SAGE Publications India Pvt Ltd
B1/I-1 Mohan Cooperative Industrial Area
Mathura Road, New Delhi 110 044, India
www.sagepub.in

SAGE Publications Inc
2455 Teller Road
Thousand Oaks, California 91320, USA

SAGE Publications Ltd
1 Oliver's Yard, 55 City Road
London EC1Y 1SP, United Kingdom

SAGE Publications Asia-Pacific Pte Ltd
18 Cross Street #10-10/11/12
China Square Central
Singapore 048423

Published by Vivek Mehra for SAGE Publications India Pvt Ltd and typeset in 10.5/13 pt Adobe Caslon Pro by AG Infographics, Delhi.

Library of Congress Control Number: 2020938403

ISBN: 978-93-5388-372-0 (HB)

SAGE Team: Rajesh Dey, Syed Husain Naqvi and Rajinder Kaur

Contents

Preface

This book originated from the author's teaching of a course on the public sector enterprises (PSEs) in India to the Advanced Professional Programme on Public Administration, which is an MPhil programme for senior government officers and defence personnel, at the Indian Institute of Public Administration (IIPA), New Delhi. Earlier, during his career in civil services, the author had the opportunity to see the working of the public sector undertakings both from inside and outside—from outside as the Assistant Comptroller and Auditor General at the Office of the Comptroller and Auditor General of India in charge of the audit of PSEs and from inside as the Chief Vigilance Officer of two central PSEs.

While preparing the lessons for this course, the author realised that there was no current book on the Indian PSEs, the last book on the subject having been published quite a few years ago. Further, most of the publications on the subject focus on different aspects of operational management of the PSEs such as their finances, human resources, production, etc., but there are very few recent academic publications dealing with their evolution, rise and decline, disinvestment and privatisation, and the reforms undertaken in them. Globalisation has exposed them to serious international competition in which many of our old champions perished or went into the red. There are a lot of lessons to learn from the PSEs of other countries and their experiences with privatisation and reforms, without which no meaningful discussion on Indian PSEs could be complete; on this aspect also, there are very few recent publications. Further, most of the existing publications and articles deal only with the central PSEs, the subject of state PSEs being almost absent from any serious academic discourse. These are the factors that drove the author to write this book in the hope of generating more public debate on the direction of reforms that the Indian PSEs must undertake, including the state PSEs. The focus of this book is on policy reforms and the restructuring of our PSEs, which had driven our economy and directed our industrial growth ever since Independence; they can again be revived energetically with a set of pragmatic measures and some imagination.

The PSEs in India are now passing through churning times, just as the economy is currently in the midst of a severe slowdown, with all core sectors as well as export being on a steep downward spiral. Consumption, which is the major driver of our economy, has slowed down substantially, with credit and investment both taking a hit. The slowdown cannot just be blamed on the global headwinds or on cyclical factors; there are major structural issues and inefficiencies of the factor market that are also equally contributing to the slowing growth, which must be addressed to revive growth. A part of the structural problems also relates to the sub-optimal performance of our PSEs where again the absence of structural reforms is a major constraint, and this is where this subject becomes more relevant now than ever before.

The government seems at last to be biting the bullet of privatisation of the public sector, forced by the compelling task of raising a humongous amount, ₹1.05 lakh crore, from disinvestments of PSEs during the fiscal year 2019–2020, if our fiscal deficit is to be contained at the budgeted level of 3.3 per cent of GDP. With economic growth plummeting well below 5 per cent and the revenue collections, especially from the GST, falling short of expectations, the renewed focus on monetisation of government assets is therefore inevitable to bridge the budgetary gap. The point to note is that this has not emerged from any coherent and consistent policy related to disinvestment or privatisation of the PSEs but from the urgency of the fiscal constraints faced by the government, mostly to finance its burgeoning social sector welfare expenditure. Governments in the past had often changed their stance regarding disinvestment, and this sort of dithering has characterised our disinvestment programme ever since it was launched in the 1990s after the economy was liberalised and the private sector was allowed entry into the areas hitherto reserved exclusively for the public sector.

Until date, some 50 PSEs have been identified by the NITI Aayog, the government's economic think tank, for strategic sale by letting go of the government's control over their management. In its latest announcement in November 2019, the government has spelled out its intent to divest its stakes from five PSEs, including its 53.29 per cent stake in the BPCL, a Maharatna PSE. This is probably the right time for such disinvestment, as the end of the oil age is looming on the horizon and BPCL, which still commands a high price for its shares, can fetch handsome gains; if this is delayed further, BPCL may approach the same fate as BSNL or Air India. But at the same time, another Maharatna PSE, NTPC, is being forced to acquire a smaller PSE, the TDHCIL, a joint venture between the Government of India and the Uttar Pradesh government. This acquisition will put some cash in the hands of the government without adding any value or gain in efficiency to either NTPC or the economy, and the asset will only change hands without the government's control in it being affected in any way. In the process, NTPC's cash reserves will get depleted and the company probably will have to borrow from the banks in future for its working capital or even to pay the salaries of its employees. The flagship oil exploration company ONGC, another Maharatna, suffered the same fate after being nudged to acquire an 80 per cent stake in the KG basin gas block of the Gujarat State Petroleum Corporation, a state PSE under the Government of Gujarat, during 2017–2018, and acquire the refining major HPCL in 2018–2019, which saw ONGC's cash reserve dwindling from ₹13,100 crore in March 2017 to only ₹500 crore in March 2019.

These are classic examples of the multiple conflicts of interest that infest the landscape of the public sector in India, where the government's role as the owner of the PSEs overlap with its roles as their regulator and policymaker. The efficiency, objectivity and profitability of the PSEs suffered as a result for no fault of their own, and they have all along been blamed unfairly for mismanagement and efficiency, for which the government was actually responsible. Despite the veneer of autonomy given to them, the government never refrains from interfering with every aspect of their functioning, often at the cost of their profitability. Bureaucratic and political control as well as interference continue to encroach upon their autonomy, affect their efficiency and stymie their growth. In the landscape of the Indian public sector, even if there is a semblance of autonomy for the central PSEs, at the level of the states, the PSEs permanently remain hostage to the rent-seeking behaviour of unscrupulous politicians and bureaucrats; governments, irrespective of their political dispensation, conveniently use them as instruments for distribution of patronage and buying of loyalty. Any meaningful reform, therefore, most take into consideration both the central and state PSEs, which together account for around 1,600 entities, many of which are dysfunctional, especially at the level of states.

In the context of the Indian public sector, reform has become synonymous with disinvestment and privatisation, driven by the government's need for cash to bridge its fiscal deficit, as already stated. Reform does not necessarily mean privatisation; in accordance with the philosophy of the public sector, even in the context of the liberalised and globalised world of today, the state needs to maintain its presence in the 'strategic areas'—it may even coexist with the private sector in these and other areas. The complete rolling back of the public sector may be fraught with unforeseen risks and may expose the citizenry to merciless exploitation by the private sector. The state also exists to ensure the availability of certain services for its citizens at affordable costs, which the private sector cannot be expected to provide, at least most of the time. Experiences across the world prove that even the public sector can be made as vibrant and efficient as the private sector if appropriate administrative and governance structures are put in place and there is an institutional mechanism to ensure a clear separation in the government's multiple roles in relation to the public sector. We have never bothered to learn from these experiences, even when the government-appointed committees had recommended such reforms. The use of the proceeds of disinvestments has never been for strengthening the entities themselves or for increasing their productivity and profitability. Except a few significant reforms like introduction of MOUs for central PSUs, all other reforms undertaken so far have mostly been of cosmetic nature. The book discusses all these and other relevant issues, based on current data.

The book is divided into seven chapters, the first of which deals with the evolution of the philosophy behind the public sector itself, to provide a proper context to the subject of PSEs. This chapter describes systematically the rise of capitalism and the rise of socialism and communism as a reaction to the pitfalls of unbridled capitalism that creates unprecedented inequality in society, which eventually led to the philosophy of the state ownership of the means of production and distribution, which is how the public sector evolved. This chapter traces the evolution and spread of social democracy and Fabian socialism and the developments in the post-colonial world in which the public sector played a vital role, especially in the newly liberated countries in all parts of the world.

In the second chapter, the nature and scope of the public sector in India have been discussed in the global context. Despite the global predominance of free market economy and structural transformations of national economies leading to downsizing of the public sector, PSEs are still retaining their position as enduring features of the economic landscapes in many countries across the world and are likely to remain so for a long time. On the basis of cross-country data, this chapter then traces the historical evolution of the public sector in India since independence through the various plan periods, the way they are classified and, finally, their administrative and accountability structures.

The third chapter critically examines the performance of the central public sector enterprises (CPSEs) in India, using data from the latest Public Enterprise Survey as well as reports of the Comptroller and Auditor General of India. This chapter also discusses the corporate governance in the CPSEs, especially after the enactment of the new Companies Act, 2013, as also their Corporate Social Responsibility. Likewise, the fourth chapter deals with the performance of the state public sector enterprises (SPSEs) in India using data from the Comptroller and Auditor General's reports relating to different states and other sources as well. This chapter attempts to bring out the anomalies in their structure and functioning, highlights the absolutely laxity in their control and accountability structures and reflects on their use by the respective state governments for own their political ends rather than for the public purposes for which they were created. The recommendations of the various Finance Commissions regarding the SPSEs have also been discussed in this chapter, along with the fact that the states have done precious little to implement these recommendations.

The fifth chapter discusses the central financial sector public undertakings. The financial sector public undertakings include public sector banks, insurance companies and developmental financial institutions. Finance is a complex area, and each of these groups merits a separate book to cover the entire range of issues concerning them. Public sector literature is usually silent on these entities, but given that the banking scenario in India is still overwhelmingly dominated by the public sector banks, which account for more than 60 per cent of the total banking business in India, the author thought leaving these out would render incomplete any discussion on the public sector. Similar logic also applies to the insurance companies. The author has left the developmental financial institutions out of the scope of this book and, in this chapter, has only focussed on reforms and restructuring of the public sector financial institutions and the challenges faced by them, so as to not to render the discussion on the subject unwieldy.

The sixth and the seventh chapters, dealing respectively with privatisation and reforms of the PSEs in India, constitute the focus of this book. In the sixth chapter, the privatisation experiences in India have been compared with similar experiences in different countries across the world, bringing out the lessons we need to learn. Since privatisation is an integral part of the reform process but not the whole of it, we need to nuance our approach very carefully, taking into account all the drawbacks of indiscriminate privatisation that may harm the economy more in the long run, including unintended creation of powerful private conglomerates and hence concentration of wealth in a few hands, leading to a more unequal society. This chapter also discusses the issue of industrial sickness of the PSEs and the institutional architecture to deal with it, including the provisions of the new Companies Act and the Insolvency and Bankruptcy Code, 2016. The observations and recommendations of the Fourteenth Finance Commission have been discussed in detail as also the inputs given by the NITI Aayog on the strategies and plans for future disinvestments.

The last chapter of the book discusses the reform experiences and strategies followed by those countries that have successfully reformed and transformed their PSEs into vibrant and productive entities, with many of these today becoming reputed global brands. They have successfully separated the roles of the government as the owner, regulator and policymaker in respect of the public enterprise, through appropriate institutional mechanisms, to ensure that the public sector always remains at an arm's length from the government, and shields its enterprises from the influence of politicians and bureaucrats. One of these models, the holding company structure, was recommended by a government-appointed panel in India, the Roongta Panel, whose report, ignored so far by successive governments, has also been discussed in detail. The chapter concludes by laying out a roadmap for reforming and rejuvenating our public sector.

Rather than advocating wholesale privatisation and disinvestment of the PSEs and the complete rollback of the state from economic and welfare activities, which we can ill afford at this stage of our development, the book suggests a middle course involving a drastic reduction in the size of the public sector, major reforms at the level of the states, which has become a wasteland of PSEs, to be followed by meaningful reforms in the light of the knowledge and insight gained from similar experiences of other countries. If the book succeeds in generating a debate at a time when the economic and fiscal compulsions are forcing the government to undertake large-scale privatisation even of profitable entities, it will render the effort of writing it a worthy venture.

Acknowledgements

I am grateful to the IIPA for giving me an opportunity to teach a course on Public Enterprises Management in their flagship programme—the Advanced Professional Programme on Public Administration (APPPA)—of which I was the Programme Director of its 45th edition. This interdisciplinary, 10-month-long MPhil programme is attended by senior-level civil service officers from all over the country as well as senior-level officers from all wings of our armed forces. Their long and rich experiences in different areas of administration and governance always lead to newer areas of investigation, and I gained much from these discourses. But for my engagement with this exceptionally bright and talented group of individuals, many of the gaps in my knowledge and analysis would have remained unbridged. I also express my gratitude to my colleagues, especially Professor Geethanjali Nataraj, Professor Ashok Vishandass and Dr Saket Bihari as well as to my friend and former colleague, Pramode Mishra, retired Director General (Commercial) from the Office of the Comptroller and Auditor General of India, for providing constant support and encouragement while writing this book. Shri Sagar Jaiswal of IIT Roorkee provided valuable help in collecting much of the data used in Chapter 2 of this book.

I express my deep gratitude to Dr B. P. Mathur, former Deputy Comptroller and Auditor General of India (Commercial), whose 1999 book *Public Enterprise Management* was one inspiration for this volume, for providing many useful insights. I also benefited hugely from many discussions with my friend Pramathesh Purkayastha, former Executive Director of the NTPC, and learnt many things from his long experiences of working with a major public sector company.

Without support from the rich IIPA library, it would not have been possible to write this book. I express my deep gratitude to all the library staff, especially H. C. Yadav, for tirelessly searching and supplying me with whatever materials and books I needed. I am also grateful to the IIPA management for procuring all the books that I needed.

Last but not least, I owe my gratitude to my wife, Dr Rakhee Bhattacharjee, Associate Professor at JNU, who has been my constant support and critic for the last quarter of a century and whose opinions always matter in improving both my person and my output.

CHAPTER 1

Concept and Philosophy behind the Public Sector

'The difficulty lies not so much in developing new ideas as in escaping from old ones'.

—John Maynard Keynes, *The General Theory of Employment, Interest and Money*

In 1651, Thomas Hobbes wrote in *Leviathan*:

> During the time men live without a common power to keep them all in awe, they are in that condition called war; and such a war, as if of every man against every man. To this war of every man against every man, nothing can be unjust. The notions of right and wrong, justice and injustice have there no place. Where there is no common power, there is no law, where no law, no injustice. Force, and fraud, are in war the cardinal virtues. No arts; no letters; no society; and which is worst of all, continual fear, and danger of violent death: and the life of man, solitary, poor, nasty, brutish and short.

It is because society cannot progress and prosper without order, discipline and peace that we need a state to ensure security of life and property and basic liberties, without which human life would not be worth living. The difficulty lies in the fact that the state's role cannot be confined within predefined limits and boundaries; by the very nature of its political power, a state often exceeds any artificial limits. In other words, states have an inherent tendency to become authoritarian and start controlling people's lives, and developed societies find a way to get through a system of appropriate checks and balances to curb the role of the state so that it does not become a monster. It is another matter that states often still do become authoritarian despite the best of checks and controls, and history is replete with many such examples where the state has penetrated too deep into the socio-economic fabric of society. Whenever this happens, individual liberties are curbed and economic growth takes a beating.

Till the 17th century, nations believed that the productive capacity of the economy and hence the total wealth of a nation was limited by it resources; in any case, even in a nation of abundant resources, the size of the pie was limited since, as population grew, the size of the pie available to each individual would necessarily diminish. To ensure order and stability in society, the value system that evolved associated wealth with vices and poverty with morality. The nations that did not have enough resources had to seek them elsewhere—often in overseas colonies—to increase the size of the total pie available to their people. The idea was not to cut the pie and distribute pieces equally but to ensure that everybody received a piece of the pie big enough for them not to disturb the social order. To finance the colonising ventures, astronomical resources in terms of money, materials, ships and adventurous men willing to risk uncertain voyages and even their lives for the sake of wealth were required. Limited liability joint stock companies were invented in order to raise these resources from not one but multiple individuals, each investing a small sum and receiving profits proportional to that sum so that, in the event of a failure, each risked losing not his/her entire wealth but a small part of it. Some of these companies such as the Dutch East India Company (*Vereenigde Oost-Indische Compagnie* or VOC) established in 1602, Dutch West India Company (*Geoctroyeerde Westindische Compagnie* or GWC) established in 1621, British East India Company established in 1600 or French East India Company established in 1664 would grow to become some of the earliest multinational companies of the world, turning in huge profits for their host countries that still did not know how to use these profits except for financing new such colonising ventures and trading with these colonies in their terms. While the size of the pie available to the people of these countries increased substantially, the basic assumptions remained the same: import was discouraged because it would drain away national wealth, reducing the size of the pie, and export was encouraged because it added to the size. The economic system captured and integrated these assumptions, levying taxes on imports, providing subsidies to exporters and ensuring protection for domestic industries. What applied to countries applied equally to provincial and local governments; hence, people were discouraged from trading even with other cities and provinces within the same country. Any commercial exchange was suspect.

In 1776, the year of the American Declaration of Independence, a Scottish academic, Adam Smith, published a book titled *An Inquiry into the Nature and Causes of the Wealth of Nations*. It would turn out to become one of the most influential books ever written in human history and fundamentally alter the way people and nations thought about economy and relations between the state, society and the individual. The book, the first edition of which sold out in just 6 months, and which proclaimed that a nation's wealth can be increased indefinitely and without any limit, would change the course of history. The secret of abundant wealth is exchange and trade without any barrier. 'Man is an animal that makes bargains: no other animal does this - no dog exchanges bones with another', Smith wrote, and therefore: 'Give me that which I want, and you shall have this which you want', leading to mutual benefit and satisfaction, which will ensure prosperity for all.

Theory of the wealth of nations, Smith's theory, is based on three simple basic tenets: pursuit of self-interest, division of labour and free trade. Underlying all three is the use of capital—surplus profits from any economic activity—which needs to be recycled in the activity to increase its scale to generate more profits, and so on in an increasing spiral to create limitless wealth for a nation. In the process everyone benefits as any economic activity requires the collective effort of a lot of people for the production of goods and services useful to others. The logic of limitless collective wealth thus lies in the basic human instinct for furthering self-interest in the form of profit—it may be called greed—but this greed drives economic activities, and higher greed begets higher profits and greater wealth for everyone. Capitalism stops working the moment profits stop getting recycled in the business. With this realisation, wealth acquired a new dimension—it is not something to be labelled as immoral because it is capable of helping the poor labourer make a living and progressively bettering his lot. Capital is the ebb and flow of wealth; only the wealth that is not invested again is to be shunned. Money is not important; it has no intrinsic value except as a measure for wealth. Human self-interest, which drives all this and lies at the root of all activities, is a benevolent force, a force for the good of society. To quote Smith:

> It is not from the benevolence of the butcher, the brewer, or the baker that we expect our dinner, but from their regard to their own self-interest. We address ourselves not to their humanity but to their self-love, and never talk to them of our own necessities, but of their advantages.

> Adam Smith, *Wealth of Nations*, Book I, Chapter II

Since not everyone is adept at making everything and efficient production warrants specialisation, division of labour is imperative. Division of labour is practically as old as mankind—that is how every adult member of a society has made himself/herself useful and productive—and is a prerequisite for wealth creation. As Smith said: 'It is the great multiplication of the productions of all the different arts, in consequence of the division of labour, which occasions, in a well-governed society, that universal opulence which extends itself to the lowest ranks of the people'. Specialisation increases efficiency, and efficiency reduces the cost of production; hence, economic prudence dictates that one should not produce what costs less to buy from the market. It naturally follows that: 'What is prudence in the conduct of every private family, can scarce be folly in that of a great kingdom', as Smith asserted. But the cycle of wealth stops if the goods so produced are not traded such that everyone gets what everyone needs. Naturally: 'If any branch of trade, or any division of labour, be advantageous to the public, the freer and more general the competition, it will always be the more so'. Hence, trade should be free—without any coercion or state-imposed artificial barriers in the form of tariffs and controls. As the state withdraws from trade, individuals will start asserting their liberties, leading to wider choices, lesser controls and more freedom to diversify in newer activities to generate more wealth. Smith thus reasoned:

> [Without trade restrictions] the obvious and simple system of natural liberty establishes itself of its own accord. Every man... is left perfectly free to pursue his own interest in his own way.... The sovereign is completely discharged from a duty [for which] no human wisdom or knowledge could ever be sufficient; the duty of superintending the industry of private people, and of directing it towards the employments most suitable to the interest of the society.
>
> Ibid, Book IX, Chapter IX

Thus, individual liberty and freedom are inherent in the doctrine of capitalism propounded by Smith from which everyone—the rich and the poor alike—benefit.

Trade takes place between the buyer who needs a good and the seller who has it; they are brought together by the market where the exchange of the good takes place either for money or for other goods, and because there are different buyers and sellers there is competition, which determines the price of the traded good. If the exchange is free from coercion—by a state or by anybody else—and if the competition is free and fair, everyone benefits; the seller gets a fair price and the buyer gets the good at a reasonable price. Thus, both the producer of the good and the consumer are satisfied in the exchange. As Smith said: 'Consumption is the sole end and purpose of all production; and the interest of the producer ought to be attended to, only so far as it may be necessary for promoting that of the consumer.' Governments should not interfere in the process by placing curbs on production and trade or by imposing oppressive taxes. In this economic exchange, then, the national borders and governments become redundant:

> The proprietor of stock is properly a citizen of the world, and is not necessarily attached to any particular country. He would be apt to abandon the country in which he was exposed to a vexatious inquisition, in order to be assessed to a burdensome tax, and would remove his stock to some other country where he could either carry on his business, or enjoy his fortune more at his ease.
>
> Ibid, Book V, Chapter II

A nation's wealth, therefore, should be measured not by the assets in its possession but by the total value of its production and exchange through trade and commerce. Thus, with his theory on capitalism, Smith also laid down the concept of what we today call Gross National Product (GNP) and Gross Domestic Product (GDP), without which economists and policymakers today would stare vaguely at an empty no man's land. Exchange implies cooperation between individuals and groups, which in turn calls for harmony and peace, which can be compatible with individual liberties and freedom only in a rule-based, orderly society based on mutual respect as well as respect for the rule of law. Thus, social order and harmony would not need a government to be established; they would grow organically as people come together to utilise the nation's resources for the ends and purposes most beneficial to society, as if guided by the 'invisible hand' of the market that always brings people together. The state's role needs to be limited to facilitating this process by ensuring enforcement of the rule of law through legislative and judicial processes. This does not require any extra effort on the part of the individual either. As Smith said:

> Every individual...neither intends to promote the public interest, nor knows how much he is promoting it...he intends only his own security; and by directing that industry in such a manner as its produce may be of the greatest value, he intends only his own gain, and he is in this, as in many other cases, led by an invisible hand to promote an end which was no part of his intention.

> Ibid, Book IV, Chapter II

Smith's theory dealt a death blow to mercantilism, which was the dominant prevailing doctrine of his time. Mercantilism is based on taxes, tariffs and a multitude of controls—quotas, price controls, production controls, monopolies, cartels, guilds, royal charters, lobbies and special interest groups, influence peddling—that today we consider as restrictive and monopolistic practices. The wealth of a nation was measured by the strength of its merchant fleet and the gold and silver earned from trading, which grew with every export and reduced with very import. Mercantilism considers imports as bad and exports as good without realising the symbiotic relationship between the two. Smith held that a free market, free exchange and free enterprise were the only requirements for an affluent society, accompanied by 'peace, easy taxes and a tolerable administration of justice' for creating unlimited wealth for everyone. A free market economy necessarily implied *laissez-faire* or a 'let alone' style of indifference from the government. It represented maximum freedom to the individual to conduct all economic activities without any limits on investment, production, trade or consumption—a perfectly free individual enterprise system giving absolute right to property and liberties to every individual. Private property and an individual's absolute right over it occupy a central place in capitalism, for the protection of which the rule of law and administration of justice are essential prerequisites:

> Commerce and manufactures can seldom flourish long in any state which does not enjoy a regular administration of justice, in which people themselves do not feel secure in the possession of their property, in which the faith of contracts is not supported by law, and in which the authority of the state is not supposed to be regularly employed in enforcing the payment of debt.
>
> Ibid, Book V, Chapter III

The state is not supposed to interfere in the market but exists only to ensure that the rules of a free market are enforced. If there is no property, there is no need for law: 'Where there is no property,… civil government is not so necessary.' Private property is not capital unless it is used in production.

Theory and practice diverge everywhere, and we know the downsides of capitalism all too well to embrace it wholeheartedly. In fact, Smith himself was not unaware of what an unbridled market could do for society:

> Wherever there is great property there is great inequality. For one very rich man there must be at least five hundred poor, and the affluence of the few supposes the indigence of the many. The affluence of the rich excites the indignation of the poor, who are often both driven by want, and prompted by envy, to invade his possessions.
>
> Ibid, Book V, Chapter I

This inequality will create social turmoil and disturb the very order which is a prerequisite to the creation of greater wealth. No society can surely be flourishing and happy', he said, 'of which the far greater part of the members are poor and miserable.

In a capitalist system, capital and hence the means of production are privately owned, and the owner is free to use his factor resources—land, labour, capital and entrepreneurship—to maximise his profit in order to serve his self-interest. Labour could be substituted or augmented by the use of machines. Under the mercantile system, machines were subsidised by the state, and credit was made available to expand the merchant fleet by bankers. Capitalism viewed subsidies as distortions, just like heavy taxes, indicative of state interference in both the production process and hence in the free market competition. Before capitalism, ownership of land was equated with political and economic power, and since land was limited, so was power. But capitalism substituted money with land in this power equation, and since supply of money, being a measure of ever-increasing wealth of the nation, was virtually unlimited, power could become infinite. Economic power, wielded by the capitalists, thus got separated from political power, wielded by the government or the king being the ultimate owner of all land and hence had the right to tax it. While political power became limited due to various factors including territoriality of jurisdiction, economic power became unbridled.

The unbridled economic power and *laissez-faire* created distortions that were inevitable. If self-interest of individuals or companies is allowed a free rein, it can have disastrous consequences for the others. For one thing, unbridled economic power leads to concentration of wealth in a few hands, and hence to cartels and monopolies preventing free competition, which necessarily leads to low wages for labour and their exploitation. Moreover, the furtherance of self-interest and obsession for maximising the profits often leads to severe exploitation and misery of large groups of people, of which there are plenty of examples in history. VOC's conquest of Indonesia or British East India Company's conquest of India are examples of exploitation of millions of people for maximising the profits of companies; profit maximisation also was the sole motive behind the trans-Atlantic slave trade of the 18th and 19th centuries that led to the untold misery and ruthless exploitation of the Africans forced to work in abominable conditions in the sugar plantations owned by white Americans. The market does not provide protection against exploitation; it has no ethics or soul. It does not care whether profits are earned or distributed in a fair manner. The prospect of endless profit to satisfy the capitalist greed of individuals and corporations can kill millions with a cold indifference, which it has done all over the world, throughout time, and is doing even now. Some of the multinational companies are more powerful than most governments, and they can make and unmake governments in many countries. They are completely unconcerned about the misery and sufferings and even extermination of large sections of people in other societies so long as their profit continues to flow, as seen in the colonies of Western powers, established by their corporations that were driven by the primary motive of earning profits from these colonies.

Even in their own societies, capitalist practices create extreme inequality, ever widening the gap between the rich who invest their capital and the poor who work in the rich's factories and buy the goods produced in those factories to keep the profit flowing into the pockets of their masters. The system led to the unrestrained exploitation of labourers, with long working hours at the factories and appalling living conditions without the most basic facilities that make human life worth living. If competition was free, labourers could move to other factories, as Smith postulated, owned by other capitalists, but capitalists always connived with other capitalists, and often with the state, which they controlled, to form large cartels and monopolies that effectively stopped labour movement in search of better wages and conditions. The means of all production and distribution were owned by the capitalists, and the working class only toiled hard in dismal, inhuman conditions to perpetuate the overwhelming capitalist control of the entire production and distribution machinery, from whose profits they received nothing. They were not really free individuals, having been actually reduced to a mere cog in the gigantic production wheel of the capitalist system from which they were completely alienated. The institutions of capitalism—democracy or parliament, market and private property—all bring misery in the long run; parliament is often controlled by the majority who are rich, the market generates cut-throat competition and selfishness and private property breeds and nurtures inequality in society.

The rise of capitalism coincided with the industrial revolution in Europe that was gathering momentum. It was breaking the traditional pastoral societies in Europe, driving workers in hordes to urban centres that developed around the mines and factories located near the sources of raw materials for production where they lived in ghettoised surroundings. It made their conditions progressively worse and was breeding resentment. By the middle of the 19th century, political scientists and thinkers and even governments were becoming sensitised to the fact that private self-interest needed to be regulated, and that some sort of state intervention was necessary to restrain the unbounded greed of the capitalists that brought misery to their subjects. It was then that Marxism emerged as an alternative to capitalism to address its ills, inequality and exploitation of labourers, but ultimately, it proved to be too ineffective even at that. But the advent of Marxism was preceded by utopianism and anarchism, which were important movements in Europe as the earliest forms of socialism, a term derived from the Latin *sociare,* meaning 'to combine' or 'to share'. In fact both utopian socialism and anarchism propagated the idea of sharing and cooperation through community living. Community is at the heart of socialism, which is based on the idea, known broadly as 'collectivism', that collective endeavour is preferable to individual striving and has far greater moral authority. Socialism is rooted in equality and cooperation between individuals and on the common ownership of property since humans, being primarily social creatures, are better placed to address their socio-economic problems successfully by acting as a community rather than as individuals with limited resources.

Utopian socialism was propagated by French socialist thinkers of the 19th century Robert Owen (1771–1858), Count Henri de Saint-Simon (1760–1825) and Charles Fourier (1772–1837). Utopianism was based on the concept of an ideal or utopian society, a perfect society with unlimited possibility of human development, a society without want, scarcity, conflict, oppression or violence. Utopianism starts with critiquing the existing order and then coming up with an alternative perfect model, howsoever fanciful or unrealistic that model is. However, in general, the concept of perfection of human beings went counter to the Christian belief in original sin propagated by the Church, and the utopian ideas did not find much resonance with people, especially the middle class, in a society over which religion held an overwhelming sway. The ideas were also against the *laissez-faire* approach of capitalism since they required responsible and compassionate behaviour from employers towards their workers. Utopians believed in the total transformation of society rather than partial and *ad hoc* reforms, but violence was not part of their scheme of things to bring about transformation in the society.

In contrast, anarchists like Pierre-Joseph Proudhon (1809–1865) in France and Mikhail Bakunin (1814–1876) in Russia believed that a utopian society based on decentralised communities could be ushered in only through violent revolution. All governments are intrinsically oppressive, and for the establishment of order and creation of a perfect society, use of anarchy and even terror should not be shunned. Proudhon's slogan, 'What is property? Property is theft' (1840), was one of the most prominent revolutionary slogans of the 19th century. Anarchists wanted to abolish the entire structure comprising the state, government, political parties, property, credit and exchange to usher in an egalitarian society based on the sharing and exercise of power by the workers.[1] The revolutionary approach found favour with the working classes in Europe and posed a challenge to Marxism to influence the working class movements in Europe; however, it lost to Marxism eventually.

Thus, we see that even the early socialists had opposed the idea of private property and advocated self-governing communities run by workers, though they did not envisage state control over means of production and distribution, the phenomenon that would eventually lead to the creation of state-controlled public sector enterprises (PSEs) in many countries. The theory that aggressively advocated this approach was of course Marxism, which offered a logically coherent and scientific explanation of the way society works, and which quickly spread across the entire continent of Europe and beyond. The theory developed by Karl Marx (1818–1883) and Friedrich Engels (1820–1895) was not only the most important theory in the history of socialism,

---

[1] 'To be governed is to be watched over, inspected, spied on, directed, legislated at, regulated, docketed, indoctrinated, preached at, controlled, assessed, weighed, censored, ordered about, by men who have neither the right nor the knowledge nor the virtue… That's government, that's its justice, that's its morality'. (Proudhon, *The General Idea of the Revolution.*

but perhaps one of the most influential theories in the history of the 19th and 20th centuries. It has altered the course of history in many ways, and its relevance is still not lost 170 years since the publication of *The Communist Manifesto* by Marx and Engels in 1848.

Marx gave an entirely new interpretation of history and showed that laws of history that define the course of development of society operate in the same manner as the laws of physical sciences, and these can be used just like the latter to predict the future and act accordingly. These laws do not operate at the level of individuals but at that of collectivities or groups. The individuals that behave in similar ways in the social milieu constitute a class—this is not the capitalist concept of class of individuals possessing common attributes usually defined in terms of economic factors, but is related to the collective consciousness of people arising from the commonality of their relations to the process of production. As Marx said: 'It is not the consciousness of men that determines their being but, on the contrary, their social being that determines their consciousness.'[2]

Production is a social enterprise and hence entails social relationships that define what Marx called the 'relations of production'. The social relationships in a hunter-gatherer society were intrinsically different from those in a feudal society, which again were fundamentally different from those in the capitalist society. While in the feudal society there were many classes, in the capitalist society there are only two classes that, by their very nature, are 'hostile' to each other: the bourgeoisie, comprising the 'owners of the means of social production and employers of wage labour', and the proletariat, 'the class of modern wage-labourers who, having no means of production of their own, are reduced to selling their labour-power in order to live.'[3] There is a constant struggle between these two classes. 'The history of all hitherto existing society', Marx asserted, 'is the history of class struggles' only. The struggle between the classes is the major driving force behind the development of society, but 'the division of society into classes and the rise of new classes, depends on the stage

[2] Marx, *Preface to A Contribution to the Critique of Political Economy*.
[3] Marx and Engels, *The Communist Manifesto*, 50.

of development of the productive forces used by man to produce the things he needs for life'.[4]

The feudal society in Britain disintegrated because of the struggle between the new rising industrial capitalist class and the industrial labour class during the 17th century when an armed revolution led by Oliver Cromwell dethroned King Charles I in 1649 and temporarily abolished monarchy. This was not because of an isolated conflict between the despotic monarch and the freedom-seeking Cromwell supported by the people for whom the freedom was being sought. It was rather the culmination of the struggle between the capitalists on the one hand and the feudal lords and the monarch on the other, which had been continuing for centuries before its culmination in an armed revolution. But because the stage was premature for the capitalist revolution, the capitalists' victory was not decisive, and the monarchy reasserted and re-established itself in 1660, even though the old feudal relations were destroyed. In France, however, when the revolution took place in 1789, the stage was mature for the capitalist revolution to succeed. Thus, the French revolution was also the result of class struggle between feudalism and capitalism and not because of lofty ideals like equality, fraternity or liberty for the people, even though the leaders of the new class might sincerely believe so. Property is at the heart of capitalism, as we have already seen, and the 'French Revolution', as Marx said, 'abolished feudal property in favour of bourgeois property'.[5]

Classes are structured by the social relations between the owners of the means of production and the workers employed by them, who are only paid the wages. These relations are specific to the means or forces of production at a given stage of development, which include land, raw materials, technology, machinery, organisation, etc. This relationship Marx called the relations of production. 'The social relations within which individuals produce, are altered, transformed, with the change and development of the material means of production, of the forces of production',[6] as he said. Under feudalism, which arose in response

---

[4] Burns, *An Introduction to Marxism*, 12.
[5] Marx and Engels, *The Communist Manifesto*, 67.
[6] Marx, 'Das Capital', Chapter 5.

to an agrarian economy, the main force of production was land, which was substituted by machinery, technology and raw materials under the industrial production system of capitalism, owned by a small minority of people in society—the bourgeoisie. Each system creates its own class structure: 'The modern bourgeois society that has sprouted from the ruins of feudal society has not done away with class antagonisms. It has but established new classes, new conditions of oppression, new forms of struggle in place of the old ones'.[7]

According to Marx, the relations of production specific to capitalism are two-fold. First:

the labourer works under the control of the capitalist to whom his labour belongs; the capitalist taking good care that the work is done in the proper manner, and that the means of production are used with intelligence, so that there is no unnecessary waste of raw material and no wear and tear of the implements beyond what is necessarily caused by the work.

The second is more general:

the labour process is a process between things that the capitalist has purchased, things that have become his property. The product of this process belongs, therefore, to him, just as much as does the wine which is the product of a process of fermentation completed in his cellar.[8]

The sum total of the relations of production, according to Marx, constitutes the economic base or infrastructure of a society, which in turn shapes the nature of the legal, political or educational institutions and also the belief and value systems of society; all these together constitute the superstructure of a society.[9] This view that material circumstances

---

[7] Marx and Engels, *The Communist Manifesto*, 51.

[8] Marx, 'Das Capital', Chapter 7.

[9] 'The economic structure of society is always the real basis, starting from which we can alone work out the ultimate explanation of the whole superstructure or juridical and political institutions as well as of the religious, philosophical and other ideas of a given historical period'. (Engels, Anti-Duhring).

or economic conditions structure all aspects of social existence and institutions is called 'historical materialism' in the Marxist parlance.

History is the product of tensions and conflicts that are inherent in every society, and change is never a smooth process. Here, Marx contradicted the ideas of Hegel who believed that history is driven by 'dialectical movement' of thoughts and ideas (thesis) which were often incompatible with each other. Society moves forward through a process in which every thesis creates its own antithesis. A synthesis of the opposing ideas of thesis and antithesis is needed to resolve the tensions between the two, and this provides direction to society to move forward. History is a record of the movement of society. Marx believed that the movement of history is caused by contradictions in the prevailing economic system itself and not in conflicting ideas. Both Hegel and Marx viewed history as a process, a movement towards change, transformation and development of society and not a series of disjointed events orchestrated by individuals. For Marx, it was the struggles between classes that was the principal driver of history.

Conflicts between the classes arise due to the changes in the mode of production, driven by new knowledge and advances in technology which usher in changes in the relations of production. In response to these changes, change in the character of social institutions is called for, which creates a conflict of ideas and interests and throws a challenge to the existing institutions. This is what causes the movement of history. The feudal institutions of control like monarchy and vassalage and also the Church could not adjust to the demands of the capitalist mode of production—no divine right for anyone but legal or constitutional rights and liberties of individuals, 'no taxation without representation', the right to trade freely, more decentralisation, free movement of labour to meet the demands of production in place of remaining bound to the land, etc.—and hence had to crumble and give way to capitalism. 'But what seemed to be free men fighting to the death for abstract rights and religious forms was in fact the struggle between rising capitalism and dying feudalism; the conflict of ideas was secondary'.[10] Most ideas in society, according to Marx, are

---

[10] Burns, *An Introduction to Marxism*, 13.

ideas of the dominant class—the owners of the means of production and hence controllers of society—which they then impose upon the rest of society. These ideas in turn are determined by the forces and relations of production.

When ideas change in response to changes in the forces of production, contradictions surface and conditions for change are created. A feudal society had thus itself created the conditions of capitalism, and in a similar manner, capitalism will create conditions for socialism due to its own contradictions when the existing class relations will prove to be a formidable barrier to the new forces of production and hold back social progress. Then, what hitherto was an unconscious and unplanned process of change will erupt with full force and tear asunder the entire edifice of capitalism. But with sufficient knowledge and understanding of the process of historical change, it might be possible to direct this process in a conscious and planned manner. As Engel said: 'The objective, external forces which have hitherto dominated history will then pass under the control of men themselves. It is only from this point that men, with full consciousness, will fashion their own history'.[11] Thus, when the inherent contradictions of the capitalist society become serious enough, the 'weapons with which the bourgeoisie felled feudalism to the ground' can be 'turned against the bourgeoisie itself'.[12]

These contradictions arise from the very nature of the capitalist mode of production, which is based essentially on the premise of maximising profits and hence continuous growth of production. For these products, new markets are to be sought, often beyond national boundaries, and if necessary, through forcible imperialist occupation of another country to supply raw materials and natural resources.

> The need of a constantly expanding market for its products chases the bourgeoisie over the entire surface of the globe. It must nestle everywhere, settle everywhere, establish connections everywhere. The bourgeoisie has through its exploitation of the world market

---

[11] Engels, *Anti-Dühring*. Quoted in Burns, *An Introduction to Marxism*, 15.
[12] Marx and Engels, *The Communist Manifesto*, 58.

given a cosmopolitan character to production and consumption in every country.[13]

Capitalist production demands continuous expansion of capital in order to produce more and make ever more profits, and this greed for endless profits will in due course lead to what Marx called 'the epidemic of over-production', with disastrous consequences. Because of overproduction, new production will decline and workers will become unemployed or be paid less. Unemployment or lesser wages will cause further reduction of demand for the goods produced, eventually leading to a spiral of economic recession. Once the stocks are cleared or deliberately destroyed, production will begin and grow till another crisis of overproduction occurs. As the Manifesto says:

> And how does the bourgeoisie get over these crises? On the one hand by enforced destruction of a mass of productive forces; on the other, by the conquest of new markets, and by the more thorough exploitation of the old ones. That is to say, by paving the way for more extensive and more destructive crises, and by diminishing the means whereby crises are prevented.[14]

Capitalist production attracts competition, and competition inevitably leads to the increasing use of machines and technology in order to continuously lower the cost of production. In the ruthless, cut-throat competition in the market, smaller firms will either perish or merge into bigger firms, leading to the establishment of monopolies to the detriment of workers who will stand to lose their bargaining power with employers. Monopolies also intensify another contradiction in capitalism which, as we have seen, is based on free competition. The lowering of production cost will also certainly warrant saving on account of workers' wages, and often, retrenchment by replacement of human labour with machines. This will further add to the crisis of overproduction.

> The bourgeoisie cannot exist without constantly revolutionising the instruments of production, and thereby the relations of production,

---

[13] Ibid, 54.
[14] Ibid, 58.

and with them the whole relations of society..... Constant revolutionising of production, uninterrupted disturbance of all social conditions, everlasting uncertainty and agitation distinguish the bourgeois epoch from all earlier ones. All fixed, fast-frozen relations, with their train of ancient and venerable prejudices and opinions, are swept away, all new-formed ones become antiquated before they can ossify.[15]

The process inevitably leads to unending exploitation of workers. Here, Marx came up with one of his most important concepts, surplus value of labour. The analysis in fact derives from the classical labour theory of value, which says that the value of a product is determined by the amount of labour that has gone into the making of it. But while in the pre-capitalist societies products were exchanged between sellers and buyers because of their utility to the buyers, in a capitalist society, they were exchanged for money and profit. The labour also was a commodity to be bought and sold in the market—what Marx called the 'objectification of labour' that produces alienation in the worker—but the exchange value of labour was less than that of the product that it makes. Marx distinguished between labour and labour power and introduced the concept of constant capital and variable capital. While constant capital comprises items land, buildings, materials, machinery etc. that do not change value in the process of production, variable capital, which is labour power, or the capacity of the worker to produce, does change its value. First, the variable capital produces the equivalent of its own value, which is paid to the worker as wages and is just enough for his subsistence. But his labour power can produce more value, which is appropriated by the capitalist. This, Marx called the 'surplus value', which is the additional value the worker has produced, over and above his wage. A part of this goes towards augmenting the constant capital or its economic depreciation, and the rest is appropriated by the capitalist as profit.

In his selfish motive of earning more profit from each unit of capital employed in production, the capitalist tries to maximise this surplus value in every conceivable way—by minimising the worker's

[15] Ibid, 54.

wage, by making him work for longer hours and by making him work and live under dismal conditions, devoid of the most basic facilities. The rate of surplus value, which Marx also called the rate of exploitation of labour, is the fundamental driver of class struggle, and this makes the capitalist system inherently prone to crisis. This is because the capitalist would tend to invest continuously in constant capital, which comprises the fixed assets, in order to contain his production cost, which increases the productivity of labour but not the worker's wages. This leaves the worker with less purchasing power and hence less demand for the products, which ultimately leads to the epidemic of overproduction as discussed earlier. Every crisis created by overproduction causes more strain on the system than the previous one till the whole system collapses irrevocably under the weight of its own contradictions. Thus, the capitalist system carries the seeds of its own destruction and its eventual transformation to a socialist system which is free from these contradictions.

Thus:

> The various interests and conditions of life within the ranks of the proletariat are more and more equalised, in proportion as machinery obliterates all distinctions of labour, and nearly everywhere reduces wages to the same low level. The growing competition among the bourgeois, and the resulting commercial crises, make the wages of the workers ever more fluctuating. The increasing improvement of machinery, ever more rapidly developing, makes their livelihood more and more precarious; the collisions between individual workmen and individual bourgeois take more and more the character of collisions between two classes.

Marx and Engels, *The Communist Manifesto*, Signet Classic, 1998, 61.

To prevent the exploitation, workers will first unite to form trade unions, which will continue to expand to include more and more workers because of the improved means of communication created by the capitalists for their industries. As the proletariat are brought together in greater numbers, their strength grows and they become aware of their increased strength. The 'numerous local struggles, all of the same character' thus ultimately converge into 'one national struggle between classes'. Just as 'each step in the development of the bourgeoisie was accompanied by a corresponding political advance of that class',[16] every class struggle is also necessarily a political struggle, and at an advanced stage, the workers will form a political party to wrest power from the capitalists through a violent armed revolution to move to the next stage of social development and organisation of society under a new system of production—socialism, establishing what Marx termed the 'Dictatorship of the proletariat'.

And thus: 'The development of Modern Industry, therefore, cuts from under its feet the very foundation on which the bourgeoisie produces and appropriates products. What the bourgeoisie therefore produces, above all, are its own grave-diggers. Its fall and the victory of the proletariat are equally inevitable'. But the revolutionary process that will see the workers take absolute control of the 'commanding heights' of industry and commerce from their capitalist owners will be the culmination of a much longer evolutionary process; any pre-mature attempt to bring about any social revolution will only end in failure. Violent overthrow of the existing order is not an essential element of Marxism; Marx believed that in advanced capitalist societies, conditions could exist for even a peaceful and non-violent socialist revolution.

What will be the essential elements of this revolution to bring about a transformation into an egalitarian society that will take from each according to his ability and give to everyone according to his need?[17] The first prerequisite is the abolition of all private property.

---

[16] Ibid, 76.

[17] 'In a higher phase of communist society, after the enslaving subordination of the individual to the division of labour, and therewith also the antithesis between mental and physical labour, has vanished; after labour has become not only a means of life but life's prime want; after the productive forces have also increased with the all-around development of the individual, and all the springs of co-operative wealth flow more abundantly—only then can the narrow horizon of bourgeois right be crossed in its entirety and society inscribe on its banners: From each according to his ability, to each according to his needs'. (Marx, *Critique of the Gotha Program*, Part 1, 1875)

Property is a means for exploitation; the wage labourer does not create any property for the labourer but creates capital for the capitalist to exploit him. Every increase in property creates conditions for more wage labourers to be employed, and hence more exploitation. Further, private ownership of capital may not be the most efficient way of realising their productive potential, only a planned and conscious development of the productive forces can unleash their full potential for growth. Thus, under the socialist system, the means of production are taken from private ownership and used for the society as a whole.

> From the moment when labour can no longer be converted into capital, money, or rent, into a social power capable of being monopolised, i.e., from the moment when individual property can no longer be transformed into bourgeois property, into capital, from that moment, you say, individuality vanishes.[18]

By 'individual', Marx meant only the bourgeoisie, the owner of property.

As *The Communist Manifesto* declares:

> These measures will, of course, be different in different countries. Nevertheless, in most advanced countries, the following will be pretty generally applicable. 1. Abolition of property in land and application of all rents of land to public purposes. 2. A heavy progressive or graduated income tax. 3. Abolition of all rights of inheritance… 5. Centralisation of credit in the hands of the state, by means of a national bank with State capital and an exclusive monopoly. 6. Centralisation of the means of communication and transport in the hands of the State. 7. Extension of factories and instruments of production owned by the State; the bringing into cultivation of waste-lands, and the improvement of the soil generally in accordance with a common plan. 8. Equal liability of all to work… 9. Combination of agriculture with manufacturing industries;…[19]

---

[18] Marx and Engels, *The Communist Manifesto*, 65.
[19] Ibid, 76.

Here, we can find the first clear philosophical basis for the public sector of the later day.

Marx believed that socialism[20] would take production to undreamt-of heights, but there would be no overproduction as all the increased production—the total output of the forces of production—would be allocated to the people in a planned manner and used to raise their living standards, the material basis on which depends their cultural and intellectual progress. The plan would cover creating additional means of production, the increased output of which would be used for the purpose of development and not for profit. In the socialist society, there would be no private ownership of property and no profit required for the expansion of capital.

Ushering in a socialist society would also signal the end of class struggles. Classes exist due to their conflicting interests in the process of production where one class works only for the prosperity of another. But under the dictatorship of the proletariat, there would no longer be any class living off the labour of another.

When, in the course of development, class distinctions have disappeared, and all production has been concentrated in the hands of a vast association of the whole nation, the public power will lose its political character. Political power, properly so called, is merely the organised power of one class for oppressing another. If the proletariat during its contest with the bourgeoisie is compelled, by the force of circumstances, to organise itself as a class, if, by means of a revolution, it makes itself the ruling class, and, as such, sweeps away by force the old conditions of production, then it will, along with these conditions, have swept away the conditions for the existence of class antagonisms and of classes generally, and will thereby have abolished its own supremacy as a class. In place of the old bourgeois society, with its classes and class antagonisms, we shall have an association, in which the free development of each is the condition for the free development of all.[21]

---

[20] Socialism and communism were practically synonymous during the 19th century.
[21] Ibid, 65.

In such an egalitarian society, the means of production would be shared by all, and all individuals would equally serve the society that would be classless, and live in harmony. Since there would be no private property to be protected and no classes to be subjugated, the state would no longer be needed either. It would then slowly 'wither away' by itself. As Engels said: 'The society which organises production anew on the basis of free and equal association of the producers will put the whole state machinery where it will then belong—into the museum of antiquities, next to the spinning wheel and the bronze ax'.[22]

Ideas of Marxism were spreading fast throughout Europe and beyond from the late 19th century. Deriving inspiration from them, the first communist regime in the world was established in Russia by overthrowing the autocratic regime of Czar Nicolas II in 1917. The communist USSR survived two world wars, and for nearly the next seven decades, extended its influence on many countries, helping establish and supporting the communist regimes in them. During this period, the world effectively became divided into two competing ideo-logical blocks: the capitalist block led by the USA and the communist block led by the USSR. But the latter was unable to ensure economic growth and ruthlessly suppressed the individual liberties of its people. As its economy nosedived, with growth reaching almost zero levels, factories became decrepit, agricultural production plummeted and living conditions became abysmal. By the mid-1980s, people were no longer afraid of denouncing the regime openly. To control public resentment and anger, in March 1985, the ageing leadership had brought in a young, energetic Mikhail Gorbachev as General Secretary of the Communist Party, who immediately embarked upon his famous *Perestroika*—a radical restructuring of the economy along with politi-cal reforms, introducing liberal democratic freedoms or *Glasnost*. It opened the floodgates of pent-up anger and unfulfilled aspiration of the people, shaking the foundation of the Soviet Union to the core, which led to the ultimate dismantling and dissolution of the USSR.

Meanwhile, in October 1985, Gorbachev had told USSR's Eastern European allies that they must now take responsibility for their affairs

---

[22] Engels, *Origins of the Family, Chapter IX.*

without any more support—military or otherwise—from the USSR. While massive protests erupted in Czechoslovakia and East Germany, displacing their entrenched communist leaders, the oppressive communist regimes in Bulgaria and Romania crumbled. In Poland, anti–communist union solidarity was swept to power after the 1989 elections.

The year 1989 in many ways determined the course of history as far as the future of Marxism was concerned. That year witnessed several defining moments, beginning with the June 4 massacre of students demanding democracy at the Tiananmen Square in China, fall of the Berlin Wall and the subsequent collapse and eventual disintegration of the USSR.

A hunger strike by 3,000 students in Beijing had metamorphosed into a mammoth protest of more than a million people crying for free-dom and democracy at the Tiananmen Square in Beijing, daring the might of the communist empire that ruled with an iron grip and went by the name of People's Republic. The People's Republic despatched hundreds of soldiers of the People's Liberation Army to silence the voice of the people. On 4 June 1989, their tanks surrounded the square occupied by the students who had camped there and fired volley after volley at the unarmed students, killing hundreds, maybe thousands, and silencing their voice of protest.

At the end of World War II in June 1945, the defeated Germany was divided into four sectors between Russia and the other three Allied powers, USA, UK and France. While the eastern half of the country (East Germany) came under the control of Soviet Russia, the western half (West Germany) came under the Allied Western powers. Even though the pre-War capital, Berlin, was located entirely within the Soviet-controlled territory of East Germany, the city was also split into similar sectors. Within a short time, however, living conditions between the two Germanys became vastly different. While West Germany experienced an economic miracle, growing rapidly with the support of the capitalist Western powers and offering a high living standard to its people, East Germany continued to languish in pov-erty. As the economy failed, individual liberties came under increasing restraints in East Germany. The prospect of a better life continued to attract people from East Germany to the West, and in July 1961,

30,000 people fled to West Germany. On a single day—12 August 1961—2,400 people escaped to West Germany. The very next day, the border was sealed, and within just 2 weeks, East Germany constructed a barbed wire fence and reinforced it later with a concrete wall, which would ultimately become the most hated symbol of the Cold War as the Berlin Wall. The wall divided families, lovers, friends and neighbourhoods. A second wall was constructed in 1962. The space in between known as the 'Death Strip'—the strip of soft sand for catching footprints—was kept under the strict vigil of vicious dogs, floodlights, trip-wire machineguns and patrolling guards who shot mercilessly at everyone attempting to cross over into West Berlin. An even more formidable wall was built in 1975. Yet, people continued to flee, and 171 people laid down their lives while attempting to do so.

In 1987, US President Ronald Regan visited West Berlin. In a speech in front of the Brandenburg Gate, he exhorted, 'Mr. Gorbachev, tear down this wall'. On 9 November 1989, the East German government suddenly announced the removal of all travel restrictions between East and West Germany. Thousands of people immediately flocked to the checkpoints along the wall, chanting, '*Tor auf!*' ('Open the gate!'), forcing the guards to leave. As celebrations broke out, people began chipping at the wall with hammers and chisels, and with each stroke of the hammer, one piece of the ultimate state tyranny symbolised by economic and political oppression, denial of individual freedom and suppression of democratic rights irrevocably fell apart, ending an era of senseless and cruel separation between people, and reuniting families. Almost the entire Berlin Wall was eventually chipped away into smaller pieces to be kept as mementoes of a world no longer real. The fall of the wall paved the way for the re-unification of Germany on 3 October 1990.

The Berlin Wall that divided Germany fell a quarter of a century ago, on 9 November 1989, and in falling, it took along with it the last vestiges of the old world—a world dominated by a rigid command and control structure enforced by a brutal, coercive state, a world wrecked by the misery of divided people and torn by the hostility of the Cold War that brought the possibility of a nuclear conflagration dangerously close to reality.

Forces of history operating in different countries and continents often work in conjunction with each other, unknown to the players whose destinies they shape. It was probably no coincidence that less than 2 years later, in March 1991, India, a country that was suffocating under the License Permit Raj of a state-controlled, centrally planned economy, would resolutely dismantle that command and control structure, ushering in a new era of liberalisation, privatisation and globalisation of its economy, letting in the fresh air of freedom, unleashing the immense entrepreneurial talent of its people, boosting growth and lifting a quarter of a billion people out of poverty within the next two decades.

The fall of the Berlin Wall not only marked the end of the Cold War and held before the world the dream of a society based on economic and political liberalisation, consensual democracy and human rights, but also paved the way for a new, multipolar world and ushered in a new worldview. It ended the debate over communism, which some said made everyone 'equally poor', and capitalism, which they said made people 'unequally rich', and gave unfettered rein to free market capitalism the world over. The market was recognised as the ultimate God.

After the collapse of the USSR, in his 1989 article, "The End of History?", Francis Fukuyama, an American author and bureaucrat, celebrated the 'triumph of the West' and 'Western idea', arguing that 'the end point of mankind's ideological evolution' had been reached 'in an unabashed victory of economic and political liberalism', in deregulated markets and Western democracy. These, of course, proved to be fanciful ideas, as evidenced by subsequent events in a world in which inequality is growing by the day. But the events of 1989 and the breakdown of the Soviet regime did create doubts and raised questions about the future of Marxism. An elaborate discussion on these aspects is outside the scope of this book, but a few important points may be mentioned.

First, social theories do not exist and operate in isolation—society being in a state of dynamic equilibrium and always changing, theories need to be adapted to the dominant currents of change. It would be wrong to assume that Soviet-style communism was Marxist, just as it would be equally wrong to assume that the class structure of society, as Marx envisaged, would always remain unchanging. The class structure of society today is much more complex and cannot be divided into two hostile camps of bourgeoisie and proletariat. A significant middle class, having substantial numbers, wealth and power, and which cannot be said to belong to either of these two camps, has emerged in most countries, and their voice today largely determines the course of politics and economy of the 21st-century world.

Second, capitalism has also responded positively to the changes in society; it has shown remarkable resilience and the capacity to reinvent itself. Capitalism today is much less exploitative—today's workers in advanced capitalist countries are paid better wages and have much better living conditions than was conceivable in Marx's times. Capitalism has successfully countered the spread of communism by inventing and institutionalising the 'welfare State', which shall be discussed later in this chapter. The state now plays a much more effective regulatory role to prevent the excesses of capitalist exploitation as pointed out by Marx. Most states today provide free education and basic healthcare to their citizens and social security and pension for the old and infirm, though some are struggling to improve the quality of these deliveries.

Third, one of the central points in Marx's theory was control of social and economic institutions, which he called superstructure, by the economic base or infrastructure. But today, in most countries, especially those ruled by democracy, the state has successfully created institutions and provided them with sufficient autonomy and authority to check its own excesses and propensities for becoming authoritarian, such as an independent judiciary, public audit, independent central bank, free media, constitutional liberties that cannot be abrogated, etc. These institutions cannot be said to be under the control of the ruling elite or the so-called bourgeoisie that they can be made to act in a manner that promotes and protects their interests.

The socialist experiments in the world have not ushered in a classless society with freedom and liberty of the individual where all individual needs are satisfied and people live in harmony. It has rather been just the opposite in all these countries. While it can be argued that they were not ready for socialist revolution, Marx's economic determinism—the theory that economic forces alone determine all political, social, cultural, intellectual, and technological developments in a society and define the course of history—is also open to question as other factors—cultural, religious and sociological, for example— also seem to play a significant role. Each society responds to changes, brought about by capitalism or any other device, in a unique way. As American sociologist Robert Nisbet said:

> How easy it is, as we look back over the past—that is, of course, the 'past' that has been selected for us by historians and social scientists—to see in it trends and tendencies that appear to possess the iron necessity and clear directionality of growth in a plant or organism... But the relation between the past, present, and future is chronological, not causal.[23]

Though inequality shows no signs of diminishing in the modern world, the emergence of financial markets and financial interme- diation by modern banking and financial institutions have helped disperse wealth across all sections of society rather than allow its concentration in a few hands; this has enabled even the relatively poor to be a part of the capitalist mode of production and earn a share, howsoever small, in its profit. Labour has been diversified rather than homogenised, and wages today depend on the skill and knowledge of workers, which have given them greater power of bargaining. Labour and capital today are complementary to each other in most produc- tive enterprises rather than being in permanent opposition, as Marx had assumed. Across the globe, the standards of living of workers and the leisure time at their disposal in the 21st century are far better than in any previous century. Rising standards of living have created a new consciousness among people, for example, towards climate, sustainability and the environment. The knowledge and information society of the 21st century may also find Marxist principles a little dated. New challenges like terror and Islamic fundamentalism have emerged as major threats to world peace, and new determinants of

[23] Quoted in Ebeling, 'Karl Marx and the Presumption of a "Right Side" to History'.

human behaviour like nationalism and religion are influencing policy and polity in many countries, which do not find any place in the Marxist philosophy. Alternative models like neo-liberalism, mixed economy, welfarism, social democracy, market economy combined with socialist polity, etc. have been successfully experimented in different countries. So far, all experiments with the use of a uniform system of absolute state control have proved equally unpopular and disastrous. The dominant ideas of the 21st century are restraining the power of the state to commit excesses and guaranteeing individual rights and liberties while promoting individual entrepreneurship.

Many of Marx's predictions failed to materialise, especially his prediction about the imminent collapse of capitalism. Social scientists and political activists also started questioning the base-superstructure binary and Marx's concept of class struggle as the be-all and end-all of all social analysis; many were also appalled by the Russian-style communism and its ruthless suppression of civil liberties and systematic abuse of human rights. An alternative view of Marxism known as neo-Marxism thus evolved in Europe in the first decades of the 20th century. Among its chief proponents were Georg Lukacs (1885–1971) in Hungary, Antonio Gramsci (1891–1937) in Italy, Theodor Adorno (1903–1969), Max Horkheimer (1895–1973) and Herbert Marcuse (1898–1979) in Germany. But a complete break with Marxism saw the emergence of social democracy as an alternative to Marxism only in the middle of the 20th century, arising from the attempts to reconcile Marx's revolutionary doctrine with electoral and parliamentary politics.

The ideas and concept of social democracy first started taking shape in Europe 'resulting from the tendency among western socialist parties not only to adopt parliamentary strategies, but also to revise their socialist goals. In particular, they abandoned the goal of abolishing capitalism and sought instead to reform or "humanize" it'.[24] Social democracy thus aimed to achieve a balance between the market economy and state control. Being thus a compromise between two opposites, it lacks a consistent underlying theory as its backbone, unlike Marxism, but focuses on the redistribution of wealth created by

---

[24] Haywood, *Political Ideologies*, 123.

capitalism through state intervention in order to reduce the inequality, which is another by-product of capitalism. Social democracy, unlike Marxism, does not believe in revolution or armed struggle being essential for social change but instead propagates the view that social change is to be ushered in by peaceful and constitutional means. In several European countries, social democratic parties emerged as legitimate political parties—many of these have since been elected to power in several countries.

The market crash of 1929 had created a consensus that *laissez-faire* capitalism had by and large failed and that governments should intervene in the economy to regulate corporations and redistribute wealth. The new deal was to pool collective wealth to build just societies. Especially in the post-War period, by and large, the Western powers agreed that market economies should not be left totally unregulated and also that there was an obvious need to guarantee basic livelihood of the workers with dignity. In many countries, governments started owning corporations for producing essential goods and services to usher in a model of mixed economy, the origin of the public sector. As a result, governments stepped in in many countries—USA, UK, France, Germany, Canada, Australia and many others as well—to provide social security, public healthcare and workers' protection. In this process, welfarism emerged as a major instrument of state policy, and gradually, the welfare state became the accepted norm. Social democracy would also integrate the concepts of a welfare state in an organic manner, as a basic tool for the implementation of the social democratic ideas.

The early social democrats believed that instead of being self-correcting, market-driven economies are often prone to recession, and that government intervention is necessary to correct the market distortions. Governments can do so through macro-economic stabilisation—either by increasing or by decreasing total spending on output or through taxation, which can also increase or decrease consumption and hence influence demand and, consequently, output. Governments also need to spend substantially on social welfare programmes, especially those targeted at the poor, as these are actually investments in human capital that will eventually increase the national wealth by increasing the productivity of labour, and hence boost everyone's income.

Modern social democrats, however, hold that such simple fixes make no sense, and that deeper economic problems cannot be permanently resolved by addressing such simple technicalities. A system based on mindless pursuit of profit and individual self-interest can only lead to economic inequality, which in turn will cause social turbulence. Hence, without transforming the economic system in a fundamental way, a just society cannot be established, and thus, individual profit and self-interest must give way to collective pursuit of the common good and promotion of social justice through a process to be directed by the state, within the framework of a liberal democratic polity and capitalist economy. According to this view, social welfare cannot be separated from political economy and will depend on the interaction between economic, political and ideological forces, whereas the early social democrats believed that social and economic policies are all about choices and alternatives in public expenditure allocations, and are concerned with allocating goods, services and opportunities to enhance social welfare.

Among the traditional social democrats, the most prominent was the British economist John Maynard Keynes (1883–1946), who accepted the capitalist market as the only reliable agency for generating wealth and its regulation by macro-economic means as the best prescription for correcting the distortions caused by the market for creating the conditions for full employment. His magnum opus, *The General Theory of Employment, Interest and Money*, was published in 1936.[25] The traditional economic theory could neither explain the causes nor prescribe a viable remedy for the economic recession of the 1930s, and free markets proved to be incapable of providing full employment. Keynes came up with his ideas that were thought to be revolutionary at that time.

Keynesian economics is based on the simple premise that aggregate demand—the sum total of spending by households, businesses and the government—is the major driver of economy. Recession and

[25] Keynes had an astute political sense also. In 1919, in *The Economic Consequences of the Peace*, he predicted that the crushing conditions imposed on Germany in the Versailles Peace Treaty Germany after World War I would lead to another war, when he made his legendary statement, 'Vengeance, I dare predict, will not limp'.

unemployment are caused only by inadequate demand. Aggregate demand can be boosted only through purposeful government intervention in public policies in order to achieve price stability with full employment. Further, the fiscal policy of the government should be countercyclical so that during the boom times, too, government intervention is necessary to moderate the impact of high growth. Thus, during economic downturns, the Keynesian prescription is to increase government spending, especially on labour-intensive infrastructure projects, to increase employment, while during boom times, the remedy is to increase taxes so as to arrest high inflation when the growth is demand-driven. Fiscal policy does not work in isolation; it has to be applied in conjunction with monetary policy, for example, by lowering or raising the interest rates to achieve the same objectives.[26] These policies are likely to yield results in the short run unlike the market forces that take a longer time to recover and adjust, and in the Keynesian perspective, short, and not long run, is important since, as he said famously, 'In the long run, we are all dead'. Keynesian policies, of course, had their critics who pointed out, not without logic, that recessions and booms were but the natural order of economic laws, and that government intervention only worsens the process of economic recovery.

In the post-War years, that is, from the mid-1940s to the early 1970s, when Western European economies applied Keynesian ideas, they experienced prolonged periods of economic growth averaging nearly 5 per cent every year, accompanied by continuous improvement in the living standards of people. Governments could significantly raise their social expenditure as a percentage of the GDP. As higher proportions of government budgets were being allocated to welfare expenditure, the focus was turned towards efficient delivery of welfare services such as education, healthcare, social security, etc. The Nordic countries followed a model of high-level taxes combined with the efficient delivery of public goods and services at a very affordable cost. Successes following from these policies pushed social democracy in these countries to pursue the goals of social reform with even more vigour and to integrate welfare as one of its abiding principles to reduce inequality and improve the lot of the working classes while still

[26] Jahan, Mahmud, and Papageorgiou, 'What Is Keynesian Economics?'

retaining the capitalist structure of the economy. The sectors identified as vital for attaining the welfarism objectives were increasingly brought under government control and regulation. This process culminated in the government-controlled production and distribution of public goods and services in these sectors and the creation of a public sector, following from Keynes's ideas of government intervention in the economy.

After the 1970s, however, the situation changed completely, due to the combination of various factors. Following the Arab-Israeli War in 1973, oil prices shot up, and the Bretton Woods mechanism based on the convertibility of dollar with gold was replaced by the establishment of the universal dollar exchange system. Following the abolition of controls on the outflow of capital in USA in 1974, private financial institutions emerged as the pivot of a new international financial order. The resulting exchange rate instability and other factors led to the plummeting of growth in most advanced economies; for example, the OECD countries registered negative growth in 1975 compared to an average 2 per cent growth the year before, and unemployment doubled during the next decade. As inflation combined with slow growth, or 'stagflation', started afflicting the advanced economies, cutting taxes and boosting government spending were no longer working; they rather caused higher inflation and higher unemployment. The Keynesian theory was thus faced with an unprecedented crisis.[27]

This was also the crisis of social democracy as austerity measures, reduction of social welfare expenditure and privatisation of the public sector became the buzzwords for the neoliberal policies in developed countries.[28] Mrs Margaret Thatcher in the UK went on an aggressive

---

[27] Newman, *Socialism: A Very Short Introduction*, 118–120.

[28] The crisis was not limited to the developed countries. The weaker, developing nations also faced balance of payments crises and were forced to borrow from international financial institutions like the IMF. IMF loans came with trademark conditions of privatisation, steep increases in taxation, government deregulation and deep cuts in governments' social spending on the poor, in the pretext of stabilising their fiscal and monetary policies. These conditions unfairly opened the vast markets of developing countries to Western business interests by removing tariff barriers, in the process destroying local business enterprises and exposing their people to acute hardships.

spree of privatisation, and even Francois Mitterrand's socialist government buried the ideas of Keynes.[29] The focus was on deregulation now rather than state welfarism, and by the mid-1980s, a new philosophy had emerged in the developed world that the cost of welfare should be reduced and that individuals must take most responsibility for their own welfare. Welfare state was no longer viable in the face of globalisation, liberalisation and an ageing population with a much higher life expectancy leading to spiralling social security expenditure. The wheel had turned full circle.

This new philosophy, described as the 'Third Way' or the *Neue Mitte* (New Middle), emerged as an alternative to social democracy and was more neoliberal in outlook. In this philosophy, top-down state intervention was discarded, the community's role was highlighted and social inclusion was emphasised. The state was conceived as a 'market state' with focus on social investment, that is, on improving infrastructure and strengthening the skill and knowledge of the workforce in an economy that was increasingly acquiring the character of a 'knowledge economy'. Government's role was being redefined as a facilitator rather than an actor in economic activities, to promote employability rather than being an employer, to improve people's skill and knowledge rather than carry out social engineering through massive welfare expenditure.[30]

The global financial crisis of 2007–2008 brought the focus back to Keynes in some way. Attempts are now being made to integrate the role of the financial system into the Keynesian theory. At the same time, consensus seems to be that more careful targeting is needed for social welfare expenditure so that the state is not unnecessarily overburdened and the poor do not feel excluded. A complete dismantling of the welfare state seems to be out of the question, as this is the only mechanism for balancing the risks created by a capitalist free market economy.

By the late 19th century, the plight of the industrial workers in Western Europe was much different than what it was earlier.

---

[29] Ibid, 120.
[30] Haywood, *Political Ideologies*, 130–133.

Capitalism was also showing signs of maturity as industrial wages and living standards of workers were rising, and workers were able to organise themselves into trade unions and political parties that protected their interests. With universal suffrage being introduced in most industrial economies by the end of World War I, the workers also got political rights to vote. All these developments had the effect of making armed insurrection and violent revolution less and less appealing to the workers and weaning the workers' movements away from militant socialism. There was a new realisation that socialism also had an alternative route through multiparty parliamentary democracy, through peaceful means. This was the view propagated by the so-called Fabian Society,[31] which was formed in 1884 in UK, led by Beatrice Webb (1858–1943) and Sidney Webb (1859–1947) and supported by towering intellectuals like George Bernard Shaw and H. G. Wells; even India's first Prime Minister, Jawaharlal Nehru, was an ardent believer and follower of Fabian socialism. The ideas of the Fabian Society gave birth to the Labour Party in the UK in 1900, and many of their intellectuals were either members of the society or closely associated with it.[32]

The Fabian socialists believed in the peaceful development of capitalism in the natural process of evolution of liberal capitalism through a combination of political action through formation of a socialist political party and education and spread of awareness among the masses that socialism is morally superior to capitalism. As against Marx's concept of the state as an agent of class oppression, Fabians held the state to be a neutral arbiter. Fabian ideas gradually spread from the UK to Germany and deeply influenced the social democratic party there, which would grow to emerge as the largest socialist party in Europe.[33] Fabians believed in gradualism, the belief that social change could be ushered in through a gradual process that was legal, constitutional and peaceful rather than through a violent upheaval,

---

[31] The Fabian Society took its name from the 3rd century Roman commander Fabius Maximus known for his defensive tactics against the superior invading army of Hannibal.

[32] Haywood, *Political Ideologies*, 110.

[33] Ibid, 111.

that workers could use the ballot box to effect reform of the political system. These were the ideas that gradually spread throughout Europe and beyond. Fabians believed in the state ownership of the means of production, leading to the birth of the public sector in the UK and other countries. As one of the prominent leaders of the movement in UK, Clement Attlee wrote:

> The dominant issue of the twentieth century is Socialism... It is essentially the outcome of the economic and social conditions. The evils that capitalism brings differ in intensity in different countries, but the root cause of trouble once discerned, the remedy is seen to be the same... The cause is private ownership of the means of life, the remedy is public ownership.[34]

After World War II, the Labour Party, under Attlee, was voted to power in the UK in 1945 on the promise of public ownership of key industries as spelled out in the manifesto, and carried out a major nationalisation drive of key industries during 1945–1951, including coal, railways, steel and electricity.

Thus, we see that the allocation of economic resources towards fulfilling national objectives, and state control and ownership of the means of production and distribution, had emerged as a result of historical developments, political debates and the emergence of different ideologies in Europe since the 19th century. Different economic models emerged as a result, and each dominant and competing ideology—communism, democratic socialism or Fabian socialism—contributed to the idea of a vibrant public sector under the control of the state in sectors important for economic growth, not only for increasing the national output but also to end the exploitation of the workers and to protect their interests. In many countries, both developed and developing, the public sector started playing a significant role in the economy. Driven by socialist ideologies that were commanding popular support in these countries, the governments started to act against those who wielded disproportionate economic powers. In the process, the state itself assumed overbearing powers and became an instrument

[34] Atlee, *The Labour Party in Perspective*, 15.

of coercion, as in the case of Russia. But by the middle of the 19th century, there emerged a general consensus among states that the concentration of economic power in a few hands must be prevented at all costs, that active state intervention was needed to reduce the ever-widening disparity between the rich and the poor and rising economic inequalities, and that it was the responsibility of the state to reduce, and if possible, to eliminate the endemic poverty among the masses. The intervention could be regulatory or participatory, or both. This led to different types of socialism, command economies and centralised planning, and the public sector emerged as a product of this process.

The public sector came to occupy vital roles in the creation of infrastructure and in the production and distribution of public goods and services in many advanced Western European economies such as Great Britain, France, Italy and Germany. The underlying concept was that only the state was in a position to mobilise the massive resources needed for building infrastructure and public utilities like railways and telecommunications, harnessing mineral wealth and generating and distributing power. In the war-ravaged European nations, it was considered a priority to mobilise whatever resources were left and use these for rebuilding their economies through state intervention, as the private sector driven by its profit motive was considered unequal to this task. Besides, infrastructure and other core sector industries have a long gestation period during which no economic returns could be expected, and the private sector was considered unlikely to be interested in investing the huge amounts needed to set up industries in these sectors.

After World War II, the colonial powers, exhausted of their economic or military might to retain their hold on colonies, were staring at the imminent loss of their colonial empires. As the colonies in the third world in Asia, Africa and South America started gaining their independence, they were miserably underdeveloped. Their governments found themselves in charge of territories completely robbed of their economic wealth, with practically no industry or infrastructure, endemic and abject poverty of their masses, crippling food shortages and abysmal economic growth. Colonial empires were not interested in their development but only in the extraction of raw materials from the colonies to fuel higher production in their own countries, and exporting their finished products to the colonies that were captive buyers. The challenge to the national governments in all these countries was to set up industries to transform the economy in the shortest possible time in order to lift their people out of poverty.

Since the colonial empires thrived on the export of their raw materials, in the post-colonial times, any export was viewed with extreme suspicion in the newly independent countries. Thus, inward-looking industrialisation became the natural order of things, and export of natural resources was discouraged, as were the imports. It was almost like going back to the mercantilist days, with the focus on developing import substitution industries and indigenous technologies to use the natural resources. For this purpose, the key natural resources like oil, coal and minerals were nationalised, and industries were set up in all key areas like power, energy, infrastructure, heavy machinery, etc., allowing limited private sector participation in other areas. The whole process of development was primarily to be led by the government. This was the mixed economy model adopted in India, too, a marriage between a centrally planned economy and market economy, with the former occupying, and almost monopolising, the 'commanding heights' of economy.[35]

This was how the public sector emerged not only in India, but in most of the third world, too. It became the primary mover of economy in many countries including India; in most of these countries, planned economic development was adopted and the public sector became an inseparable part of this, as it was only through the public sector that planned development could be achieved. Thus, strategic sectors like defence, power, atomic energy, etc. were kept outside the reach of the private sector, and control was established over extraction and utilisation of natural resources. Even the few sectors where private industries were allowed were subjected to debilitating state control and regulation. Eventually, banking and insurance industries were also nationalised, bringing almost the entire financial architecture of

---

[35] As early as 1931, the Indian National Congress had adopted a resolution at its Karachi session advocating nationalisation of key industries.

the country under government control, leading to further corruption and cronyism. The industrial development was steered by a Planning Commission that prescribed ridiculously, following unrealistic and faulty models, and determined and dictated how much was to be produced in which sectors and by following which technology.

The downside to this process was closing the country, which had very limited capital at that stage, and its industries to foreign capital and technology, which were so essential for increasing productivity. Without access to capital and technology and without having any viable industrial infrastructure, the newly created public sector was at a huge disadvantage from the start. The overbearing state control also turned the state organs into instruments of unbridled power, which not only opened the floodgates of corruption but also made resource utilisation extremely inefficient, leading to low productivity and non-fulfilment of objectives in most of these countries. The less the objectives were fulfilled, the stronger became the command and control structure of the economy. In India, this led to the suffocating License Permit Raj that stifled growth and stymied entrepreneurship.

The first half of the 20th century saw the burgeoning growth of the public sector in both developed as well as developing countries, and the second half of the 20th century saw its gradual decline. But by the 1970s, the public sector had become globally so important that the United Nations Development Organisation (UNIDO) constituted an expert group to identify 'The Role of the Public Sector in the Industrialisation of the Developing Countries'. In its meeting in Vienna in May 1979, it examined, *inter alia*, the genesis and growth of the public industrial sector, its role and interlinkages in the industrialisation process and the government policies and strategies in this context.[36] It identified a vast, rather an astounding range of developmental objectives of the public sector for the developing countries, far beyond their capacity, defined at three levels—national, sectoral and enterprise. These included adopting a socialistic model of development, evolving into a balanced economic structure, controlling and managing natural monopolies as well as strategic sectors of the

---

[36] https://open.unido.org/api/documents/4690986, accessed 12 June 2019.

economy, developing backward areas and weaker sections of society, generating employment, earning foreign exchange, improving income distribution, increasing the availability of essential consumer goods, undertaking tasks beyond the capability of private enterprise and also for readying them for competition, assimilating technology, stimulating agricultural development, helping stabilise prices, taking over the management of ailing private sector firms (under the assumption that governments could manage them better), exploitation of unused natural resources, etc.[37]

Indeed, in many third world countries, including India, Brazil, China, Malaysia, Mexico, Nigeria, Pakistan, Sri Lanka, Zambia, etc., the public sector was made to undertake many of these activities, often with disastrous results. Globalisation would ultimately change this scenario in most countries, often accompanied by disruptive economic reforms. In the globalised world of today, the public sector is undergoing disruptive transformation in many countries to change their ethos to reflect the demands of fast-changing times.

---

[37] Report of the Expert Group Meeting on the Role of the Public Sector in the Industrialization of the Developing Countries, Vienna, 14–18 May 1979 (https://open.unido.org/api/documents/4682968), accessed 12 June 2019.

CHAPTER 2

Nature and Scope of the Public Sector in India and the World

Public sector in its widest connotation means the entire government sector, though for the purpose of this book, we shall use it in a limited sense meaning government-controlled corporate sector. The public sector in this sense has different names in different countries—PSE or public enterprise (PE), parastatal, government controlled enterprise (GCE), state-owned enterprise (SOE), public sector undertaking (PSU) or public undertaking (PU) or simply state enterprise or state undertaking (SE or SU). In India, we use the term PSE or PSU; in this book, all these terms will be used interchangeably. Definitions of public enterprises also vary from country to country, with different legal connotations.

A PE is created for serving a public purpose, but it has two facets—public and enterprise—and these two dimensions need to be blended properly. As a business enterprise, a PE has shareholder(s) who contribute to its capital assets, which are distinct from the personal or other assets of the shareholders. It also has a formal system of management with key officials appointed by the shareholder(s). As a public enterprise, the government is the principal shareholder of the PE and hence, unlike in the case of a private enterprise, the objective of a PE may not necessarily be only commercial, which is of course earning the maximum profit from operations. A PE has social objectives as well in accordance with the government's policy; in fact, the socio-economic objectives of a PE often eclipse its commercial objectives. In recent times, however, the commercial viability of PEs is becoming increasingly important, though the emphasis on public purpose remains undiminished. Like any private company, a PE is also a legal entity or a corporate person.

Classical thinkers defined a public enterprise in very broad terms. The distinguished Bulgarian jurist Konstantin Katzarov dealt with the subject of nationalisation in his *The Theory of Nationalisation,* which had significantly influenced government thinking in Europe. Government intervention in the economy is generally designed to serve three under-lying interests: the financial or fiscal interest of the state, the economic interest of the nation and the political interest of the political party in power, of which the fiscal interest, though important sometimes, is obviously not the *'essentialia negotii* of nationalisation'; the decisive motives for nationalisation are economic, political or moral in character, and these are inextricably interwoven.[1] The public purpose is essentially 'establishing equality between men by enabling goods to be share out by the community in a socially equitable manner', while it does not seek 'to eliminate private property, private enterprise and private capital'.[2]

Three conditions are generally recognised as characteristics of a public enterprise: government control over the entity, which even 'need not be synonymous with majority ownership', 'production of goods and services for sale' as the primary activity of the entity and a policy that a substantial part of the costs of operation of the entity should be covered by its revenues.[3] The International Monetary Fund (IMF) classifies them as public financial institutions and non-financial public enterprises, of which the former is primarily engaged in collecting deposits and 'incurring liabilities and assets in the market', while the latter is engaged in production or selling of 'industrial or commercial

---

[1] Katzarov, *The Theory of Nationalisation,* 13.
[2] Ibid, 14–15.
[3] Floyd, Gray, and Short, *Public Enterprise in Mixed Economies,* 41.

goods and services to the public on a large scale'.[4] The International Centre of Public Enterprise defines the public sector as 'any commercial, financial, agricultural or promotional undertaking owned by public authority, either wholly or through majority shareholding engaged in sale of goods and services'. It is interesting to note that profit is not mentioned anywhere in these definitions.

Government investment in the public sector comes either through equity on investment in the entity's capital or through debt, that is, long-term loans. Ownership is exercised through majority shareholding of equity by the government. There are many organisational forms for the public sector: departmentally managed commercial enterprises, statutory public corporations, limited liability joint stock companies, autonomous organisations and even non-profit organisations. The nature, form and pattern of ownership vary widely across the globe, but being financed from public funds, they are accountable to the parliament through statutory standing committees or bodies constituted for the purpose of enforcing public accountability. They are also subject to the rules and accountability mechanism like every other private company. Usually, they are managed by a Board of Directors, the majority of them appointed by the government.

Their management involves issues which are exogenous as well as endogenous. The former pertain to macro level public policies determined by the socio-economic objectives, market structure and supply constraints, while the latter concern the micro issues like day-to-day operation and management, falling within the jurisdiction of the local management. Operationalisation of corporate governance has, however, obliterated many of the distinctions between the public and the private sector enterprises.

The noted German-American scholar of international law Wolfgang Friedmann gave a more practical and workable legal definition of a public enterprise as:

> an institution operating a service of an economic and social character on behalf of the Government but as an independent legal

[4] Ibid, 42.

entity, largely autonomous in its management, though responsible to the public through government and parliament and subject to some direction by the government, equipped on the other hand with independent and separate fund of its own and the legal and commercial attributes of a commercial enterprise.[5]

The Organisation for Economic Co-operation and Development (OECD), an intergovernmental economic organisation headquartered in Paris and having 36 members including most advanced economies of the world, defines SOE as an autonomous public entity involved in commercial activities, controlled directly or through other government-controlled units, by the central or federal level of the government, control being defined as the ability to determine general policy or programme of the entity. This definition excludes public entities controlled by the sub-national government, whereas in many countries like India, sub-national entities are also classified as public enterprises. The OECD classifies SOEs as majority- or minority-owned enterprises, depending on whether the government controls 50 per cent or more of the shares of the entities, or between 10 and 50 per cent shares, respectively. The latter is also known as a partially state-owned enterprise. They may or may not be listed in the stock exchange. In many countries, they may be owned partly by a government—central, provincial or local—and partly by another government company. They may also be a wholly owned subsidiary of another government company. Government shareholding in them can be through multiple routes—through direct investment in the authorised capital of the company, or though other vehicles like government pension funds, asset management funds, restructuring corporations or government-controlled development lenders—and they may have complex ownership or regulatory structures. The International Public Sector Accounting Standards Board (IPSASB) is trying to harmonise the way state-owned companies are legally defined and to adjust their financial reporting standards accordingly,

---

[5] Friedmann, *The Public Corporation: A Comparative Symposium*, 576, quoted in Mathur, *Public Enterprise Management*, 17.

which in turn might facilitate a more systematic corporate governance of the PEs.[6]

Even in these days of privatisation, liberalisation and deregulation, with the market ruling the roost globally and structural transformations of national economies leading to downsizing of the public sector, PEs still seem to retain their position as enduring features of the economic landscapes in many countries across the world and are likely to do so for a long time, as can be seen from the cross-country data in Table 2.1.[7]

Even though the private sector is being recognised as the main engine of growth, PEs continue to occupy important roles in most economies—developed as well as developing. In the underdeveloped countries of sub-Saharan Africa and in many countries in South Asia and Eastern Europe, where the private sector has not yet grown adequately, PEs continue to be the principal provider of many essential goods and services, and also of employment, and are facilitating the achievement of the United Nation's Millennium Development Goals. It is therefore imperative that they continue to fulfil the social and economic objectives for which they were created, in full measure, and be alert to the changes taking place in the market at the same time. It is not only the economic space that they occupy in different national jurisdictions but also their share in global production that remains significant. An analysis by the accounting firm PWC shows that SOEs have been claiming an increasing share of the world's largest companies; for example, their share in the Fortune Global 500

---

[6] PriceWaterhouseCoopers, 'State-owned Enterprises: Catalysts for Value Creation?'

[7] Because of different definitions and structure of control and ownership, cross-country comparisons are often extremely difficult, if not impossible. Comparable cross-country data are also very difficult to get. Lack of data makes it almost impossible to assess the impact of privatisation and the diminished importance of state enterprises in the national economies since the 1980s. Available databases like the OECD database of member countries are also far from perfect. Apart from differing definitions of SOEs, the quality of reporting also varies widely. While most countries include only majority central government holdings, some may even include minority stakes and holdings at the sub-national levels.

Table 2.1 SOEs Across the World: 2015

Countries	Total No. of SoEs	Total No. of Employees	Total Value of SOEs (US$ Million)
Australia	8	42,607	13,602
China	51,341	20,248,999	29,201,079
Japan	8	256,265	82,365
India	270	3,284,845	338,518
South Korea	56	147,833	217,811
UK	16	153,604	114,639
France	51	826,967	76,908
Germany	71	370,440	72,000
Sweden	49	124,133	37,115
Russia	32,586*	22,300,000#	NA
Italy	20	499,765	207,507
Spain	51	94,635	36,700
Poland	126	128,016	15,700
USA	16	535,981	−21,692
Canada	44	83,462	30,316
Mexico	78	73,686	21,332
Brazil	134	597,505	145,000
Argentina	59	130,776	27,610
Chile	25	50,361	20,811

Source: OECD dataset on the size and sectoral composition of national state-owned enterprise sectors (2015), except for Russia.
Note: *Bella, Dynnikova, and Slavov, 'The Russian State's size and its footprint'. #Estimated figure for 2014 from Abramova et al., 'State-owned enterprises in the Russian market'.

companies has grown from 9 per cent in 2005 to 23 per cent in 2014, securing them a greater presence in the top rankings. This increased SOE presence in the Fortune Global 500 has, however, been driven primarily by Chinese companies (3% and 15%, respectively).[8] SOEs

[8] Ibid, 9.

collectively account for revenues worth more than US$ 7,000 billion. The actual share and contribution of SOEs would be higher since Fortune Global 500 only includes the listed companies. Their importance in the global economy has been on the rise over the last decade.

The public sector is still dominant not only in the emerging economies, but in developed economies as well. In 2011, more than 10% of the world's largest firms were state-owned (204 firms from 37 countries) and their combined turnover represented more than 10 per cent of the combined sales of the Forbes Global list of the 2,000 largest companies, equivalent to 6 per cent of the world's GDP, more than the GDPs of countries such as Germany, France or the UK.[9] Even today, many governments spanning both the developed and developing world own or control majority shares in mammoth public sector undertakings that are established global brands and major drivers in the economy in their respective countries, such as Baosteel and China Mobile (China), EdF (France), Deutsche Bahn (Germany), ENI (Italy), Posco (South Korea), Pertamina (Indonesia), Gazprom and Rosimuschestvo (Russia), Petronas and Khazanah (Malaysia), Transnet (South Africa), etc. Many countries have become global industrial powers through state patronage and active participation, protection and support to PSUs. Some of the biggest companies in the world are still in the public sector. Thirteen of the biggest oil companies which control three-fourths of the world's oil reserves are all state-owned. In some countries, some SOEs have even been renationalised after their privatisation. One example is New Zealand, whose national airline Air New Zealand was privatised in 1989 after which it merged with the loss-making Ansett Australia Airline. However, partly to rescue it from losses, and also fearing that this was lowering the number of flights of international airlines to New Zealand that was necessary for its burgeoning tourism industry, the government renationalised it in 2001. Between 2000 and 2013, international arrivals to New Zealand had increased by 51 per cent, and in 2014, Air New Zealand was ranked the top airline in the world.[10]

[9] Büge, 'State-owned Enterprises in the Global Economy'.
[10] PriceWaterhouseCoopers, 'State-owned Enterprises: Catalysts for Public Value Creation?', 9.o

The reverse has also happened, like in the case of General Motors (GM), which had to be bailed out by the US Government during the global financial crisis of 2008 through injecting US$ 49.5 billion, which was subsequently converted into a 61% equity stake in the company. The bailout was to prevent the feared shutdown of the US automobile industry and consequent loss of an estimated 2.63 million jobs. But the government takeover eroded the investor confidence, and GM's share prices continued to fall before the government decided to exit in 2012. On the day of sale of the final GM shares in December 2013, the company's shares closed at a record high of $40.90, up from a low of $18.80 in July 2012, bringing back investor confidence in the company.[11]

Table 2.2 shows the respective shares of SOEs among the top 10 firms of different countries in 2011 which ranges from 96 per cent for China to 11 per cent for Germany.[12]

The 40 rich countries included in the database of OECD, or the club of rich countries, had 2,467 fully owned or majority-owned SOEs with 9.2 million employees at the end of 2015. Their combined value is

Table 2.2 SOE Share Among Countries' Top 10 Firms in 2011 (%)

Country	SOE Share Among Top 10 Firms (%)	Country	SOE Share Among top 10 Firms (%)
China	96	Norway	48
UAE	88	Thailand	37
Russia	81	Singapore	23
Indonesia	69	France	17
Malaysia	68	Ireland	16
Saudi Arabia	67	Greece	16
India	59	Finland	13
Brazil	50	Germany	11

Source: Büge, Egeland, Kowalski, and Sztajerowska, *State-owned enterprises in the global economy.*

[11] Ibid, 17.
[12] Computed on equally weighted average of shares of state-owned enterprises in sales, assets and market value of the country's top 10 firms.

estimated at $2.4 trillion. Till the late 1980s or early 1990s, before the new *mantras* of privatisation and deregulation started sweeping across nations around the globe, the public sector had significant presence and shares in GDP and employment in most countries (Tables 2.2A–2.2C).

Table 2.2A *Share of State-owned Enterprises in Economic Activity, 1978–1991*

Economies	1978–1985	1986–1991	1978–1991	1978–1985	1986–1991	1978–1991
	Share in GDP (%)			Share in Employment (%)		
Asia						
India	10.8	13.8	12.1	8.2	8.5	8.3
China	7.4	6.2	6.9	2.2	2	2.1
Indonesia	15.4	14.1	14.8	NA	1	1
South Korea	9.6	10.3	9.9	1.6	1.9	1.8
Malaysia	NA	17.0	17.0	NA	NA	NA
Europe						
UK	5.9	3.0	4.6	NA	NA	NA
France	10.7	10.0	10.5	NA	NA	NA
Germany	7.1	NA	7.1	NA	NA	NA
Spain	4.0	NA	4.0	NA	NA	NA
Africa						
South Africa	13.9	14.7	14.2	NA	NA	NA
Egypt	37.1	30.0	34.1	13.7	13.6	13.7
Tanzania	10.8	13.7	12.1	22.3	22.3	22.3
Nigeria	13.5	14.8	13.8	NA	NA	NA
North America						
USA	1.3	1	1.2	NA	NA	NA
Mexico	12	11	11.6	3.6	3.4	3.5
South America						
Venezuela	23.1	23	23.1	NA	NA	NA
Chile	13.6	12.9	13.3	3.3	1.1	2.8
Peru	8.5	5.3	7.1	2	2.5	2.2
Brazil	5	8.6	6.5	1.2	—	1.2
Argentina	4.7	4.7	4.7	3.1	2.5	2.8

Source: World Bank, *Bureaucrats In Business Database.*

Table 2.2B *Share of State-owned Enterprises in Economic Activity, 1978–1991 (% Share in GDP)*

S. No.	Group (of Economies)	1978–1985	1986–1991	1978–1991
1	40 Developing economies	10.6	11.2	10.9
2	8 Industrial economies			7.8
3	15 Low income economies	13.7	14.2	13.9
4	25 Middle income economies	8.8	9.4	9
5	18 Latin America and the Caribbean	9.2	10.2	9.6
6	14 Africa	14	13.9	13.9
7	8 Asia	7.9	8.8	8.3

Source: World Bank, *Bureaucrats in Business Database.*

Table 2.2C *Share of State-owned Enterprises in Employment, 1978–1991 (%)*

Group (of Economies)	1978–1985	1986–1991	1978–1991
21 Developing economies	10.2	10.7	10.4
11 Low income economies	14.8	15.6	15.2
6 Middle income economies	6	6.2	6.1
9 Latin America and the Caribbean	2.8	2.3	2.6
15 Africa	19.9	21.5	20.6
13 Asia	2.9	2.9	2.9

Source: World Bank, *Bureaucrats in Business Database.*

Till that period, the SOEs' shares in the manufacturing sector in their respective countries were also significant across the globe, as shown in Table 2.3.

However, compared to the overarching role of SOEs in the economy during the 1970s and 1980s, the range of their activities seems to have shrunk to a few sectors of the economy. In 2017, only a few sectors such as electricity and gas, transportation, telecoms and other utilities accounted for 51 per cent of all SOEs by value and 70 per cent by

Table 2.3 Shares of PEs in the Manufacturing Sector (%)

Country	Share of Manufacturing in	Year	Share (%)
Australia	GDP	1978–1979	4.0
France	GDI	1971	11.4
Italy	GDI	1978	18.6
UK	GDI	1978–1981	5.3
Ethiopia	GDP	1979–1980	60.9
Ghana	GDP	1970	32.9
Tanzania	GDP	1974–1977	37.9
Kenya	GDP	1970–1973	13.1
Egypt	GDI	1979	80.4
Iraq	GDI	1975	96.7
Syria	GDI	1975	95.9
Tunisia	GDP	1982	31.4
Turkey	GDP	1979	30.1
Bangladesh	GDP	1981–1982	46.1
Myanmar (Burma)	GDP	1980	56.2
India	GDP	1978	15.7
Pakistan	GDP	1974–1975	7.8
Singapore	GDP	1972	14.2
Sri Lanka	GDP	1974	33.2
Taiwan	GDP	1985	12.0
Venezuela	GDP	1985	16.2

Source: Balassa, *Public Enterprise in Developing Countries.*

employment. Most SOEs (92% by value and 84% by employment) are incorporated according to companies' laws in different countries and hence are subject to the same laws and regulations in their countries that the private companies are subjected to. About half of these companies by value are listed at their respective national stock exchanges.[13]

[13] https://www.oecd.org/industry/ind/Item_6_3_OECD_Korin_Kane.pdf, accessed 17 June 2019.

Different countries have devised and followed different models for the role of their public enterprises in their economic development. Some countries such as Japan, Mexico and Taiwan limited the state's role only for the creation of infrastructure; some like China prior to the 1970s and the erstwhile USSR believed in complete state control over all means of production and distribution and in the total absence of any private sector. Others such as India prior to 1991, Tanzania and Iraq believed in a mixed economy where the private sector functioned along with the public sector, though the role of the public sector in almost every sector of the economy remained predominant while the growth of the private sector remained stymied. Most countries in the world today follow a diluted version of the mixed economy model wherein the public sector competes with the private sector on a level playing field, giving both equal opportunities for success in competition. Since the beginning of the new century, disinvestment, deregulation and privatisation of the public enterprises have become the global trend—a subject that will be addressed later in greater detail. This trend is of course in consonance with the current philosophy and global political predilection towards gradual withdrawal of the state from economic activities and the state becoming more of a facilitator rather than an actor while allowing the private sector and individual entrepreneurs to flourish.

Despite their diminishing importance, many SOEs, spanning both the developing and the developed world, have remarkable success stories to tell. They also have diversified into many fields beyond the traditional banking, insurance and manufacturing sectors. For example, sovereign wealth funds (SWFs)—state-owned funds invested in various financial assets—emerged in the last century, with the objective of funnelling the budgetary surpluses into investments, but their importance increased immensely after the global financial crisis as they were found useful for recapitalising some of the world's largest banks like Morgan Stanley and Merrill Lynch. These state-owned investment funds are being used by the European governments for solving the Eurozone debt crisis. The SWFs have acquired very sophisticated, risk-calculated governance structures and investment policies. They have grown in size as well as in number, with their investment size exceeding US$ 5 trillion worldwide. Their operations are transnational; for example, in March 2014, 69 per cent of the portfolio of Singapore's SWF—Temasek Holdings—was invested outside Singapore.[14] One of the largest global SWFs is Norway's Government Pension Fund Global (GPFG). Norway gets most of its revenue from oil, and the fund was set up in the 1990s to help the government absorb the effects of any sudden fall in the global oil price. Its stated mission is to 'safeguard and build financial wealth for future generations', and it has a robust governance structure to hedge any unforeseen risks. GPFG has ownership stakes in 1.3% of the world's listed companies spanning 73 countries, their number exceeding 9,100.

Besides these public investment companies, the model of public–private partnership (PPP) has also emerged as a major driver of construction projects for infrastructure building in many countries, though the model has often been criticised for being heavily skewed in favour of the private sector to the detriment of the public sector. But PPPs are used by many countries as an alternative to privatisation and also to upgrade the capacity of the SOEs. They are an example of joint ventures between the public and the private sectors. China, for example, has used joint ventures with foreign companies to get access to foreign technology and capital, foreign management and marketing techniques, besides undertaking joint research and development. One major joint venture project in China was the expansion of telecommunications equipment facilities in Shanghai area, facilitated through the joint venture between the China's Ministry of Posts and Telecommunications, the Belgian Government and the company Alcatel Bell. Joint ventures are also used to build telecommunications, transport, shipping, airport and utility infrastructure in many countries, using various models like build-operate-transfer (BOT) or build-operate-own (BOO).[15]

At independence, India inherited endemic poverty and widespread unemployment. The immediate concerns were to face the challenges

---

[14] PriceWaterhouseCoopers, 'State-owned Enterprises: Catalysts for Public Value Creation?', 12.

[15] Rondinelli, 'Can Public Enterprises Contribute to Development?', 35–36.

to growth, to create avenues for employment, to alleviate poverty and address the concerns that poverty inevitably brings such as lack of food, sanitation, health and education and to provide to the citizens the minimum basic goods and services. An appropriate development strategy had to be chalked for the purpose, given the huge constraints of capital, skill, foreign exchange and access to technology that the country was facing. At the same time, given the colonial experience of exploitation through export of natural resources and import of the finished products, any export was viewed with suspicion, and the focus was on substitution of imports. Another big challenge was to create the basic infrastructure of roads, power, irrigation, etc. Save a few industries in steel, textile, sugar, etc. managed by large business houses like Tata, Birla and a few others, India possessed hardly any industrial base. There were few private industries at independence, institutional financing was very limited and the private sector could not be expected to invest in these sectors due to the huge scale of investment required, long gestation periods and the attendant risk factors involved.

To Prime Minister Nehru, the only way to overcome the endemic poverty and food crisis that bedevilled post-Independence India was through establishing overwhelming state control over the means of production and distribution, in the Soviet style, to serve broad macro-economic objectives of achieving higher economic growth, self-sufficiency in production, import substitution and long-term equilibrium in foreign trade, besides meeting other socio-economic obligations. In a speech before the National Development Council in November 1954, he stated: 'The means of production should be socially owned and controlled for the benefit of society as a whole'. Under Nehru's stewardship, the Indian Parliament passed a resolution in December 1954, adopting a goal of 'socialistic pattern of society' for India, to be achieved through a mixed economic model, with the PSEs occupying and dominating the 'commanding heights' of the economy. The objectives of economic growth, self-reliance, social justice and alleviation of poverty were to be achieved in a planned manner, for which a Planning Commission was created in 1950, through an executive order, with powers to allocate national resources for the purpose of development. As stated by B. S. Minhas, a member of the Planning

Commission, during 1971–1973: 'Securing rapid economic growth and expansion of employment, reduction of disparities in income and wealth, prevention of concentration of economic power and creation of the values and attitudes of a free and equal society have been among the objectives of all our plans'.[16]

The Planning Commission derived its legitimacy from the Directive Principles of the State Policy of the Constitution that laid down that the state must direct its policy to ensure citizens' right to 'adequate means of livelihood', distribution of the 'ownership and control of the resources of the community' to 'subserve the common good' and to prevent concentration of 'wealth and means of production to the common detriment'. However, created by an executive order, the Planning Commission was an extra-constitutional mechanism, giving a body created outside the Constitution vast and unusual powers, which, over the course of the next several decades, would produce huge distortions in the economy. The objectives of development were to be achieved through the Five Year Plans (FYPs) to be formulated, implemented and monitored by the Planning Commission. The FYPs were discontinued in 2017 after the implementation of 12 such plans; the Planning Commission itself was disbanded in 2014 by the newly elected NDA government.

However, at independence, the realities were quite different, and hence the first Industrial Policy Resolution of 1948 outlines the priorities of the government in declaring the objectives of PSEs to:

1. establish a social order with justice and equality for all;
2. promote rapid rise in the living standards of citizens through exploitation of national resources;
3. accelerate production to meet the needs of a growing population and
4. provide opportunities for employment

The First FYP, launched in 1951, set the direction of growth for the next 5 years, focusing on agriculture and also beginning the process

---

[16] Minhas, *Planning and the Poor*, vii.

of industrialisation through PSUs. This was based on the Keynesian Harrod–Domar model that regards capital accumulation as a key factor in the process of growth and seeks to explain growth in terms of the level of saving and productivity of capital. But a definite strategy for development came into being with the Second FYP (1956–1961) that was formulated on the so-called Mahalanobis Model developed by the renowned Indian statistician Mr P. C. Mahalanobis, borrowing the philosophy and experiences from the USSR's Gosplan. The plan allocated investments among different sectors of the economy in order to optimise sectoral outputs for overall long-term economic growth.[17] Industrialisation was recognised as the principal engine for rapid economic growth and industrialisation was reckoned synonymous with creation of basic and heavy industries. This was the philosophy behind India's PSUs. As Nehru himself later stated: 'If we are to industrialise, it is of primary importance that we must have the heavy industries that build machines'.[18] Thus, the focus of planning shifted from agriculture towards industrialisation, and several PSUs were

---

[17] The Mahalanobis model, known as the four-sector model, depends on a set of equations like:

$$Y_k + Y_{c1} + Y_{c2} + y_{c3} = ₹2,900 \text{ crore}$$
$$I_k + I_{c1} + I_{c2} + I_{c3} = ₹5,600 \text{ crore}$$
$$n_k + n_{c1} + n_{c2} + n_{c3} = 11 \text{ million,}$$

where the Ys are the stipulated income increases in the four sectors: k (basic investment goods), c_1 (factory consumer goods), c_2 (household industries including agriculture), and c_3 (services); Is are the respective investments and ns represent the allocation of manpower to the respective sectors. In addition, there are various structural coefficients of Ys, Is and ns. The first three equations express the boundary conditions for creating additional income amounting to ₹2,900 crores and additional employment of the order of 11 million on an aggregate new investment of ₹5,600 crores. The system assumes that the structural constants are known and only the Ys, Is and ns are to be determined. Mahalanobis determined that one-third of the total investment must take place in the investment-goods sector, and the rest of the quantities needed to be determined. (Source: Mitra, 'A Note on the Mahalanobis Model', 372–374.) The model, based on many simplistic and unrealistic assumptions of a closed economy, has been severely criticised by economists, and many have held it responsible for the so-called 'Hindu rate of growth' during the first four decades after independence.

[18] Speech in the Parliament, 22 August 1960.

established in different parts of the country, especially in the steel and power sectors.[19] The Mahalanobis Model, with minor modifications, would guide resource allocation during the next three plans as well, with consequences that would prove disastrous for the economy.

The Third Five Year Plan (1961–1966) brought the focus back to agriculture, but during its period, two wars—in 1962 with China and in 1965 with Pakistan—took their toll on the economy, which was accentuated by a severe drought in 1965. The result was high inflation and low growth; the growth in fact plummeted to 2.4 per cent as against the target of 5.6 per cent. The FYP was abandoned during the next 3 years during which only annual plans were drawn. It was revived in 1969, and during the Fourth Five Year Plan (1969–1974), 14 major Indian banks were nationalised. However, the growth remained at only 3.3 per cent during the plan period. The Fifth Five Year Plan (1974–1979) was abandoned after the Janata Government was elected to power following the Emergency, which introduced a new Sixth Five Year Plan (1978–1983). This was again abandoned after the Congress Government returned to power in 1980, with the period 1978–1980 being treated as the Rolling Plan. Though during the new Sixth Five Year Plan (1980–1985) and Seventh Five Year Plan (1985–1990) the growth exceeded 5 per cent, the country had come to the brink of economic collapse, having almost completely run out of its foreign exchange reserves, and by then the overall failure of the planning process was apparent to everyone. In 1991, India would make a break with the past and launch its deregulation, liberalisation, globalisation and privatisation process, ushering in transformational economic reforms that would eliminate the License Permit Raj regime that was characteristic of the planning era, boosting economic growth to nearly double digits. The FYPs would, however, continue for another quarter of a century before the distinction between plan and non-plan expenditure would be removed for good.

---

[19] 'In the long run, the rate of industrialisation and the growth of the national economy would depend upon the increasing production of coal, electricity, iron and steel, heavy machinery, heavy chemicals and heavy industries generally which would increase the capacity for capital formation. One important aim is to make India independent as quickly as possible of foreign imports...' (Second Five Year Plan, The Framework, 43)

The plans were duly backed by industrial policies, and as the focus changed from plan to plan, a series of Industrial Policy Resolutions were adopted. The First Industrial Policy Resolution in 1948 essentially laid down the contours of the mixed economy—a hybrid between the market economy and a centrally planned economy. It divided industries into four categories, of which defence production, atomic energy and railways would be reserved for the public sector. In respect of coal, iron and steel, aircraft manufacture, shipbuilding, mineral oil, telephones, cable and wireless, the private sector would be allowed to operate its existing industries, but new undertakings in these industries would be created only by the State. In respect of 18 industries including motor vehicles, heavy machine tools, cotton textiles, cement, sugar, paper, shipping material and tractor, private industries would be allowed to operate under government control, while private ownership would be allowed in respect of the rest. This was the beginning of the infamous License Permit Raj.

As the Second FYP was introduced in 1956, a new industrial policy resolution replaced the 1948 policy. The Industrial Policy Resolution of 1956, which would guide industrialisation in the country for the next two decades, stated emphatically:

> the adoption of the socialistic pattern of society as the national objective, as well as the need for planned and rapid development require that all industries of basic and strategic importance or in the nature of public utility services should be in the public sector. Other industries which are essential and require investment on a scale, which only the state, in the present circumstances, could provide, have also to be in the public sector.

The new policy essentially focused on establishing basic and heavy industries, accelerating the pace of industrial development and reducing income and wealth inequalities. It classified industries into three categories, broadly retaining the old structure of classification but expanding the lists. The 'Schedule A' industries would include 17 industries that were to be in the exclusive domain of the public sector, such as arms and ammunition, atomic energy, iron and steel, heavy machinery, mineral oil, coal, etc. 'Schedule B' included 12 industries such as aluminium, machine tools, drugs, chemical fertiliser, road and sea transport, mines and minerals, etc., in which the state would set up new industries but the private sector could supplement the effort of the state. The remaining industries would come under 'Schedule C' that would be left to the initiative and enterprise of the private sector. They would of course be subject to the government's laws, rules and regulations like the Industries (Development and Regulation) Act, 1951 and a plethora of other legislations. Another legislation was the Monopolistic and Restrictive Trade Practices Act, 1969, enacted to ensure that the operation of the economic system did not result in the concentration of economic power in the hands of a few, to provide for the control of monopolies and to prohibit monopolistic and restrictive trade practices. Since repealed, its provision would be considered draconian by today's standards.

After the Emergency, the Janata Government introduced the new 1977 Industrial Policy Statement, laying heavy emphasis on cottage and small scale industries as the drivers of employment. The intention was to prevent the concentration of wealth among the large industrial houses, while envisaging a larger role for the public sector in the development of ancillary industries as well as consumer goods industries, besides the production of important and strategic goods, and also to augment the growth of the small scale sector by making available to the sector its managerial and technological expertise. The policy was disowned by the incumbent Congress Government in 1980, which reinforced the 1956 policy with some changes. Admitting that there was an erosion of faith in the public sector, the new policy focused on the 'effective operational management' of the public sector. The next was the Industrial Policy Resolution of 1991 that finally dismantled the command and control structure of the economy characterised by the License Permit Raj regime.

July of 1991 was indeed a momentous month in the economic history of India. The rupee was devalued by 7 per cent and again by 11 per cent within the first 3 days to bring it closer to its real market value. On 9 July 1991, the Prime Minister addressed the nation, highlighting the need for reforms and promising to remove the cobwebs that hindered the economy. A new industrial policy and a path-breaking budget defining the course of reforms the country was to embrace were presented together on 24 July 1991. It was this industrial policy that actually freed the economy from the suffocating License Permit Raj architecture of the Nehruvian socio-economic philosophy and polity, built around a complex labyrinth of licenses, permits and controls that dictated every facet of production and distribution, setting up entry barriers at every stage, and built a strong bias towards state ownership of the means of production. The License Permit Raj viewed all private enterprises with extreme suspicion and believed in the domination of the public sector over every economic activity. It abhorred international trade and erected tariff barriers to prevent India's integration into the global economy, which in its myopic vision was capitalist and hence repugnant. It had infinite trust in the wisdom of its redoubtable bureaucrats and Planning Commission members and their ability to control and direct the market forces towards India's growth.

The defined objectives of the new industrial policy were to liberalise industries from all regulatory devices like licences and controls and unshackle them 'from the cobwebs of unnecessary bureaucratic controls', enhance support to the small scale sector, increase competitiveness among industries, ensure running of public enterprises on business lines and ensure rapid industrial development in a competitive environment. The cornerstones of this policy were: (a) abolition of all industrial licensing, irrespective of the level of investment, except for certain industries related to security and strategic concerns; (b) de-reservation of industries for the public sector and allowing the private sector in all areas to reserve three industries—arms and ammunition, atomic energy and rail transport (till then, the public sector had exclusive reservation over as many as 17 sectors); (c) disinvestment of the public sector and its restructuring by giving it more autonomy, closing sick units and reducing government stake in them to 26 per cent or less; (d) free entry to foreign direct investment (FDI) and foreign technology for modernisation, and providing products and services of international standards, through a new FDI policy; and (e) abolition of MRTP clearance for large industries and liberalising industrial location approvals.

There were many other facets to the reforms process, and each of these contributed to the creation of a competitive industrial climate, built around the private and not the public sector by unleashing the former's immense energy, innovation and entrepreneurship to create wealth and jobs for millions, and by attracting financial capital from across the seven seas. The most pronounced and visible impacts of the economic reforms unleashed in July 1991 have been the drastic fall in our poverty ratio, the dramatic improvement in our growth rates and the miraculous increase in the inflow of foreign capital and the consequent development of our foreign exchange reserves. The India of 2019 is far more integrated in the global economy, and indeed, it is an economic force to reckon with in today's world. Stagnation and despair of the 1990s are things of the past, and India today aspires to be counted among the top economies in the world within the next decade.

Jawaharlal Nehru hailed public sector undertakings (PSU) as 'temples of modern India'. It cannot be denied that PSUs had indeed helped the infant nation in its formative years. Save a handful of companies, the private sector, inherently averse to risk, was almost non-existent then, and could not be expected to invest in infrastructure and heavy industries that entailed long gestation periods, more so in the insular economy of the post-Independence days. PSUs have grown luxuriantly since then, from only five Central PSUs (CPSUs) with a total investment of ₹29 crore during the First Plan to as many as 444 in 2016–2017, with a total investment of ₹16 lakh crore. Besides these, there are also 192 companies controlled by the government indirectly, in association with state governments. The states of India together have as many as 1,136 PSUs as of March 2017, with a total public investment of about ₹15 lakh crore.[20] But the philosophy behind the PSUs has undergone a sea change since then, with the redefinition of the state's role as a catalyst and facilitator rather than as a producer. Today, most of our PSUs, especially those owned by the state governments, remain haplessly trapped in the vast no man's land between the state and the market.

The term Central Government Public Sector Enterprises (CPSEs) includes the union government–owned companies set up under the

---

[20] Data collected from the Union Report No. 2 of 2018 of the CAG of India for the year 2016–2017.

Companies Act, 2013, and statutory corporations set up under the statutes enacted by the parliament. A government company is defined in section 2(45) of the Companies Act, 2013 as a company in which not less than 51 per cent of the paid-up share capital is held by the central government or by any state government or governments, or partly by the central government and partly by one or more state governments, and also includes a company which is a subsidiary of a government company. Besides, the departmental commercial undertakings like Railways and Posts and Telecommunications, which are financed by annual appropriations from the Union Budget, would also come under the broad definition of the public sector. Statutory corporations are wholly owned by the government,[21] while government companies would be mostly in the nature of joint-stock companies, with the controlling stake being held by the government under the Companies Act, as defined above. Banking and insurance companies as well as non-banking financial institutions controlled by the government would thus come under the definition of public enterprise if they satisfy the conditions stipulated in the Companies Act, as discussed above. The Comptroller and Auditor General of India (CAG) in his report treats all these companies as public enterprises.

The Department of Public Enterprises (DPE) under the Ministry of Heavy Industries and Public Enterprises brings out an annual survey of public enterprises under the Government of India, known as the Public Enterprises Survey. This traditionally covers, besides certain statutory corporations, those government companies wherein more than 50 per cent equity is held by the central government. The survey, however, does not include the departmentally run public enterprises, banking and insurance companies, which may also be government companies—in fact, most of them are indeed controlled by the government. Thus, there is a difference in the number of companies considered as CPSEs by CAG and by DPE, and the latter is understated and unrealistic, being not perfectly aligned with the definition

---

[21] There are six Statutory Corporations under the Union Government: Airports Authority of India, Central Warehousing Corporation, Damodar Valley Corporation, Food Corporation of India, Inland Waterways Authority of India and National Highways Authority of India.

of government companies under the Companies Act. In this book, whenever we are constrained to use data from both the sources, this distinction should be borne in mind. However, we are excluding the departmentally run commercial undertakings, banking and insurance companies, as well as financial institutions from the scope of our discussion on public enterprises, which require a separate book to discuss the issues related to them.

Over the years, the PSEs in India have grown luxuriantly. Table 2.4 shows the gradual proliferation of the CPSEs over the years. The

Table 2.4 *Growth of the Public Sector*

Year	No. of Units	Total Govt. Investment (₹ Crore)	Employment (Lakh)	Event
1950–1951	5	29		Beginning of 1st plan
1955–1956	21	81		Beginning of 2nd plan
1960–1961	47	948		Beginning of 3rd plan
1968–1969	73	2,415		Beginning of 4th plan
1974–1975	122	6,237	9.2*	Beginning of 5th plan
1980–1981	179	18,150	19.3	Beginning of 6th plan
1985–1986	215	42,673	21.5	Beginning of 7th plan
1990–1991	244	99,329	22.2	Economic reforms launched
1992–1993	246	135,445	21.5	Beginning of 8th plan
1997–1998	240	231,024	19.6	Beginning of 9th plan
2000–2001	240	252,745	17.4	Turn of century
2002–2003	240	324,614	18.7#	Beginning of 10th plan
2007–2008	247	420,771	15.6	Beginning of 11th plan
2012–2013	277	850,599	14.0	Beginning of 12th plan
2016–2017	331	1,245,819	11.4	End of planning era
2017–2018	339	1,373,412	10.9	Beginning on non-plan era

Source: Economic Survey and Public Enterprise Survey, respective years, and Department of Public Enterprises, 'Public Sector in India'.
Notes: *1972–1973 Figure for employment. #No. of employees had increased due to the corporatisation of DOT in 2001–2002.

Table 2.5 *Savings and Investment as Shares of GDP*

	Gross Domestic Savings				GFCF		
	Household Sector	Private Corporate Sector	Public Sector	Total	Private Sector	Public Sector	Total
Base year 2004–2005							
1950–1951	6.5	0.9	2.1	9.5	6.8	2.5	9.3
1955–1956	9.2	1.2	2.2	12.6	6.7	5.4	12.1
1960–1961	6.8	1.6	3.2	11.6	6.0	6.8	12.8
1965–1966	9.0	1.4	3.8	14.2	7.2	8.1	15.3
1970–1971	9.5	1.4	3.4	14.3	7.9	5.8	13.7
1975–1976	11.3	1.2	4.8	17.3	8.6	7.4	16.0
1980–1981	12.1	1.6	4.1	17.8	8.8	9.1	17.9
1985–1986	12.7	1.9	3.9	18.5	9.3	11.3	20.6
1990–1991	16.5	2.4	2.4	21.3	13.6	10.2	23.8
1995–1996	16.2	4.8	2.6	23.6	15.4	8.6	24.0
2000–2001	21.3	3.7	-1.3	23.7	16.0	6.7	22.7
2005–2006	23.5	7.5	2.4	33.4	23.4	7.9	31.3
2010–2011	23.1	8.0	2.6	33.7	23.1	7.8	30.9
Base year 2011–2012							
2015–2016	19.2	11.9	1.3	32.4	21.9	7.4	29.3

Source: Economic Survey, Government of India, 2016–2017.

contribution of the public sector to the Gross Domestic Savings and investment as measured by the Gross Fixed Capital Formation (GFCF) also remained substantial till the mid-1980s. After that, even though their contribution to savings declined, their contribution to investment remained significant throughout (Table 2.5). In fact, by 1990–1991, the share of the public sector GFCF in GDP was twice as much as that of the private corporate sector. The contribution of the PSEs, however, came down after 1991 due to the policy of gradual privatisation and disinvestment, which we shall deal with later.

CPSEs vary widely in terms of their size, activities, scale of operations, profitability and employee compensation, geographical dispersion, product range and their strategic significance to the national economy. There cannot be a common standard to assess either their performance or their policies, and this calls for a system of classification of the CPSEs.

There are generally three types of classification of the CPSEs followed by the Department of Public Enterprises, namely (a) cognate group-wise classification; (b) grouping of CPSEs into four schedules— A, B, C and D—for the purposes of determining the compensation of executives and (c) their categorisation into 'Ratnas', for example, Navratna, Miniratna–I, Miniratna–II, etc., for the purpose of autonomy and delegation of powers.[22] While the cognate group-wise classification is somewhat analogous to the sectoral classification of industries in the private sector, the schedule-wise classification system, introduced in 1965, was based on their relative importance to economy, which determined the compensation of their Board-level executives. The Ratna classification was introduced in 1997 with nine CPSEs having been identified as Navratnas, and different categories were introduced subsequently. The Ratna status of a company has no bearing on the compensation structures, and is also not sector-specific. Thus, these three systems of classification are mutually independent. Besides these three systems, CPSEs are also classified ministry/ department-wise, according to the ministries/departments vested with their administrative controls. They may also be classified as central or state public sector enterprises depending on whether they are owned by the union or the state governments respectively.

As regards the cognate group-wise classification, 21 cognate groups have been identified under five sectors, as shown in Table 2.6.

The schedule-wise classification, introduced in 1965, is decided by the concerned administrative ministry in consultation with Department of Public Enterprises (DPE) and the Public Enterprises Selection Board (PSEB), which recruits the Board-level executives

[22] Department of Public Enterprises, *Classification and Categorisation of CPSEs.*

Table 2.6 *Cognate Group-wise Classification of CPSEs*

| | | No. of CPSEs as on | |
| | | 31 March 2018 | 31 March 2017 |
Sectors	*Cognate Group*		
Agriculture			
	Agro-based industries	3	5
Mining and exploration			
	Coal	8	8
	Crude oil	5	5
	Other minerals and metals	11	11
	Sub-total	24	24
Manufacturing, processing and generation			
	Steel	4	4
	Petroleum (refinery and marketing)	6	6
	Fertilizers	7	7
	Chemicals and pharmaceuticals	17	17
	Heavy and medium engineering	36	35
	Transportation vehicle and equipment	1	1
	Industrial and consumer goods	13	13
	Textiles	4	4
	Power generation	12	12
	Sub-total	100	99
Services			
	Power transmission	9	8
	Trading and marketing	20	20
	Transport and logistic services	23	21
	Contract and construction and technical consultancy services	43	42
	Hotel and tourist services	7	9

(Table 2.6 Continued)

(Table 2.6 Continued)

Sectors	Cognate Group	No. of CPSEs as on	
		31 March 2018	*31 March 2017*
	Financial services	20	21
	Telecommunication and IT	8	8
	Sub-total	130	129
Enterprises under construction			
	Enterprises under construction	82	74
	Grand total	339	331

Source: Department of Public Enterprises, *Public Enterprise Survey 2017–2018*, Vol. I, Box 1.2, p. 3.

for the CPSEs. There are laid-down criteria for this categorisation based on quantitative factors like investment,[23] capital employed,[24] net sales, profit, number of employees, number of units, etc., as well as qualitative factors like strategic importance of the company for national economy, the complexity of its operations, the level of technology employed, competition, etc. Other factors like Ratna classification of the Company, if any, its productivity, profitability, share price (if it is a listed company), etc. are also factored in to decide the classification. Subsidiary companies are categorised at least one schedule below that of the holding company. As of March 2019, there were 65 Schedule A, 66 Schedule B, 44 Schedule C and 5 Schedule D operating companies; the rest were either unclassified or non-operating companies. The schedule-wise list of companies is appended at Annexure 2.1 to this chapter.

Finally, for delegation of higher financial and operational autonomy to CPSEs that have developed the potential to become global players, nine CPSEs were identified in 1997 and accorded the status of

[23] Government's contribution for equity and long-term loans
[24] Net block + Net working capital

Navratnas. Subsequently, a separate category of Maharatnas was created and seven companies were accorded the status of Maharatnas. The list of Navratnas was expanded to include 16 CPSEs. Two more categories, Miniratna–I and Miniratna–II, were also created. As of March 2018, there were 8 Maharatna, 16 Navratna and 75 Miniratna CPSEs (60 Miniratna–I and 15 Miniratna–II companies).[25] The eligibility criteria for the granting of Maharatna, Navratna or Miniratna status to CPSEs are as follows:

A CPSE is eligible to be considered for the grant of Maharatna status, if

1. it has a Navratna status already;
2. it is listed on the Indian stock exchange with minimum prescribed public shareholding under SEBI regulations;
3. its average annual turnover exceeded ₹25,000 crore during the last 3 years;
4. its average annual net worth exceeded ₹15,000 crore during the last 3 years;
5. its average annual net profit after tax exceeded ₹5,000 crore during the last 3 years; and
6. it has a significant global presence and international operations.

Similarly, a CPSE is eligible to be considered for the grant of Navratna status if it is a Miniratna–I and Schedule 'A' CPSE, obtained an 'excellent' or 'very good' rating under the Memorandum of Understanding system in three of the last 5 years and scores more than 60 in respect of the following six selected performance parameters, namely:

1. Net profit to net worth;
2. Manpower cost to total cost of production/services;
3. Profit before depreciation, interest and taxes to capital employed;
4. Profit before interest and taxes to turnover;
5. Earnings per share; and
6. Inter-sectoral performance.

---

[25] Press Information Bureau, Government of India, Ministry of Heavy Industries & Public Enterprises Press Release dated 21 July 2014.

CPSEs that have made profits in the last 3 years continuously and have a positive net worth are eligible for the grant of Miniratna status. In case the pre-tax profit is ₹30 crore or more in any one of the last 3 years, the CPSE is classified as Miniratna-I; otherwise, it is a Miniratna-II company.

As regards the delegation of power, a Maharatna company can invest up to ₹5,000 crore in one project autonomously. In contrast, a Navratna company can invest only up to ₹1,000 crore or up to 15 per cent of its net worth, whichever is less, in a single project, or up to 30 per cent in all joint ventures or subsidiaries, and has the powers to incur capital expenditure on purchase of new items or for replacement without any monetary ceiling. A Navratna CPSE has also been delegated the powers for mergers and acquisitions subject to certain conditions.

A Miniratna-I company can invest up to ₹500 crore or up to an equal amount of their net worth, whichever is less, in projects during a year. On the other hand, a Miniratna-II company can invest up to ₹300 crore or 50 per cent of their net worth, whichever is less, autonomously, during a year. Thus, the basis on which such status is accorded is more structured and unambiguously defined than the schedule classification. The list of these categories of companies is appended at Annexure 2.2 to this chapter.

Even though the state is the owner of the PSUs, there are different ways in which this ownership function can be exercised. OECD countries follow one of the three existing ownership models: decentralised, centralised and dual. In the centralised model, as in Denmark, Norway, Sweden, Netherlands, Belgium or Spain, one government body, either a single ministry (Finance/Industry) or a holding company, exercises the ownership functions. This establishes a clear line of accountability from the PSU to the government while enabling the government to exercise effective control through coherent policies or strategies. The risk here is that this may blur the distinction between the government's roles as regulator and as owner, the owner exerting undue influence over the regulator, besides the risk of over-centralisation that could inhibit innovation and enterprise. A well-known and well-managed example of a centralised agency is Temasek of Singapore, which is one of the two investment arms of the government (the other being the

Government Investment Corporation responsible for forex). After its independence in 1965, Singapore pursued economic growth by taking stakes in many companies, including start-ups. Temasek was established in 1974 to take over the government's stakes in companies held by the Ministry of Finance and holds stakes in a wide range of areas including telecommunications, financial services, energy and natural resources, transport and semiconductors industries, biopharma and healthcare, etc. We shall return to Temasek later in this book.

In the decentralised or sectoral model, PSUs have the responsibility of different ministries such as in India, Germany, Czech Republic, etc., the idea being that decentralisation brings greater sectoral expertise to the PSUs dealing with sectoral ministries. But the downside is the difficulty in separation of the ownership from the regulatory function of the state and risk of interference in the autonomy of PSUs, instances of which have been seen aplenty in India. In the dual form, practised in New Zealand, Switzerland, Mexico, Turkey etc., responsibility is shared between a sector ministry and a single central ministry like the Ministry of Finance. Division of the roles is likely to usher in more rigorous checks and balances than a single ministry, besides facilitating developmental technical oversight from the sectoral ministry and fiscal and financial oversight from the finance ministry, but the dividing line for responsibility and accountability may often get blurred. Among the three, the centralised model seems to be preferred because of its transparency.[26]

Under the decentralised model practised in India, the list of CPSEs under various ministries/departments is shown in Annexure 2.3.

The Department of Public Enterprises (DPE) under the Ministry of Heavy Industries and Public Enterprises, Government of India, acts as the nodal agency for the CPSEs in formulating the policy pertaining to their role. It also lays down the policy guidelines in respect of their performance and evaluation thereof, and in other areas related to finance, accounts, procurement, human resources, etc. DPE was set up in 1965 as a centralised coordinating unit known as the Bureau of Public Enterprises (BPE) for the purpose of continuous appraisal of

---

[26] 'The Role of State-owned Enterprises'.

performance. It was made into a full-fledged Department—DPE—in 1990 and is now organised under five constituent divisions: (a) Financial Policy Division; (b) Management Policy Division; (c) MOU Division; (d) Administration & Coordination Division and (e) Permanent Machinery of Arbitration.

Although the CPSEs are created and put under the control of different ministries under the Government of India, only the DPE acts as their coordinating and monitoring agency and issues directives and guidelines to them in that capacity. The instructions issued to CPSEs may be mandatory or advisory. There are two types of these: (a) Presidential directives that are generally instructions issued to the CPSES by the controlling administrative ministries, which are mandatory in nature and (b) Guidelines issued by the DPE or the administrative ministries, which are advisory in nature and generally pertain to good corporate governance, greater transparency and stronger accountability. However, compared to the 1970s or 1980s, now, very few guidelines are issued by the government, and there is hardly any interference in their operational or tactical decisions, with substantial delegation of powers and autonomy being provided to the CPSEs. The top management of the CPSEs are selected by the Public Enterprises Selection Board (PESB), which functions under the Department of Personnel & Training Ministry of Personnel, Public Grievances and Pension, Government of India, and advertises the vacancies from time to time. The selected individuals are appointed by the government to the CPSE boards, which also has the powers to remove any of them after following the due process of law. Each CPSE board also includes an independent director not concerned with the day-to-day operation and management of the entity.[27]

The interactions between the government and the CPSEs take place through a Memorandum of Understanding (MOU), which

[27] There is a body called the Standing Conference of Public Enterprises (SCOPE) that was recognised by the Union Cabinet in 1976 as an apex professional organization representing the CPSEs. It aims to promote excellence in its members that also include some state PSEs as well as Public Sector Banks (PSBs), to enable them to be globally competitive. It facilitates dialogue and engagement between the government, PSEs, international organisations and competitors.

is a negotiated agreement and contract between the CPSE and the Government of India represented by the Administrative Ministry/ Department, or, in other words, between the majority shareholder and the management of the CPSE on selected parameters, with specific targets assigned for at the beginning of each financial year and performance measured at the end of the year against a set of critical indicators.

The MOU system originated in France in 1967, with the objective of creating a level playing field for the public sector enterprises *vis-à-vis* the private corporate sector. It was introduced in the CPSEs in 1986 following the recommendations of the Arjun Sen Gupta Committee Report of 1984. The report recommended that the CPSEs should enter into 'performance' agreements with their Administrative Ministries for 5 years in respect of three financial parameters, namely, price fixation, investment planning and financial management, with progress to be reviewed annually while giving their management adequate autonomy for improving the operational efficiency within the overall government control. Apart from operational autonomy, the other objectives of the MOU system were to remove the haziness in goals and objectives, to design objective evaluation criteria and also to incentivise the CPSEs for better future performance, which was later manifested in their Ratna classification discussed earlier.

At the time of its introduction in India, the core sectors of steel, heavy engineering, coal, power, petroleum and fertilisers were considered vital in the FYPs, and the committee recommended MOUs in respect of CPSEs in these sectors only. Accordingly, the first set of MOUs was signed by four CPSEs for 1987–1988. Following the New Industrial Policy of 1991, the system was extended to other CPSEs. It remained ineffective till it was revamped again in 2004–2005; the system now covers almost all the CPSEs, as shown in Table 2.7.

Under the current guidelines, equal weights are given to financial and non-financial parameters (50% each). While the financial parameters are expressed both in terms of absolute values like the gross margins (profits) or turnover as well as financial ratios, the non-financial parameters are further classified into dynamic parameters (30% weightage), enterprise-specific parameters (20% weightage)

Table 2.7 No. of MOUs *Signed: 2014–2015 to 2018–2019*

Year	No. of MoUs Signed
2013–2014	197
2014–2015	214
2015–2016	215
2016–2017	231
2017–2018	196

Source: Department of Public Enterprises, *Public Enterprises Survey 2017–2018.*

and sector-specific parameters (10% weightage).[28] All parameters are required to be SMART (i.e., Specific, Measurable, Attainable, Result-oriented, Tangible) and objectively verifiable.

The parameters, however, get revised every year. As per the latest guidelines for the year 2018–2019,[29] there would be three mandatory and uniform parameters for most CPSEs for measuring financial performance such as turnover (i.e., revenue from operations), operating profit and return on investment (e.g., ratio of PAT[30]/Net Worth), carrying a total weightage of 50 per cent. For the remaining 50 per cent of weightage, a menu of parameters was indicated for selection by the individual CPSEs[31] depending on their respective sectors—financial or non-financial. For the purpose of performance evaluation, different weights are assigned to different parameters in a five-point scale, and

[28] As per DPE's guidelines for the year 2010–2011, Corporate Social Responsibility (CSR), R&D and Sustainable Development were included in non-financial parameters with a mandatory 5 per cent weightage against each. non-financial parameters are to be decided jointly by the CPSE, the concerned Administrative Ministry and the task force.

[29] DPE OM No M-03/0017/2016-DPE (MOU) dated 19 January 2019. https://dpemou.nic.in/MOUFiles/Revised_mou_guidelines.pdf, accessed 31 August 2019.

[30] Profit after tax.

[31] To be suggested by the Pre-Negotiation Committee to the Inter-Ministerial Committee.

the final evaluation is the composite score based on the targets and the actual results.

MOUs are finalised through a multistage consultative process involving the CPSE management, the administrative ministry, an Inter-Ministerial Committee (IMC) comprising NITI Aayog CEO and the Secretaries to the Ministry of Finance and the Department of Investment and Public Asset Management (DIPAM),[32] which is the final arbiter in the matter, and which is assisted and supported by a Pre-Negotiation Committee (PNC) comprising representatives from the DPE, the concerned Administrative Ministry and the Ministry of Statistics and Programme Implementation besides the concerned Adviser, NITI Aayog. A draft MOU is first prepared, which is overseen by a task force appointed by the DPE. Currently, there are about 68 task force members who are divided into sector-wise syndicate groups. For the evaluation of the performance of CPSEs, a High Power Committee (HPC) of secretaries is set up as the 'apex committee', with support given by the administrative ministries/departments.

The MOU system is believed to have increased the profitability of CPSEs significantly. Between 1994–1995 and 2007–2008, before the global economic meltdown had affected all sectors including the CPSEs, their profits increased from ₹12,013 crore to ₹91,062 crore. MOUs have also been instrumental behind the turnaround of many sick enterprises like NBCC, ECIL, EPIL, Mecon, MECL, PDCIL, HIL, etc. Overall, the system has helped improve the performance of CPSEs by upgrading their systems and processes, increasing autonomy and enforcing accountability, besides addressing the corporate governance imperatives.[33]

The MOU system was adopted from France, but the experiences of many countries have shown that it could be instrumental in

---

[32] Earlier known as the Department of Disinvestment, which was set up as a separate department in 1999 and was later renamed Ministry of Disinvestment in 2001. In 2004, it functioned under the Ministry of Finance as a department and was renamed DIPAM in 2016, reflecting the new philosophy of the government, bringing the focus on management of assets rather than disinvestment.

[33] Mohapatra, 'Road Ahead for the MoU System'.

transforming PEs; some have even viewed the MOU and privatisation as complementary to each other. In South Korea, for example, an MOU-like system was used to improve the performance and thereby increase the value of PEs before actually selling them to the private sector. The extent of social obligations being discharged by a PE should determine the precise route to be taken; in case of high social commitment, MOU should be the answer; otherwise, the privatisation route could be a viable option. In fact, the MOU mechanism could be used to reduce the losses without taking the extreme step of privatisation of a PE. MOU also enables the government to compare the performances of essentially dissimilar enterprises to establish an environment of competitiveness among them, some of which often function in monopolistic conditions, and to improve their performance across the board.[34]

However, there still remains the scope for incorporating global best practices in the MOUs, like the following five major global trends in performance management in public financial management:

1. Moving away from the Administrator Model to the Management Model, which represents an 'internal culture of making managers manage, as opposed to the Administrative Model which values compliance to pre-determined rules and regulations';
2. Moving away from the Bureaucratic Model to the Market Model, 'which represents greater use of market-type mechanisms as opposed to rendering public services as a monopoly provider';
3. Helping the CPSEs reinvent themselves—something like 'changing the very DNA of public organisations so that they habitually innovate and continually improve performance without external pressure';
4. Promoting 'knowledge management and knowledge sharing within the public sector' for overall performance improvement and
5. Transformation through 'extensive use of e-governance tools'.[35]

Indicators for these will be mostly intangible as opposed to the quantitative SMART parameters now being used in the MOUs for

---

[34] Kumar, 'Non-Privatizing Reforms of Public Enterprises', 143–146.
[35] Ibid.

the evaluation of CPSE performance. Until these trends are suitably reflected in the evaluation indicators in the MOUs, the CPSEs cannot be nudged towards their adoption. The challenge is to develop a set of tangible parameters for measuring the intangible aspects of CPSE performance.

In most modern private sector organisations and companies, a balanced scorecard approach involving an array of performance measurement parameters are used, each of which aligns with the overall objectives of the entity. CPSEs also might adopt such an approach by including non-financial parameters like human capital (knowledge, skill and attitude), organisation capital (organisational culture, leadership, style, etc.), information capital (systems, database and networks), process efficiency, resource utilisation, etc. Another global trend that may be adopted is knowledge management. But unless the MOU captures and reflects all these parameters, these are unlikely to be adopted by the CPSEs.[36]

CPSEs, being under the control of the government, are obviously accountable to the government. Being financed by the exchequer, they are also accountable to the parliament. The accountability to the government is ensured through the system of MOUs and the administrative control exercised by the concerned administrative ministries/departments, as already discussed, and also through the institution of the Central Vigilance Commission (CVC). The accountability to the parliament is ensured through the external audit conducted by the institution of the Comptroller and Auditor General of India (CAG) and the examination of the reports of the CAG by the parliamentary Committee on Public Undertakings (COPU). Accountability through the CVC is ensured by posting an independent Chief Vigilance Officer (CVO) at each CPSE, usually from among the civil servants, who will report to the CMD of the government company but has sufficient autonomy in matters pertaining to internal oversight, vigilance and controlling the environment and is responsible for investigating all complaints and irregularities which might come to his/her notice, and report on these independently to the CVC as well as to the secretary

[36] Ibid.

of the administrative ministry/department concerned. The CVC was established in 1964, under recommendations of the Santhanam Committee, as an apex body for exercising vigilance and control in matters related to public administration. It was given a statutory status by the Central Vigilance Commission Act passed by the parliament in 2003, section 8(1)(h) of which empowers the CVC to exercise superintendence and vigilance over ministries/departments/corporations/companies/authorities and bodies functioning under the control of the central government.

The CAG derives his/her authority from the articles 148–151 of the Indian Constitution and the provisions of the Comptroller and Auditor General's (Duties, Powers and Conditions of Service) Act, 1971 (DPC Act), enacted under Article 149. The audits of government companies and corporations are conducted under Section 19 of the DPC Act, which states that the duties and powers of the CAG in relation to the audit of the accounts of government companies shall be conducted in accordance with the provisions of the Companies Act, while his/her duties and powers in relation to the audit of government corporations (not being companies) established by or under law made by the parliament shall be performed and exercised by him in accordance with the provisions of the respective legislations. The CAG can also take up the audit of any state PSE or a PSE established by a union territory (with legislature) at the request of the governor of the state or the administrator of the union territory as the case may be. In such cases, he/she will have unrestricted access to the books of accounts and other records of the entity being audited.

Section 19A of the DPC Act deals with the laying of CAG's reports in relation to the accounts of government companies and corporations, stating that the CAG will submit these reports to the union or the state/UT government as the case may be, which will then cause each such report to be laid 'as soon as may be after it is received, before each House of Parliament' or the legislature of the state/UT. It is interesting to note that there is no time limit defined for laying of the CAG reports before the parliament or state/UT legislature after their submission by the CAG, and there are instances of these reports being deliberately delayed for placement in the legislature, especially by certain state governments facing elections, in cases where the reports were perceived to be critical of those governments and hence carrying the potential of causing electoral damage to the political party in power.

As per provisions of Section 139 of the new Companies Act, 2013 (Section 619 of the earlier Companies Act, 1956), CAG is also required to appoint the auditor of a government company or deemed government company,[37] duly qualified to be appointed as auditor, within 180 days of the commencement of the financial year, who shall hold office till the conclusion of the next Annual General Meeting (AGM) of the company. The first auditor, however, shall be appointed by the CAG within 60 days from the date of registration of the company. This constitutes the statutory audit of the company, and the CAG is authorised to issue instructions/guidelines to the auditor so appointed in relation to the audit of the government company concerned. The auditor is required to submit a copy of his/her report on the accounts of the company to the CAG who shall evaluate the report and take penal action against the auditor, if warranted, for any breach of professional conduct and ethics, including debarring him/ her from conducting further audit of government companies for a specified period.

Once the auditor submits the report, the CAG shall, within 60 days of the receipt of the audit report, have the right to conduct a supplementary audit of the company's accounts, over and above the statutory audit, and comment upon the audit report submitted by the statutory auditor or supplement the same with his/her own observations. The observations emanating from the supplementary audit by the CAG will be placed before the AGM along with the audited accounts and statutory auditor's report. Section 394 of Companies Act, 2013 mandates that the annual reports on government companies will have to be laid before both houses of the parliament together with a copy of the audit report and comments upon or supplement to the audit report

---

[37] Deemed Government Companies are those in which the combined stakes of central and state government as well as of the companies under their controls exceed 51 per cent.

made by the CAG. A similar procedure is followed in respect of the PSEs controlled by the state/UT with legislature.

The CAG conducts three kinds of audit: financial audit, which involves the audit of financial accounts, compliance audit, which consists of checking the compliance to rules, regulations, systems and procedures, all of which mostly pertain to internal controls within the entities audited, and performance audit, which involves scrutinising the activities and transactions of the entity from the overall perspective of economy, efficiency and effectiveness. Both the statutory audit and the supplementary audit are in the nature of financial audit. The CAG will separately prepare a report on the CPSEs, including observations on the supplementary audit as well as their compliance and performance audits, and submit the same to the president under Section 151 of the Constitution, who shall cause it to be laid before both the houses of the parliament. Once the report is placed before the parliament, a specialised standing committee of the parliament, called the COPU, takes up the report for further examination and makes its recommendations for addressing the deficiencies and irregularities pointed out by the CAG. A similar system exists for all the states, too.

In countries across the globe, parliamentary control over the PSEs are exercised with varying degrees of oversight; the nature of public audit institutions and the independence, power and authority given to them also vary from country to country. Some, mostly the Anglophone and Commonwealth countries, follow what is called the Westminster model of audit institution, very much like in India, with a central audit institution headed by the Comptroller and Auditor General, called the Auditor General in some countries, who is an independent authority reporting to the parliament.

The Francophone countries follow the Napoleonic court system, having several members (like the Cour de Comptes or Court of Accounts in France). The courts have both judicial and administrative powers; they are integral parts of the judiciary and make legal judgements on compliance to rules and regulations, besides exercising budget control functions for ensuring the proper use of public funds. Many continental European countries also have the court system, for example, the Corte did Conti (Court of Accounts) in Italy, Federal Court of Auditors (Bundesrechnungshof) in Germany, Court of Audit of Belgium or the Austrian Court of Audit. These courts are multi-member bodies equipped with wide powers that function on the basis of collegiate decision-making, and they are entrusted with the audit of PEs in their respective countries.

In other countries, there is a board system, wherein a Board of Audit—generally a constitutional body independent of the executive with several members—collectively decides on all policy matters, such as the state audit office called Riksrevisionen in Sweden, the Japanese Audit Commission and other similar systems in South Korea and Indonesia. The president/chairman of the board or the commission acts as the *de facto* Auditor General. South Africa follows a hybrid system where an Audit Commission establishes the Office of the Auditor General as an independent body. In most countries, however, irrespective of the specific model of their audit institutions, the public audit institution, also known as the Supreme Audit Institution (SAI) of the country, is primarily responsible for audit of PEs and reporting thereon, unlike in UK or India where the primary audit is delegated to the statutory auditor rather than to the CAG, for reasons which can best be described as historical.[38]

Many entities, especially in the financial sector, like the nationalised banks, or financial institutions such as IDBI, IFCI, LIC etc., have been kept outside the purview of the CAG's audit from the beginning as it was felt that the CAG audit would rather constrain the commercial operations of these entities, which necessarily involves taking certain risks that may lead to losses in an uncertain market scenario which may not be viewed objectively by the public auditor.

---

[38] In USA, the PREs are audited by the General Accounting Office (GAO), in France by the Cour de Comptes, and by the Corte did Conti in Italy. In the Asia Pacific Region, too, SAIs' mandate extends to the PEs in many countries from Australia and New Zealand to China, Japan, South Korea, Malaysia, Pakistan and Thailand. In India, the CAG is the statutory auditor in respect of State Electricity Boards, State Transport Corporations and some Central Statutory Corporations like the International Airports Authority of India, but not all. The audits of statutory corporations are guided by the provisions under the respective statutes.

In the UK, too, nationalised industries were kept outside the CAG's audit from the beginning.

A consultation paper 'Efficacy of Public Audit System in India: C & AG—Reforming the Institution' prepared by Dr B. P. Mathur, a former Deputy Comptroller and Auditor General of India, under the aegis of the National Commission to Review the Working of the Constitution, in 2001, mentioned the historical reasons for the peculiar auditing arrangement of CPSEs while questioning the government policy towards diluting their stakes in some of them:

> Audit of public enterprises by C&AG has always remained a controversial issue. In the 50's when PSU's were being set-up first time, there were attempts to bar C&AG's jurisdiction but the then C&AG resisted and the matter was resolved by amending the Companies Act and providing for supplementary audit of government companies by C&AG. Subsequently in the 70's, as a result of recommendation of Administrative Reforms Commission, an Audit Board system was introduced to provide commercial type audit for PSU's. In the wake of current privatisation programme, government is making policy pronouncements that government portion of equity will be brought down to a level of 49 or 26 percent. This is ostensibly being done to free them from government control including audit as they would no longer fall within the definition of government company. Will this not tantamount to evasion of public accountability as by retaining sizable share-holding government could still exercise policy control over these companies but will not be answerable to Parliament?

In the 1950s, the then CAG Mr Narahari Rao had pointed out that dispensing with CAG audit of CPSEs would be unconstitutional, and the government had agreed. But in 2005, the J. J. Irani Committee again recommended that CAG audit should be abolished as it duplicates the audit of the statutory auditors without adding much value, and that it cripples the independence of the CPSEs. In a liberalised and globalised economy where the public sector is exposed to the same competition as the private sector, CPSEs' survival depends essentially on the interplay of market forces. It is therefore argued that they should be given the same autonomy and flexibility as the private companies that do not have to face any audit other than the statutory audit, and that therefore the supplementary audit by the CAG should also be dispensed with.

In the wake of several scams that shook the Indian corporate world and the stock market in the recent past, especially the Satyam Scam of 2009 that exposed the serious weaknesses that bedevilled the accounting and auditing systems of companies and their control environment, and also the overall dismal failure of checks and balances under which the companies operated in India, there was a persistent demand for reassessing and revising our auditing and accounting systems in order to realign them for improved corporate governance and greater assurance about their integrity and credibility. It led a corresponding churning in the CAG's systems and processes also.

Audit of CPSEs was being conducted by the CAG through the institution of the Audit Board, which provided a mechanism for three-way interaction between the Chairman of the Board, who was the Deputy CAG in charge of Commercial Audit, the secretary to the administrative ministry concerned and the top management of the CPSE. This mechanism was revamped in 2005 by drastically changing the structure and composition of the board and by making it a permanent body that was responsible for all major decisions regarding the audit of CPSEs, especially their performance audit. There are nine ex-officio Members of the Audit Board (MAB) whose jurisdictions have been geographically defined and who are primarily responsible for the audit of the CPSEs and for certifying their accounts. Beginning with 2008–2009, a three-phased auditing system was introduced, in a focused and result-oriented manner, for 78 companies including the listed government companies like BPCL, HPCL, ONGC Videsh and Shipping Corporation of India, the Navratnas, category-I Miniratnas and statutory corporations including the Airports Authority of India and the National Highways Authority of India. This was aimed at introducing higher transparency and ensuring timeliness in preparing the accounts of CPSEs, and at precluding any impact of the adverse comments of the CAG on their accounts upon their share prices.

In the first phase, the auditor was only required to review the general accounting policy of the PSUs and steps taken by them on previous audit observations, based on which the CAG would issue directions to statutory auditors and the management of CPSEs in case corrections in accounting practices were warranted. Once the draft accounts or schedules were ready, usually by April every year, the second phase would begin, during which a detailed examination of the books of accounts would be undertaken by the supplementary auditor—hitherto, the auditor only undertook the audit of finalised accounts—audited by the statutory auditor and presented in the AGM. The third and final phase of audit would commence after the finalisation of accounts by the Board of Directors of the CPSE on the basis of the reports of the statutory auditors. The new system was designed to help the companies avoid adverse comments by the CAG on their annual accounts by rectifying the same on time. Additional directions were also issued to the statutory auditors for conducting the audit of accounts of CPSEs.[39]

As already stated, the report of CAG is examined and discussed by the COPU for making recommendations to the government for rectification of the irregularities pointed out by the CAG in his/her reports and for improvement in the functioning of CPSEs in general. COPU is one of the two watchdog committees of the parliament, the other being the Public Accounts Committee (PAC). Parliamentary oversight over CPSEs is exercised through COPU.[40] The PAC and COPU, along with the Estimates Committee, whose job it is to examine the budgetary estimates and suggest policies to effect greater economy and efficiency in administration, constitute the three financial committees of the parliament.

COPU consists of 22 members—15 elected by the Lok Sabha every year from among its members, excluding ministers, according to the principle of proportional representation by means of a single transferable vote and seven nominated by the Rajya Sabha. The committee is reconstituted every year, with or without the same members, with the Chairman being appointed by the Speaker. Its scope is specified in the Fourth Schedule to the Rules of Procedure and Conduct of

---

[39] As of March 2018, 87 listed CPSEs are covered under the three-phased audit.
[40] A similar arrangement also exists at the level of states.

Business in the Lok Sabha. Its duties are to examine the reports and accounts of CPSEs—primarily the reports of the CAG on the public undertaking—and to examine 'in the context of the autonomy and efficiency of the Public Undertakings whether the affairs of the Public Undertakings are being managed in accordance with sound business principles and prudent commercial practices', and to exercise such other functions that may be allotted to the committee by the Speaker from time to time.[41]

The committee selects such subjects as it may deem fit, in consultation with the CAG, and frames a questionnaire. The ministry and the CPSE concerned are then asked to furnish the necessary material relating to these questions. The committee may also appoint one or more study groups for carrying out a detailed examination of various subjects, and even make spot visits for study tours, during which it can collect information, evidence or testimony from all relevant sources, including the representatives of Chambers of Commerce and Industry, non-official organisations and bodies that are concerned with the subject under examination. Finally, formal sittings of the committee take place, usually in Parliament House/Parliament House Annexe, where all concerned persons including the secretaries of the administrative ministries/departments, the top management of the CPSE concerned, the CAG and/or his/her representatives and other non-official and official witnesses are invited to give evidence. The committee's sittings are held in camera and its proceedings are also confidential. The observations/recommendations of the committee are made in its reports, which are presented to the parliament, upon which the ministry and the CPSE concerned are required to take action and report back to the parliament in the form of an Action Taken Note (ATN). The replies of the government contained in the ATN are examined by an Action Taken Sub-Committee/Committee and finally, the Action Taken Report is presented to the House. The COPU does not have any executive powers, and its recommendations can be accepted or rejected by the government at its discretion.

---

[41] http://loksabhaph.nic.in/Committee/CommitteeInformation.aspx?comm_code=27&tab=0, accessed 13 July 2019.

Since their inception, the various COPUs have so far presented 604 reports to the parliament till the end of tenure of the 16th Lok Sabha, of which 301 are Original Reports and 303 are reports on action taken by the government on Original Reports of the Committee. Out of 301 Original Reports, 37 are horizontal studies on various aspects of working of the CPSEs. Many of its recommendations have been able to effect significant improvements in the performance of the CPSEs and led to the redesigning of their systems and procedures and, consequently, better output and higher profits. Thus, the supplementary audit by the CAG, examination of his/her reports by COPU and implementation of their recommendations by the government and the CPSE concerned complete the cycle of parliamentary oversight and accountability of the CPSEs.

Annexure 2.1. Schedule-wise List of Companies

Schedule A

1. Airports Authority of India
2. Air India Ltd.
3. BEML Ltd.
4. Bharat Electronics Ltd.
5. Bharat Heavy Electricals Ltd.
6. Bharat Petroleum Corporation Ltd.
7. Bharat Sanchar Nigam Ltd.
8. Central Warehousing Corporation
9. Coal India Ltd.
10. Container Corporation of India Ltd.
11. Dedicated Freight Corridor Corporation of India Ltd.
12. Electronics Corporation of India Ltd.
13. Engineers India Ltd.
14. Fertilizers & Chemicals (Travancore) Ltd.
15. Food Corporation of India
16. GAIL (India) Ltd.
17. Heavy Engineering Corporation Ltd.
18. Hindustan Aeronautics Ltd.
19. Hindustan Copper Ltd.

20. Hindustan Paper Corporation Ltd.
21. Hindustan Petroleum Corporation Ltd.
22. HMT Ltd.
23. Housing & Urban Development Corporation Ltd.
24. ITI Ltd.
25. Indian Oil Corporation Ltd.
26. IRCON International Ltd.
27. Indian Railway Finance Corporation Ltd.
28. Konkan Railway Corporation Ltd.
29. Kudremukh Iron Ore Company Ltd.
30. MMTC Ltd.
31. Mahanagar Telephone Nigam Ltd.
32. Mangalore Refinery & Petrochemicals Ltd.
33. Mazagon Dock Shipbuilders Ltd.
34. MECON Ltd.
35. MOIL Limited
36. Mumbai Railway Vikas Corporation Ltd.
37. National Aluminium Company Ltd.
38. National Building Construction Corporation Ltd.
39. National Fertilizers Ltd.
40. NHPC Ltd.
41. National Mineral Development Corporation Ltd.
42. National Textiles Corporation Ltd.
43. NTPC Ltd.
44. Neyveli Lignite Corporation Ltd.
45. North Eastern Electric Power Corporation Ltd.
46. Oil & Natural Gas Corporation Ltd.
47. Oil India Ltd.
48. ONGC Videsh Ltd.
49. Power Finance Corporation
50. Power Grid Corporation of India Ltd.
51. Power System Operation Corporation Ltd.
52. RITES Ltd.
53. RailTel Corporation of India Ltd.
54. Rail Vikas Nigam Ltd.
55. Rashtriya Chemicals and Fertilizers Ltd.
56. Rashtriya Ispat Nigam Ltd.

57. Rural Electrification Corporation Ltd.
58. Satluj Jal Vidyut Nigam Ltd.
59. Security Printing & Minting Corporation of India Ltd.
60. Shipping Corporation of India Ltd.
61. State Trading Corporation of India Ltd.
62. Steel Authority of India Ltd.
63. Telecommunications Consultants (India) Ltd.
64. THDC India Ltd.

Schedule B

1. Andrew Yule & Company Ltd.
2. Balmer Lawrie & Company Ltd.
3. Bharat Coking Coal Ltd.
4. Bharat Dynamics Ltd.
5. Bharat Petro Resources Ltd.
6. Bharat Pumps & Compressors Ltd.
7. Brahmaputra Crackers & Polymers Ltd.
8. Brahmaputra Valley Fertilizer Corporation Ltd.
9. Biotechnology Industry Research Assistance Council
10. Braithwaite & Company Ltd.
11. Bridge & Roof Company (India) Ltd.
12. British India Corporation Ltd.
13. Burn Standard Company Ltd.
14. Cement Corporation of India Ltd.
15. Central Coalfields Ltd.
16. Central Electronics Ltd.
17. Central Mine Planning & Design Institute Ltd.
18. Chennai Petroleum Corporation Ltd.
19. Cochin Shipyard Ltd.
20. Cotton Corporation of India Ltd.
21. Dredging Corporation of India Ltd.
22. Eastern Coalfields Ltd.
23. Engineering Projects (India) Ltd.
24. Kamarajar Port Ltd.
25. Fertilizer Corporation of India Ltd.
26. Garden Reach Shipbuilders & Engineers Ltd.

27. Goa Shipyard Ltd.
28. Handicrafts & Handlooms Export Corporation Ltd.
29. Hindustan Cables Ltd.
30. Hindustan Fertilizer Corporation Ltd.
31. HLL Lifecare Ltd.
32. Hindustan Newsprints Ltd.
33. Hindustan Organic Chemicals Ltd.
34. Hindustan Shipyard Ltd.
35. Hindustan Steelworks Construction Company Ltd.
36. HMT (International) Ltd.
37. HMT Machine Tools Ltd.
38. HMT Watches Ltd.
39. India Tourism Development Corporation Ltd.
40. India Trade Promotion Organization
41. Indian Drugs & Pharmaceuticals Ltd.
42. Indian Railway Catering & Tourism Corporation Ltd.
43. Indian Rare Earths Ltd.
44. Indian Renewable Energy Development Agency Ltd.
45. Instrumentation Ltd.
46. MSTC Ltd.
47. Madras Fertilizers Ltd.
48. Mahanadi Coalfields Ltd.
49. Mineral Exploration Corporation Ltd.
50. Mishra Dhatu Nigam Ltd.
51. National Handloom Development Corporation Ltd.
52. National Jute Manufacturers Corporation Ltd.
53. National Projects Construction Corporation Ltd.
54. National Seeds Corporation Ltd.
55. National Small Industries Corporation Ltd.
56. Northern Coalfields Ltd.
57. Numaligarh Refinery Ltd.
58. Orissa Mineral Development Company Ltd.
59. PEC Ltd.
60. Pawan Hans Helicopters Ltd.
61. Projects & Development India Ltd.
62. Scooters India Ltd.
63. South Eastern Coalfields Ltd.

64. Uranium Corporation of India Ltd.
65. WAPCOS Ltd.
66. Western Coalfields Ltd.

Schedule C

1. Andaman & Nicobar Islands Forest & Plantation Development Corporation Ltd.
2. Artificial Limbs Mfg. Corporation of India
3. BBJ Construction Ltd.
4. Bengal Chemicals & Pharmaceuticals Ltd.
5. BHEL Electric Machines Ltd.
6. Bharat Wagon & Engineering Company Ltd.
7. Bisra Stone Lime Company Ltd.
8. Broadcast Engineering Consultants India Ltd.
9. Central Cottage Industries Corporation of India Ltd.
10. Central Inland Water Transport Corporation Ltd.
11. Central Railside Warehouse Company Ltd.
12. Certification Engineers International Ltd.
13. Delhi Police Housing Corporation
14. Educational Consultants (India) Ltd.
15. FCI Aravali Gypsum & Minerals (India) Ltd.
16. Ferro Scrap Nigam Ltd.
17. Hindustan Antibiotics Ltd.
18. Hindustan Insecticides Ltd.
19. Hindustan Photo Films Manufacturing Company Ltd.
20. Hindustan Prefab Ltd.
21. Hindustan Salts Ltd.
22. HMT Bearings Ltd.
23. HMT Chinar Watches Ltd.
24. Hooghly Dock and Port Engineers Ltd.
25. HSCC (India) Ltd.
26. Hotel Corporation of India Ltd.
27. Jute Corporation of India Ltd.
28. Karnataka Antibiotics & Pharmaceuticals Ltd
29. Nagaland Pulp & Paper Company Ltd.
30. National Backward Classes Finance & Development Corporation

31. National Film Development Corporation Ltd.
32. National Handicapped Finance & Development Corporation
33. National Minorities Development & Finance Corporation
34. National Research Development Corporation of India
35. National Safai Karamcharis Finance & Development Corporation
36. National SC Finance & Development Corporation
37. National ST Finance & Development Corporation
38. NEPA Ltd.
39. North Eastern Handicrafts & Handloom Development Corporation Ltd.
40. North Eastern Regional Agricultural Marketing Corporation Ltd.
41. Rajasthan Electronics & Instruments Ltd.
42. Richardson & Cruddas (1972) Ltd.
43. STCL Ltd.
44. Tungabhadra Steel Products Ltd.

Schedule D

1. Birds Jute & Exports Ltd.
2. Hindustan Fluorocarbons Ltd.
3. Indian Medicines Pharmaceutical Corporation Ltd.
4. Orissa Drugs & Chemicals Ltd.
5. Rajasthan Drugs & Pharmaceuticals Ltd.

Annexure 2.2. List of Ratna CPSEs

Maharatna CPSEs

1. Bharat Heavy Electricals Limited
2. Bharat Petroleum Corporation Limited
3. Coal India Limited
4. GAIL (India) Limited
5. Indian Oil Corporation Limited
6. NTPC Limited
7. Oil & Natural Gas Corporation Limited
8. Steel Authority of India Limited

Navratna CPSEs

1. Bharat Electronics Limited
2. Container Corporation of India Limited
3. Engineers India Limited
4. Hindustan Aeronautics Limited
5. Hindustan Petroleum Corporation Limited
6. Mahanagar Telephone Nigam Limited
7. National Aluminium Company Limited
8. National Buildings Construction Corporation Limited
9. NMDC Limited
10. Neyveli Lignite Corporation Limited
11. Oil India Limited
12. Power Finance Corporation Limited
13. Power Grid Corporation of India Limited
14. Rashtriya Ispat Nigam Limited
15. Rural Electrification Corporation Limited
16. Shipping Corporation of India Limited

Miniratna Category-I CPSEs

1. Airports Authority of India
2. Antrix Corporation Limited
3. Balmer Lawrie & Co. Limited
4. Bharat Coking Coal Limited
5. Bharat Dynamics Limited
6. BEML Limited
7. Bharat Sanchar Nigam Limited
8. Bridge & Roof Company (India) Limited
9. Central Warehousing Corporation
10. Central Coalfields Limited
11. Chennai Petroleum Corporation Limited
12. Cochin Shipyard Limited
13. Dredging Corporation of India Limited
14. EdCIL (India) Limited
15. Kamarajar Port Limited
16. Garden Reach Shipbuilders & Engineers Limited

17. Goa Shipyard Limited
18. Hindustan Copper Limited
19. HLL Lifecare Limited
20. Hindustan Newsprint Limited
21. Hindustan Paper Corporation Limited
22. Housing & Urban Development Corporation Limited
23. HSCC (India) Limited
24. India Tourism Development Corporation Limited
25. Indian Rare Earths Limited
26. Indian Railway Catering & Tourism Corporation Limited
27. Indian Railway Finance Corporation Ltd
28. Indian Renewable Energy Development Agency Limited
29. India Trade Promotion Organization
30. IRCON International Limited
31. KIOCL Limited
32. Mazagaon Dock Shipbuilders Limited
33. Mahanadi Coalfields Limited
34. Manganese Ore (India) Limited
35. Mangalore Refinery & Petrochemical Limited
36. Mishra Dhatu Nigam Limited
37. MMTC Limited
38. MSTC Limited
39. National Fertilizers Limited
40. National Small Industries Corporation Limited
41. National Seeds Corporation
42. NHPC Limited
43. Northern Coalfields Limited
44. North Eastern Electric Power Corporation Limited
45. Numaligarh Refinery Limited
46. ONGC Videsh Limited
47. Pawan Hans Helicopters Limited
48. Projects & Development India Limited
49. RailTel Corporation of India Limited
50. Rail Vikas Nigam Limited
51. Rashtriya Chemicals & Fertilizers Limited
52. RITES Limited
53. SJVN Limited

54. Security Printing and Minting Corporation of India Limited
55. South Eastern Coalfields Limited
56. State Trading Corporation of India Limited
57. Telecommunications Consultants India Limited
58. THDC India Limited
59. Western Coalfields Limited
60. WAPCOS Limited

Miniratna Category-II CPSEs

61. Artificial Limbs Manufacturing Corporation of India
62. Bharat Pumps & Compressors Limited
63. Broadcast Engineering Consultants (I) Limited
64. Central Mine Planning & Design Institute Limited
65. Central Railside Warehouse Company Limited
66. Engineering Projects (India) Limited
67. FCI Aravali Gypsum & Minerals India Limited
68. Ferro Scrap Nigam Limited
69. HMT (International) Limited
70. Indian Medicines & Pharmaceuticals Corporation Limited
71. MECON Limited
72. Mineral Exploration Corporation Limited
73. National Film Development Corporation Limited
74. PEC Limited
75. Rajasthan Electronics & Instruments Limited

Annexure 2.3 Ministry/Department-wise List of Operating PSUs

S. No.	Name of the Ministry/Department	No. of CPSEs
1	Ministry of Agriculture and Farmers Welfare	2
2	Ministry of Ayush	1
3	Ministry of Chemicals and Fertilizers	20

(Annexure 2.3 Continued)

(Annexure 2.3 Continued)

S. No.	Name of the Ministry/Department	No. of CPSEs
4	Ministry of Civil Aviation	10
5	Ministry of Coal	11
6	Ministry of Commerce and Industry	9
7	Ministry of Communication	9
8	Ministry of Consumer Affairs, Food and Public Distribution	3
9	Ministry of Defence	13
10	Ministry of Development of North Eastern Region	2
11	Ministry of Electronic and Information Technology	1
12	Ministry of Environment, Forests Climate Change	1
13	Ministry of Finance	4
14	Ministry of Health and Family Welfare	5
15	Ministry of Heavy Industries and Public Enterprises	29
16	Ministry of Home Affairs	1
17	Ministry of Housing and Urban Affairs	6
18	Ministry of Human Resource Development	1
19	Ministry of Information and Broadcasting	2
20	Ministry of Micro Small and Medium Enterprises	1
21	Ministry of Mines	3
22	Ministry of Minorities Affairs	1
23	Ministry of New and Renewable Energy	2
24	Ministry of Petroleum and Natural gas	22
25	Ministry of Power	25
26	Ministry of Railways	24
27	Ministry of Road Transport and Highways	1
28	Ministry of Science and Technology	5
29	Ministry of Shipping	6
30	Ministry of Social Justice and Empowerment	2
31	Ministry of Steel	14
32	Ministry of Textiles	9
33	Ministry of Tourism	8

(Annexure 2.3 Continued)

(Annexure 2.3 Continued)

S. No.	Name of the Ministry/Department	No. of CPSEs
34	Ministry of Tribal Affairs	1
35	Ministry of Water Resources, River Development and Ganga Rejuvenation	2
36	Department of Atomic Energy	4
37	Department of space	1
	Total	**264**

Source: Department of Public Enterprises, *Public Enterprise Survey 2018–2019*, 7–18 Vol. 1, Annexure Statement 1, S1–8.

CHAPTER 3

Performance of the Central Public Sector Enterprises

India's first Prime Minister, Jawaharlal Nehru, was the architect behind the creation of PSEs in India, giving them an imperious position in driving the economy after independence; he hailed them as temples of modern India. Nehru was deeply influenced by the centrally planned economic model of the Soviets based on ownership of the means of production and distribution by the state, which he introduced in India. With his deep knowledge of history, Nehru must not have been oblivious to the experiment of another Asian nation Japan at rapid industrialisation during the Meiji era of 1868–1912, which completely transformed the Japanese state and society through modernising and Westernising its traditional education system, ending the feudal structure of society and production and training its students in Western science and technology by sending them abroad, to eventually beat the Western world in their own game. The Meiji Restoration in Japan was based on abolition of feudal fiefs, state-led focus on engineering and scientific education, establishment of a private banking system and encouragement of private investment in rails, roads and manufacturing through imported technology. But after setting the country on the road to rapid industrialisation and steering the economy successfully through the Meiji era, Japan withdrew gradually from the overwhelming state control over economy. It supported and encouraged private business houses to grow, mature and take control of industry and businesses, which ultimately made the tiny island nation an economic powerhouse and the second largest economy after the United States, even after absorbing the shocks of a devastating loss in World War II. It remained so for a long time till China overtook it only in the 2010s, after two 'lost decades' since the 1990s, during which the growth in its productivity had plummeted to less than 2 per cent, taking a toll on its competitiveness.

India's growth trajectory was quite different from Japan's. The crisis of the 1990s compelled the Narasimha Rao government to embark upon a wave of transformational reforms ushered in by the New Industrial Policy of 1991, which liberalised and opened up the economy to the private sector. But for a long time afterwards, rather than gradually withdrawing from production, the Indian state continued with its control over a large swathe of industry. Some of the companies that grew as monopolies in the absence of competition earlier have in fact become too big to be divested of state control, but not too big to fail.

In 1961, several employees of HMT Watches, a newly created division of another CPSE Hindustan Machine Tools Ltd that was established in 1953 with a factory in Bangalore, were sent to Japan to undergo training with its Citizen Watch Company to develop skills and competence in micro-engineering to give India cheap wristwatches, and possibly a sense of punctuality in a country then left way behind by time's onward march. The same year, the first batch of 800 watches—500 'Citizen' men's watches and 300 'Sujata' women's watches—were produced at its factory established in collaboration with Citizen Watch Co., initially only by assembling imported components. The first batch of these watches was in fact released by Prime Minister Nehru himself. Over the next decade, as HMT developed indigenous capabilities, it was making a full 84 per cent of the watches in-house. Most Indians at that time proudly sported an HMT watch, as did the author—for 15 long years after passing out of high school. At one point, HMT was commanding at least 70 per cent of the Indian watch market share and employed thousands of workers across its five factories, around which developed small townships. It was a success story of the Nehruvian model—to inculcate capability, self-sufficiency and pride. HMT truly became what its advertising slogan proclaimed, 'Timekeepers to the Nation'.

Today, however, all lies in shambles among the desolate ruins of a success story gone haywire. The townships are all deserted, and HMT Watches could not withstand its first serious competition with the private sector in a liberalised economy. Unable to anticipate the market trend that was giving way to automatic quartz watches, it continued with its old mechanised products, lost its vast market share in no time, accumulated colossal losses and slowly withered away. On 1 May 2016, the last of its employees were sent into voluntary retirement as the company was declared defunct. The plight of HMT Watches in many ways symbolises the plight of public sector enterprises in India in general, save a few exceptions. Despite the pretensions of operational autonomy of the PSEs, it is a story of excessive government control and politicisation of these entities and their milking by successive governments to fund their own populist agenda—not to mention their extortion by politicians and bureaucrats. Naturally, all these drain their resources, turning them sick and making them ever more dependent on government largesse on a *quid pro quo* basis. And of course, disinvesting the government stake while retaining control has become a standard *modus operandi* for bridging the burgeoning fiscal deficit of the central government.

Nehru wanted the public sector to seize the 'commanding heights of Indian economy', a phrase that was coined in 1922 by Vladimir Lenin. Later, Yevgeni Preobrazhensky (1886–1937), a Russian revolutionary and economist who championed rapid industrialisation of peasant Russia through state-owned heavy industries, fervently advocated for complete state control over the 'commanding heights of economy' to promote 'primitive socialist accumulation'. He was executed during Stalin's Great Purge in 1937, but the idea continued to inspire the leaders of newly independent third world nations, which inherited an ocean of poverty, deindustrialisation and undeveloped agrarian economy left over by their colonial masters. To Nehru, the only way to overcome the endemic poverty and food crisis that bedevilled post-Independence India was through overwhelming state control over economy in the Soviet style. PSEs were established to serve broad macro-economic objectives of achieving higher economic growth, self-sufficiency in production, import substitution and long-term equilibrium in foreign trade, besides meeting other socio-economic obligations.

In the book *The Commanding Heights: The Battle for the World Economy* (1998), Daniel Yergin and Joseph Stanislaw recount the incredible story of a CPSE, Hindustan Fertilizer Corporation, which was part of the 26 per cent of Indian economy that was state-owned during the 1970s. Its gigantic plant at Haldia, built during 1971–1979 with public funds, used machinery from nine Eastern European countries with financing from export credits. For a dozen years, 1,200 employees clocked in every day, but the plant never produced any fertiliser because the Eastern European machinery did not fit in; yet, everyone pretended, for 12 years, that the plant was operating until it was closed in 1986 and finally shut down in 2002. This author has seen for himself the desolate state of the company during an official visit in 1987, its vast infrastructure with modern facilities lying unutilised, empty and abandoned. The book tells the story of the battle between the government and the marketplace. Most of our PSEs today, especially those owned by the state governments, are haplessly trapped in the vast no man's land between the state and the market.

Nehru's Fabian socialist vision is spelled out in the Industrial Policy Resolution of 1956: 'the adoption of socialistic pattern of society as the national objective, as well as the need for planned and rapid development, require that all industries of basic and strategic importance, or in the nature of public utility services should be in the public sector'. This formed the plank of industrialisation efforts during successive plans till 1991 when the command and control economic structure was found too overbearing and had to be dismantled. The New Industrial Policy of 1991 redefined the role of the public sector in view of its increasing sickness and limited its growth to strategic priority areas like essential infrastructure, defence, exploration and exploitation of natural resources and development of technology and capacity in crucial areas where private sector investment was inadequate. It was a new understanding based on the realism that public enterprises were not only controlled and financed by the public but were also enterprises that had to function in commercial lines and compete with others in an open economy, which required a redefinition of their roles, activities and obligations. If CPSEs are still struggling to carve an identity for themselves in the changed environment, the state public sector fits nowhere in the new changed paradigm.

It cannot be denied that CPSEs indeed helped the infant nation in its formative years. Save a handful of companies, the private sector, inherently averse to risk, was almost non-existent then and could not be expected to invest in infrastructure and heavy industries that entailed long gestation periods, more so in an insular economy dependent on discretionary handouts by the government. At the beginning of the First Five Year Plan, there were only five central CPSEs with a total investment of ₹29 crore in the areas of strategic importance like capital-intensive oil and natural gas, heavy engineering, steel and mining. PSEs have grown luxuriantly since then, as already discussed in the previous chapter, to as many as 444 including six statutory corporations in 2016–2017, with a total investment of ₹16 lakh crore in equity and long-term loans. Besides these 444 PSEs, there are also 192 companies controlled by the government indirectly, in association with state governments. But the philosophy behind them has undergone a sea change since then, with the redefinition of the state's role as a catalyst and facilitator rather than a producer or distributor.

Till 1991, CPSEs were functioning in a highly protected environment characterised by extensive bureaucratic controls over production and inward-looking policies that made the economy almost seem like a closed one. They enjoyed a monopolistic position in a captive market and naturally inculcated the inefficiencies that functioning in a competitive market would otherwise have prevented. Most of them had low profitability and low returns on the capital employed; they were also badly managed with many vested interests eating into their profitability. Once the economic reforms opened up sectors hitherto forbidden to the private sectors for investment and operation, CPSEs found themselves in a situation where they faced competition from the private sector they were ill prepared for. Many of them became sick and perished as a result, while others managed to adjust and survive, albeit with lower margins, but the role and importance of CPSEs in the economy obviously diminished. However, a few of the CPSEs, especially the larger ones, could take advantage of the liberalised environment, learnt from their competitors to improve their efficiency and profitability and were able to expand their footprints in the liberalised market. CPSEs still dominate many sectors, from banking and insurance to basic infrastructure like roads and power, petroleum, steel and aluminium, mining, heavy machinery, pharmaceuticals, etc. Their role in making India technologically self-reliant is undeniable.

Following the New Industrial Policy of July 1991, the market environment had suddenly changed completely. Free entry of the private sector into the arena hitherto reserved for the public sector most significantly affected the CPSEs operating in sectors like telecommunication, petroleum extraction, refining and marketing, power generation and distribution, several basic goods industries like steel, aluminium, etc. and mining and transportation. The policy also called for disinvestment of the government's stake while still not diluting government control over the CPSEs, their listing in the stock exchanges and consequent changes in the accounting architecture including disclosure norms, improvement in corporate governance and withdrawal of budgetary support to loss-making or 'sick' enterprises which warranted laying off workers to improve commercial viability, failing which they had to be closed.[1] The restructuring of CPSEs followed as a result, with many becoming privatised. The subject of privatisation will be discussed in detail later in this book.

What were the basic underlying causes for the decline of the public sector? Much has been written on this, and hence it would suffice to list out some of the important causes without getting into the details. In the changed scenario after 1991, CPSEs were required to reinvent themselves continuously in order to remain relevant and adjust their objectives in sync with the changed national priorities. They had to improve corporate governance, upgrade the skills of their employees

---

[1] Khanna, 'The Transformation of India's Public Sector'.

and adapt to the new technologies available for production, account-ability norms and internal control mechanisms while aligning themselves to the market, and these challenges proved too much for many of them. Their governance structure with overwhelming control by a bureaucracy that little understood the demands of the market was the biggest hurdle. Conflicts between ownership and management continued to plague the CPSEs from the very beginning, with frequent interference by the government through their administrative ministries, thereby preventing these entities to function as professional organisations managed by a competent board and leading to slow and poor decision-making as well as poor planning and investment. Long gestation for important projects, faulty project appraisal, major investment decisions without proper appreciation of demand-supply situations and feasibility studies, huge cost and time overruns for most projects and occasional launching of projects without any clear objective led to huge losses and drying up of the order books. Besides, outdated technology and the inability to update the same for lack of funds led to many CPSEs being saddled with vintage plants operating with obsolete technology and hence being unable to compete in the market. Overcapitalisation and underutilisation of capacity, ineffective materials management with huge capital being blocked in inventories far in excess of requirement, excessive overheads, especially the huge expenditure on social overheads like maintaining townships for staff members with all modern facilities, overstaffing, which led to recruitment without the assessment of actual requirements, and lack of a clear pricing policy or appropriate pricing guidelines were also responsible for the low rates of return, inefficiency and high cost of production of the CPSEs. The quality of output also suffered in the process. Adding to the losses was the fact that some CPSEs were forced by the government to take over sick units of some private sector companies to protect the jobs of the workers, like SAIL taking over the Visvesvaraya Iron and Steel Company in 1988. The capital structure of many CPSEs was highly skewed with the ratio of loans to equity being far larger than optimal, with the result that the interest burden was eating into their profits, making them unviable.

Management and leadership further left much to be desired. Over-centralisation led to uninspiring leadership in the organisation and rigid bureaucratic control stifled innovation, stymied initiative and affected the motivation and morale of the workforce. Many of the CPSEs had problematic industrial relations with militant labour unions that were politically affiliated and hence could not be controlled. There was also political and administrative interference in day-to-day affairs and poor delegation. All this created the ideal situation for the breeding of vested interests, entrenched lobbies, corruption, wastes and leakages, which perpetuated in the absence of a strong, regulatory environment—at least prior to the 1990s. Most of the regulatory bodies, barring the RBI that has been in existence since 1935 and the Registrar of Companies since 1956, which is now a part of the Ministry of Corporate Affairs (MCA), came up after the economic reforms of the 1990s. The Securities and Exchange Board of India (SEBI), the security market regulator, was created in 1988 but became a statutory body only in 1992 when the SEBI Act was passed by the Parliament. Other regulators like Pension Fund Regulatory and Development Authority (PFRDA), Insurance Regulatory and Development Authority (IRDA), Competition Commission of India (CCI), Telecom Regulatory Authority of India (TRAI), Central Electricity Commission (CEC), Airports Economic Regulatory Authority (AERA), Food Safety and Standards Authority of India (FSSAI), etc. came later. Still other regulators like Insolvency and Bankruptcy Board of India (IBBI), Real Estate Regulatory Authority (RERA), etc. were created only recently.

Things improved later only when greater autonomy was allowed to the CPSEs, with delegation of greater powers to make their own strategic decisions—but this was by and large restricted to the better functioning entities, including the Ratna CPSEs. Many CPSEs are still continuing with their old work cultures, being unable to reinvent themselves and adjust to the demands of globalised markets of the 21st century.

Let us take a look at the performance of the Central PSEs. As per the CAG report,[2] which covers all the CPSEs from all sectors including the financial and insurance CPSEs, about half—212 of the 444

[2] CAG report No 18 of 2018 on CPSEs, 1–19.

CPSEs—earned net profits of ₹1.6 lakh crore in 2016–2017 while 157 incurred net losses of ₹30,700 crore, SAIL (loss of ₹3,187 crore) and MTNL (loss of ₹2,941 crore) leading the pack of the loss-making entities. One hundred and eighty-eight CPSEs had accumulated losses exceeding ₹1.23 lakh crore over the years, and the net worth of 77 companies has completely been eroded by their accumulated losses. The government earned ₹46,000 crore from selling a part of its stakes in 25 of these CPSEs during 2016–2017. Fifty-nine CPSEs are listed in the stock exchange as of June 2019. Of the seven Indian companies that made it to the coveted Fortune 500 list in 2018, four were PSEs: Oil India (ranked 137), ONGC (197), SBI (216) and Bharat Petroleum (314)—the others being Reliance Industries (148), Tata Motors (232) and Rajesh Exports (405). Fifty-seven CPSEs were either defunct or under liquidation or did not make their accounts, so their operational results remained indeterminate. CPSEs contributed ₹3.86 lakh crore to the public exchequer in 2016–2017 in taxes, cess and dividends and earned forex worth ₹87,616 crore through exports while paying ₹4.59 lakh crore on imports on royalty, technical knowhow, interest, consultancy, etc. CPSEs provided regular employment to 11.31 lakh people (excluding casual and contractual workers) during 2016–2017.[3]

The information for 2017–2018 are available in the Public Enterprises Survey brought out by the Department of Public Enterprises, which shows the top 10 profit-making and loss-making CPSEs during 2017–2018 (Tables 3.1 and 3.2).

The two major oil companies (IOC and ONGC) accounted for more than a quarter of the total profits made by profit-making CPSEs, while only the top 10 profit-making companies accounted for nearly 62 per cent of the total profits, the remaining 174 profit-making companies contributing a total of only 38 per cent of the net profits. Of the loss-making companies, only three companies—the two telecom

[3] As explained in the last chapter, CAG's data are more comprehensive than the data provided in the Public Enterprises Survey. However, most of the information provided in the tables in this chapter are not available from the CAG reports and hence both the sources had to be used. The latest data sources have been used, which is the Public Enterprises Survey for 2017–2018.

Table 3.1 Top 10 Profit-making CPSEs during 2017–2018 (₹ Crore)

S. No.	CPSE Name	Net Profit	% Share
1	Indian Oil Corporation Ltd.	21,346	13.4
2	Oil and Natural Gas Corporation Ltd.	19,945	12.5
3	NTPC Ltd.	10,343	6.5
4	Coal India Ltd.	9,293	5.8
5	Power Grid Corporation Ltd.	8,239	5.2
6	Bharat Petroleum Corporation Ltd.	7,919	5.0
7	Hindustan Petroleum Corporation Ltd.	6,357	4.0
8	Power Finance Corp Ltd.	5,855	3.7
9	Mahanadi Coalfields Ltd.	4,761	3.0
10	Rural Electrification Corporation Ltd.	4,647	2.9
	Total (1–10)	**98,707**	**61.8**
	Other CPSEs (174)	**60,928**	**38.2**
	Total Profit of profit making CPSEs (184)	**159,635**	**100.0**

Source: Department of Public Enterprises, *Public Enterprises Survey 2017–2018*, Vol. I, Box 1.1, p. 3.

Table 3.2 Top 10 Loss-making CPSEs during 2017–2018 (₹ Crore)

S. No.	CPSE Name	Net Loss	% Share
1	Bharat Sanchar Nigam Ltd.	−7,993	25.6
2	Air India Ltd.	−5,338	17.1
3	Mahanagar Telephone Nigam Ltd.	−2,973	9.5
4	Hindustan Photo Films Manufacturing Co. Ltd.	−2,917	9.3
5	Western Coalfields Ltd.	−1,757	5.6
6	Bharat Cooking Coal Ltd.	−1,391	4.5
7	Rashtriya Ispat Nigam Ltd.	−1,369	4.4
8	India Infrastructure Finance Co. Ltd	−1,155	3.7

(Table 3.2 Continued)

(Table 3.2 Continued)

S. No.	CPSE Name	Net Loss	% Share
9	Eastern Coalfields Ltd.	−931	3.0
10	STCL Ltd	−657	2.1
	Total (1–10)	−26,480	84.7
	Other CPSEs (61)	−4,781	15.3
	Total Loss of loss making CPSEs (71)	−31,261	100.0

Source: Department of Public Enterprises, *Public Enterprises Survey 2017–2018,* Vol. I, Box 1.1, p. 3.

companies BSNL and MTNL together with the beleaguered Air India—contributed more than 52 per cent of the total losses incurred by 71 companies. All three companies have huge wage bills with a much higher number of employees than their private sector counterparts and low employee productivity. Besides, the government itself was responsible for their plight to a very large extent.

Take the case of Air India, for example. Air India began its journey as Tata Airlines before independence, which began the first airmail service in India on 15 October 1932 with Mr J. R. D. Tata flying a small British monoplane carrying the postal mail of Imperial Airways from Karachi to Juhu aerodrome in Mumbai. During its first year, it flew 155 passengers and carried 10.71 tonnes of mail over 160,000 miles; it made a profit of ₹60,000 only. During the next few years, the fleet was expanded and new routes added with an increase in flight frequencies. Tata Airlines was converted into a public limited company in July 1946 and renamed Air India. International services were started in 1947 after the formation of Air India International Limited with government participation, which flew its inaugural flight to London via Cairo and Geneva on 8 June 1948. In 1953, India nationalised all Indian airlines, creating two corporations—one for domestic service, called Indian Airlines Corporation (merging Air India Limited with six lesser lines), and one for international service, Air India International Corporation, which was abbreviated to Air India in 1962. As the national flag carrier, Air India extended its international outreach to all continents except South America and Australia, along with its cargo operations.

The Government of India merged Indian Airlines and Air India in 2007. It can be cited as an example of how mergers should not be effected. It was done without any proper understanding of the lack of synergies between the two national carriers and in total disregard of the different work cultures and employee expectations in the two airlines, which made employee integration a very complex issue. This also resulted in an excess number of employees per aircraft (214, compared to the industry standard of around 170), thereby reducing employee productivity and increasing employee cost unsustainably. The two entities had different scales and allowances, and the merger led to huge infighting between their employees' unions, with each demanding the best of the wages and perks of the other without sacrificing any of their existing privileges. Besides, before the merger, both the airlines had placed orders for a huge number of aircraft—50 by Air India in 2004 from Boeing at an estimated cost of ₹46,000 crore (US$7.2 billion), besides 18 chartered aircraft for the VVIPs, and 43 by Indian Airlines from Airbus at an estimated cost of ₹8,400 crore (US$ 1.8 billion)[4]—goaded by the government of the day. These procurements at huge financial costs are at the root of Air India's current trouble and running losses. Within just 2 years, its combined losses shot up 10 times, from ₹770 crore in 2006–2007 to over ₹7,200 crore in 2008–2009. The government also allowed private airlines like Etihad and Jet to fly on the profitable routes hitherto served by Air India, especially the Middle East and America, from which it was gradually withdrawn. It has been alleged, not without reason, that the Middle-Eastern Airlines (Emirates, Etihad and Qatar) were huge beneficiaries of this and could capture an ever-increasing overseas market hitherto served by Air India, with a huge chunk of westward Indian travellers transiting via the Middle East. Allegations of cronyism and kickbacks have been raised repeatedly, but a serious probe into the matter is yet to be undertaken.

All strategic decisions—right from the merger to the purchase of an unjustifiable number of aircraft, or deciding the routes—were taken by the Ministry of Civil Aviation, making a mockery of autonomy without which no company can function profitably. Possibly, this involved kickbacks involving the ministers and bureaucrats who ran

---

[4] CAG Report No 18 of 2011, Performance Audit on Civil Aviation, 22.

the ministry at that time, and only a proper and detailed investigation will uncover truths. The stressed airlines kept steadily losing its market share to private players that had entered the Indian sky way back in the 1990s, with low-cost carriers snatching away Air India's business. Today, it commands a market share of less than 13 per cent, from 60 per cent a few years ago. With four subsidiaries[5] and huge liabilities—an annual finance cost of about ₹4,500 crore, or 15 per cent of total expenditure, accumulated losses over ₹53,000 crore, outstanding liability of ₹55,000 crore (₹30,000 crore on account of long-term borrowing only)—it is failing to attract any buyers, despite the government's best intentions and efforts.

The plight of state-run telecom companies BSNL and MTNL is not much different. BSNL came into existence in October 2000, taking over the business of providing telecom services and network management when, as per the National Telecom Policy, 1999, the Government of India had decided to separate the policy and licensing functions of the Department of Telecommunication from its service provisioning function. About 3.75 lakh employees were transferred *en masse* to BSNL at the time of corporatisation as per options exercised by them. Ever since, this huge number has been the bane of BSNL and a permanent drag on its functioning. The last time BSNL earned any operating profit (EBIT) was way back in 2007–2008; today, its operating losses exceed ₹57,000 crore (2017–2018). Since then, it has been incurring losses continuously, and with 1.84 lakh employees, the employee cost (salary, wages and retirement benefits) alone account for nearly 44 per cent of its total expenditure and 57 per cent of total income, as of 2017–2018. For private operators, the employee cost is between 2 and 5 per cent of their income. The huge number of employees is at the root of BSNL's problems, to address which the government does nothing.

Once the seventh largest telecom company in the world and a market leader with huge assets and a pan-India network, BSNL did not invest enough cash on upgrading its crumbling network hardware

[5] Air India Air Transport Services Ltd., Air India Engineering Services Ltd., Air India Express Ltd., Airline Allied Services Ltd.

assets. At a time when the country is going to offer 5G services, BSNL is yet awaiting the government decision for allotment of 4G spectrum. Once a shining diadem of India's telecom ecosystem and a Navratna PSE, earning profits exceeding ₹10,000 crore annually, today, it the largest loss-making PSE, without enough cash to pay its employee salary on time, as happened in February 2019. Poor maintenance of installations, failure to replace decades-old cables and the resultant poor quality of services are driving customers to other networks, and BSNL is struggling to keep its market share while steadily losing customers. Besides, it is in no position to withstand the competition from aggressive players like Reliance Jio. Its accumulated losses have reached almost ₹60,000 crore (2017–2018) and its outstanding debt is more than ₹18,000 crore.

MTNL provides telecom services in Delhi and Mumbai circles. High employee cost is also the cause of MTNL's problems. With around 25,000 employees and a monthly wage bill of ₹200 crore, its employee cost exceeds 78 per cent of its income. With declining revenues and mounting losses, MTNL is clearly unable to survive a fiercely competitive market and may have run out of options already. As of March 2018, the two public sector telecom companies, BSNL and MTNL, together commanded only 10.86 per cent of the market share in the country in telephones (landlines plus mobile connections). The possibility of merging MTNL with BSNL was earlier explored and abandoned due to the huge liabilities of both the debt-laden and loss-incurring companies, and the government is now exploring the option of monetising its land, buildings and tower assets. To renew its license in 2019, MTNL needs to pay an unaffordable ₹11,000 crore, which it is in no position to pay. With total outstanding liabilities exceeding ₹14,600 crore in 2018–2019 and a negative net worth of about ₹9,900 crore, even the auditors are doubting its ability to continue as a going concern. One reason for the huge liability was again the government. The UPA government forced MTNL, operating only in two metros, to buy spectrum worth ₹10,000 crore in 2008, for which MTNL had to raise loans. Today, the cash-stripped company does not have the money to pay salaries to its employees. The comparative financial position of these three companies as of 2017–2018 is shown in Table 3.3.

Table 3.3 *Comparative Financial Positions of Three Top Loss-making CPSEs: 2017–2018 (₹ Crore)*

Items	Air India	BSNL	MTNL
Total income	23,900	25,071	3,116
Total expenditure, of which	29,126	33,809	6,090
Employee cost	2,913	14,837	2,446
Finance cost	4,464	48	1,505
Net loss	5,338	7,993	2,973
Outstanding long-term liability	30,228	18,361	10,293
Total current liability	44,091	23,201	9,055
Cash and bank balances	743	758	66
Net worth	−24,894	31,840	−6,337
Contribution to exchequer	NA	NA	183
Operating margin (%)	−3.3	−34.7	−61.9
Net profit margin (%)	−22.3	−31.9	−95.4
Return on capital employed (%)	−16.4	−8.0	−37.1

Source: Financial Statements of the Companies and Public Enterprises Survey, Vol. 2, 2017–2018.
Note: Net worth of BSNL computed by the author from financial statements.

In October 2019, the government has decided to merge both BSNL and MTNL, India's largest and third largest loss-making CPSEs respectively, into a single entity, at a humongous cost of ₹69,100 crore of revival package, of which ₹30,000 crore will finance the VRS package to their employees alone who are over 50 years of age, at the rate equivalent to 10 years' pay for each. BSNL has about 1.65 lakh employees (1.16 lakh above the age of 50) and MTNL has about 21,700 employees (19,000 above the age of 50). After VRS, the staff cost is expected to get reduced by 35 per cent for BSNL and 43 per cent for MTNL. The two companies together account for 14 per cent market share of the mobile business in India. MTNL being a listed company, some regulatory and operation issues will have to be sorted out before the merger takes place. The package is meant to make the unified entity competitive again by giving it access to the 4G spectrum, curtailing the number of employees through the

VRS package to reduce employee cost (amounting to 77% and 87%, respectively, for BSNL and MTNL) and monetising their assets like large swathes of land and telecom towers. The government considers BSNL and MTNL as 'strategic assets', not to be closed, disinvested or hived off to a third party, as the Telecom Minister has stated on 23 October 2019. Apart from the VRS cost of ₹30,000 crore, the package will comprise sovereign guarantee for long-term bonds for ₹15,000 crore, capital infusion towards 46 spectrum acquisition for ₹20,140 crore and adjustments towards GST pay-out for ₹4,000 crore. Thus, most of it will have to be financed by taxpayers' money.[6]

Even profit-earning companies have been bled by the government systematically. Take the case of Hindustan Aeronautics Ltd. (HAL), which dominated the newspaper headlines before the 2019 Lok Sabha elections, courtesy Rafale and Mr Rahul Gandhi. It is presently facing an acute cash crunch because of lack of orders from the government despite the government's assertions to the contrary. Being a PSE under the Ministry of Defence, the government has been its only buyer. As of March 2013, 2014 and 2015, HAL had cash and cash equivalents for ₹13,378 crore, ₹16,935 crore and ₹17,671 crore, respectively. In 3 years flat, the cash-rich company was struggling for cash to pay salaries to its employees, being forced to buy back its shares from the government during 2015–2016 and 2017–2018 for a total amount of ₹6,394 crore. This, and the payment of dividends of ₹3,013 crore out of a total net profit of ₹6,546 during 2015–2018 without leaving sufficient reserves, saw its cash and cash equivalents dwindling to only ₹6,525 crore in March 2018.[7] In October 2018, the cash balance was less than ₹1,000 crore, not enough to pay the salaries of its 29,000-plus staff, and it had to borrow from the banks.

---

[6] *Times of India*, 24 October 2019, New Delhi. As of December 2019, over 92,000 employees of BSNL and MTNL (78,000 for BSNL and 14,000 for MTNL) have opted for VRS, far exceeding the target set for the purpose. This will reduce the employee cost of BSNL by an estimated ₹7,000 crore and of MTNL by an estimated ₹1,800 crore. "BSNL MTNL to be merged; Centre lines up ₹70000 crore revival package"; https://timesofindia.indiatimes.com/business/india-business/bsnl-mtnl-to-be-merged-centre-lines-up-rs-70000-crore-revival-package/articleshow/71730263.cms

[7] Source: Balance sheets of HAL for respective years.

It was the same case with all cash-rich CPSEs, whose surplus cash was squeezed out by a government perpetually looking for funds to contain its soaring fiscal deficit. Share buybacks has become one of the most preferred modes for the Centre to meet its disinvestment target. Coal India and NMDC had cash and bank balance of ₹38,313 crore and ₹14,809 crore, respectively, in 2015–2016. During 2016–2017, they were made to buy back their shares worth ₹3,650 crore and ₹7,527 crore, respectively. Shares were also bought back by NALCO (₹2,835 crore), Manganese Ore India Ltd (₹863 crore), Bharat Dynamics Ltd (₹450 crore) and Bharat Electronics Ltd (₹2,171 crore) during 2016–2017.

The cash and bank balances of ONGC Ltd, India's main state-owned oil explorer that accounts for over 60 per cent of the country's crude oil production, has systematically dipped from ₹9,957 crore in March 2016 to ₹9,511 crore in March 2017, ₹1,013 crore in March 2018 and a record low of ₹504 crore in March 2019, severely restricting its capex spends. This steady slide has come as a result of two deals the government had forced the company into—acquiring the down-stream oil marketing company Hindustan Petroleum Corporation Ltd (HPCL) and Gujarat-based GSPC—which severely dented the ONGC's cash reserves. During the last 6 years, however, ONGC's expenditure on exploratory wells has almost halved from ₹11,687 crore in 2013–2014 to ₹6,016 crore in 2018–2019, though its expenditure on developmental wells has remained steady over the last 6 years (₹8,518 crore in 2013–2014, ₹9,362 crore in 2018–2019). The decline in exploratory expenditure was accompanied by a steady decline in domestic crude oil production, from 38.09 MMT in the FY 2012 to 35.68 MMT in the FY 2018. The decline in exploration expenditure was all the more necessary to offset this decline in crude production through exploration and discovery of new sources of oil.[8]

The Union Budget, 2016–2017 focused on the need to migrate from the 'disinvestment based approach' to 'investment based approach' for CPSEs. The thrust of the government also shifted from disinvestment towards efficient management of its investment

---

[8] *Indian Express*, 'ONGC Cash Reserves at Record Low'.

in CPSEs, as symbolised by the change of name in the Department of Disinvestment to 'Department of Investment and Public Asset Management' (DIPAM), with an expanded mandate. DIPAM laid down comprehensive 'Guidelines on Capital Restructuring of CPSEs' in May 2016 by addressing various aspects such as payment of dividend, buyback of shares, issuance of bonus shares and splitting of shares. Later, the government put in place a mechanism/procedure along with indicative timelines for the listing of CPSEs in February 2017.

The new guideline mandates every CPSE with a net worth of at least ₹2,000 crore and a cash and bank balance of ₹1,000 crore to exercise the option of share buyback. Some unlisted companies were also forced to buy back their shares, such as Mazagon Dock Shipbuilders, IRCON, Garden Reach Shipbuilders & Engineers, HSCC (India), Security Printing and Minting Corporation of India (SPMCIL), and the ISRO's commercial arm, Antrix Corporation. The buyback automatically led to a reduction in their outstanding shares, all of which were in any case held by the Centre. The government's stake in them remained 100 per cent even after the buyback. As a matter of principle, there may be nothing wrong in such buybacks, but the business or capex requirements of the companies must take priority over the government's demand for funds. But with the government being in the driver's seat, as far as PSEs are concerned, their business interests are always subservient to the government's will. The scant regard paid to PSEs is evident from the shabby manner in which their CMDs are treated by the middle level bureaucrats of their controlling ministries when they come to meet them for official purposes. The CMDs can be seen loitering in the corridors of power, waiting patiently to meet the concerned Joint Secretary, as if pursuing some favours. It is common knowledge that many bureaucrats and ministers routinely extract their pound of flesh from the PDUs under their administrative control. Non-interference in their autonomy is a pure myth; PSEs function under a structure where their management remains permanently and unquestioningly compliant to directives and orders of government functionaries.

As discussed in the last chapter, one objective behind the creation of public sector enterprises covering all major strategic sectors of the economy was generation of employment. In the deindustrialised post-colonial economy inherited at independence, there was hardly any scope for gainful employment except in agriculture, which already had significant underemployment and low labour productivity besides not requiring much skilled labour. The CPSEs not only provided an avenue for employment of skilled manpower, but also served as the training ground for the development of skills that were essential for laying down the foundation on which would be raised the architecture of manufacturing and industrialisation in the country. CPSEs throughout have remained the major employers of technical manpower, and since employment in them was securely protected by labour-friendly laws, the advantage of technology could not be harnessed by their management to reduce employee cost and increase profitability. The author recalls a personal experience of visiting the SAIL plant in Durgapur during the mid-1990s when demand for steel in China, a major importer of Indian steel, was falling sharply without any prospect of picking up in the near future—the trend would in fact continue almost till the end of the decade—and the Durgapur plant was unable to run the three shifts it was running earlier due to the lack of adequate demand. Mostly, it was able to run only a single shift but was unable to retrench the huge number of workers who were being paid without having any work to do. No industry can survive with two-thirds of the labour being paid without any productivity, but the management was powerless. SAIL, which booked a loss of ₹482 crore in 2017–2018, still happens to be one of the major public sector employers, in fact second after only BSNL, another public sector behemoth that has been continuously incurring losses for more than decade now. Table 3.4 shows the list of top 20 employers among the CPSEs, and the list contains seven loss-making enterprises whose total losses during 2017–2018 amount to ₹14,366 crore.

Table 3.5 shows the aggregate real investments as measured by the Gross Block in top 10 CPSEs; of the total ₹19.84 lakh crore of gross block for all CPSEs, the top 10 alone account for as much as 71 per cent, the remaining 294 accounting for only 29 per cent. Most investments, thus, have been concentrated in only a handful of CPSEs.

Table 3.4 *Top 20 CPSEs in Terms of Employment: 2017–2018*

S. No.	CPSE Name	Employment	% Share	Profit/ Loss During 2017–2018 (₹ Crore)
1	BSNL Ltd.	183,522	16.9	−7,933
2	Steel Authority of India Ltd.	76,870	7.1	−482
3	Eastern Coalfields Ltd.	61,796	5.7	−931
4	South Eastern Coalfields Ltd.	58,143	5.3	+2,370
5	Bharat Coking Coal Ltd.	48,747	4.5	−1,391
6	Western Coalfields Ltd.	45,663	4.2	−1,757
7	Central Coalfields Ltd.	40,777	3.7	+790
8	Bharat Heavy Electricals Ltd.	37,540	3.4	+807
9	Indian Oil Corporation Ltd.	33,157	3.0	+21,346
10	Oil and Natural Gas Corporation Ltd.	32,265	3.0	+19,945
11	Hindustan Aeronautics Ltd.	29,362	2.7	+2,070
12	MTNL Ltd.	25,191	2.3	−2,973
13	Mahanadi Coalfields Ltd.	22,430	2.1	+4,741
14	FCI Ltd.	22,370	2.1	0
15	NTPC Ltd.	19,739	1.8	+10,343
16	Rashtriya Ispat Nigam Ltd.	17,617	1.6	−1,369
17	AAI	17,535	1.6	+2,802
18	Northern Coalfields Ltd.	15,057	1.4	+2,685
19	Andrew Yule & Co. Ltd.	14,731	1.4	+17
20	NLC India Ltd.	14,446	1.3	+1,849
	Total (1 to 20)	**816,958**	**75.1**	**+67,395**
	Other CPSEs (218)	**271,182**	**24.9**	**−14,466**
	Total Employment in CPSEs (238)	**1,088,140**	**100.0**	

Source: Department of Public Enterprises, *Public Enterprises Survey, 2017–2018*, Vol. 1, Statement 14, p. S111.

Table 3.5 *Top 10 CPSEs in Terms of Gross Block (₹ Crore)*

S. No.	CPSE Name	Gross Block	% Share
1	BSNL Ltd.	251,056	12.7
2	NTPC Ltd.	218,921	11.0
3	Power Grid Corporation India Ltd.	207,407	10.5
4	Oil and Natural Gas Corporation Ltd.	196,122	9.9
5	Indian Oil Corporation Ltd.	146,035	7.4
6	Steel Authority of India Ltd.	113,913	5.7
7	ONGC Videsh Ltd.	108,684	5.5
8	Nuclear Power Corporation India ltd.	62,295	3.1
9	Bharat Petroleum Corporation Ltd.	53,526	2.7
10	Hindustan Petroleum Corporation Ltd.	49,676	2.5
	Total (1–10)	**1,407,635**	**70.9**
	Other CPSEs (294)	**576,987**	**29.1**
	Total Gross Block of CPSEs (304)	**1,984,622**	**100.0**

Source: Department of Public Enterprises, *Public Enterprises Survey 2017–2018,* Vol. 1, Statement 15, p. S117.

The government's financial investments[9] in the CPSEs stood at ₹13,73,412 crore as at the end of 2017–2018. Most of the investments (45%) have taken place in the manufacturing, processing and generation sectors, followed by services (33%), mining and exploration (20%) and construction sectors (2%). Agriculture has negligible share in the total investments. The corresponding figures for financial investments are 28 per cent, 61 per cent, 7 per cent and 3 per cent, respectively.

CPSEs contribute to the public exchequer in various ways—through dividend, tax on dividends and income tax on profits earned by them, through indirect taxes, interest on loans, cess on petrol by petroleum marketing companies, etc. Table 3.6 shows the top 10 contributors to the exchequer during 2017–2018, who contributed

[9] Include paid up capital, shares pending allotment, funds received against share warrants and long term loans.

Table 3.6 Top 10 Contributors to the Exchequer: 2017–2018 (₹ Crore)

S. No.	CPSE Name	Net Contribution	% Share
1	Indian Oil Corporation Ltd.	103,361	29.5
2	Bharat Petroleum Corporation Ltd.	46,900	13.4
3	Hindustan Petroleum Corporation Ltd.	31,004	8.9
4	Mangalore refinery & Petrochem. Ltd.	15,961	4.6
5	Oil and Natural Gas Corporation Ltd.	13,346	3.8
6	Chennai Petroleum Corporation Ltd.	12,741	3.6
7	Mahanadi Coalfields Ltd.	9,817	2.8
8	Coal India Ltd.	8,521	2.4
9	South Eastern coalfields Ltd.	8,360	2.4
10	Airports Authority of India	7,014	2.0
	Total (1 to 10)	**257,025**	73.4
	Other CPSEs (233)	**93,027**	26.6
	Total Contribution of CPSEs (243)	**350,052**	100.0

Source: Department of Public Enterprises, *Public Enterprises Survey 2017–2018*, Vol. 1, Statement 28, pp. S200–S206.

more than 73 per cent of the total contribution made by all CPSEs to the public exchequer. The 233 other CPSEs contributed less than 27 per cent of the total contribution to public exchequer during the year.

As regards the distribution and spread of assets and employment of CPSEs among the Indian states, it can be seen from Table 3.7 that the 18 general category states account for over 69 per cent of the assets while the 11 special category states share less than 10 per cent. The seven union territories account for only 4 per cent, almost the whole of which is in Delhi (3.9%). Of the total employment, again, the distribution is skewed heavily in favour of the general category states, which account for nearly 86 per cent of the total employment in CPSEs, with the small, special category states accounting for only 6 per cent. The union territories account for 5.5 per cent of employment, with Delhi

Table 3.7 State-wise List of CPSE Assets and Employment: 2017–2018

States	No. of PSUs Having Offices/ Branches in the State	Gross Block (₹ crore)	Number of Employees	Overall Percentage Share in All-India	
				Gross Block	Employees
General-category states					
Andhra Pradesh	97	105,418	50,174	5.3	4.6
Bihar	74	68,670	12,254	3.5	1.1
Chhattisgarh	64	100,976	77,365	5.1	7.1
Goa	34	2,970	3,457	0.1	0.3
Gujrat	79	81,377	34,640	4.1	3.2
Haryana	65	46,524	16,779	2.3	1.5
Jharkhand	75	58,870	127,252	3.0	11.7
Karnataka	106	89,868	57,435	4.5	5.3
Kerala	75	47,234	27,906	2.4	2.6
Madhya Pradesh	87	91,056	63,448	4.6	5.8
Maharashtra	121	167,970	125,404	8.5	11.5
Odisha	84	121,247	60,034	6.1	5.5
Punjab	61	21,154	14,525	1.1	1.3
Rajasthan	80	54,761	18,796	2.8	1.7
Tamil Nadu	112	131,546	64,772	6.6	6.0
Telangana	78	16,041	17,916	0.8	1.6
Uttar Pradesh	106	128,254	47,989	6.5	4.4
West Bengal	129	92,772	111,801	4.7	10.3
Sub-total		**1,377,423**	**931,947**	**69.4**	**85.6**
Special-category states					
Arunachal Pradesh	30	18,461	1,494	0.9	0.1
Assam	71	75,341	35,938	3.8	3.3

(Table 3.7 Continued)

(Table 3.7 Continued)

States	No. of PSUs Having Offices/ Branches in the State	Gross Block (₹ crore)	Number of Employees	Overall Percentage Share in All-India	
				Gross Block	Employees
Himachal Pradesh	39	34,475	6,323	1.7	0.6
Jammu & Kashmir	46	20,398	5,840	1.0	0.5
Manipur	27	1,092	589	0.1	0.1
Meghalaya	32	346	1,071	0.0	0.1
Mizoram	21	1,706	236	0.1	0.0
Nagaland	20	1,185	553	0.1	0.1
Sikkim	16	3,665	513	0.2	0.0
Tripura	34	5,617	1,674	0.3	0.2
Uttarakhand	54	28,574	13,372	1.4	1.2
Sub-total		**190,860**	**67,603**	**9.6**	**6.2**
Union territories					
Delhi	163	76,561	55,935	3.9	5.1
Chandigarh	39	249	582	0.0	0.1
Pondicherry	20	1,054	2,013	0.1	0.2
Lakshadweep	4	40	154	0.0	0.0
Daman & Diu	9	273	50	0.0	0.0
Andaman & Nicobar Islands	19	698	1,124	0.0	0.1
Dadra & Nagar Haveli	7	589	77	0.0	0.0
Sub-total		**79,464**	**59,935**	**4.0**	**5.5**
Unallocated	49	**287,590**	**28,655**	**14.5**	**2.6**
Grand total		**1,984,622**	**1,088,140**	**100.0**	**100.0**

Source: Department of Public Enterprises, *Public Enterprises Survey 2017–2018*, Vol. 1, Statement 11, pp. S51–S99.
Note: This does not include nationalised banks and financial corporations like the LICI, etc. Contributions of less than ₹1 lakh have also been ignored while computing the number of contributing PSEs.

alone accounting for 5.1 per cent. Distribution is not uniform even among the respective groups—thus, Jharkhand accounts for 3 per cent of assets but almost 12 per cent of employment because of the coal mines that employ a huge labour force. Only a few states have more than 5 per cent of the total assets, like Andhra Pradesh, Chhattisgarh, Maharashtra, Odisha, Tamil Nadu and Uttar Pradesh.

In Chapter 2, the concept of MOU, by which the CPSEs are given performance targets every year and evaluated against specified parameters, has been explained. The MOU is, in fact, 'a performance contract'—a mutually negotiated agreement between the CPSE management and the Government of India. It is a mechanism for ensuring the accountability of the CPSEs to the government. The performance parameters that were applied since 2004–2005 included financial or static parameters and non-financial parameters with equal weightages. While financial or static parameters included profit, turnover, productivity, etc., the non-financial parameters included dynamic parameters like project implementation, investment in R&D, extent of globalisation, etc. with 30 per cent weightage and enterprise-specific and sector-specific parameters with 10 per cent weightage each. In 2010–2011, the non-financial parameters were expanded to include Corporate Social Responsibility (CSR), R&D and sustainable development. The performance is graded on a 5-point scale (Excellent, Very Good, Good, Fair and Poor) on the basis of a composite score comprising all these parameters. The MOU rating forms the basis of incentivising the CPSE executives through Performance Related Pay (PRP), with all the key result areas identified in the MOU.

The guidelines prescribing parameters have since been revised many times, and as per the latest guidelines issues in January 2019, financial parameters now include three parameters: turnover (10% weightage), operating profit/loss (20% weightage) and Return on Investment (20% weightage). The non-financial parameters have been diversified and differentiated for the financial and non-financial companies; while for the finance sector companies the parameters include those related to loans, NPAs, outstanding liabilities including contingent liabilities, HR-related parameters, etc., for the non-financial companies, the included parameters relate to capacity utilisation, production

Table 3.8 MOU Rating of PSUs: 2014–2017

Rating	No. of PSEs		
	2014–2015	*2015–2016*	*2016–2017*
Excellent	73	57	49
Very good	53	58	54
Good	41	28	40
Fair	26	22	31
Poor	7	26	24
Total	200	191	185

Source: Department of Public Enterprises, *Public Enterprises Survey 2017-2018,* Vol. 1, p. 184.

efficiency, exports, capex, inventory, debtors and creditors, market share, HR-related parameters, R&D, technology upgradation, innovation, etc.[10]

The MOU rating during the last 5 years is shown in Table 3.8, and Annexure 3.1 shows the rating for the year 2017–2018 for the individual CPSEs. As profitability carries only 20 per cent weightage, many loss-making CPSEs have also earned ratings like Excellent or Very Good.

Sector-wise performance of the CPSEs shows wide variation across sectors and also across cognate groups, as seen from Tables 3.9 and 3.10, and Figure 3.1. The manufacturing sector recorded the maximum profit during 2016–2017 and 2017–2018, followed by the mining and exploration and services sectors, in that order. The profit of the manufacturing sector was lagging behind that of mining and exploration in 2015–2016 but improved by a third during the next year due to increase in profits from the petroleum CPSEs. Among this sector, however, only petroleum, power generation, heavy and medium engineering and transportation PSEs consistently earned profits during

[10] GoI Circular No. M-03/0017/2016-DPE (MoU), dated 17 January 2019, Department of Public Enterprises, Govt. of India.

Table 3.9 Sector and Cognate Group-wise Net Profit and Loss of CPSEs (₹ Crore)

S. No.	Sector	Cognate Group	Net Profit/Loss			Percentage Change over Previous Year (%)	
			2015–2016	2016–2017	2017–2018	2016–2017	2017–2018
	Agriculture						
1		Agro-based Industries	–69	–29	–103	58.4	–258.4
	Mining and exploration						
2		Coal	30,361	23,598	15,821	–22.3	–33.0
3		Crude oil	14,697	19,985	23,432	36.0	17.3
4		Other minerals and metals	3,650	3,875	5,685	6.2	46.7
	Sub-total		**48,708**	**47,458**	**44,938**	**–2.6**	**–5.3**
	Manufacturing, processing and generation						
5		Steel	–5,466	–3,946	–1,711	27.8	56.6
6		Petroleum (refinery and marketing)	25,123	40,129	40,804	59.7	1.7
7		Fertilizers	9,107	168	253	–98.2	51.1
8		Chemicals and pharmaceuticals	–1,358	–1,361	–707	–0.2	48.1
9		Heavy and medium engineering	2,990	8,693	9,306	190.7	7.1
10		Transportation (vehicle and equipment)	64	84	129	32.7	53.3

11	Industrial and consumer goods	-2,529	-2,684	-2,733	-6.1	-1.8
12	Textiles	-90	868	-412	–	-147.5
13	Power generation	19,085	20,573	21,399	7.8	4.0
	Sub-total	**46,926**	**62,522**	**66,328**	**33.2**	**6.1**
	Services					
14	Power transmission	6,018	7,555	8,351	25.6	10.5
15	Trading and marketing	-997	-156	-77	84.3	50.5
16	Transport and logistic services	3,217	1,906	3,700	-40.8	94.2
17	Contract and construction and technical consultancy services	2,252	2,413	2,885	7.1	19.6
18	Hotel and tourist services	156	164	185	5.0	12.7
19	Financial services	14,618	11,113	12,894	-24.0	16.0
20	Telecommunication and IT	-6,591	-7,448	-10,728	-13.0	-44.0
	Sub-total	**18,673**	**15,547**	**17,211**	**-16.7**	**10.7**
	Grand total	**114,239**	**125,498**	**128,374**	**9.9**	**2.3**

Source: Department of Public Enterprises, *Public Enterprises Survey 2017–2018*, Vol. I, p. 25.

Table 3.10 *Sector-wise Key Financial Ratios*

Sector	Return on Net Worth (%) 2016–2017	Return on Net Worth (%) 2017–2018	Return on Assets (%) 2016–2017	Return on Assets (%) 2017–2018	Net Profit Margin (%) 2016–2017	Net Profit Margin (%) 2017–2018	Operating Profit Margin (%) 2016–2017	Operating Profit Margin (%) 2017–2018
Agriculture	−8.8	−39.3	−1.5	−5.1	−2.3	−10.5	7.1	−0.9
Mining and exploration	16.2	14.8	8.0	6.9	20.5	18.2	28.9	27.1
Manufacturing, processing and generation	14.4	14.3	4.8	4.7	5.5	5.1	9.3	9.0
Services	4.6	5.0	1.0	1.0	3.4	3.6	11.8	11.7
Total	**11.8**	**11.6**	**3.7**	**3.4**	**6.9**	**6.3**	**12.4**	**11.9**

Source: Department of Public Enterprises, *Public Enterprises Survey 2017–2018,* Vol. I, p. 5.

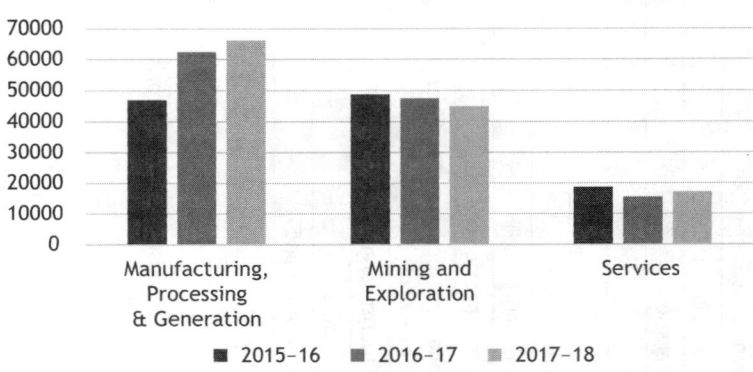

Figure 3.1 *Sector-wise Net Profit/Loss (₹ Crore)*
Source: Based on Table 3.9.

all 3 years, while the rest remained mostly in the red. CPSEs in the steel, chemicals and pharmaceutics groups were, however, able to reduce their losses over the 3-year period, whereas the CPSEs in the industrial and consumer goods as well as those in the textile groups were not able to control their losses. Among the mining and exploration sector, crude oil and other minerals and metals increased their profits while the profits from coal PSEs showed a steep declining trend over the period. Oil PSEs saw their profits jump in 2016–2017 due to the moderation in oil prices and the government's giving them full immunity from under-recoveries. Demand for coal depends on the production of steel, and therefore it is no wonder that both the sectors were suffering from depressed demands. Returns on net worth and assets as well as the profit margins for the mining and exploration sector were higher than the other sectors.

Table 3.11 shows the overall performance of the CPSEs during the last 5 years. Of the 257 CPSEs operating in 2017–2018, almost 72 per cent, or 184 PSEs earned profits in 2017–2018 amounting to almost ₹1.6 lakh crore; in contrast, 71 CPSEs incurred losses amounting to ₹31,261 crore. CPSEs' contribution to the GDP has however come down, from more than a fifth of the GDP in 2013–2014 to only 12.6 per cent in 2017–2018. The total dividend earned by the government from the CPSEs in 2017–2018 was ₹76,578 crore. Both the profits earned by profit-making companies and dividend paid by them increased only marginally—by about ₹10,000 crore—over this 5-year period. Taking into account the losses, the overall profit of the 257 CPSEs, in fact, declined marginally, from ₹1.5 lakh crore to ₹1.3 lakh crore during these 5 years. From Table 3.12, it can be seen that the Petroleum (Refinery & Marketing) CPSEs contribute more than half the gross revenues earned by all the CPSEs, with trading and marketing at a distant second position with 8.3 per cent of gross revenues.

The comparison of the public sector companies with their private sector counterparts brings out many interesting features. As far as production of basic minerals like coal, crude oil and natural gas are concerned, CPSEs overwhelmingly dominate the scene (Table 3.13) even after the private sector has been allowed in oil exploration, production and distribution; in coal, private sector still has a nominal presence. However, the CPSEs' shares in the other sectors like steel, fertilisers, power and telecommunication are very small—these sectors are overwhelmingly dominated by private players, and CPSEs' market shares are continuously being eroded in these sectors. Capacity utilisation

Table 3.11 Overall Performance of CPSEs (₹ Crore)

Particulars	2013–2014	2014–2015	2015–2016	2016–2017	2017–2018
No. of operating CPSEs	234	236	244	257	257
Capital employed	1,710,453	1,833,274	2,037,318	2,138,069	2,273,969
Total gross turnover	2,266,057	1,995,176	1,834,635	1,955,675	2,155,948
GDP (Economic Survey, 2018–19)	11,233,522	12,467,959	13,771,874	15,362,386	17,095,005
Turnover as % of GDP	20.2	16.0	13.3	12.7	12.6
Total net income	2,056,336	1,965,638	1,764,113	1,821,971	203,3545
Net worth	92,6663	962,518	1,079,953	1,066,885	1,108,595
Operating profit (PBIT)	234,861	195,083	209,133	225,936	240,961
Profit before taxes	183,223	150,141	157,684	178,707	187,659
Tax provisions	55,178	47,230	43,653	53,183	59,661
Overall net profit/loss	128,045	102,911	114,031	125,523	127,997
No. of profit-making CPSEs	164	159	164	175	184
Profit of profit-making CPSEs	149,636	130,364	144,991	152,978	159,635
No. of loss-making CPSEs	70	76	79	81	71
Loss of loss-making CPSEs	21,341	27,498	30,756	27,480	31,261
No. of CPSEs without profit/loss	0	1	1	1	2
Dividend paid	65,115	56,527	68,583	78,129	76,578
Dividend tax paid	8,709	8,642	10,598	14,419	12,935

Source: Department of Public Enterprises, *Public Enterprises Survey 2017–2018*, Vol. I, p. 27.

Table 3.12 Percentage Share of Cognate Group in Revenue Generation

Cognate Group	Share of Gross Revenue (%)	Cognate Group	Share of Gross Revenue (%)
Petroleum (refinery and marketing)	53.4	Coal	4.0
Trading and marketing	8.3	Heavy and medium engineering	3.7
Power generation	5.7	Financial services	3.3
Transport and logistics	5.2	Steel	3.5
Crude Oil	5.0	Others	7.9

Source: Figure 3.3, Public Enterprises Survey, 2017–18, Vol. I p. 22, Govt. of India.

Table 3.13 CPSEs' Share in Production: 2016–2017

Commodities/Services	CPSEs	Private Sector	Total
Total production in MMT			
Coal	623.9	34.1	658
Crude oil	25.6	10.4	36
Natural gas	25.0	7.0	32
Steel	33.5	180.5	214
Fertilisers*	87.0	296.0	480
Power generation (GW)#	103.0	159.1	346
Telecommunication (millions)$	122.6	1072.4	1,195
Share in total production (%)			
Coal	94.8	5.2	100
Crude oil	71.1	28.9	100
Natural gas	78.5	21.5	100
Steel	15.7	84.3	100

(Table 3.13 Continued)

(Table 3.13 Continued)

Commodities/Services	CPSEs	Private Sector	Total
Fertilisers	20.4	61.7	82.1
Power generation	29.8	45.0	74.8
Telecommunication	10.3	89.7	100

Source: Department of Public Enterprises, *Public Enterprises Survey 2017–2018,* Vol. I, pp. 10–17; PIB press release on coal production in private sector dated 25 July 2018.
Notes: *In addition, the cooperative sector produced 108 MMMT of fertilisers during 2016–2017. Also includes that of State PSEs for 103 GW.
#Measured by Iinstalled Ccapacity, which also includes that of Sstate PSEs for 103 GW.
$Measured by the number of telephone/mobile connections.

by the CPSEs has also been very high in the core sectors—steel, coal, electricity and crude oil, while in the other sectors such as metals, medical formulations, cement, etc., which have substantial private sector participation, the capacity utilisation has been sub-optimal and rather poor (Table 3.14).

Table 3.15 shows the comparison of the financial performance between private and public sectors in 2017–2018. For the purpose of comparison, three parameters have been used: net profit margin, return on assets and long-term debt/equity ratio. In the telecom sector, both the CPSEs have registered dismal performances. Though they lag far behind their private sector counterparts, even the latter just cruised through with minimal margins. In the mining sector, CPSEs are as competitive as the private sector companies, while in the metals sector, their performance is far below that of their private sector counterparts. In petroleum and power generation, CPSEs outshine their private sector competitors by huge margins, while in the fertiliser sector, cooperatives and private sectors seem to do better.

Corporate governance in CPSEs was not an issue till the 1980s. Corporate governance is to ensure commitment to the ethical conduct of business, transparency and accountability, adequacy of internal

Table 3.14 Capacity Utilisation by CPSEs Across Sectors

CPSE	Product	Installed Capacity	Capacity Utilisation (%)		
			2015–2016	2016–2017	2017–2018
SAIL	Saleable steel	17.85 MT	82	92	79
RINL	Saleable steel	5.57 MT	73	77	81
Hindustan Copper Ltd.	Copper wire rod	60,000 MT	43	30	37
CIL	Coal	0.6 MT	42	52	134
Northern Coalfields Ltd.	Coal	95.5 MT	72	89	98
Western Coalfields Ltd.	Coal	59 MT	96	84	80
NTPC	Electricity	40,355 MW*	79	79	78
IOC	Crude	69 MT	102	94	99.7
MRPL	Crude	15 MT	104	108	108
National Fertilisers Ltd.	Urea	3.23 MT	118	118	118
Hindustan Antibiotics Ltd.	Formulation	610 MT	3	1	15
BHEL	Boiler	8.3 billion tonne	39	40	45
HEC	EOT crane	6,940 tonnes	55	42	10
Cement Corporation of India	Cement	3.9 billion tonne	23	20	19
GRSEL	Shipbuilding	5107 tonne	87	28	55

Source: Department of Public Enterprises, *Public Enterprises Survey 2017–2018*, Vol. I, pp. 47–59; PIB press release on coal production in private sector dated 25 July 2018.
Note: *NTPC generated 266 BU of electricity during 2017–2018 as against 250 BU during 2016–2017 while another PSE, NHPC, generated 1.3 BU of electricity during 2017–2018 as against 4.7 BU during 2015–2016.

Table 3.15 *Comparison of Performance Between Private Sector and CPSEs: 2017–2018*

Sector	Sector and Companies	Public/ Private	Net Profit Margin (%)	Return on Assets (%)	Long-term Debt: Equity Ratio
Telecom	BSNL	Public	−31.9	−6.0	−0.11
	MTNL	Public	−95.4	−18.3	—
	Reliance Jio Infocomm Ltd.	Private	3.6	0.3	0.3
	Bharti Airtel	Private	0.2	0.04	0.5
Mining	NALCO	Public	13.5	9.2	0
	ONGC	Public	21.5	6.9	0
	NDMC	Public	31.4	13.3	0
	Hindalco	Private	3.2	1.7	0.4
	Vedanta	Private	14.6	4.9	0.2
	Hindustan Zinc	Private	38.2	21.6	0
Metals	SAIL	Public	−0.8	−0.4	0.8
	RINL	Public	−10.0	−4.3	0.9
	Tata Steel Ltd.	Private	6.8	3.3	0.4
	JSW Steel Ltd.	Private	7.0	5.4	1.1
Petroleum	IOC	Public	4.2	7.6	0.2
	BPCL	Public	2.8	7.9	0.4
	Reliance Petro Marketing Ltd.	Private	0.7	8.8	0
Fertilisers and chemicals	National Fertiliser Ltd.	Public	2.4	2.2	0.1
	RCFL	Public	1.1	1.2	0.1
	Coromandel International Ltd.	Private	6.0	6.8	0
	IFFCO	Coop.	4.0	3.1	0.1
Power generation	NTPC	Public	12.1	4.0	1.1
	NHPC	Public	5.2	32.7	0.6

(Table 3.15 Continued)

(Table 3.15 Continued)

Sector	Sector and Companies	Public/ Private	Net Profit Margin (%)	Return on Assets (%)	Long-term Debt: Equity Ratio
	NPCIL	Public	28.9	4.9	0.9
	Adani Power Ltd.	Private	−0.3	−0.1	0.2
	Tata Power Co. Ltd.	Private	−37.2	−8.6	0.6

Source: Department of Public Enterprises, *Public Enterprises Survey 2017–2018*, Vol. I, pp. 11–21; PIB press release on coal production in private sector dated 25 July 2018.

controls, compliance to the law of the land, adequate disclosures about the financial state of affairs and informed decision-making to protect the interest of all stakeholders. CPSEs were entirely owned by the government; they were generally tax compliant, followed the laws and rules and generally conformed to ethical business practices. They were also subject to audit by the CAG of India and hence irregular practices, if any, were generally detected on time and corrected. Being cent per cent government-owned, there was no conflict between the management and owners and there was no question of protecting the interests of minority shareholders as the government was their sole owner. The institutional oversight mechanisms provided by COPU, CAG and CVC also worked satisfactorily, ensuring accountability and transparency. These issues of corporate governance, therefore, were not affecting their functioning. However, once they were exposed to competition from the private sector after the economic reforms of the 1990s, the scenario started changing, and with stock exchange listing and then privatisation, the need for instituting formal mechanisms for corporate governance became urgent to enable them to function as business entities managed by competent professionals. Corporate frauds in India and abroad also forced the Indian corporate sector to adopt the best global practices of corporate governance that evolved in the advanced countries.

Poor standards of financial reporting had caused corporate scams the world over during the earlier decades—the 1980s and the 1990s.

In the UK, this had led to the setting up of the 'Cadbury Committee' headed by Sir Adrian Cadbury in 1991 by the Financial Reporting Council, the London Stock of Exchange and the accountancy profession to address this disturbing aspect of corporate functioning and to impart greater confidence, both in financial reporting and in the ability of auditors, to provide the safeguards. The objective was to raise the standards of corporate governance and hence improve investor confidence.[11] Known as the 'Committee on Financial Aspects of Corporate Governance', the report had identified the basic elements of the corporate governance in Para 2.5:

> Corporate governance is the system by which companies are directed and controlled. Boards of directors are responsible for the governance of their companies. The shareholders' role in governance is to appoint the directors and the auditors and to satisfy themselves that an appropriate governance structure is in place.[12]

The report stated, *inter alia,* that there should be a clear division of responsibilities at the top, that the Board should have a strong presence of independent elements, that outside directors should comprise the majority of the Board and that there should be an Audit Committee appointed by the Board including at least three non-executive directors.

The Enron scam in 2001 and the Worldcom scam in 2002 shook the US financial world. Both involved cooked-up accounts that were overlooked by the auditors. The spate of corporate crimes led to the enactment of the Sarbanes-Oxley Act in USA in July 2002, which strengthened disclosure requirements and penalties for fraudulent accounting. The Sarbanes-Oxley Act passed by the US Congress in 2002 introduced significant changes in the corporate governance scenario in US and profoundly improved the way companies functioned. It established a Public Company Accounting Oversight Board to oversee the accounting industry. It required the public companies to establish and strengthen audit committees, fortified their internal control systems, prescribed stringent disclosure norms, imposed stricter criminal penalties

---

[11] http://cadbury.cjbs.archios.info/report, accessed 30 July 2019.
[12] https://ecgi.global/sites/default/files/codes/documents/cadbury.pdf, accessed 30 July 2019.

for frauds and made the directors and management personally liable for the accuracy of financial statements. The Act also protected the whistle blowers from victimisation. The landscape of accounting, auditing and corporate governance vastly improved as a result in the United States.

In 2004, the OECD had codified the Principles of Corporate Governance built around six principles: (a) basis for an effective corporate governance framework including specifying the division of responsibilities at different levels of authority: supervisory, regulatory and enforcement; (b) protecting shareholders' rights and facilitating the exercise of those rights including mechanism for redressal for violation of those rights; (c) specifying the role of stakeholders in corporate governance and recognition of their rights as per law; (d) equitable treatment of all shareholders including minority and foreign shareholders; (e) disclosure and transparency requirements to ensure timely and accurate disclosure on all material issues affecting the operation and governance of the entity; and (f) specifying the responsibilities of the Board as well as its accountability to the company and the shareholders. These still remain the cornerstones of all corporate governance frameworks.[13]

After the global economic meltdown of 2008, the volatility in the financial markets across the globe had affected Indian companies also, and general retail investors were beginning to lose their trust in stock markets. Several scams started rocking the market around this time, most important of them being the Satyam scam of 2009. In India, too, the Satyam scam and other scams emphasised the need for the strengthening of corporate governance standards. According to a study of 4,867 companies listed on the BSE and 1,288 companies listed on the NSE conducted by the Pune-based Indiaforensic Consultancy Services in 2008, at least 1,200 listed companies had forged their financial results, which included 20–25 firms on Sensex and Nifty indices. The study called 'Early Warning Signals of Corporate Frauds' pointed to various accounting irregularities indulged in by these firms.[14]

---

[13] https://www.oecd.org/daf/ca/corporategovernanceprinciples/31557724.pdf, pp. 17–25, accessed 31 July 2019.
[14] https://indiaforensic.com/research.htm, accessed 30 July 2019.

Till then, corporate governance in India was being ensured only for the listed companies for whom the Securities and Exchange Board of India (SEBI) had made it mandatory to follow the corporate governance code formulated by it in the Clause 49 of the Listing Agreement of SEBI. The clause was incorporated in 2000 following the recommendations of the Kumar Mangalam Birla Committee on Corporate Governance constituted by SEBI in 1999. Following the recommendation of the Narayana Murthy Committee set up by SEBI in 2002 to review Clause 49, a revised Clause 49 came into effect in 2005. It strengthened the earlier provisions and prescribed elaborate guidelines on the issue of corporate governance. As per the revised Clause 49, for a company with an executive Chairman, at least 50 per cent of the board should comprise independent directors. In the case of a company with a non-executive Chairman, at least one-third of the board should be independent directors. The board is to meet at least 4 times in a year, with the maximum gap between two successive meetings not exceeding 4 months. The clause also prescribes the minimum information to be made available to the Board. The Board is to lay down a code of conduct for all Board members and senior management, to be posted on the website of the company.

The SEBI guidelines make it mandatory to appoint a qualified and independent audit committee with the chairman of the audit committee being an independent director. The audit committee's role shall include, *inter alia*, the 'oversight of the company's financial reporting process and the disclosure of its financial information to ensure that the financial statement is correct, sufficient and credible'.[15] The clause provides specific guidelines about disclosure norms regarding the basis of related party transactions, disclosure of accounting treatment of an item or transaction in case of any deviation from the accounting standards, procedures to inform Board members about risk assessment and mitigation thereof, proceeds from public issues, rights issues, preferential issues, remuneration of directors, etc. The relationship between the holding company and its subsidiaries in terms of financial transaction must be disclosed including any loan giving by the holding company to the subsidies.

[15] Clause 49, (D) 1, SEBI Listing Agreement.

Item VI of Clause 49 prescribes:

There shall be a separate section on Corporate Governance in the Annual Reports of company, with a detailed compliance report on Corporate Governance. Non-compliance of any mandatory requirement of this clause with reasons thereof and the extent to which the non-mandatory requirements have been adopted should be specifically highlighted.

It also suggests a list of items to be included in the report on corporate governance. Clause 49 also includes a list of non-mandatory requirements that include setting up a remuneration committee, a mechanism for evaluating the performance of non-executive Board members and a whistle blower policy, among others.[16] A 2014 amendment made it mandatory for companies to put in place a whistle blower policy to establish a process through which employees can report to the management concerns about unethical behaviour, suspected fraud or violation of the company's code of conduct and be protected against disclosure of their identities or victimisation or retaliation by the authorities reported against.[17] This amendment laid down elaborate guidelines covering all aspects of corporate governance, further strengthening the pre-existing provisions of Clause 49. The amended Clause 49 included

[16] The non-mandatory Whistleblower Policy followed from the Narayana Murthy Committee's recommendations in the wake of the murder of Satyendra Dubey, an IIT-trained engineer who was killed for exposing the corruption in the Golden Quadrilateral project in Bihar in 2003 by writing a letter to the Prime Minister's Office that was leaked out. The Committee had, however, suggested a mandatory Whistleblower Policy, which was diluted in the Clause 49 revised in 2005.

[17] 'F. Whistle Blower Policy
  1. The company shall establish a vigil mechanism for directors and employees to report concerns about unethical behaviour, actual or suspected fraud or violation of the company's code of conduct or ethics policy.
  2. This mechanism should also provide for adequate safeguards against victimisation of director(s)/employee(s) who avail of the mechanism and also provide for direct access to the Chairman of the Audit Committee in exceptional cases.
  3. The details of establishment of such mechanism shall be disclosed by the company on its website and in the Board's report'. (Source: SEBI Circular No. CIR/CFD/POLICY CELL/2/2014 dated 17 April 2014.)

provisions for shareholders' rights, including equitable treatment of all shareholders including minority and foreign shareholders, disclosure and transparency requirements, and clearly spelt out the responsibilities and key functions of the board and role of independent directors, their performance evaluation, role and powers of the Audit Committee, risk management and disclosures about related party transactions, report on corporate governance, etc.

The amended Clause 49 has further strengthened the original intent of protecting the interests of investors through best practices and disclosures to promote transparency and accountability and nudged companies to adopt global best practices. The new Companies Act, 2013, together with Companies Rules under the new act, incorporated many of the key provisions of Clause 49 and gave statutory backing to the principles of corporate governance, which will also apply to the unlisted companies that are equally governed by the Companies Act, and aligned the corporate governance practices in Indian companies with global practices in this regard. Thus, section 134 requires the Board to lay down the policy for regulatory compliance and risk management and ensure that these are operating effectively, to devise proper systems to ensure compliance with the provisions of all applicable laws and to ensure that such systems are adequate and operating effectively. Further, the Board is also required to make annual assessments of the internal financial controls and consider getting expert assistance from outside for such evaluations. While Section 138 mandated the internal audit for certain classes of companies, Section 177 mandated constitution of the Audit Committee in both private and public companies. The mandatory establishment of Corporate Social Responsibility Committee (Section 135), Nomination and Remuneration Committee and Stakeholders Relationship Committee (Section 178) were also prescribed. Section 173 mandated the holding of a minimum of four meetings of the Board every year with a gap of not more than 120 days between two consecutive meetings. Section 211 (1) required the establishment of an office called the Serious Fraud Investigation Office to investigate frauds relating to companies; this has since been established. Section 149 dealt with the appointment of Independent Directors in companies.

CPSE disclosure standards are now comparable to those in many OECD countries, as a World Bank Report had admitted in 2010, with the RTI Act pushing the frontier further on transparency and accountability.[18] Implementing these disclosure requirements, however, still remains a challenge, particularly in light of relatively weak internal audit and internal controls in many CPSEs, especially the non-listed ones, the CAG Report No. 18 of 2018 on General Purpose Financial Reports of CPSEs testifies. The report examined 52 CPSEs and found 37 without the required number of Independent Directors and four without any independent director. Delays exceeding 3 months were observed in filling vacancies of Independent Directors in 23 CPSEs, and delays exceeding 6 months were observed in filling up vacancies of functional Directors in the Board in 16 CPSEs. One CPSE did not have any Audit Committee and there was no whistle blower mechanism in place in three CPSEs.[19]

With a view to bringing in greater transparency in disclosure norms in the accounting practices of the companies, in 2015, the MCA notified the Companies (Indian Accounting Standards) Rules, 2015 for the adoption and application of Indian Accounting Standards (IND AS) by all companies (other than the banking companies, insurance companies and NBFCs, for which RBI would take the necessary steps) in a phased manner beginning with 2016–2017. The 2015 Rules have been amended thrice by the MCA since, in 2016, 2017 and 2018. The IND AS are standards harmonised with the International Financial Reporting standards (IFRS) to make reporting by Indian companies aligned with global standards and practices. Indian companies now have gained a much wider global reach compared to the earlier times, necessitating the convergence of their reporting standards with international standards. IND AS was developed as a result.

The adoption and application of IND AS are to be based on the listing status and net worth of a company, beginning with companies with a net worth equal to or more than ₹500 crore, with effect from

---

[18] World Bank, *Corporate Governance of Central Public Sector Enterprises*, 19.
[19] CAG Report No. 18 of 2018, 61–62.

1 April 2016 in the first phase. Listed companies as well as others having a net worth equal to or more than ₹250 crore will follow from 1 April 2017 onwards during the second phase. Both phases will also include the holding, subsidiary, joint venture or associate companies of companies covered under the respective phases.

A provision on Corporate Social Responsibility (CSR) was incorporated in the new Companies Act, 2013 and Companies (Corporate Social Responsibility) Rules, 2014, for the first time. But the concept of social responsibility of business in India was not new; in fact it dated back to the ancient times. Business is insulated from society, and companies cannot exist and operate in isolation. Ancient Indian wisdom dictates that the purpose of money is to serve the needs of society and its best use is as donation for the welfare of others. Thus, corporate philanthropy was a part of India's culture, and many industrialists in pre-Independence India such as Tata, Birla, Modi, Godrej, Bajaj, Singhania, Shriram, Mahindra, etc. contributed significantly to setting up charitable foundations, educational and healthcare institutions and trusts for community development. Gandhiji had urged the industrialists to share their wealth for the benefit of the society. He gave the concept of trusteeship:

> Supposing I have come by a fair amount of wealth—either by way of legacy, or by means of trade and industry—I must know that all that wealth does not belong to me; what belongs to me is the right to an honourable livelihood, no better than that enjoyed by millions of others. The rest of my wealth belongs to the community and must be used for the welfare of the community.[20]

The egalitarian idea of trusteeship had inspired many industrialists who contributed significantly towards nation-building and self-reliance in the pre-independence years and after independence also. But at that time nobody had thought of integrating the idea in law, and never did it emerge as a business concept. But the modern concept of CSR is of a rather recent origin and is based on the concept that

---

[20] *Harijan*, 3 June 1939, p. 145, http://www.gandhiashramsevagram.org/gandhi-views/on-theory-of-trusteeship.php, accessed 31 July 2019.

since companies derive their profits from society, they also have certain obligations towards society while trying to maximise their own profit.

Capitalists have discarded the concept of any social responsibility of companies. Milton Friedman famously wrote:

> the doctrine of 'social responsibility' taken seriously would extend the scope of the political mechanism to every human activity. It does not differ in philosophy from the most explicitly collectivist doctrine. It differs only by professing that collectivist ends can be achieved without collectivist means. That is why in my book Capitalism and Freedom, I have called it a 'fundamentally subversive doctrine' in a free society, and have said that in such a society, 'there is one and only one social responsibility of business—to use its resources and engage in activities designed to increase its profits so long as it stays within the rule of the game, that is to say, engages in open and free competition without deception or fraud'.[21]

But this view in some way obscures the real relationship between business and society, and in modern times, CSR has emerged as a business concept that can help in furthering the commercial interest of the company by earning the goodwill of society, which is an intangible asset for the company. In a liberalised economy, companies are guided by a multi-stakeholder approach, making companies responsible to all stakeholders, including financial stakeholders, employees and the community, where they have to compete successfully with transnational corporations that have taken significant CSR initiatives and they have no alternative but to integrate CSR into a coherent and sustainable business strategy. Both public and private sector companies now realise that their long-term survival and success can be ensured only by the satisfaction of all stakeholders, without which their future prospects in the community could be jeopardised. Hence, it makes sound business sense to invest in CSR activities.[22]

The concept of CSR is based on ethics and morality in the way a company behaves towards society. The idea that businesses have

[21] 'The Social Responsibility of Business is to Increase Its Profits', 89.
[22] Sharma, 'Corporate Social Responsibility in India: An Overview'.

a social responsibility occurred in modern literature in Chester Barnard's *The Functions of the Executive* (1938) and Theodore Krep's *Measurement of the Social Performance of Business* (1940). The modern concept of CSR is often attributed to Howard R. Bowen. His seminal work, *Social Responsibilities of the Businessman* (1953) explored the connection between business ethics and social responsibility. He defined the Social Responsibilities of the Businessman as 'the obligations of businessmen to pursue those policies, to make those decisions, or to follow those lines of action which are desirable in terms of the objectives and values of our society'. In 1961, R. Eells and C. Walton in *Conceptual Foundations of Business* talked about 'the ethical principles that ought to govern the relationship between the corporation and society'. In *Corporate Social Responsibilities* (1967), Clarence C. Walton advocated that CSR should be practised voluntarily by the companies. During the 1980s, the idea of CSR was further promoted by R. Edward Freeman through his *Strategic Management: A Stakeholder Approach* (1984) and also by Archie B. Carroll, Peter F. Drucker, who suggested converting social problems into economic opportunities, and many others. The Enron scandal of 2001, and especially the global financial crisis of 2008–2010 that followed the meltdown of many large corporations, brought CSR again in focus for reassessing corporate behaviour and responsibility towards society. This also forced businesses to become more sensitive to the social concerns and expectations.

In 1971, the Committee for Economic Development used a model comprising three concentric circles to indicate the approach towards CSR, where the inner circle represented the basic economic functions of a company like growth, products and jobs, the intermediate circle represented 'the sensitive awareness of changing social values and priorities' and the outer circle represented the responsibilities that an organisation must discharge towards actively improving the social environment like reducing poverty, etc.[23]

Some writers focussed on social responsiveness of companies rather than social responsibilities, but reconciliation between the economic

---

[23] Carrol, 'The Pyramid of Corporate Social Responsibility', 91.

and social orientations of a business enterprise remained somewhat amorphous. Carrol, in 1979, made a significant contribution with his CSR Pyramid, in which he tried to combine the corporation's economic and legal obligations with ethical and philanthropic obligations, simply expressed as 'the CSR firm should strive to make a profit, obey the law, be ethical and be a good corporate citizen', which involves engagement in activities that 'enhance the community's "quality of life"' and reconciles its concern for profit with concern for society also.[24] The pyramid has guided many an organisation in designing their CSR policies.

Empirical studies have pointed towards a positive correlation between CSR activities and corporate performance through image building and reputation. Evidence also points that CSR can create shareholder values—with some firms and some management strategies at least—and that CSR can promote customer satisfaction.[25]

Another dimension was added to CSR with the advent of the concept of Triple Bottom. In traditional accounting parlance, 'Bottom Line' refers to the profit earned (or loss incurred) by a company, ignoring how that profit has been earned. Corporate profits are sometimes earned at great social cost and by inflicting great damages to the environment. Thus, the Bottom Line should be expanded to include social and environmental dimensions as well. Freer Spreckley first articulated the TBL in 1981 by arguing that business entities should report on their financial performance as well as social wealth creation and environmental responsibility so that it becomes a 'full cost accounting'.[26] In 1997, John Elkington articulated the TBL concept more comprehensively, arguing that the TBL should comprise people, the social equity bottom line, planet, the environmental bottom line and profit, the economic bottom line.[27] The concept was taken forward with the Integrated Bottom Line (IBL) to encourage companies to assimilate their financial, environmental and social

---

[24] Ibid, 92–94.

[25] Cowe and Hopkins, 'Corporate Social Responsibility: Is there a Business Case?', 107–109.

[26] Spreckley, *Social Audit: A Management Tool for Co-operative Working.*

[27] Elkington, *Cannibals with Forks.*

costs and benefits into a unified measure of business activity reflected in one integrated balance sheet, which would provide a more holistic assessment of the company's performance in long-term value creation in society.[28]

Two other important guidelines in this regard—the UN Global Compact and the OECD Guidelines for Multinational Enterprises—which articulate the principles of responsible business conduct based on international standards and consensus, also provide comprehensive, though non-binding guidelines for voluntary corporate responsibility initiatives for multinational enterprises (MNEs). They cover all relevant areas like human rights, disclosure of information, anti-corruption, taxation, labour relations, environment, competition and consumer protection based on the same set of core values. These are two of the world's foremost corporate responsibility initiatives that complement and reinforce each other.[29]

Formal CSR activities or CSR reporting in India is of recent origin. Though some companies have been carrying on similar activities, there was no formal structure or requirement for these. In December 2009, as a first step towards mainstreaming the concept of CSR, the Ministry of Corporate Affairs, Government of India, issued voluntary guidelines for CSR, which enumerated its fundamental principle that each business entity should formulate a CSR policy to guide its strategic planning and provide a roadmap for its CSR initiatives as an integral part of its overall business policy and aligned with its business goals. The core elements of this policy should include (a) care for all stakeholders and protection of their interests; (b) ethical functioning with transparency and accountability; (c) respect for workers' rights and welfare, including providing a safe, hygienic and humane workplace environment, and giving access to training and development of necessary skills for career advancement, on an equal and non-discriminatory basis; (d) respect for human rights; (e) respect for the environment;

---

[28] https://sustainabilitydictionary.com/2006/03/06/integrated-reporting/, accessed 31 July 2019.

[29] http://www.oecd.org/investment/mne/34873731.pdf, accessed 31 July 2019.

and (f) activities for social and inclusive development. The CSR policy of the business entity should provide for an implementation strategy that should include identification of projects/activities, setting measurable physical targets with timeframe, organisational mechanism and responsibilities, monitoring, etc. It also suggested that companies should allocate a specific amount in their budgets for CSR activities, related to their profits after tax or any other suitable parameter. These guidelines were further refined as 'National Voluntary Guidelines on Social, Environmental and Economic Responsibilities of Business' in 2011. Though these guidelines were basically prescriptive and not mandatory, many CPSEs, especially most Ratna CPSEs, implemented these guidelines and started spending in socially crucial areas like pollution control, slum development, improvement of localities they operated in, etc. which would benefit the underprivileged or larger section of the community.

Until the Companies Act, 2013, the CSR activities in India were purely voluntary. Some corporations including big public sector companies like ONGC, NTPC, etc. had integrated CSR into their business strategy, and through their CSR activities brought many tangible benefits to society which earned them substantial credibility and goodwill. But India is the perhaps the first country in the world to give CSR a statutory backing through the new Companies Act, 2013.

According to Section 135 of the Companies Act, 2013, all companies—holding, subsidiary or foreign—operating in India and having net worth of ₹500 crore or turnover of ₹1000 crore or net profit of ₹5 crore or above have to spend in every financial year at least 2 per cent of the average net profits made during the three immediately preceding financial years. Such companies are also liable to constitute a Corporate Social Responsibility Committee comprising three or more directors, including at least one independent director, which will formulate and recommend to the Board a CSR policy that shall indicate the activities to be undertaken by the company as specified within the purview of Schedule VII of the Companies Act, 2013, and institute a transparent monitoring mechanism for the implementation of the CSR projects or programmes or activities undertaken by the company, after approval by the Board.

Thus, CSR is not mandatory for every company—only the companies that fall within the ambit of Section 135 of the Companies Act, 2013 are required to spend 2 per cent of average net profits earned in the last three financial years. While doing so, a company is to give preference to the areas where they operate for spending the amount earmarked for CSR activities. The CSR activities would not include the normal business activities of the company, and neither would these be undertaken exclusively for the benefit of its employees. Contribution to political parties would not qualify for CSR expenditure. It is to be noted that the term CSR has not been defined by the Companies Act, 2013.

Schedule VII of the Companies Act, 2013 specifies the eligible activities as eradicating extreme hunger and poverty; promoting education; promoting gender equality and empowering women; reducing child mortality and improving maternal health; combating human immunodeficiency virus, acquired immune deficiency syndrome, malaria and other diseases; ensuring environmental sustainability; employment enhancing vocational skills; social business projects; contributing to the Prime Minister's National Relief Fund or any other fund set up by the central government or the state governments for socio-economic development and relief and funds for the welfare of the Scheduled Castes, Scheduled Tribes, other backward classes, minorities and women; and such other matters as may be prescribed.[30] Most CSR activities undertaken by companies include contribution to the *Swachh Bharat Kosh* set up by the central government for the promotion of sanitation and making available safe drinking water, skill development and livelihood enhancement projects, environmental sustainability and conservation projects including contribution to the Clean Ganga Fund set up by the central government for rejuvenation of river Ganga, national heritage protection, projects for the benefit of armed forces veterans, war widows and their dependents, promotion of rural sports, slum area development, etc.

The Companies (Corporate Social Responsibility Policy) Rules, 2014 mandates that the Board shall include in its annual report a report on CSR activities undertaken during the year in a prescribed format,

---

[30] Schedule VII to Companies Act, 2013.

indicating a brief outline of the company's CSR policy and providing an overview of projects/programmes/activities undertaken by the company. The report should also include the composition of the CSR committee, prescribed CSR expenditure for the financial year and details of amounts spent and reasons in case of failure to spend the prescribed amount.

Penalties have been provided for non-compliance to the CSR provisions in the Companies Act, 2013, which shall not

> be less than fifty thousand rupees but which may extend to twenty-five lakh rupees and every officer of the company who is in default shall be punishable with imprisonment for a term which may extend to three years or with fine which shall not be less than fifty thousand rupees but which may extend to five lakh rupees, or with both.[31]

The prudence of such provisions is open to question, and the CSR provisions are already being criticised, for right reasons, as being akin to an additional tax. Where fostering a CSR culture through persuasion may yield better results, draconian penal provisions may backfire. Certainly, it is not business-friendly and does not augur well for attracting investments.

The COPU of the 16th Lok Sabha had examined the CSR activities undertaken by 13 CPSEs and made some recommendations in their 8th report of 2015–2016. Since the compliance report to Section 135 of the Companies Act was not available till the COPU completed their examination, still their report was one of the very first attempts to evaluate the CSR activities undertaken by the CPSEs. As per this report, during 2013–2014, 131 CPSEs exceeded the threshold limits for undertaking CSR as prescribed in Section 135, and the 2 per cent average net profits of these companies in the three immediately preceding years worked out to ₹3,684 crore. The 13 CPSEs examined by COPU had allocated ₹2,160 crore under CSR including the amount of unspent balance carried forward from the previous year, out of which ₹1,021 crore could be spent during 2014–2015.

---

[31] Section 134(8), Companies Act, 2013. The Companies Amendment Bill, 2020, introduced in the Lok Sabha in May 2020 seeks to amend this section by withdrawing the penal provision related to imprisonment.

In 2017–2018, the CAG examined the CSR activities in 77 CPSEs including seven Maharatna, 17 Navratna, 50 Miniratna-I and three Miniratna-II companies under the administrative control of 24 ministries/departments.[32] As per the CAG's Report No. 8 of 2018, these 77 CPSEs undertook as many as 8.84 lakh CSR projects during 2016–2017 and spent ₹3,150 crore on them, including the amounts carried forward from previous years. Interestingly, even though there is no obligation on the part of the loss-making CPSEs to spend on CSR, the CAG found that out of the 11 loss-making CPSEs, five CPSEs also had allocated an amount of ₹18 crore for CSR. It seems the culture is slowly making inroads into the CPSEs. Most of the CSR spending by CPSEs were on education and skill development (₹1,036 crore), healthcare (₹826 crore), rural development (₹417 crore) and environment sustainability (₹394 crore). Focus on other areas given in Schedule VII was rather limited. As regards the distribution of CSR spending among the states, the CAG reported that CPSEs had spent more in Andhra Pradesh, Odisha, Uttar Pradesh, Gujarat and Chhattisgarh. Expenditure in Punjab and north-eastern states such as Mizoram, Manipur, Nagaland and Sikkim was insignificant.

Among the major CPSEs, ONGC entrusted maintenance activity of toilets in 5,592 schools constructed under *Swach Vidyalaya Abhiyan* to the Auroville Foundation, which had undertaken Information, Education & Communication (IEC) activities to bring behavioural change and inculcate hygienic sanitation practices among the students of the schools and communities. The focus was on institutionalising the mechanisms by inculcating habits in a sustainable way. BPCL had undertaken a rainwater harvesting project to convert the 21 tribal villages from water-scarce to water-positive in Boond district of Madhya Pradesh, while OIL had undertaken a cluster-based livelihood project for sustainable income generation in Arunachal Pradesh aimed at imparting skill development and up-gradation training to 400 targeted households on bee-keeping, honey processing and processing of mustard, buck-wheat and local pulse as well

---

[32] CAG's Report No. 8 of 2018, 63–81.

as for generation of alternate sources of income and formation of self-sustaining livelihood clusters. HPCL had undertaken project ADAPT in Maharashtra to support special children, under which 315 special children were provided therapeutic support along with education and skill development. Under another project in Andhra Pradesh, 12,000 girls from underprivileged families were provided quality education through academic, material and social support. For improving rural livelihood through farmer-centric, integrated watershed management in Karnataka and Andhra Pradesh, PGCIL developed a storage capacity of 12,000 cu m and conservation of 45,000 cu m of rainwater. This resulted in about a 10–22 per cent rise in crop productivity. CIL had taken an initiative for a community-based integrated programme with a special focus on marginalised children and youth in Naxalite and insurgency-affected districts of Jharkhand and Assam, in collaboration with an NGO.[33]

CSR activities undertaken by CPSEs have just begun to make some impact upon society, and they are picking up. But a lot still remains to be done before they become integrally and organically involved in social welfare. The performance of CPSEs in CSR as in all other areas, as we have seen in this chapter, is a mixed bag, with a few doing extremely well, some showing sub-optimal performance and a majority facing existential problems. Only a few CPSEs account for most of the profits, and another few account for most of the losses. A few again account for most of the jobs, though they may be well-performing CPSEs. Sector-wise results are also skewed; while in some sectors CPSEs seem to be doing well and competing successfully with their private sector counterparts, in other sectors their performance has been dismal. Government interference makes things worse, and it raises questions about the desirability of their continued existence. We shall examine these questions later; for the present, however, let us turn our focus towards the wasteland of public sector enterprises, those functioning under the various state governments.

[33] Ibid.

Annexure 3.1 MOU Rating: 2017–2018

#	Excellent			Very Good	Good		Fair		Poor
1	AAI	IRCONPBTL	Antrix Corporation	NLCTNPL	AYCL	OIL	BBNL	NTL	BNVNL
2	BLCL	IRCONSGTL	ALMCI	NMDC	BRBCL	PEC	BIBCL	NBCCECL	BVFCL
3	BEL	KRCL	BDL	NPCIL	CEL	REIL	BBJCCL	NUPPL	BCL
4	BELTSL	MRPL	BPRL	ONGC	CWC	SAILRCL	CCIL	PFCCL	BSUL
5	BELOP	MMTC	BIRAC	ONGC Videsh	DFCCIL	SPMCIL	EPIL	PLIL	GAPL
6	BEML	MOIL	BCPL	PPCL	DCIL	TCIL	FCT	SCICL	HOCL
7	BHEL	NALCO	BRCIL	PDIL	ECGCL	THDCIL	HEC		HSL
8	BPCL	NBCFDC	CEIL	RCIL	EDCIL	VIL	HCL		HPL
9	CRWCL	NMDFC	CIL	RINL	ECIL		HIL		HMT Machine Tools
10	CIAL	NSTFDC	CAL	RECTPCL	FCIAG		HSCL		LDHCL
11	CPCL	NBCC	GAIL Gas Ltd.	RECL	FSNL		HLLLL		MFL
12	CSL	NTPC	HSL	SCIL	Hindustan Antibiotics Ltd.		HMTIL		MRVCL
13	CONCOR	NTPCVVNL	HLLITSL	SECI	HFL		HMTIL		NHDCL

14	EIL	NRL	ITPO	SAIL	HLLBL	Hooghly Printing Co. Ltd.	REL
15	GAIL	PFC	IRCTC		ITI	HPCLBL	RCFL
16	GRSEL	PSOCL	IRCONISL		JCIL	ITDC	SSL
17	GSL	PGCIL	KPL		KIOCL	IL	SIL
18	HAL	RVNL	MDSL		MECON	KAPL	STC
19	HPCL	REMCL	MIDHANI		MTL	KBUNL	
20	HUDCO	RECPDCL	NSKFDCL		MECL	KTPO	
21	IOC	Rites Ltd.	NSICL		MTML	KMRCL	
22	IRFCL	SJVL	NBCCSL		NSCFDC	MSTC	
23	IREL	UCIL	NHPC		NSCL	MTNL	
24	IREDA	WAPCOS	NLCIL		NHDC	NPCCL	
25	IRCONIL				NEEPCO	NRDC	

Source: Department of Public Enterprises, *Public Enterprises Survey 2017–2018*, Vol. I.

CHAPTER 4

Wasteland of State Public Sector Undertakings

In the last chapter, we have reviewed the financial performance of CPSEs. Though the overall picture regarding CPSEs remains somewhat discouraging, many CPSEs have well adjusted themselves in the post-globalised scenario and demonstrated their ability to compete successfully with the private sector in an open economy; they indeed have the potential to grow into global brands with the right mix of deregulation, technology and empowerment. But in contrast, the landscape of our state public sector enterprises (SPSEs) reflects a dismal and sorry state of affairs. They have been rendered helpless pawns in the hands of unimaginative and greedy bureaucrats and politicians. SPSEs are devoid of logic, vitality, sustenance and *raison d'être*. They continue to consume substantial amounts of the scarce resources of the states, thereby impeding the development and growth of the states as a whole. They, in fact, constitute the wasteland of our states' economy.

While there was an ideology behind the creation of CPSEs, SPSEs lack any such ideological background. Their initial creation was rather guided by historical and practical reasons, partly to substitute the activities that were earlier undertaken by provincial governments or princely states, partly to access funds from financial institutions which were not available to the state government departments, or in areas where substantial investments were required for the creation of basic infrastructure like power, irrigation and roads or to provide basic services like road transport for which there was no other agency—private or public.[1] Gradually, however, their numbers proliferated greatly as they moved out of these core areas and started venturing into all activities and abandoned all logic. In the process, for most of these entities, losses accumulated till their net worth was completely eroded, rendering them sick or dysfunctional. States continued to provide budgetary support to them—often to avoid lapses in the budgetary funds or to serve as conduits for off-budget borrowings of the state governments. They became convenient instruments for loot by corrupt politicians and bureaucrats and sinecures for those who were closer to power. And thus, they lost their vitality and forfeited the reason for their existence.

Various finance commissions and studies made by different agencies—notably the study conducted by the Institute of Public Enterprise (IPE) and the Study Group on Reforms in State Public Sector Undertakings—had pointed to the depressing performance of the SLPEs time and again and stressed on the urgent need for their restructuring and reforms, which went unheeded.

State Electricity Boards (SEBs) and State Road Transport Corporations (SRTCs) were the earliest public sector undertakings created by the states, and have always claimed the major share of government investments in both equity and loans right from the beginning. Right from the beginning, their performance and rates of return remained a matter of concern. In 1964, the Venkataraman Committee had prescribed a return of 11 per cent for the electricity boards after full adjustment of their operation and maintenance costs as well as depreciation. As the report of the Seventh Finance Commission (1980–1985) noted, these boards had been saddled with huge transmission and distribution (T&D) losses ranging from 11 to 26 per cent in different states, huge establishment costs due to the large number of employees, uncollected arrears, poor management and, consequently,

---

[1] Ganesh, *State Level Public Enterprises in India*, 1.

poor returns.[2] There were some genuine constraints also like the large gestation periods of power projects requiring the boards to incur interest charges without any return for longer periods, besides being made to fulfil certain social objectives like providing subsidised power to agriculture, etc. Section 59 of the Electricity Supply Act, 1948, which was amended in 1983, required the electricity boards to generate a revenue surplus of 3 per cent, which roughly corresponded to the 11 per cent rate of return suggested by the Venkataraman Committee way back in 1964. Another committee, Rajadhyaksha Committee (1980), prescribed an even rate of return of 15 per cent.[3] The actual rates of return were, however, far less and varied widely from state to state.[4]

Similarly, large sums of money were spent in the Road Transport Corporations by the states, which were perpetually saddled with ageing and over-aged vehicles, large workforce, high operational costs, low fleet utilisation, low occupancy and high repair and maintenance costs, rendering their operations commercially unviable.[5] But they continued to operate without addressing these issues, and consequently, their losses kept on mounting. The Ninth Finance Commission (1990–1995) noted:

> Section 22 of the Road Transport Corporation Act stipulates that the Corporations should carry on their activities on 'business principles'. This requirement has not been fulfilled by most of the Corporations... some of the Undertakings are not in a position to cover even their working expenses.[6]

There were several constraints here, too, like compulsions of social obligations, which the corporations were obliged to discharge by incurring losses.

Other than the electricity boards and road transport corporations, there were financial corporations set up under the State Financial

---

[2] Report of the Seventh Finance Commission, 26–31.

[3] Report of the Eighth Finance Commission, 15.

[4] For example, the range varied from 0.15 per cent in Bihar to 1.3 per cent in UP, to 11.7 per cent in MP in 1974–1975.

[5] Report of the Seventh Finance Commission, 31–34.

[6] Report of the Ninth Finance Commission, 9.

Corporations Act, 1951, as well as enterprises eligible for refinancing by the Industrial Development Bank of India (IDBI). There were also promotional corporations engaged in promoting developmental and other industries through providing infrastructural facilities and financial, managerial and technical assistance—especially for the backward section of society; this category included a host of different types of companies from industrial development corporations to corporations for the development of handlooms, handicrafts, cottage industries, backward areas and certain industrial sectors like drugs and pharmaceuticals and even films. Strictly speaking, most of these areas do not fall under the domain of the state governments in the sense that the state has neither the expertise nor the means to carry out these activities that the banks and established financial institutions were in a much better position to carry out. Thus, no mechanism could be established to review the performance of these corporations or to suggest remedial measures if their performance was sub-optimal, which was often the case, and monitor them. An accountability structure was conspicuously absent from the very beginning, which characterised the functioning of these entities.

The Tenth Finance Commission (1995–2000) also echoed the same concerns expressed by the earlier finance commissions. Regarding the SEBs and SRTCs, it noted:

> Most of these enterprises have not been functioning in a satisfactory manner and they have incurred huge losses over the years. In fact, we have ben distressed to note that in State after State, even the accounts of many Undertakings have not been finalised for long periods ranging from 5–20 years. Clearly, such a state of affairs reduces accountability and is hardly an incentive for good management. It is expected that the State Governments would take up this task in right earnest and bring the accounts up-to-date in time bound fashion.[7]

It further noted: 'It has been the view of successive Finance Commissions that the substantial investments made in these enterprises should yield a reasonable return. Most Finance Commissions have set very modest

---

[7] Report of Tenth Finance Commission, 10.

goals but the actual yield has been much below even these.'[8] A study commissioned by it and conducted by the Hyderabad-based IPE to report on the performance of the SPSEs during 1985–1986 to 1993–1994 recommended that the enterprises should be classified as commercial, commercial-cum-promotional and promotional, to which classification the Finance Commission agreed. The study also recommended the minimum expected rates of return from these three categories at 7.5 per cent, 5 per cent and 2.5 per cent respectively, which the Commission moderated to 6, 4 and 1 per cent during 1995–2000. The study also drew attention to the skewed capital structure of the SPSEs with huge amounts of loans eating into their profitability due to the heavy interest burden. The Finance Commission firmly stated that there should be no more addition to the existing number of SPSEs. In fact, it opined that 'there might well be a case for reverting certain functions of a purely promotional nature to other Government departments or even to non-government organisations'; indeed, it noted that non-achievement of the intended performance goals had often led to erosion of accountability. The Commission recommended that all the states should devise appropriate disinvestment strategies and use the proceeds of such disinvestment partially towards the retirement of the debt of their SPSEs, which was owed mostly to the central government.[9] These observations and recommendations had fallen on deaf ears, and the performance of the SPSEs continues to slide—most of them were indeed on an irreversible downward spiral by then.

The Study Group on Reforms in State Public Sector Undertakings chaired by Dr N. J. Kurian was appointed in 1999 by the Planning Commission primarily for the purpose of building a database by identifying some crucial parameters of performance of the SPSUs and also to study the reforms undertaken in the SPSUs in India. Its terms of reference included study of the performance pattern and management practices in the enterprises, among other things. Its report indicated the scope for divesting public ownership of nonstrategic SPSUs in order to release financial resources for bridging the fiscal gap of state governments and for enhancing the much needed public spending on

[8] Ibid.
[9] Ibid.

social sectors like health and education. The study was necessitated by the severe resource crunch faced by the centre as well as the states during the final years of the Seventh Plan.

The Group, which also consulted the IPE study referred to above and other studies and data available, finally submitted its report to the government in 2002. The report classified the SPSEs into six categories: financial, manufacturing, promotional, trading and services and welfare. Based on data collected by it from all the 747 enterprises in the country, it found that in the 8 years between 1990–1991 and 1998–1999, the SPSEs' debt/equity ratio had worsened from 4.3 to 2.8, net losses increased from ₹934 crore to ₹3,377 crore and profit before interest and taxes declined from 10.24 per cent to 6.64 per cent, as against the norm of 20 per cent. The dividend paid by them amounted to a negligible 0.6 per cent of the states' investments on equity, which increased from ₹11,146 crore to ₹45,982 crore during this period. The total government investment on them including loans increased from ₹44,173 crore to ₹1,04,449 crore between 1990–1991 and 1998–1999, while the accumulated losses soared from ₹11,296 crore to ₹31,267 crore. It was also noticed that the enterprises in promotional, welfare and trading and services sectors attracted the major share of investments compared to those in the manufacturing or financial sectors. The utility enterprises like the SEBs and SRTCs, which accounted for the biggest chunk of investments, were also the biggest loss makers. That was the scenario before the turn of the century.[10] At the beginning of the new millennium, about half of these were either running with severe losses or already had become dysfunctional (Annexure 4.1). The accounts of many of the SPSEs had also fallen into arrears by several years, some by decades. Because of the lack of accounts, the data about the SPSEs were also very sketchy, and a complete picture was never available; this situation continues even now.

The Study Group on Reforms in State Public Sector Undertakings made a series of recommendations including the setting up of a statutory Disinvestment Commission by every state, in addition to a State Renewal Fund to be financed from the proceeds of disinvestments

[10] Ganesh, *State Level Public Enterprises in India*, 8–10.

of SPSEs, introduction of the MOU system akin to that existing one in the CPSEs and reforms such as fixed tenure CEOs for each enterprise and also the professionalisation of their management. An important recommendation was also to compensate them for the cost of meeting their social obligations as dictated by the government policies and instructions, which often landed them in the red. As expected, there was very little follow-up on most of these recommendations, and the SPSEs continued their journey down the slippery slope while their numbers continued to grow unchecked.[11] Some states did take some baby steps for closure of their dysfunctional PSEs, but the process could not yield any result for the lack of accounts and the consequent uncertainty about the status of their assets and liabilities. Similarly, the states' effort at disinvestment did not attract many buyers for reasons of their non-viability and the high level of debt in their capital structure, besides other liabilities and the poor state of their assets.

As the Eleventh Finance Commission (2000–2005) noted, many States such as Orissa, Punjab, Rajasthan, UP, etc. understood the need for the restructuring of their PSEs, of disinvestment and reduction of their excess manpower through voluntary retirement schemes as well as an appropriate exit policy. States were also coming to the realisation that their power sector needed urgent restructuring for the viability of the finances of power sector SPSEs. The Commission noted:

> With deregulation of the economy and moves towards privatisation, we presume that the finances of the public sector undertakings will be shaped increasingly by the market and not be dominated by government decisions. Public sector undertakings, both with the Centre and the States, barring a few exceptions, were moving more and more into the red and loss-making had taken the place of profitability quite universally. The electricity boards, the transport corporations and many other public ventures were scenes of stark inefficiency and non-profitability and were making little contribution to the revenue budgets.[12]

---

[11] Ibid.
[12] Report of Eleventh Finance Commission, 37.

The slide of the SPSEs continued unabated, while their numbers exceeded 1,000 by 2004. The Twelfth Finance Commission (2005–2010) reported that out of 1,003 SPSEs, as many as 599 were either non-functioning or running with losses. The Commission reported that out of a total 785 SPSEs, 332 (about 42%) were engaged in the manufacturing sector, 149 (19%) in the promotional sector, 74 (9.4%) in the trading sector, 69 (8.8%) in the financial sector and only 38 (5%) in the welfare sector. The services sector accounted for the remaining 16 per cent or 123 SPSEs (details are given in Annexure 4.2). Like all the previous Finance Commissions, it also noted that their returns were either 'non-existent or low' and that a large number of them had failed to finalise their accounts. It wanted the states to restructure their finances and noted: 'In the period of restructuring, that is 2005–2010, state governments should draw up a programme that includes closure of almost all loss making SLPEs'. The process should be accompanied by the reforms of SEBs and SRTCs and by 'the end of 2009–2010, states should have a small but viable set of SLPEs'.[13]

The terms of reference (ToR) of the Thirteenth Finance Commission (2010–2015) required it to examine the issue of commercial viability of SPSEs. It conducted an in-house study of the status and performance of SPSEs as of 2006–2007 based on data provided by the CAG reports and the states and also enumerated the reform measures initiated by the states to restructure their public sector enterprises during the period 2002–2007. Data was a major constraint in all SPSE studies as most of these entities have arrears of accounts running into several years, and obtaining uniform and reliable data pertaining to a given year was therefore well-nigh impossible. However, based on their latest finalised accounts–which pertained to several years back for most SPSEs—the information as presented in Tables 4.1–4.3 have been compiled from this Study Report as of March 2007.

Thus, we see that as of March 2007, there were altogether 1,119 SPSEs in the country, of which 306, or 27 per cent, were dysfunctional. The total investment of the governments in equity and loans in the working PSUs amounted to nearly ₹3.5 lakh crore, of which

[13] Report of Twelfth Finance Commission, 84.

₹1.3 lakh crore pertained to equity and ₹2.2 crore to loans, indicating a skewed debt/equity ratio on the whole as average. The 813 working PSUs earned a total net profit of only ₹503 crore, the SPSEs of 17 general category states earning a total net profit of ₹1,649 crore and the 11 special category states incurring a net loss of ₹1146 crore. Thus, the average rate of ROI amounted to 0.001 per cent.

The total investment of the governments in the 306 non-working PSUs amounted to ₹5,616 crore–₹5,442 crore in the general category states and ₹174 crore in the special category states. During 2006–2007, only 379 SPSEs earned some profits, while 359 entities incurred losses. As regards the SRTCs, their losses during the 3 years from 2005 to 2008 amounted to ₹1,077 crore, ₹792 crore and ₹253 crore respectively. The total budgetary support given by the governments during 2007–2008 amounted to 2.87 lakh crore (Equity ₹0.92 lakh crore, Loan ₹1.7 lakh crore and Subsidies and Grants ₹0.25 lakh crore).

Their accounts were in arrears for periods ranging up to 36 years—none of the states could compile the accounts of all their PSEs for the year 2006–2007 during 2007–2008. Rajasthan was the only state where the arrears in accounts did not exceed 1 year for any PSE. Even in mainstream states like UP or West Bengal that had invested substantial sums in their PSEs, the arrears ranged up to 25 and 23 years respectively for some PSEs. Only 244 out of 1,119 SPSEs had their accounts up-to-date. They paid a meagre ₹167 crore as dividend and ₹1,685 crore as interest to their respective governments during 2007–2008.[14] Table 4.1 shows the summarised performance of SPSEs as per their latest finalised accounts as of 31 March 2007.

Most of the investments—as much as two-thirds—have been made in the power sector, that is, in the State Electricity Boards and their successors. The investments made in the other sectors were marginal (Tables 4.2, 4.3 and Figure 4.1)—in fact so little that hardly any impact could be created in the economy at such low levels of investments in transport (SRTCs), industry, infrastructure, finance, construction, textiles, backward area development or agriculture. Low capitalisation

[14] Study Report on State Level Public Enterprises, Report of Thirteenth Finance Commission, 62–90.

Table 4.1 Summarised Performance of SPSEs as per Their Latest Finalised Accounts, as of March 2007

	No. of Working PSEs	Total Govt. Investment (₹ Crore)		Profit/ Loss (₹ Crore)	Arrears in Accounts (No. of Years)
		Equity	Long-term Loans		
General-category States					
Andhra Pradesh	38	7,013	26,182	95	1–10
Bihar	21	473	7,457	−122	1–19
Chhattisgarh	10	33	2,277	137	1–5
Goa	16	220	256	1	0–6
Gujrat	45	23,860	22,310	1243	0–8
Haryana	21	3,838	8,334	261	0–6
Jharkhand	6	8	2,466	−48	1–4
Karnataka	65	18,893	22,309	936	0–4
Kerala	89	3,442	4,955	40	3–17
Madhya Pradesh	35	5,488	14,820	556	0–17
Maharashtra	55	19,372	14,191	−183	0–21
Odisha	32	1,973	7,425	398	2–36
Punjab	27	3,669	10,227	−11	0–16
Rajasthan	22	5,099	11,373	269	0–1
Tamil Nadu	55	2,523	15,232	−1,488	0–14
Uttar Pradesh	55	19,318	8,754	−500	0–25
West Bengal	66	6,620	28,357	65	0–23
Sub-total	**658**	**121,842**	**206,925**	**1,649**	
Special-category States					
Assam	39	1,260	1,363	−1032	1–22
Arunachal Pradesh	3	9	7	−4	1–13
Himachal Pradesh	19	749	3,137	−60	0–3
Jammu & Kashmir	20	399	4,022	152	0–19
Manipur	15	29	10	0.45	10–24
Meghalaya	13	398	892	−99	1–15

(Table 4.1 Continued)

(Table 4.1 Continued)

	No. of Working PSEs	Total Govt. Investment (₹ Crore)		Profit/ Loss (₹ Crore)	Arrears in Accounts (No. of Years)
		Equity	Long-term Loans		
Mizoram	5	55	33	−5	1–8
Nagaland	5	23	39	−2	9–26
Sikkim	9	82	77	−4	1–5
Tripura	9	337	8	−16	1–13
Uttarakhand	18	774	1,951	−76	1–20
Sub-total	**155**	**4,115**	**11,539**	**−1145.55**	
Grand total	**813**	**125,957**	**218,464**	**503.45**	

Source: Study Report on State Level Public Undertakings, Thirteenth Finance Commission.

Table 4.2 *Investment of State Governments in Non-working PSEs: March 2007*

	No. of Non-Working PSEs	Total Investment (₹ Crore)
General-category States		
Andhra Pradesh	18	263
Bihar	34	718
Chhattisgarh	0	0
Goa	0	0
Gujrat	12	839
Haryana	7	139
Jharkhand	0	
Karnataka	17	594
Kerala	25	165
Madhya Pradesh	9	229
Maharashtra	22	794

(Table 4.2 Continued)

(Table 4.2 Continued)

	No. of Non-Working PSEs	Total Investment (₹ Crore)
Odisha	32	155
Punjab	19	165
Rajasthan	4	14
Tamil Nadu	14	87
Uttar Pradesh	40	879
West Bengal	20	401
Sub-total	**273**	**5,442**
Special-category States		
Assam	10	83
Arunachal Pradesh	2	3
Himachal Pradesh	2	5
Jammu & Kashmir	3	3
Manipur	7	72
Meghalaya	0	
Mizoram	0	
Nagaland	1	5
Sikkim	3	3
Tripura	1	0.04
Uttarakhand	4	0.39
Sub-total	**33**	**174.43**
Grand total	**306**	**5,616.43**

Source: Study Report on State Level Public Undertakings, Thirteenth Finance Commission.

thus constrained most of the SPSEs from the very beginning and turned them into potential non-performers. This was compounded by other issues like skewed financial leverage and high interest outgo, bureaucratisation and lack of professionalisation of their management, interference in their autonomy by the state government forcing them to absorb the high and uneconomical social costs of governments' welfare programmes, which mostly were designed to serve electoral purposes, excess manpower and operational issues.

Table 4.3 Sector-wise Investment in State PSEs (₹ Crore)

	Power	Transport	Manufacturing	Agriculture	Finance	Others
General-category States						
Andhra Pradesh	21,542			447		11,206
Bihar	7,007			37	451	435
Chhattisgarh	2,263				22	25
Goa		71	13	6		386
Gujrat	41,624	1,386	1,156	195	1,651	158
Haryana	10,947		329	24	256	616
Jharkhand	2,461			10		3
Karnataka	10,179	1,485	498	25,766*	2,818	456
Kerala	4,052	698	258	645	620	2,124
Madhya Pradesh	18,273	602			1,143	290
Maharashtra	18,322	1,266		133	689	13,153
Odisha	7,604				629	5,775
Punjab	11,856	294	712	589	338	107
Rajasthan	14,781	384	1,055	17		235
Tamil Nadu	11,271	1,430	311		734	4,009
Uttar Pradesh	22,686		3,597	1,305	220	264
West Bengal	20,482	821		192	10,654	2,828
Sub-total	225,350	8,437	7,929	29,366	20,225	42,070

Special-category States

Assam	1,635	332	301	189	24	142
Arunachal Pradesh						16
Himachal Pradesh	2,401	437		84	253	711
Jammu & Kashmir	2,162	438	367	72	790	592
Manipur			19			20
Meghalaya	1,066	66				158
Mizoram				4		84
Nagaland			58			4
Sikkim	53				29	77
Tripura	10	131	190	2		12
Uttarakhand	2,386	97	80		34	128
Sub-total	**9,713**	**1,501**	**1,015**	**351**	**1,130**	**1,944**
Grand total	**23,5063**	**9,938**	**8,944**	**29,717**	**21,355**	**44,014**
Percentage share	**67**	**3**	**3**	**9**	**6**	**13**

Source: Study Report on State Level Public Undertakings, Thirteenth Finance Commission.
Note: *Investments made in irrigation.

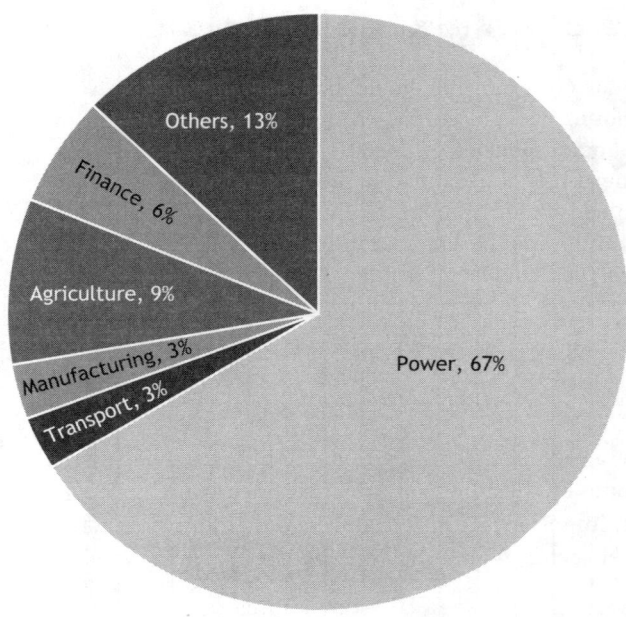

Figure 4.1 *Sectoral Share of Investments: 2006–2007*
Source: Table 4.3.

By 2007, the total turnover of ₹3.07 lakh crore of the SPSEs
constituted about 6 per cent of the country's GDP and their total
employment had reached 18 lakh. Their aggregate accumulated losses
had mounted to ₹65,924 crore. All but nine states reported aggregate
losses from their PSEs, with the loss exceeding more than ₹2,000
crore for some states. More than 70 per cent of their accounts had
fallen in arrears, and what was more disturbing, the arrears were on the
increase. States continued to invest in them even without the assurance
of audited accounts and without caring to know what was happening
to their investments. As regards the non-working companies, the
situation was indeed alarming, with many of their accounts remaining
incomplete and unaudited since 1992–1993; the Thirteenth Finance
Commission (2010–2015) came across one SPSE whose accounts were
not finalised for the last 37 years.

The Commission recommended:

All State Governments should draw up a road map by March 2011 for closure of non-working companies in consultation with the Accountant General. All pending commercial and other disputes empowering the Board to approve a settlement scheme. States could consider setting up of a holding company which would be responsible for the liquidation of all nonworking PSUs. Such a holding company could employ legal, management, and account-ancy experts, thereby obviating the need to appoint individual liquidators for each company. This company would also take over the assets and liabilities of the non-working PSUs, thus simplifying the process of closing them down.[15]

This was a very sensible suggestion, but like all other suggestions given to the states by all earlier commissions, once again, nothing happened. The only important reforms that were brought in after 2003 concerned the power sector, which shall be discussed later in detail.

Between 2002 and 2007, some states did introduce Voluntary Retirement Schemes (VRS) for retiring their excess public sector employees, which got lukewarm responses from most states; some states also retrenched some of their employees under the Early Retrenchment Scheme (ERS) or otherwise. Seventeen states could retire or retrench altogether 91,418 excess employees at a cost of ₹1,654 crore (Table 4.4). Kerala also created a Social Safety Net for its retired employees under the VRS scheme. Most states did not for-mulate any disinvestment policy; only a handful of states took concrete actions towards disinvestment. Punjab received ₹341 crore from the disinvestment of three of their PSEs, while Maharashtra privatised one PSE. Odisha was the only state to have created a Department of Public Enterprises in the line of the central government, while Madhya Pradesh was the only state to have introduced a system of MOUs between the PSEs and the government, as of 2007. A handful of states like Punjab and Odisha had also merged a couple of their PSEs. Closure proceedings were initiated by a few other states such as Andhra Pradesh, Bihar, Karnataka and Odisha but could not be taken

[15] Report of Thirteenth Finance Commission, 103–104.

Table 4.4 *Number of Employees Retired/Retrenched by the State PSEs under VRS/ERS Schemes*

State	No. of Employees	Cost Incurred (₹ Crore)
Uttar Pradesh	24,304	361
Gujrat	21,924	490
Andhra Pradesh	18,446	322
West Bengal	6,147	—
Kerala	5,709	149
Assam	4,537	136
Madhya Pradesh	4,306	—
Maharashtra	1,701	53
Rajasthan	1,457	20
Manipur	1,178	35
Himachal Pradesh	750	25
Punjab	664	44
Nagaland	93	3
Meghalaya	83	13
Arunachal Pradesh	46	2
Tamil Nadu	51	1
Chhattisgarh	22	0.3
Total	**91,418**	**1,654.3**

Source: Prepared on the basis of information contained in the Study Report on State Level Public Undertakings, 13th Finance Commission.

forward due to the lack of certainty about the liabilities and assets of the concerned PSEs in the absence of their accounts.

The Thirteenth Finance Commission also prescribed the rating of SPSEs by an accredited rating agency to be made mandatory along with the setting up of independent regulatory authorities for proper pricing. It stated in no uncertain terms:

The State Governments should actively consider withdrawal/ reduction of SPSUs in non-welfare and non-utility sectors. There is an immediate need to reduce the number of SPSUs in most of the states as the large number of such enterprises not only engages the productive assets of the government, but also promotes inefficiency due to lack of proper monitoring by the State Governments.[16]

This called for immediate divestment and privatisation, which could not be followed through because of problems related to non-finalisation of their accounts and their skewed capital structure.

The terms of reference of the Fourteenth Finance Commission explicitly required the Commission to consider 'the need for making the public sector enterprises competitive and market oriented; listing and disinvestment; and relinquishing of non-priority enterprises' and make their recommendations, in respect of both the CPSEs and SPSEs. In fact, in their report, one entire chapter (Chapter 16) was devoted to the Public Sector Enterprises alone.

For the states, the Fourteenth Finance Commission noted that the power companies set up after the unbundling of the SEBs were the largest enterprises in terms of capital invested and sales turnover, followed by SRTCs. In their representations to the Commission, the states argued that these were public utilities that provided basic essential services while the remaining functional companies catered to the welfare of disadvantaged sections. The states, therefore, contended that assessing their performance purely in terms of commercial considerations alone would not be fair or prudent and that returns on their investments should not be the sole criteria to recommend their disinvestment. Besides, as already pointed out, most of the SPSEs except in the power and transport sectors have small sizes and inadequate capital and hence lack the scale to make their operations profitable.

While discussing the central PSEs, the Commission had taken note of the new realities, many of which applied equally to the states as well. It observed:

It needs to be seen if the objectives of public sector enterprises have been achieved, and, if not, whether the original objectives have

---

[16] Ibid., 104.

been re-defined. Public enterprises were started with the objective of leveraging resources for development and there is no continued justification for public investments unless the enterprises are generating assured resources for the government.[17]

This is true both for the central as well the state PSEs, as is the following observation:

There may be a compelling need for the presence of public enterprises in specific activities from a strategic perspective, but what constitutes strategic perspective demanding the presence of public enterprises does vary from time to time. What was once a strategic activity may cease to be so now and new areas of strategic importance may be opened up for public sector enterprises?[18]

The Commission therefore recommended that there was a need to reprioritise the PSEs by identifying them as engaged in 'high priority' activities where public ownership should predominate or simply in 'priority' activities where just a majority public ownership would suffice. The criteria for such identification may depend on the level of public interest served by their activities, use of natural resources by them or where they were fulfilling important functions due to existing market imperfections, or where they were earning higher returns on investments than in alternative investments, or public utilities whose presence was desirable 'as a reference point for getting more reliable information for the regulators'. The rest of the PSEs could be categorised as 'low-priority' and 'non-priority' based on what the Commission referred to as 'some inter-related and non-exclusionary indicative criteria of market conditions and socio-economic considerations', which might include areas where the private sector was functioning well, or where unrestricted imports are permitted, or where they were loss-making or sick, or where they were not public utilities, unless there were other compelling reasons for their functioning in these sectors.[19] These recommendations made primarily for the CPSEs are equally applicable for the SPSEs, too.

---

[17] Report of Fourteenth Finance Commission, Para 16.4 (i).
[18] Ibid., Para 16.4 (j).
[19] Ibid., Para 16.20.

As regards the SPSEs specifically, the Commission agreed that they were historically set up 'for achieving certain welfare goals or for promotional activities or as commercial enterprises' and that there are limits to their commercial viability, especially in welfare-oriented activities connected with public distribution or cottage industries or promotional activities in tourism or small scale industries sectors, and in these areas the SPSEs may need additional fiscal and financial support. Similarly, public utility enterprises entail a significant fiscal burden because of government policy, while certain other enterprises—for example, those engaged in land-based infrastructure and trading in beverages—are much better positioned to generate revenue surpluses primarily because of government patronage in a monopolistic market rather than due to operational efficiency. The utility enterprises like power companies and SRTCs had accumulated huge losses over the years which completely eroded their net worth, making them commercially unviable; yet, social considerations were forcing the state governments to provide budgetary support to them year after year, which in turn was seriously impacting the state finances—in fact, as the Thirteenth Finance Commission had noted, SPSEs remained 'a drag' on the state finances. The recommendations made by the previous commissions about the minimum rates of return expected from them had remained only on paper, and the reality was quite different.[20] The fault was not entirely on the entities but largely on the state governments that, because of their own political compulsions, forced them to provide services at uneconomical rates and did not support them to collect their dues from the consumers—often these were government departments, bodies or authorities whose dues ran into hundreds of crores of rupees.

By March 2013, the number of SPSES in the country had swelled to 1,321, with 298 being non-working. The Thirteenth Finance Commission had recommended the drawing up of a roadmap by the states for closure of the non-working companies by March 2011, and had suggested a detailed operational and administrative framework for winding up the loss-making enterprises as well. It had suggested the establishment of a holding company for facilitating the process of such liquidation, but these suggestions found no takers among the states. As already pointed out, one serious obstacle to this process was the

[20] Ibid., Para 16.50.

absence of audited accounts of most of these entities, to which previous commissions had repeatedly drawn the governments' attention without any results; the Fourteenth Finance Commission found that the position had shown no improvement; even in 2012–2013, out of 1,023 working public sector enterprises, the accounts of 696 (68%) were in arrears—the Thirteenth Finance Commission had found 70 per cent of the accounts in arrears. The Fourteenth Finance Commission reiterated the concerns expressed by the previous commissions and wanted the state governments to review the policy of continued investments in these entities and impressed upon the necessity for all working enterprises, except those in the welfare and utility sectors, to become financially viable. At the same time, it again stressed on the necessity of following the Thirteenth Finance Commission recommendations for closing the sick and non-working public sector enterprises.[21]

As already stated, the approach of understanding and adjusting to the new realities that the Commission had suggested for the CPSEs was equally applicable to the SPSEs. In the words of the Commission:

> The approach we have suggested for Central public sector enterprises related to prioritisation, disinvestment and relinquishment are equally relevant to the State public sector enterprises. Our suggestions on assessment of each entity for categorisation as per their levels of 'priority' and 'non-priority' can be used for operationalising the recommendations of the FC-XIII, with appropriate changes as required in the particular State/entity's context. We recommend that, in addition to acting upon the recommendations of the FC-XIII on state-level enterprises, the logic of our recommendations on public sector enterprises in general be adopted, to the extent appropriate, by State Governments.[22]

The ground reality hardly changed even after the Fourteenth Finance Commission so strongly advocated for the closure of sick and dysfunctional enterprises and for reducing the arrears in their accounts. The performance of the SPSUs remained as dismal in 2016–2017 as it was 10 years ago, in 2006–2007. As shown in Table 4.5, in March 2017, there were 1,136 functional SPSUs in India, with a total public

[21] Ibid., Paras 16.51–16.53.
[22] Ibid., Para 16.54.

Table 4.5 *Working State Public Sector Undertakings as of March 2017 (₹ Crore)*

| | Latest Year for Which A/c Are Available of Most PSUS | No. of Working PSUs | Total Govt. Investment | | Budget Support (Grants, Subsidy) | Total Turnover During the Year | GSDP | No. of Cos. With Negative Net Worth |
			Equity	Long-term Loans				
General-category States								
Andhra Pradesh	2016–2017	64	6,406	54,474	12,482	61,948	695,491	9
Bihar	2016–2017	30	41,979	11,161	4,477	11,278	425,888	6
Chhattisgarh	2015–2016	22	12,342	15,426	2,524	21,580	251,447	4
Goa	2016–2017	15	355	546	389	913	64,544	4
Gujrat	2016–2017	77	87,817	54,600	16,970	111,953	1,125,654	8
Haryana	2016–2017	26	11,955	32,371	14,852	36,269	434,607	5
Jharkhand	2015–2016	19	228	2,133	829	1,866	241,955	6
Karnataka	2016–2017	90	60,921	42,252	23,115	56,478	1,132,393	15
Kerala	2016–2017	115	9,154	17,842	2,323	26,463	655,205	37
Maharashtra	2016–2017	66	177,861	51,252	3,124	86,319	2,267,789	7
Madhya Pradesh	2015–2016	58	21,039	48,523	9,908	78,316	565,053	10
Odisha	2016–2017	56	4,070	8,754	1,601	21,597	314,364	9

(Table 4.5 Continued)

(Table 4.5 Continued)

	Latest Year for Which A/c Are Available of Most PSUS	No. of Working PSUs	Total Govt. Investment		Budget Support (Grants, Subsidy)	Total Turnover During the Year	GSDP	No. of Cos. With Negative Net Worth
			Equity	Long-term Loans				
Punjab	2016–2017	30	8,877	24,980	11,898	57,796	427,297	9
Rajasthan	2016–2017	45	41,460	96,192	31,116	62,186	749,642	19
Tamil Nadu	2016–2017	68	49,672	104,129	46,127	110,850	1,298,511	17
Telangana	2016–2017	47	4,141	54,813	17,839	47,329	654,294	6
Uttar Pradesh	2015–2016	65	119,623	75,595	19,794	85,282	1,153,795	19
West Bengal	2015–2016	70	13,949	28,511	2,655	30,371	1,039,923	29
Sub-total		**963**	**671,849**	**723,554**	**222,023**	**908,794**	**13,497,852**	**219**
Special-category States								
Assam	2016–2017	33	1,539	3,898	1,253	5,609	257,510	15
Arunachal Pradesh	2013–2014	5	22	8	1	6	13,491	3
Himachal Pradesh	2016–2017	21	3,933	8,645	756	8,344	124,570	8
Jammu & Kashmir	2015–2016	30	875	6,822	143	8,417	91,850	11
Manipur	2016–2017	10	53	210	634	161	23,325	4
Meghalaya	2016–2017	16	4,450	2,020	146	1,109	29,567	7
Mizoram	2013–2014	6	60	31	9	15	10,297	3

Nagaland	2013–2014	5	36	62	20	6	17,749	5
Sikkim	2016–2017	12	3,040	12,418	0	186	18,852	5
Tripura	2015–2016	13	1,291	141	127	706	33,189	3
Uttarakhand	2016–2017	22	6,607	3,910	193	7,324	195,192	9
Sub-total		**173**	**21,906**	**38,165**	**3,282**	**31,883**	**815,592**	**73**
Grand total		**1136**	**693,755**	**761,719**	**225,305**	**940,677**	**14,313,444**	**292**

Source: Reports of the Comptroller and Auditor General (CAG) of India on the Public Sector Undertakings of the respective states for respective years.

investment of ₹14.55 lakh crore. During the year, they received total budgetary support of ₹2.25 lakh crore in the form of government grants and subsidies. SPSUs had a total turnover of ₹9.41 lakh crore during 2016–2017, which was 6.57 per cent of their combined gross state domestic product (GSDP). But more than a quarter of these companies—292 out of 1,136—had their net worth completely eroded—for some, by many times over. Only two State PSUs, Gujarat Mineral Development Corporation and Punjab Communications Ltd, are listed in the stock exchange, as per available data.

Table 4.6 shows the operational results of the working SPSUs as per their latest accounts (mostly 2016–2017). Out of 1,136 working companies, only 541 had earned some profit, and the total profit earned by them amounted to ₹18,415 crore, while the net losses of all working PSUs amounted to ₹84,118 crore. Their accumulated losses amounted to a whopping ₹4.65 lakh crore as of March 2017. Only 117 of the profit-making companies had declared some dividends and paid a total dividend of ₹1253 crore during the year. The total manpower employed on a regular basis by the CPSUs as of March 2017 was 17.4 lakh.

The sector-wise break-up of government investment in these SPSUs has been shown in Table 4.7 and Figure 4.2. Power sector companies alone have claimed 78 per cent of total government invest-ments, the shares of services, manufacturing and finance being only 5, 3 and 3 per cent respectively. The power sector has been a perennial drag, being forced to absorb the losses due to government largesse to farmers and others, besides their own inefficiency, and their finances have not improved even after their unbundling into separate gen-eration, transmission and distribution companies (Discoms) and despite the government taking over 75 per cent of the Discoms' loans through the UDAY scheme. The companies with negative net worth invariably span power and transport sectors in almost every state, transport because of its high and unsustainable overheads and operational inefficiencies—for example, in 2015–2016, there were 30 per cent over-age vehicles in all State Transport Undertakings, with an average fuel efficiency of only 4 kilometres per litre of HSD/kg of CNG and occupancy less than 70 per cent.[23]

[23] Source: data.gov.in

Table 4.6 Operational Results of the State Public Sector Undertakings During 2016–2017 (₹ Crore)

	No. of Profit-making Cos.	Total Profit Made	Total Profit/Loss by All Working Cos.	Manpower Employed (Regular)	Accumulated Losses of All Working Cos.	No. of Cos. that Declared Dividend	Total Dividend Paid to Govt.
General-category States							
Andhra Pradesh	25	418	–2,354	94,000	24,045	5	20
Bihar	10	278	–1,160	16,533	4,365	2	4
Chhattisgarh	12	489	–1,108	20,317	5,880	2	5
Goa	15	54	50	3,422	–27	2	1
Gujrat	54	3,648	–14,764	109,000	11,715	8	83
Haryana	9	271	72	27,763	29,270	4	7
Jharkhand	6	38	–165	5,544	1,221	0	0
Karnataka	55	1,421	155	176,000	–299	13	12
Kerala	45	383	–1,833	119,000	6,348	9	32
Maharashtra	39	2,987	–17,355	212,000	36,771	6	5
Madhya Pradesh	31	729	–4,593	63,459	31,609	2	12
Odisha	35	2,028	1,521	21,000	–504	9	585

(Table 4.6 Continued)

(Table 4.6 Continued)

	No. of Profit-making Cos.	Total Profit Made	Total Profit/Loss by All Working Cos.	Manpower Employed (Regular)	Accumulated Losses of All Working Cos.	No. of Cos. that Declared Dividend	Total Dividend Paid to Govt.
Punjab	10	65	-8,852	47,905	9,343	4	4
Rajasthan	23	1,194	-1,615	100,000	101,242	7	63
Tamil Nadu	39	931	-8,435	284,000	78,854	20	240
Telangana	6	948	-5,165	138,000	17,560	5	70
Uttar Pradesh	33	708	-17,790	114,000	91,401	10	8
West Bengal	22	605	17	49,078	-126	4	1
Sub-total	**469**	**17,195**	**-83,374**	**1,601,021**	**448,668**	**112**	**1,152**
Special-category states							
Assam	18	106	-280	37,558	4,484	1	2
Arunachal Pradesh	5	8	-15	237	15	0	0
Himachal Pradesh	12	24	-104	36,071	3,243	2	2
Jammu & Kashmir	10	835	678	23,876	2,434	1	85
Manipur	2	0.3	-48	3,990	121	0	0
Meghalaya	4	9	-266	6,788	1,534	0	0
Mizoram	1	1	-2	269	58	0	0

Nagaland	3	2	0.5	623	49	0	0
Sikkim	3	8	-333	871	795	0	0
Tripura	5	16	-139	7,642	762	0	0
Uttarakhand	9	211	-235	20,693	2,510	1	12
Sub-total	72	1,220.3	-743.5	138,618	16,005	5	101
Grand total	541	18,415	-84,118	1,739,639	464,673	117	1,253

Source: Reports of the CAG of India on the Public Sector Undertakings of the respective states.

Table 4.7 Sector-wise Investment: 2016–2017 (₹ Crore)

	Power	Services	Manufacturing	Finance	Others*	Total
General-category states						
Andhra Pradesh	41,736	3,408	269	4,557	11,375	61,345
Bihar	49,333	1,978	447	591	1,543	53,892
Chhattisgarh	25,157	2,573	108	5	39	27,882
Goa	552	131	0	209	15	907
Gujrat	47,334	10,196	20,784	5,583	59,321	143,218
Haryana	41,177	0	0	130	3,054	44,361
Jharkhand	2,241	24	12	0	84	2,361
Karnataka	42,193	1,604	1,086	4,835	53,999	103,717
Kerala	9,953	6,360	2,034	4,969	3,790	27,106
Maharashtra	216,756	3,912	676	3,659	4,827	229,830
Madhya Pradesh	60,497	5,889	478	1,988	902	69,754
Odisha	9,830	218	380	1,156	1,337	12,921
Punjab	30,105	0	0	560	3,191	33,856
Rajasthan	127,406	4,555	0	615	5,103	137,679
Tamil Nadu	143,019	4,930	2,857	1,229	1,836	153,871
Telangana	28,579	15,710	6,340	4,477	4,106	59,212

Uttar Pradesh	188,358	813	4,097	1,383	1,627	196,278
West Bengal	31,924	2,217	1,890	5,865	1,699	43,595
Sub-total	**1,096,150**	**64,518**	**41,458**	**41,811**	**157,848**	**1,401,785**
Special-category states						
Assam	4,056	186	118	137	940	5,437
Arunachal Pradesh	12		5	10	12	39
Himachal Pradesh	11,108		11	281	1,258	12,658
Jammu & Kashmir	2,705	845	1,367	2,531	252	7,700
Manipur	224		8	18	16	266
Meghalaya	5,963	101	290	0	120	6,474
Mizoram	0	0	27	47	17	91
Nagaland	0	0	0	63	39	102
Sikkim	15,037	8	56	281	132	15,514
Tripura	666	248	297	145	76	1,432
Uttarakhand	6,729	298	326	32	3469	10,854
Sub-total	**46,500**	**1,686**	**2,505**	**3,545**	**6,331**	**60,567**
Total	**1,142,650**	**66,204**	**43,963**	**45,356**	**164,179**	**1,462,352**
Percentage share	**78**	**5**	**3**	**3**	**11**	**100**

Source: Reports of the CAG of India on the Public Sector Undertakings of the respective states.
Note: *Others mainly includes Infrastructure.

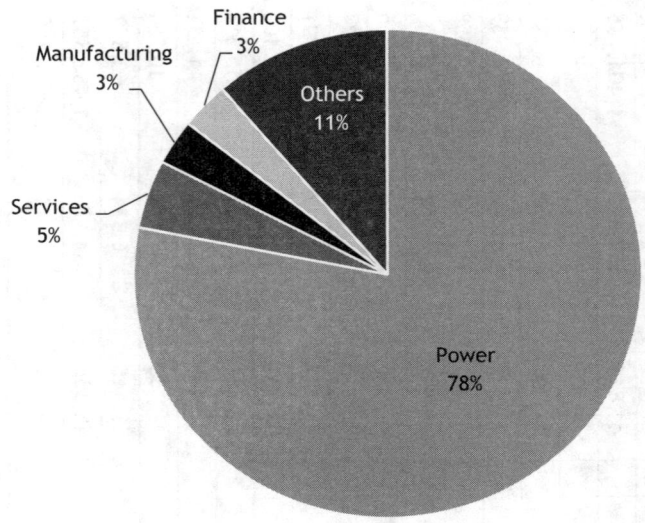

Figure 4.2 *Sectoral Share of Investment: 2016–2017*
Source: Table 4.7.

Apart from 1,136 working SPSUs, there are also 319 non-working SPSUs that produce nothing and are neither liquidated (Table 4.8). The state governments have invested ₹6,420 crore in these PSUs, all of which are virtually defunct. Many of these companies have not been working for ages now—for example, the non-working of companies of Kerala have been dysfunctional for 11–33 years, those of MP for 6–26 years, those of Tamil Nadu for 14–24 years and those of Rajasthan for 1–17 years.

A pattern can be discerned in their distribution among the states. 12 out of 29 Indian states accounted for 78, 86 and 79 per cent of all working, non-working and total SPSUs respectively in 2016–2017, as shown in Table 4.9. Leading the list is Kerala, followed by Uttar Pradesh and Karnataka, each of which had more than 100 SPSUs each, followed closely by Gujarat and West Bengal. Kerala also had the largest number of working SPSUs, 37, whose capital bases had completely been eroded, followed by West Bengal's 29. Both these states were ruled by the Left for a long time, and their political compulsions and

Table 4.8 Non-working SPSUs

	No. of Non-working PSUs	Total Govt. Investment (₹ Crore)	
		Equity	Long-term Loans
General-category states			
Andhra Pradesh	22	75	185
Bihar	44	197	554
Chhattisgarh	0	0	0
Goa	2	6	0
Gujrat	14	86	713
Haryana	5	22	4
Jharkhand	0	0	0
Karnataka	12	112	433
Kerala	15	45	67
Maharashtra	22	318	400
Madhya Pradesh	9	58	134
Odisha	28	67	31
Punjab	21	24	34
Rajasthan	3	12	16
Tamil Nadu	6	48	21
Telangana	22	75	185
Uttar Pradesh	38	704	355
West Bengal	19	169	965
Special-category states			
Assam	16	70	81
Arunachal Pradesh	2	0.4	0
Himachal Pradesh	2	19	60
Jammu & Kashmir	3	3	1
Manipur	3	2	1
Meghalaya	1	5	0
Mizoram	0	0	0
Nagaland	1	5	0

(Table 4.8 Continued)

(Table 4.8 Continued)

	No. of Non-working PSUs	Total Govt. Investment (₹ Crore)	
		Equity	Long-term Loans
Sikkim	4	56	1
Tripura	1	0	0
Uttarakhand	4	0.4	0
Total	**319**	**2,178.8**	**4,241**

Source: Reports of the CAG of India on the Public Sector Undertakings of the respective states for the year 2016–2017.

Table 4.9 *States with Largest Numbers of SPSUs, 2016–2017*

S. No.	State	Working Cos.	Non-working Cos.	Total No. of Cos.
1	Kerala	115	15	130
2	Uttar Pradesh	65	38	103
3	Karnataka	90	12	102
4	Gujrat	77	14	91
5	West Bengal	70	19	89
6	Maharashtra	66	22	88
7	Andhra Pradesh	64	22	86
8	Odisha	56	28	84
9	Tamil Nadu	68	6	74
10	Bihar	30	44	74
11	Telangana	47	22	69
12	Madhya Pradesh	58	9	67
13	Punjab	30	21	51
14	Rajasthan	45	3	48
15	All other States	255	44	299
	Total	**1,136**	**319**	**1,455**

Source: Reports of the CAG of India on the Public Sector Undertakings of the respective states.

philosophy contributed to the reckless creation of SPSUs without consideration of their viability. It was not that the non-Left-ruled states fared much better; Punjab had 19 of its 30 companies and Rajasthan 19 of its 45 companies with a negative net worth.

The accounts of working as well as non-working companies have been in arrears for a number of years, as shown in Table 4.10. At one account per year per company, SPSUs have over 2,600 arrears in accounts. For some non-working companies, the arrears date back to as many as 51 years. Many companies have never prepared their account since inception, and what happened to their assets and cash balances is anybody's guess. In Odisha, one company has arrears of accounts since 1965–1966 and another since 1966–1967. Even for some working companies, the arrears range up to 30 years. Without accounts, not only can their assets and liabilities and profit/loss position not be ascertained, but any possible fraud, misappropriation or scam would also go undetected for years. The companies also cannot be liquidated for want of accounts, by settling their liabilities, partly, or wholly, by selling off the assets.

Liquidation proceedings have, in fact, been instituted against many non-working companies, but most of these have been lying with the official liquidator for decades (Table 4.11). Section 270 of the Companies Act, 2013 prescribes two modes of winding up of a company and its liquidation: voluntarily, by passing a special resolution, which is simpler but used rarely, or by a tribunal through the appointment of an official liquidator who will liquidate its assets to pay off the liabilities. Since many of the SPSUs have never prepared their accounts, their assets and liabilities remain unknown, without which it is well-nigh impossible to liquidate them through tribunals. Liquidation proceedings have been initiated against 134 non-working SPSUs leading nowhere, with proceedings against many companies going on for 30 years or more. Obviously, for governments, this is not a priority. Only a handful of them have been closed by following the voluntary winding up route.

But the picture really turns bizarre when we look into the activities of the SPSUs, which defy all logic, as if they were created as permanent losing concerns. A large number of SPSUs were established in

Table 4.10 Status of Accounts in SPSUs as of March 2017

	Working PSUs			Non-working PSUs		
	No. of PSUs Having Arrears in A/cs	Total No. of A/cs in Arrears	No of Years for Which A/cs Are in Arrears	No. of PSUs Having Arrears in A/cs	Total No. of A/cs in Arrears	No of Years for Which A/cs Are in Arrears
General-category states						
Andhra Pradesh	51	127	1–12			
Bihar	21	142	1–5	39	1,029	1–40
Chhattisgarh	15	33	1–5			
Goa	13	46	1–11			
Gujrat	42	75	1–6	13		1–22
Haryana	23	45	1–5	4		1–3
Jharkhand	19	66	1–10	0		0
Karnataka	59	75	1–4	6	40	1–14
Kerala	101	265	1–14	15	151	1–31
Maharashtra	53	137	1–18	15		1–23
Madhya Pradesh	32	79	1–12	2		4–7
Odisha	39	64	1–8	21		1–51
Punjab	26	43	1–4			.
Rajasthan	7	9	1–2	1		3

Tamil Nadu	29	32	1–2	5		1–4
Telangana	41	79	1–14			
Uttar Pradesh	62	266	1–20	38	737	1–41
West Bengal	41	72	1–6	12	52	1–10
Sub-total	**674**	**1,655**		**132**	**980**	
Special-category states						
Assam	33	179	1–24	14	174	1 to >30
Arunachal Pradesh	5	29	1–15			
Himachal Pradesh	17	27	1–4	1		2
Jammu & Kashmir	19	183	1–19	3		16–26
Manipur	10	86	1–29	3		19–33
Meghalaya	16	46	1–12	1		10
Mizoram	6	17	1–8	0		0
Nagaland	5	18	1–5	1		36
Sikkim	9	29	1–8			
Tripura	12	20	1–2			
Uttarakhand	19	138	1–30	4	113	1–30
Sub-total	**151**	**772**		**27**	**287**	
Total	**674**	**1,655**		**132**	**980**	

Source: Reports of the CAG of India on the Public Sector Undertakings of the respective states.

Table 4.11 *Status of Liquidation of SPSUs*

	No. of SPSUs in Liquidation	Since How Many Years		No. of SPSUs in Liquidation	Since How Many Years
General-category States			*Special-category States*		
Andhra Pradesh	10	10–27	Assam		
Bihar	17	1–18	Arunachal Pradesh	2	1–2
Goa	2	1–3	Himachal Pradesh	2	1–18
Gujrat	8	1–21	Jammu & Kashmir	2	1–10
Haryana	2	13–18	Meghalaya	1	>5
Karnataka	12	1–14	Sikkim	4	NA
Kerala	4	1–28	Tripura	1	NA
Maharashtra	2	NA	Uttarakhand	4	>26
Madhya Pradesh	7	NA			
Odisha	18	NA			
Punjab	13	2–23			
Tamil Nadu	1	NA			
Telangana	10	11–27			
Uttar Pradesh	12	10–35			
West Bengal	NA	NA			
Total	**118**			**16**	

Source: Reports of the CAG of India on the Public Sector Undertakings of the respective states.

the so-called promotional and welfare sectors. UP has 103 SPSUs (38 non-functional) which include finance and development corporations for backward classes and Scheduled Castes, development corporations for almost everything from fishery, poultry, piggery, livestock, sugarcane and seed to police housing and small industries, welfare corporation for women and ex-servicemen, etc. Almost similar areas also span Bihar's 74 PSUs (40 non-functional); besides, they also include corporations for film development and finance, beverages, Panchayati Raj finance, medical services and infrastructure, development of fruits and vegetables, pharmaceuticals and chemicals, textiles, etc. Kerala's 130 PSUs (15 non-functional) include development corporations for the welfare of almost every conceivable segment of humanity—Christian converts from Scheduled Castes and recommended communities, handicapped persons, school teachers and non-teaching staff, artisans, palmyrah workers, women, backward classes, minorities, Scheduled Castes and Scheduled Tribes, and even one for forward communities. The primary activity of all these companies is to provide loans to the members of these communities for entrepreneurial and sundry purposes, which are refinanced by the government under various schemes, and their only income is from interest. The purpose can be easily served through the existing network of public sector banks by channelling the government subsidy through them or through other governments' existing delivery mechanisms without creating separate companies. The financial sector companies lack the economy of scale and are hopelessly short of the massive capital requirements as well as techno-financial expertise needed for making an impact on the specific sectors like infrastructure or MSME—scheduled commercial banks are in a much better position to do this effectively, economically and efficiently. The financial and welfare needs of specific sectors can be addressed much more efficiently by banks and financial institutions.

Needless to say, no state has the necessary expertise or resources to manage this diverse and disparate range of activities. Poultry, piggery, fishery, etc. are better left to individual entrepreneurs or firms that know how to make these profitable. There are government ministries and departments to take care of the welfare of backward classes, minorities and disadvantaged sections. Development and production of films, pharmaceuticals, seeds, chemicals, textiles, etc. are not activities mandated for the state. It is no wonder that these companies do not serve any useful purpose, and most have accumulated huge losses, eroding their capital bases many times over. The real reasons for the creation and continuance of these corporations is only to provide cushy parking places for senior bureaucrats, MLAs and powerful politicians as Chairman and Managing Directors so that state largesse can be extended to them through cars, perks and privileges, which add to the losses at the cost of the taxpayers. In a country that professes 'maximum governance and minimum government', these are the apparatuses for appeasement of potential trouble makers.

As mentioned earlier, the only significant reforms that were effected in respect of the state enterprises were in the realm of the power sector utility companies by unbundling the erstwhile state electricity boards into separate generation, transmission and distribution companies and converting the boards themselves into holding companies. The power sector dominated by the SBs was beset with many problems from the beginning, turning them into loss-making entities with huge out-standing dues owing to government policies and basic inefficiencies in their functioning. By the turn of the 20th century, these problems had assumed serious proportions. The financial performance of the power sector from 1997–1997 to 2001–2002, as depicted in Table 4.12, shows progressive deterioration with a consequent impact on the state finances as the governments had to continue pouring in subsidies and grants to sustain the financially unviable SEBs in almost every state. Their transmission and distribution (T&D) losses increased from 24.5 per cent in 1996–1997 to about 27.8 per cent during 2001–2002, which again was unsustainable and far above the industry standard of less than 10 per cent all over the world.[24]

The average tariff charged to the consumers had increased from ₹1.65 to ₹2.40 per unit (kWh) between 1996–1997 and 2001–2002; the cost of supply had increased from ₹2.16 to ₹3.50 during the same period, leaving a gap that widened from ₹0.50 to ₹1.10 per unit during this period, while the recovery of cost of supply through tariff declined from 76.7 per cent to 68.6 per cent only. The domestic and agricultural consumers were supplied power at subsidised rates much below the average tariff, and the tariff charged to agricultural consumers had increased only marginally from 21.20 paise per unit in 1996–1997 to 41.54 paise per unit in 2001–2002. As a result, the subsidy paid by the states on account of domestic consumers increased from ₹4,386 crore in 1996–1997 to ₹12,239 crore in 2001–2002, while the subsidy on account of agricultural consumers increased from ₹15,586 crore to

[24] https://data.worldbank.org/indicator/EG.ELC.LOSS.ZS, accessed 15 August 2019.

Table 4.12 Financial Performance of SEBs

	1996-1997 (Actual)	1997-1998 (Actual)	1998-1999 (Actual)	1999-2000 (Actual)	2000-2001 (RE)	2001-2002 (AP)
1 Cost of supply (₹/kWh)	2.16	2.40	2.63	3.05	3.27	3.50
2 Average tariff (₹/kwW)	1.65	1.80	1.87	2.07	2.26	2.40
3 Percent of recovery	76.7	75.2	71.0	67.8	69.2	68.6
4 Average agriculture tariff (Paise/kWh)	21.20	20.22	21.01	22.61	35.38	41.54
5 Commercial losses (₹ crore) (with subsidy)	-4,674	-7,598	-10,509	-15,088	-17,794	-24,837
6 Commercial losses (₹ crore) (without subsidy)	-11,305	-13,963	-20,860	-26,353	-25,259	-33,177
7 Net internal resources (₹ crore)	-2,091	-6,209	-8,954	-13,316	-15,621	-19,104
8 Subsidy for domestic consumers (₹ crore)	4,386	5,258	6,332	8,121	10,036	12,239
9 Subsidy for agriculture consumers (₹ crore)	15,585	19,021	22,473	24,650	26,950	30,462
10 Gross subsidy* (₹ crore)	20,211	24,750	29,261	33,145	37,331	43,060
11 Subvention received (₹ crore)	6,631	6,365	10,352	11,265	7,465	8,340
12 Uncovered subsidy (₹ crore)	5,805	9,374	10,600	16,616	24,118	28,977
13 Gross subsidy per unit of sales (₹/kWh)	0.75	0.87	0.99	1.11	1.19	1.27

Source: Government of India, *Annual Report (2001-2002)*, XV.
Note: *Gross subsidy includes subsidy for domestic consumers, agricultural consumers and on interstate sales.

₹30,462 crore over this period, raising the gross subsidy paid by the states to ₹43,060 crore in 2001–2002. Most states could barely afford this level of subsidy, and consequently, could only partially compensate the SEBs for subsidised supply of electricity. The uncovered gap of the SEBs, after taking into consideration the subvention received from the state governments, had increased to ₹28,977 crore in 2001–2002 as against to ₹58,053 crore in 1996–1997, and the commercial losses of SEBs (with subsidy) increased to ₹24,837 crore from only ₹4,674 crore over the same period. While the shares of domestic and agricultural consumers in the total power supply was increasing over the years (50% in 2001–2002 as against 49% in 1996–1997), the share of industry was declining as a result (29% as against 33% over this period).[25] At the same time, there was a power shortage that threatened to derail the industrial growth scenario in the country.

Of the total installed generation capacity of 1.1 lakh MW in the country as on March 2002, 59 per cent was owned by the states, 30 per cent by the centre and only 11 per cent by the private sector. Thermal electricity accounted for about 75 per cent of the total generation. There were slippages in capacity addition in both the thermal and hydel as well as both central and state sectors. As of March 2002, while the peak deficit of 12.6 per cent at the all-India level was improved compared to 18 per cent in 1996–1997, there was wide variation from state to state. The per capita electricity consumption of the country of 355 kWh in 1999–2000 showed no improvement over 334 kWh in 1996–1997; as a comparison, it may be mentioned that the per capita consumption in China, which was lagging far behind India's during the 1970s, was 719 kWh during 1997.[26] There were also wide variations in per capita consumption among the states in India. As of 1999–2000, the per capita consumption varied from 69 kWh in Manipur and Arunachal Pradesh to 141 kWh in Bihar, to 535 kWh, 400 kWh and 318 kWh respectively in the western, southern and northern region states.[27]

[25] Government of India, *Annual Report (2001–2002)*, xvii.
[26] Ibid., xvi.
[27] Ibid., 39.

Table 4.13 *Rate of Return of the SEBs (Without Subsidy, in %)*

Year	ROR (%)
1992–1993	(–)12.7
1993–1994	(–)12.3
1994–1995	(–)13.1
1995–1996	(–)16.4
1996–1997	(–)19.6
1997–1998	(–)22.9
1998–1999	(–)34.2
1999–2000	(–)43.1
2000–2001 (RE)	(–)39.1
2001–2002 (AP)	(–)44.1

Source: Government of India, *Annual Report (2001–2002)*, 9.

Returns on investment and assets employed by the SEBs also remained dismal throughout due to the increasing levels of commercial losses suffered by them. It was estimated that in order to break even and achieve a rate of return (ROR) of 3 per cent as stipulated in the Indian Electricity Supply Act (1948) in 2001–2002, the SEBs needed to raise the average tariff by ₹1.10 and ₹1.17 per unit respectively, which the state governments were unwilling to allow. Table 4.13 shows the trend in the rate of return (without subsidy) from 1992–1993 to 2001–2002, from which it can be seen that the rate of return progressively deteriorated to an abysmal –44.1 per cent.[28]

As the Planning Commission noted:

The unsatisfactory and deteriorating financial health of the State Electricity Boards has acted as a constraint not only for adding new capacity, improving the transmission and distribution system, carrying out renovation and modernisation programmes, but also for carrying out much needed reforms in the electricity utilities. One of the main hurdles to private sector participation gaining momentum

[28] Ibid., 8–9.

is the perceived reservations about the capacity of SEBs to pay for power purchases in view of their generally poor financial health.[29]

Some states such as Orissa, Haryana, Rajasthan, UP, Karnataka and Andhra Pradesh had already gone for restructuring and reforming their SEBs, with Odisha taking the lead in every sphere, as seen in Table 4.14. These reforms focussed on: (a) rationalisation of the tariff structure by establishing independent Electricity Regulatory Commissions and (b) restructuring of the SEBs by separating generation from transmission and distribution to bring greater efficiency in each of these areas. Reform in the power sector in fact began right in 1991 along with the liberalisation of economy, guided by the realisation that without private sector participation it would be impossible to bridge the supply-demand gap and private sector must contribute to capacity addition in this sector most vital for the economic revival. But by the end of the decade, capacity addition by private Independent Power Producers (IPPs) remained woefully short of expectations. During the 9th Plan period (1997–2002), the shortfall against the targeted capacity addition through private sector projects was as much as 71 per cent.

Government of India enacted the Electricity Regulatory Commission Act, 1998, allowing for the setting up of independent regulatory bodies like the Central Electricity Regulatory Commission (CERC) and the State Electricity Regulatory Commissions (SERCs) respectively at the central and state levels, primarily to look into all aspects of tariff structures. CERC was set up in July 1998, while 19 states constituted the SERCs; some also issued tariff orders. A few states such as Odisha, Haryana, Andhra Pradesh, Uttar Pradesh, Karnataka, Rajasthan, Madhya Pradesh and Delhi had enacted their State Electricity Reforms Acts, which provided for the unbundling and corporatisation of their SEBs. The Union Ministry of Power also entered into MOU arrangements with 20 states to undertake reforms in a time bound manner.[30] But the situation in most states still remained far from satisfactory and SEBs still were continuing to operate with all their inefficiencies and mounting losses.

---

[29] Ibid., 9.
[30] Ibid., 178–179.

Table 4.14 Status of Power Sector Reforms in the States: March 2002

Reform Path	Odisha	Haryana	UP	AP	Karnataka	Rajasthan	Delhi
Date of instituting Reform Act	April 1996	March 1998	September 1998	October 1998	June 1999	June 2000	March 2001
Regulatory commission established	Yes	Yes	Yes	Yes	Yes	Yes	Yes
Utility unbundled	Yes	Yes	Yes	Yes	Yes	Yes	In the process stage
Separate distribution companies established	Yes	Yes	No	Yes	No	Yes	In the process stage
Distribution privatised	Yes	No	No	No	No	No	No process stage

Source: Government of India, Annual Report (2001–2002), 179.

It was in this background that the Central Electricity Act was enacted by the centre in 2003 in order to promote efficiency by streamlining distribution, transmission, generation and trading operations, while also promoting transparency and accountability. The Act prohibited the SEBs from functioning as integrated power utilities and instead made it mandatory for them to unbundle themselves into separate entities for handling transmission, generation, distribution and trading functions. The Act placed no restriction on generation, distribution and trading, making it free for the states to adopt their own models, but in a manner that was neutral to all players in the power sector. While some states unbundled their SEBs into three companies—one each for power generation, transmission and distribution—some states such as Andhra Pradesh, Rajasthan and Bihar have divided the SEBs into four or more companies—one each for generation and transmission, and two or three or even four companies for distribution. The unbundling was originally mandated to have been achieved by all states within a year, but the deadline was extended several times. But by 2013, almost all states had unbundled their SEBs. Kerala is the only state that has not unbundled its electricity board into separate generation, transmission, and distribution companies but vested all these activities into the reconstituted Kerala State Electricity Board Ltd (KSEBL).

Unbundling saw a large number of private players enter generation, while transmission remained mostly in the hands of the state.[31] Only two states—Orissa and Delhi—privatised their distribution. But unbundling did not solve the structural problems faced by the SEBs; in fact, it made them worse in the absence of internal reforms and good corporate governance to make it effective. The SEBs eventually faced a paradoxical situation where distribution companies were unable

[31] The major public sector companies in power generation and transmission are NTPC, NHPC and Power Grid Corporation (PGCIL), the private sector companies in the power sector include Tata Power, CESC, Reliance Power, Adani Power, SJVN, JSW Energy, Torrent Power, Sterlite Power Transmission, L&T Power, Jaiprakash Power, Kalpataru Power, Toshiba Transmission & Distribution Systems, Unitech Power Transmission, Ratnagiri Gas & Power, Reliance Energy, GE T&D (India) Ltd. etc.

to purchase power from generation companies due to their financial problems, resulting in generation companies cutting down production, compounding the problems of the consumers. The Discoms' woes were exacerbated by the unabated T&D losses and outages due to old equipment.[32] It was estimated that 25,000 MW of capacity was lying idle by the end of 2015.[33]

To tide over the financial crisis, the Discoms started borrowing heavily from banks, which were pressurised by the government to lend to them. The result was the accumulation of humongous debts by the Discoms; by 2013, their debts accumulated to ₹2.9 lakh crore, increasing almost by ₹1 lakh crore every year. Nearly 40 per cent of this debt was owing to the losses and the rest due to tariffs not rising in sync with the rising cost of supply. This was again because independent regulators, which were established to work at an arm's length from the state governments to ensure quality of service and cost-based pricing, were not allowed to discharge their functions as they had been hijacked by the state governments by appointing compliant bureaucrats at their helm, virtually rendering them into departmental units run by the government. The governments were required under law to compensate the Discoms for the subsidised power supply, and in many cases this was not done, forcing the Discoms that were almost entirely owned by state governments to carry the loss into their books. As the Discoms were unable to pay back their loans to the banks, the banks' loans started becoming non-performing assets (NPAs). The governments' inability to correct the supply-demand gap and to curtail the T&D losses and thefts as well as their failure to revise the tariff all contributed to the ever-worsening situation. The Financial Stability Report of the RBI released in June 2015 noted that ₹53,000 crore loans to seven SEBs had a 'very high probability' of turning into NPAs by September 2015.[34] The banks' exposure to the power sector increased to ₹5.83 lakh crore by September 2015, which amounted to 22 per cent of all outstanding banking loans to industries. As of March 2015, the

---

[32] Mehta, 'Achilles Heel of the Power Sector'.
[33] Purkayastha, 'The Crisis of the Power Sector Reforms—Part I'.
[34] Mehta, 'Achilles Heel of the Power Sector'.

Discoms had accumulated losses of ₹3.8 lakh crore and outstanding debts of ₹4.3 lakh crore.[35]

Thus, the basic objective behind unbundling, which was to make the utilities more efficient and economical through competition, was completely defeated in the absence of concomitant structural reforms and commitment on the part of the state governments. Instead, the losses of the SEBs, which stood at the level of ₹2,700 crore in 1992–1993 and at around ₹25,000 crore before the Central Electricity Act mandating unbundling was enacted, had increased to ₹3.8 lakh crore by 2014–2015. This was because the underlying causes were left completely unaddressed, as explained above. Besides, the cost of electricity for the consumer remained very high.

The high cost of electricity also enticed the big international players in the power sector such as Siemens, GE, Westinghouse, ABB, Hitachi, etc., which were not interested in taking over distribution, to opt for the easier and more profitable route of building power stations and selling electricity through assured purchases to the SEBs through Power Purchase Agreements (PPAs). This also gave them the power to manipulate prices to their advantage, because electricity being a sector where supply must always balance consumption, a supplier can always hike up prices through manipulation to reduce the supply and create an imbalance in the market. Controversies and cronyism marked many of the projects under PPA, the most notorious being the Dabhol power project executed by Enron Corporation to build a $3 billion natural gas power plant in Dabhol in Maharashtra. The gas was to have been supplied from the nearby Panna and Mukta fields by a joint venture between Reliance and ONGC, which again raised many questions related to bureaucratic corruption and cronyism. The project—the single largest direct foreign investment in India till then—was touted as the poster child of economic liberalisation. Instead, it turned out to be a disaster and a scandal that imposed huge and unanticipated financial burden on the Government of Maharashtra and created huge public outrage that forced the government to close the contract in 2001. This was also the beginning of the endgame for Enron.

---

[35] Purkayastha, 'The Crisis of the Power Sector Reforms'.

The Dabhol plant was ultimately taken over by the NTPC and is today lying idle because of the high cost of gas-based electricity. About 14,000 MW of capacity created through gas-based plants are today lying almost idle due to their high cost of generation.[36]

The shortages created by inadequate investments in the power sector during the 8th, 9th and 10th plans had resulted in hiking up the prices of electricity and making the country one of the highest costing countries in the region in terms of electric power consumption, which impacted its industry, investments and economic growth very significantly. The same high prices also attracted the private sector to invest in generation. With easy finance available from the public sector banks through the government's intervention, often by disregarding all lending norms, and captive coal mines allowed to the private companies through the allocation of coal mines on a totally opaque and so-called 'first-cum-first-served basis' that would later blow up into the infamous 'Coalgate' scandal of unprecedented proportions during the UPA-II era, private and domestic industrial companies also entered the fray. They found coal more attractive and profitable than power and made windfall profits from selling coal or the licenses for coal block allocation.[37] The result was that the power projects remained incomplete and hence loan repayment could not be made, and even the coal extraction was not started in many mines in anticipation of higher prices, leading to shortages of both power and coal—two vital inputs for industrial growth in the country. As the *Indian Express* then reported:

> The projects facing potential stress include Adani (4 projects with a debt of Rs 24,100 crore), Lanco (five projects with a debt of Rs 22,100 crore), Reliance ADAG (three projects involving a debt of Rs 32,600 crore), Tata Power (one project with a loan of 14,400 crore), IndiaBulls (four projects with a debt of Rs 21,200 crore) and Essar (seven projects with Rs 21,900 crore debt).......
> The banking sector's short term exposure to state discoms is quite substantial and is estimated at Rs 1,50,000–1,70,000 crore as on

[36] Ibid.
[37] Ibid.

March 2012, which is 3–3.6 per cent of banking credit and 45–52 per cent of total power credit. A large part of these loans were taken to fund the cash losses of the discoms.[38]

All these loans and many more by other industrial houses—obtained mostly through cronyism and political connections—would later need to be written off by a benevolent government. Between 2013 and 2016, nearly ₹1.75 lakh crore of such outstanding loans—much of it owing to the power sector—were actually written off.

The demand for coal had increased substantially after 2003. Given that 70 per cent of India's power needs are supplied by thermal plants operating on coal, the assured supply of coal to all producers, public and private, was an essential prerequisite. The domestic shortfall was estimated at 70 million tonnes of coal by 2011–2012, and imports were costly. Under the Coal Mines Nationalisation Act, 1973, the mining of coal was the monopoly of Coal India Limited. An amendment to this Act made in June 1993 allowed private companies engaged in the production of power, iron and steel the right to mine coal for captive use. The entire process of allocation of coal blocks was mired in such opacity and arbitrariness that once the scandal was uncovered by the CAG in all its details, finally, the Supreme Court had to intervene to cancel all but four of 218 coal block allocations, just as it had cancelled all the 122 spectrum licences issued earlier as 'unconstitutional and arbitrary'. The nation had to pay a heavy price for such indiscretion; the power sector suffered for want of coal, and despite sitting on one of the largest global reserves of coal estimated at more than 300 billion tonnes, the country was forced to import coal at the cost of precious foreign exchange, pushing our already high current account deficit further into the red.[39]

The unbundling of the SEBs actually brought private players in the market, mainly for generation of electricity, along with central PSEs like NTPC. By 2016, the share of the private sector in total electricity generation in the country (about 3.05 lakh MW) had increased substantially—to over 41 per cent—while the central PSEs accounted

[38] Mathew, 'Banks Staring at Huge Stressed Loans of Private Power Companies'.
[39] Bhattacharjee, 'Coalgate Revisited'.

for about 25 per cent and the states accounted for only one-third of the total generation. The share of the private sector would further increase to 45 per cent at the cost of the states, whose share would shrink to 30 per cent by April 2018, when the total generation went up 3.43 lakh MW. The result is that while the states are in no position to determine the prices for generation that are dictated by private players and NTPC, which generate but does not distribute electricity, they yet have to distribute electricity at prices reasonable for the consumer, with no control over its cost, and absorb the consequent losses. Increasing the price of electricity for the consumer who is already burdened by a very high price would inevitably invite a political backlash that no state is willing to face.[40]

In 2012, to mitigate the losses of the Discoms and to enable them to turn around and become financially viable, the central government launched a scheme for their 'Financial Restructuring', outlining the steps to be taken by the state Discoms as well the governments for restructuring their debts through a 'Transitional Mechanism by the Central Government'.[41] Under this scheme, 50 per cent of the short-term liabilities of the Discoms outstanding as on 31 March 2012 would be taken over by the state governments, through issue of long-term bonds to be issued by the Discoms backed by state government guarantees. The state would support the Discoms to repay the principal and pay the interest on these bonds and would gradually take over its liability in a phased manner by issuance of special securities in favour of the lender, within the FRBMA targets. The balance 50 per cent of the liability would be rescheduled by the lenders with a moratorium on payment for 3 years on the principal. Here also, the state would provide guarantee for the repayment of principal and interest payments by the Discoms.

The restructuring of the loans is to be accompanied by 'concrete and measurable action by the Discoms/States to improve the operational performance' of the Discoms, including a commitment to carry out certain 'mandatory and recommendatory' measures like enforcing financial discipline in the Discoms, providing a commercial

---

[40] Purkayastha, 'The Crisis of the Power Sector Reforms—Part II'.

[41] OM No. 20/11/2012—APDRP dated October 5, 2012, Ministry of Power, Govt. of India.

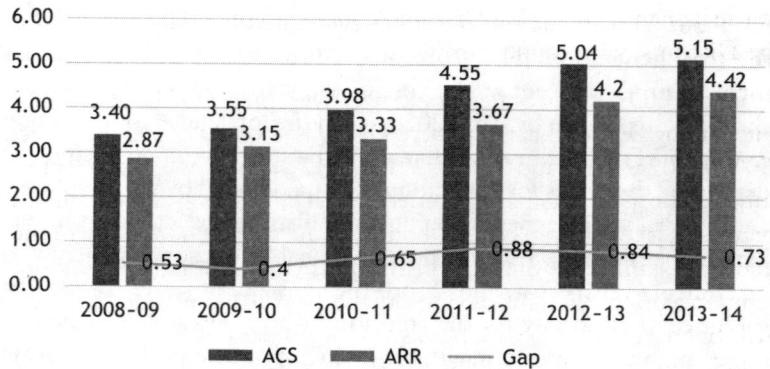

Figure 4.3 ACS–ARR Gap of Discoms

Source: R Sree Ram, "States will need to walk the talk for discom revival plan success", Livemint, 09 Nov 2015, quoting Nomura Research.

orientation to their activities, regular rationalisation of tariff, eliminating the gap between the average cost of supply (ACs) and average revenue realised (ARR), which was ₹0.76 per kWh in 2011–2012, timely audit of Discom accounts, etc. The centre promised additional incentives by way of grants equal to the value of the energy saved by reducing AT&C loss[42] and capital reimbursement of 25 per cent of the principal repayment by the states on the liability taken over by them under the scheme.

Immediately after the scheme was launched, the Discoms aggressively increased the tariffs, but the states were constrained by their own fiscal considerations and the FRBMA requirements. Thus, neither could the ACS-ARR gap be narrowed appreciably (Figure 4.3), nor could the AT&C losses be minimised.

Thus, the financial restructuring plan (FRP) could hardly improve the financial health of the Discoms, which continued to sink into the quagmire of debt and losses. By September 2015, their debts had accumulated to a whopping ₹4.8 lakh crore. In November 2015, the

[42] The National Power Portal (https://npp.gov.in/glossary) defines AT&C loss as the combination of energy loss (Technical loss + Theft + Inefficiency in billing) and commercial loss (Default in payment + Inefficiency in collection).

centre launched the Ujwal Discom Assurance Yojna (UDAY) to help the Discoms, with support from their state governments.

Under UDAY, the States would take over three-fourths of the total outstanding debt of their respective Discoms as on 30 September 2015 (50% in 2015–2016 and 25% in 2016–2017), as against 50 per cent of only the short-term liabilities under the FRP. This was to be achieved by the states by issuing 'UDAY bonds' in the market or directly to the respective banks and financial institutions (FIs) holding the Discom debts to raise money for paying off the loans; these would be non-SLR bonds, including SDL bonds.[43] Government of India would not include the debt taken over by the states as per the above scheme in the calculation of fiscal deficit of respective states in the financial years 2015–2016 and 2016–2017. The proceeds would be transferred to Discoms through a mix of grant, loan and equity, which the Discoms would use to pay back their loans to banks and FIs, with a moratorium period of up to 5 years.

The remaining 25 per cent of debt would remain with the respective Discoms and would either be issued as state-guaranteed Discom bonds or re-priced by Banks/FIs at interest rates not more than bank base rate plus 0.10 per cent. State backing could be expected to bring down the interest rates for the Discoms. States would take over future losses of Discoms in a graded manner and also fund them in a graded manner.[44]

In return for the bailout, the Discoms were required to achieve several efficiency parameter targets between 2017 and 2019, like reduction in power lost through transmission, theft and faulty metering, installing smart meters and implementing geographic information system (GIS), mapping of loss-making areas, regular and periodic revision of power tariffs, etc. The AT&C losses had to be minimised to 15 per cent by 2019 and the ACSD-ARR gap to be eliminated by the same date.

[43] To meet their statutory liquidity ratio (SLR) requirement, banks generally invest in State Development Loan (SDL) bonds, which are more buy-and-hold instruments rather than instruments for trading. They are normally quoted at a premium to G-Secs. Non-SLR bonds may get SLR bond status later. SLR is the percentage of total deposits that banks have to invest mandatorily in government securities.

[44] 5 per cent of losses in 2016–2017; 10 per cent of losses in 2017–2018; 25 per cent of losses in 2018–2019 and 50 per cent of losses 2019–2020.

States accepting UDAY and performing as per operational milestones would be given additional or priority funding through Deendayal Upadhyaya Gram Jyoti Yojana (DDUGJY), Integrated Power Development Scheme (IPDS), Power Sector Development Fund (PSDF) or other similar schemes. They would also be benefited through reduction in cost of power through central support, increased supply of domestic coal, allocation of coal linkages at notified prices, coal price rationalisation, faster completion of interstate transmission lines, power purchase through transparent competitive bidding, etc.[45]

UDAY is an optional scheme, and so far all states except Odisha and West Bengal and all union territories except Delhi and Chandigarh have joined UDAY. Over 86 per cent of the total ₹2.69 lakh crore bonds have already been issued by 2018–2019, which will mature up to 2017. While UDAY has transferred a large part of the Discom debts to the state governments and reduced their interest burden, the problem of the losses of the distribution companies have been addressed satisfactorily. There have been some hits and many misses, as a newspaper headline states in respect of UDAY targets. A research study by NIPFP reported in December 2018 found that the AT&C losses stood at 25.41 per cent in December 2018, as against the target of 15 per cent to be achieved in March 2019; only seven states—Himachal Pradesh, Andhra Pradesh, Goa, Gujarat, Kerala, Telangana, and Tamil Nadu—had losses below 15 per cent. Similarly, regarding the ACS-ARR gap, which is to be completely eliminated by March 2019, they found that this gap had, on the contrary, widened in several states, including Jharkhand, Punjab Goa, Manipur, and Jammu and Kashmir. Only a handful of high-performing states—Gujarat, Karnataka, Himachal Pradesh and Telangana—have shown consistent performance on most financial and operational parameters, but many states still suffered from a lack of effective billing procedures, poor measurement of power consumption and ineffective monitoring of power theft.[46]

---

[45] http://pib.gov.in/newsite/PrintRelease.aspx?relid=130261, accessed 18 August 2019.

[46] Kaur and Chakraborty, 'NIPFP. UDAY Scheme's Progress Shows Few Hits, Many Misses'.

The losses of Discoms were reduced by ₹17,352 crore by March 2018 or by 50 per cent annually, but their outstanding dues to generating companies (Gencos) surged by over 150 per cent to ₹32,071 crore in the same period, of which ₹27,832 crore were pending for more than 60 days. Five states—UP, Telangana, Maharashtra, Tamil Nadu and Karnataka—accounted for nearly 63 per cent of the total dues (₹20,201 crore). The problems were now shifting from the Discoms to the Gencos; irregular and often delayed payments by Discoms were the primary reasons for their assets getting stressed, and that included power projects worth ₹1.80 lakh crore. Some Gencos had accumulated NPAs worth over ₹70,000 crore. Gencos themselves owed huge amounts to the power producers—as of March 2018, they owed ₹9,479 crore to NTPC, ₹14,091 crore to 10 independent power producers (IPPs) including Tata Power, Adani Power, GMR and Jindal Steel and Power, etc., ₹7,000 crore to NHPC, DVC, NEEPCO and SJVNL, besides ₹8,000 crore to power producers as a result of appeals made by them to the respective electricity regulators.[47]

Thus, the power sector reforms have now turned full circle. UDAY has brought severe adverse impacts upon the finances of the state governments and drastically reduced their ability to continue to support the Discoms further while the problems of the power sector remain as bad as ever. Far from being financially viable, the Discoms may need another bailout in the near future, as the rating agency Crisil has observed. Crisil cautioned in May 2019:

> While Discoms enjoyed the benefit of debt reduction, structural reforms have been slow. AT&C losses came down by only 400 bps[48] by December 2018 from pre-Uday levels and average annual tariff increase were a paltry 3 per cent. With most states having limited fiscal headroom, continuous financial support to Discoms may be difficult.

It has predicted that given the funding needs for budgeted capex, the debt of Discoms might balloon to ₹2.6 lakh crore by March

---

[47] Chatterjee, 'UDAY Scheme: DISCOMS Cut Losses, But Their Dues to GENCOS Mount'.

[48] 100 basic points = 1 per cent.

2020. 'That makes structural reforms of Discoms, especially ensuring cost-reflective tariffs and a material reduction in AT&C losses using measures such as smart metering, a critical need. Any delay would increase the pain for the power sector, especially for the generating companies, investors and lenders', Crisil has warned. Otherwise, the Discoms may have to be rescued by another bailout, and the story would continue the same as ever.[49]

The 1991 reforms liberalised the economy by restricting the role of PSUs to a few strategic sectors while progressively opening up other sectors to private investment and FDIs. This was followed by privatisation and disinvestment of PSUs, listing them on stock exchanges and empowering the better performing ones by giving them Maharatna, Navratna and Miniratna status with substantial autonomy, which helped them grow abundantly. But the reforms were carried only for the CPSEs, while the SPSEs continued to languish helplessly in an environment of rent-seeking and favour-dispensing political gamesmanship.

For 29 states,[50] 1,136 SPSUs are too many to manage, and so are 444 central PSUs. For revitalising them, it is imperative first to identify the sectors the state must withdraw from, reduce their number drastically and then revamp the structure and management of the remaining ones. Wherever feasible and where synergies exist, centrals PSUs may be persuaded to manage the SPSEs that otherwise are likely to remain unviable. The essential prerequisite is to de-politicise and de-bureaucratise them, professionalise their management by appointing experienced managers and shield them from politicians or bureaucrats. The holding structure of PSEs also needs to be reworked, by following the best practices we shall discuss later in the in the book, like the Temasek Model. But for any reform, political will is essential, and so far, unfortunately, our leaders have not been able to transcend the narrow vision determined by political expediency which has prevented genuine institutional reforms from taking place. The result was that the more the things changed, the more they remained the same.

---

[49] *Business Today*, 'SEBs to Dive Deeper into Debt as they Miss Uday Scheme Targets'.

[50] Including undivided Jammu and Kashmir, which has since been organised into two union territories with effect from November 2019.

Annexure 4.1 Status of PSEs (March 2001)

S. No.	State	No. of SPSEs	Estimated Total Investment (₹ Crore)	Net Accumulated Losses (₹ Crore)	No. of Loss Making SPSEs	No. of Non-working SPSEs
1	Andhra Pradesh	40	4,444	2,894	25	14
2	Assam	42	3,649	2,792	28	10
3	Goa	12	4,869	730	NA	NA
4	Gujrat	54	23,438	965	NA	NA
5	Haryana	45	443	384	10	4
6	Himachal Pradesh	21	3,143	369	12	2
7	Karnataka	76	19,295	811	37	13
8	Kerala	109	9,805	1,280	52	13
9	Madhya Pradesh	26	7,923	NA	8	15
10	Maharashtra	65	19,196	NA	43	17
11	Manipur	14	NA	NA	10	NA
12	Odisha	68	9,796	1,180	18	34
13	Punjab	53	12,425	847	25	23

(Annexure 4.1 Continued)

(Annexure 4.1 Continued)

S. No.	State	No. of SPSEs	Estimated Total Investment (₹ Crore)	Net Accumulated Losses (₹ Crore)	No. of Loss Making SPSEs	No. of Non-working SPSEs
14	Rajasthan	24	116	261	10	3
15	Tamil Nadu	59	6,192	NA	NA	NA
16	Uttar Pradesh	45	24,753	3,110	NA	NA
17	West Bengal	82	18,241	5,068	59	6
	Total	**835**	**167,718**	**20,691**	**337**	**166**

Source: Ministry of Disinvestment, *Disinvestment in States*, quoted in Ganesh, *State Level Public Enterprises in India*, 26–27.
Note: The above figures pertain only to the SPSEs that have finalised their accounts. A large number of companies are excluded in the above figures. Further, many states such as Arunachal Pradesh, Bihar, Chattisgarh, Jammu and Kashmir, Jharkhand, Meghalaya, Mizoram, Nagaland, Sikkim, Tripura and Uttarakhand did not furnish any data.

Annexure 4.2 Sector-wise Number of PSEs (2003–2004)

S. No.	State	Manufacturing	Promotional	Trading	Financial	Service	Welfare	Total
1	Andhra Pradesh	20	11	3	2	5	0	41
2	Arunachal Pradesh	0	0	2	1	0	0	3
3	Assam	25	12	5	0	3	3	49
4	Bihar	7	7	1	2	4	0	21
5	Chhattisgarh							0
6	Goa	4	6	2	2	2	0	16
7	Gujrat	13	11	4	8	9	3	48
8	Haryana	12	2	7	4	4	2	31
9	Himachal Pradesh	6	4	6	2	2	4	24
10	Jammu & Kashmir	5	2	4	1	4	2	18
11	Jharkhand							0
12	Karnataka	30	12	4	3	10	4	63
13	Kerala	67	16	3	7	5	6	104
14	Madhya Pradesh	8	10	4	2	3	0	27
15	Maharashtra	18	7	4	6	12	7	54
16	Manipur	1	4	0	0	0	0	5

(Annexure 4.2 Continued)

(Annexure 4.2 Continued)

S. No.	State	Manufacturing	Promotional	Trading	Financial	Service	Welfare	Total
17	Meghalaya	7	1	3	1	2	0	14
18	Mizoram	2	2	1	0	0	0	5
19	Nagaland	3	1	0	2	0	0	6
20	Odisha	17	9	5	3	4	0	38
21	Punjab	4	6	3	6	8	0	27
22	Rajasthan	11	8	4	1	4	0	28
23	Sikkim	6	2	0	0	1	1	10
24	Tamil Nadu	17	7	2	3	23	1	53
25	Tripura	6	0	1	5	2	0	14
26	Uttar Pradesh	11	5	3	4	7	3	33
27	Uttarakhand	4	0	0	2	2	0	8
28	West Bengal	28	4	3	2	7	1	45
	Total	332	149	74	69	123	38	785

Source: Figures furnished by the states to the Twelfth Finance Commission, quoted in Ganesh, *State Level Public Enterprises in India,* 29–30.

CHAPTER 5

Financial Sector Public Enterprises

On 19 July 1969, the ownership of 14 major Indian banks was transferred to the government by the banking companies (acquisition and transfer of undertakings) Ordinance. In the 50th anniversary year of that landmark decision, on 30 August 2019, the Union Finance Minister Ms Nirmala Sitharaman announced the merger of 10 public sector banks (PSBs) owned by the Government of India into four large banks, reducing in a single stroke the total number of state-owned banks in the country from 27 to 12. The plan included the merger of Punjab National Bank with Oriental Bank of Commerce and United Bank of India; Canara Bank with Syndicate Bank; Union Bank of India with Andhra Bank and Corporation Bank; and Indian Bank with Allahabad Bank. The government also announced the infusion of ₹55,250 crore[1] to help the newly merged and some other public sector banks to advance more loans to their customers besides meeting the crucial regulatory norms. This followed the government's decision in 2018 to merge three banks—Vijaya

---

[1] PNB (₹16,000 crore), Union Bank of India (₹11,700 crore), Bank of Baroda (₹7,000 crore), Canara Bank (₹6,500 crore), Indian Bank (₹2,500 crore), Indian Overseas Bank (₹3,800 crore), Central Bank (₹3,300 crore), UCO Bank (₹2,100 crore), United Bank (₹1,600 crore) and Punjab and Sind Bank (₹750 crore).

Bank and Dena Bank with Bank of Baroda—to create a larger bank effective from 1 April 2019. Earlier, in 2017, State Bank of India, the country's largest bank, was also merged with five of its associate banks and the Bharatiya Mahila Bank. The present merger is expected to lead to a better scale of operations, and, as the Finance Minister said, 'We want banks with strong national presence and enhanced risk appetite'.

As pointed out by the Economic Survey, 2019–2020, Indian banks are suffering from 'dwarfism', with only one bank—State Bank of India (SBI)—among the top 100 banks in the world, whereas the fifth largest economy in the world would need at least six. USA has 18 banks among the top 100, China 12, and Japan, South Korea and the UK six each. With over 8 lakh employees including nearly 4 lakh officers and a manifold expansion of branch networks throughout the length and breadth of the country, India's banking sector is still disproportionately under-developed compared to the size of its economy. Banks are the primary providers of credit, and the credit penetration remains very low compared to the size of population of the country. This was perhaps a major reason behind the decision of merger, because no economy can realise its full potential unless it is supported by its banking sector. As the economic survey has noted:

> Over Rs 4,30,000 crores of taxpayer money is invested as Government's equity in PSBs. In 2019, every rupee of taxpayer money invested in PSBs, on average, lost 23 paise. In contrast, every rupee of investor money invested in 'New Private Banks' (NPBs)—banks licensed after India's 1991 liberalization—on average gained 9.6 paise. As PSBs and NPBs operate in the same domestic market, there is a case for enhancing the efficiency of PSBs.[2]

The consolidated Punjab National Bank, Oriental Bank of Commerce and United Bank of India (anchor bank—Punjab National Bank) would be the second largest PSB in India after the SBI, with a turnover of ₹18 lakh crore and branch network of 11,437 branches. The consolidated

---

[2] Government of India, *Economic Survey, 2019–2020*, Vol. I, Para 7.7.

Indian Bank and Allahabad Bank (anchor bank—Indian Bank) would be the seventh largest public sector bank with ₹8.1 lakh crore turnover and 6,104 branches; the consolidated Union Bank of India, Andhra Bank and Corporation Bank would be the fifth largest PSB with ₹14.6 lakh crore of business and 9,609 branches, while the consolidated Canara Bank and Syndicate Bank would be the fourth largest PSB with ₹15.2 lakh crore of business and 10,342 branches. To allay the fear of job losses emanating from this merger, the Finance Minister asserted that no retrenchment had taken place after the merger of Bank of Baroda, Dena Bank and Vijaya Bank and that all the staff had been redeployed, with best practices in each bank being replicated in others.[3] The government has assured this time, too, that there will be no retrenchment of employees, though relocation and redeployment as a result of branch rationalisation cannot be ruled out. The entire process of amalgamation is expected to take at least a year. The data regarding different performance indicators in respect of both the pre-merger individual banks and post-merger amalgamated banks are shown in Annexure 5.1.

The merger of two or more entities to form a larger one entails no explicit change in the ownership, and the government remains the majority shareholder of the merged entity as well. But apparently, the government was motivated into this action due to the slowing economy; it expected that a larger entity might be in a position to lend more money to help revive this slowing economy. Without a boost in credit growth, which has slowed down considerably in recent times, it will be impossible to achieve the target of growing India into a US$5 trillion economy in the next few years. Besides, the merger is expected to improve operational efficiency by enabling the banks to lower their costs and hence their lending rates. The merged entities will be able to achieve better synergy in terms to debt, resources, technology and assets, including stressed assets, reduce the cost of lending and hence

---

[3] Post the mega merger, the six PSBs banks that will remain independent are Indian Overseas Bank, UCO Bank, Bank of Maharashtra, Punjab and Sind Bank, Bank of India and Central Bank of India, besides the State Bank of India.

increase their domestic and global competitiveness.[4] Technology is a primary consideration for the merger, and mergers of individual banks have been decided on the basis of technology platforms used by them. The tasks that merged banks will have to complete will include the integration of the core banking technology platforms of the merging banks, amalgamation of their HR policies without compromising the staff benefits, assimilation of the diverse work cultures of employees in the merging entities while retaining the best practices and products of each, rationalisation of branches and staff deployment to achieve economies of scale, divestment of competing subsidiaries, rationalisation of multiple distribution agreements and partnerships, etc.[5] All these pose serious challenges but offer great opportunities as well for the amalgamated banks to emerge as global competitors. The merged banks are also better placed to manage their risks.

Our merger experiences so far, however, have not been particularly encouraging; in fact, the non-productive assets (NPA) or the bad loans of the SBI became worse after its merger with associates 2 years ago, with write-offs and persistent slippages eating into its profit and capital both, impeding the growth of credit. Similarly, 1 year since the merger of Bank of Baroda (BOB) with Vijaya Bank and Dena Bank, BOB's financials confirm the underlying problems with such forced mergers. Likewise, it had taken PNB years to overcome the trauma of its merger in 1993 with the New Bank of India. It is unlikely that the current mergers will also create any significant value for the shareholders, at least in the short term. As the former RBI Governor Mr Raghuram Rajan had cautioned against forced mergers: 'You have to be careful in any kind of merger that you don't get a big weak bank. You'd hope that the strong bank would clean up the weak bank's problems but there are very few banks without problems today in the public sector'. [6] The real problem, as he correctly identified, was the unresolved issue of cleaning up their balance sheet. Indeed, during his short tenure, Rajan has attempted to cleanse the balance sheets of banks and also rebuild the institutional

---

[4] https://www.thehindu.com/business/Industry/how-will-mergers-affect-public-banks/article29363041.ece, accessed 9 December 2019.
[5] *The Times of India*, PSB Mergers: Technology, HR Synergy, Key Challenges.
[6] Quote in ibid, 110.

architecture of banking in India, including by introducing new institutions like Payments Bank,[7] Small Finance Banks and Postal Bank.

For one thing, labour becoming redundant as a result of such consolidation cannot be retrenched very easily; neither can the merger of healthy banks with weak banks actually be expected to improve the health of the banking system as a whole. Rather, such forced mergers, by diluting the management of stronger banks, may deteriorate the overall health of the banking structure, adversely affecting their long-term performance as a whole. As can be seen from Table 5.1, the mergers are not leading to significant reduction of the NPA ratios of amalgamated banks. The bad loan recovery process has many structural problems including the inefficiency of our judicial system; forced mergers do not address these structural glitches. There also remains the vexed issue of political interference and crony capitalism in the corporate loans advanced by the PSBs that is at the root of their present NPA crisis. The stated objective of the 1969 nationalisation of banks was to channelise bank credit to development programmes of the government, which enabled the politicians to force the PSBs to extend loans even where they were clearly unviable and made no business sense. The project appraisal machinery of the banks was rendered useless and lost its efficiency in the process.

The history of bank merger indeed dates back to the 1960s—the primary motivation then was to bail out the weaker banks while protecting the depositors' money. Mergers have always been driven by the problem of growing 'Non-Performing Assets' that curtail the availability of bank funds, affecting investment and growth, and in the process turning the banks into loss-making entities, which ultimately pushes the burden to the government. In any case, it does not make much sense to create entities owned by the government that compete against each other. In the present case, too, the PSBs have been reeling under a severe NPA crisis for years. The total NPAs of PSBs stood

---

[7] As of December 2018, seven payments bank were operational in India, with the objective of harnessing the power of technology for financial inclusion by opening small savings accounts and providing payments/remittance services to migrant labourers, small businesses, low income households and others in the unorganised sectors through the digital medium.

at ₹7.9 lakh crore on 31 March 2019 because of default in corporate loan repayment. In fact, the entire financial sector has been reeling under multiple crises for some time, triggered by the 'twin balance sheet problems' of corporate entities and banks—the former not being able to repay the loans because of incomplete projects resulting in losses and banks not being able to extend further credit for want of repayment money—not to speak of the various scams that had hit the banks severely. Major among these scams were the ₹14,000 crore PNB scam perpetrated by Nirav Modi and Mehul Choski, which got exposed last year, and the huge ₹91,000 crore fraud perpetrated by the Infrastructure Leasing & Financial Services (IL&FS) in September 2018, when the nation learnt with amazing disbelief that the company was reeling under an outstanding debt of that amount, to repay which it was planning to sell its assets. Of the total debt, ₹57,000 crore were owed to the PSBs alone. The vicious cycle of low credit growth, low investment and low economic growth was set off by such triggers, bringing into focus the urgent need for recapitalisation and reform of the banking sector as a whole. The present attempt at restructuring the banking system through mergers is only a logical consequence of this process.

Neither is the proposal for such restructuring new; in fact, a similar proposal was recommended by the Committee of Financial System (The First Narasimham Committee) headed by Mr M. Narasimham, the 13th Governor of the RBI, way back in 1991:

The Committee is of the view that the system should evolve towards a broad pattern consisting of:

a) 3 or 4 large banks (including SBI) which could become international in character:

b) 8 to 10 national banks with a network of branches throughout the country engaged in 'universal' banking;

c) Local banks whose operations would be generally confined to a specific region; and

d) Rural banks (including RRBs) whose operations would be confined to the rural areas and whose business would be predominantly engaged in financing of agriculture and allied activities.[8]

---

[8] Quoted in Warrier, *India's Decade of Reforms*, 103.

Successful mergers will certainly provide impetus to the reform in the banking system and increase its momentum, enabling the Indian banks to compete effectively with the giant foreign banks; only then will Indian banks become truly globalised, which is the objective of the mergers. But the process cannot be expected to transform our banking scenario overnight; besides, the entire process has to be carefully negotiated and managed, protecting the interest of all stakeholders, among them, most importantly, the employees.

Public enterprises in the financial sector comprise the Public Sector Banks and the government-owned insurance companies as well as developmental financial institutions (DFIs).[9] In independent India, the first bank to have been nationalised was the Imperial Bank in 1956, which became the State Bank of India, the largest bank. Then, in 1969, the Congress government under Mrs Indira Gandhi had nationalised 14 major banks, and in one fell swoop, 'the operating system of the country changed, not just in politics which moved from party to person but also the economy which moved from private hands to state'.[10] There were compelling reasons for the move at that point in time—indeed, there was a 1966 before 1991. The 1965 war with Pakistan followed by two successive droughts in 1965 and 1966 afflicting almost two-thirds of the country had brought it almost to the brink of economic collapse and almost completely drained out its foreign exchange reserves due to food imports in 1966. With food crisis looming on the horizon and spiralling prices, empty forex reserves and economic growth at its lowest point in two decades, an economic crisis of an unprecedented dimension was staring at the face of the country. Just like in 1991, on 6 June 1966, the rupee was devalued by 57 per cent, from ₹4.76 to ₹7.50 to a dollar.

The response of the politicians and bureaucracy to the crisis was, however, just opposite to that in 1991. While in 1991 the command and control structure of the economy was dismantled with the help of the bureaucracy, 'In 1966, the bureaucrats did what they are best trained to do in the absence of a clear political direction: bring things

---

[9] DFIs are outside the scope of this book.
[10] Srinivasa Raghavan, *Dialogue of the Deaf*, 85.

to a halt while they figure out what they do next'.[11] Therefore, further controls were imposed, turning the country into a 'virtual autarchy'. Since there was no money to finance the 5-year plans, the Fourth Plan was given up, and a plan holiday was declared in 1966, which would continue for 3 years. With sub-zero economic growth in real terms, the Nehruvian model lay tattered at its first crisis since the independence. To salvage the economy from the brink of a collapse, Nehru's daughter, who had become the Prime Minister in January 1966 after the death of Lal Bahadur Shastri at Tashkent, would take her first major economic step by nationalising 14 banks, each with a deposit above ₹50 crore, on 19 July 1969.[12] These 14 banks[13] used to account for more than 80 per cent of the banking business in India among themselves, all of which were then to receive their orders directly from the government, that is, the Ministry of Finance.[14] Ever since, the banking sector in India has remained captive to the wills and wiles of politicians and bureaucrats. In 1980, six more banks[15] were nationalised, bringing over 90 per cent of the banking business of the country under the government's control.

The government exercises control over the banks through the Department of Financial Services headed by the Finance Secretary whose mandate covers the functioning of banks, financial institutions, insurance companies and the National Pension System. The Department coordinates the initiatives related to financial inclusion, social security and credit flow to the key sectors of the economy, especially in the rural areas, and insurance as a risk transfer mechanism; it is

[11] Ibid, 86.

[12] Bank nationalisation was done through an Ordinance initially; later, on 30 March 1971, the Ordinance became law after receiving the presidential assent. This enabling Act was the Banking Companies (Acquisition and Transfer of Undertakings) Act, 1970, which was made operative with effect from 19 July 1969.

[13] Allahabad Bank, Bank of Baroda, Bank of India, Bank of Maharashtra, Central Bank of India, Canara Bank, Dena Bank, Indian Bank, Indian Overseas Bank, Punjab National Bank, Syndicate Bank, UCO Bank, Union Bank and United Bank of India.

[14] Srinivasa Raghavan, *Dialogue of the Deaf*, 89–90.

[15] Punjab and Sind Bank, Vijaya Bank, Oriental Bank of India, Corporate Bank, Andhra Bank and New Bank of India. In 1993, New Bank of India was merged with the Punjab National Bank, bringing the number of PSBs to 19.

also responsible for managing the flagship schemes of the government[16] that require constant flow of funds through the banks. The department is responsible for policy support to PSBs, public sector insurance companies (PSICs) and DFIs like National Bank for Agriculture and Rural Development (NABARD), Small Industries Development Bank of India (SIDBI), India Infrastructure Finance Company Ltd (IIFCL), National Housing Bank (NHB), Export-Import Bank of India (EXIM Bank), Industrial Finance Corporation of India (IFCI), etc., as well as for monitoring the performance of these organisations. The legislative and policy issues pertaining to the concerned regulatory bodies, that is, the RBI, the Insurance Regulatory and Development Authority of India (IRDAI) and the Pension Fund Regulatory and Development Authority (PFRDA), are looked after by the Department as also the legislative framework relating to debt recovery.[17]

There are deep divisions among economists about whether the bank nationalisation was necessary to rescue the country from an imminent economic ruin or it was disastrous to the economy; some hold it responsible for bringing the country on the verge of a greater economic collapse in 1991. Truth probably lies somewhere in between. In 1969, the financial market was non-existent in India, more than 70 per cent of India was unbanked, globalisation was still two decades away and banking regulation was at a primitive stage, with RBI setting the bank interest rates twice a year, in April and October, aligned with the *Rabi* and *Kharif* cropping seasons respectively. Banks mostly lent their money to the government, and hence there was no motivation to expand the rural network of branches. Starved of funds, the government wanted to tap every possible source, including the rural deposits.

[16] Pradhan Mantri Jan Dhan Yojana (PMJDY), Pradhan Mantri Suraksha Bima Yojana (PMSBY), Pradhan Mantri Jeevan Jyoti Bima Yojana (PMJJBY), Pradhan Mantri Mudra Yojana (PMMY), Atal Pension Yojana (APY), Pradhan Mantri Vaya Vandana Yojana (PMVVY) and the Stand Up India Scheme, etc.

[17] In 2016, the government created the Banks Board Bureau (BBB) as an autonomous body for improving the governance of PSBs. It recommends the selection of chiefs of PSBs and government-owned financial institutions and helps banks in facing competition effectively through developing strategies and capital raising plans. The BBB emerged out of the recommendations of the P. J. Nayak Committee (Committee to Review Governance of Boards of Banks) in 2014.

The nationalisation of banks indeed had altered the banking scenario in the country by converting 'class banking' into 'mass' banking and extending the outreach of banking to the remotest parts of country, bringing banking facilities to the doorstep of the weakest sections and also leading to massive recruitment to man the newly opened branches. With profits no longer being the driving force behind banking, branch expansion became the major objective of the operations of nationalised banks to tap the money lying outside urban centres where the banks had hitherto concentrated their activities. Just before the nationalisation in June 1969, there were only 1,833 rural and 3,342 semi-urban bank branches; by March 1991, the numbers had grown to 35,206 and 11,344, respectively, and the total number of branches increased from 8,262 to 60,220. Annexure 5.2 shows the number of branches and ATMs of scheduled commercial banks (SCBs) as of June 2018.

The non-urban areas were practically unbanked before nationalisation and massive expansion in bank branches took banking into the rural areas. It would never have been possible without the nationalisation of banks, which also channelled 40 per cent of the lendable funds to what the government had defined as the priority sector, comprising agriculture, small scale industries (SSI), micro, small and medium enterprises (MSME), housing, educational loans, etc. The ratio of priority sector credit to total credit rose from 14 per cent to 38 per cent between 1969 and 1991, which was significant because a vast majority of Indian people derived, and still derive, their livelihood from these 'priority sectors', which were practically excluded from bank credit by private banks before the nationalisation. It certainly loosened the vice-like grip of private moneylenders in the rural areas, if not eliminating them altogether. PSBs helped the poorest of the poor through their Differential Rate of Interest (DRI) loans, which carried only 4 per cent interest, extended loans to thousands of women's self-help groups (SHGs) and funded rural infrastructure through the Rural Infrastructure Development Fund (RIDF). Without the PSBs, financial inclusion and the opening of 31 crore Jan Dhan Accounts would have remained a fantasy.

The 'Lead Bank' concept, designating one bank (either a PSB or a private bank) having a wide network of branches in a district as the

Lead Bank in that district, was introduced in 1969; the scheme gave a lead role to the bank to facilitate development of the district; it brought a paradigm shift in the way rural credit was disbursed and managed. The Lead Bank was supposed to act as a leader in coordinating the efforts of all credit institutions in their respective districts to increase the flow of credit to agriculture, small-scale industries and other priority sectors of the economy through the district credit plans (DCPs), and also for routing government subsidies.[18] State Level Bankers' Committees (SLBCs) were formed in all states for inter-institutional coordination and joint implementation of programs and policies by all financial institutions operating in the state. SLBC holds quarterly meetings with various banks operating in the state, and acts as an interface between the banks and the state government authorities. SBI is the convenor of SLBCs in respect of 12 states. Regional Rural Banks (RRBs), each owned by a commercial bank that would run it on commercial principles, were introduced in 1975, soon after the Emergency was imposed, initially through an Ordinance promulgated on 26 September 1975 that was later converted to an Act, the Regional Rural Banks Act, 1976, piloted by Mr Pranab Kumar Mukherjee, then a junior minister in Mrs Gandhi's Cabinet. Its stated objective was to develop the rural economy by providing credit and other facilities to agriculture, trade, commerce, industry and other productive activities in the rural areas, particularly to small and marginal farmers, agricultural labourers, artisans and small entrepreneurs. There are today 56 operational RRBs; the government is now considering bringing their numbers down to 38 or below by consolidating them through mergers with their sponsoring banks.[19] To streamline the institutional arrangements for credit flow for agricultural and rural development, the National Bank for Agriculture and Rural Development was set up in 1982.

All these expansion activities were premised on the availability of money with rural folks, on the expectation that the supply of branches

---

[18] The SBI, the country's largest lender, is the Lead bank in respect of as many as 238 districts as of August 2018.

[19] https://economictimes.indiatimes.com/industry/banking/finance/banking/consolidation-of-regional-rural-banks-on-government-agenda/articleshow/70352683.cms?from=mdr, accessed 14 December 2019.

would create the demand for their services, which did not happen for obvious reasons. Thousands of accounts were opened with minimal deposits which then became dormant. During the 1970s and 1980s, credit growth was driven not by demand from the private sector or private businesses, which would have become the real drivers of the economy, but in a control and command economy that stymied all entrepreneurial energy; private business was discouraged and the credit growth continued to be driven by public sector enterprises and the government sector, especially the state governments.[20] After the 1991 opening up of the economy and subsequent reforms since then, credit growth has been driven by the demands of the private sector; it picked up as the economy became gradually unshackled and then entered the high growth zone. Today, the slowing economy is again suffering from a low demand for credit, low investment and low consumption, each of these reinforcing the other and in turn dragging the economy in a vicious downward spiral.

While whether nationalisation has served its objectives remains a highly debatable issue, everyone agrees that the conditions have since changed, and today, nationalisation is no longer an option. Demands for privatisation of the nationalised banks are becoming stronger. The government has already diluted its stake on these banks, all of which are listed in the stock exchange, while retaining a majority stake in each, and their shares are available for purchase to the general public. But these banks have been facing stiff competition from the new generation private sector banks like the ICICI Bank, Axis Bank, HDFC Bank, etc. that are leveraging technology in a way that the PSBs cannot match. The new-age private banks are extensively using FinTech, the convergence of finance and technology to provide various banking and financial services, which has come to dominate the financial landscape and is becoming increasingly popular for the ease with which it can be used by an average, computer-literate customer. Being unable to match the service standards of the private banks, PSBs are continuously losing their market shares to them. They are also adapting to FinTech, but the private banks have established an edge in the market in this regard, which they are exploiting to eat

[20] Srinivasa Raghavan, *Dialogue of the Deaf*, 98–101.

deeper into the PSBs' market share. The Jan-Dhan-Aadhaar-Mobile trinity can extend FinTech for 'last mile' connectivity to include the rural sector into a modern banking network driven by technology, and PSBs, having a much wider rural network than any private sector bank, must use this to their advantage, even though the new technology may offset their locational advantages to some extent.[21] The Economic Survey, 2019–2020 had suggested that banks should share corporate data amongst themselves through a GSTN like PSB network and leverage big data analytics to improve their efficiency and recovery of NPAs.

The current banking scenario in India is shown in Table 5.1. While the overall credit growth in the banking sector has slowed down considerably since March 2019 for the PSBs, the slide down has been much more pronounced than in any other segment of commercial banking in India. Even after the series of rate cuts by the RBI, the demand for credit of PSBs has not picked up. The RBI has reduced the repo rate—the rate at which it lends money to SCBs—as many as five times in 2019, bringing it down from 6.5 per cent in February 2019 to 5.15 per cent in October 2019 to stimulate a sagging economy by making credit cheaper, and joined most central banks in the world to lower the cost of funds to beat a global economic slowdown, induced by trade wars as well as sluggish demand in domestic economies in Europe and other continents as well. Both in terms of growth in deposits and credits, PSBs lag way behind private sector and foreign banks. It is no wonder that they have ceded a considerable part of their market share to their private sector counterparts, even though they still dominate in the banking sector in India (Table 5.2). To quote the Economic Survey, 2019–2020 again:

> As on 20th January 2020, we note that every rupee of this taxpayer money fetches a market value of 71 paise. In stark contrast, every rupee invested in NPBs fetches a market value of ₹3.70, i.e., more than five times as much value as that of a rupee invested in PSBs.[22]

---

[21] Ranade, 'Role of "Fintech" in Financial Inclusion and New Business Models', 125–127.

[22] Government of India, Vol. I, Para 7.9.

Table 5.1 Indian Banking Sector at a Glance

	September 2019	March 2019	September 2018	March 2018	September 2017	June 2017
No. of scheduled commercial banks	141	147	149	149	148	144
Of which, Regional rural banks	45	53	56	56	56	56
			Number of reporting offices			
Rural	51,709	50,081	49,616	49,384	49,022	48,774
Semi-urban	41,202	39,063	38,674	38,481	38,120	38,230
Urban	26,523	25,498	25,438	25,307	25,067	25,131
Metropolitan	27,776	27,114	27,077	26,961	26,835	• 27,105
Total	**147,210**	**141,756**	**140,805**	**140,133**	**139,044**	**139,240**
			Annual growth rates (%)			
Aggregate deposits	10.1	9.4	8.4	6.8	8.2	12.6
Bank credit	8.9	13.1	13.1	9.5	6.5	8.0
			Population group-annual growth rates (%)			
Rural						
Aggregate deposits	12.1	10.9	9.2	8.3	17.0	20.5
Bank credit	14.8	12.4	12.9	13.0	6.5	12.3

Semi-urban

Aggregate deposits	11.2	10.1	8.9	7.8	16.2	19.7
Bank credit	12.3	12.4	14.8	16.2	11.2	12.6

Urban

Aggregate deposits	10.7	10.2	9.3	8.2	12.4	16.6
Bank credit	9.9	12.1	16.0	15.1	9.8	11.6

Metropolitan

Aggregate deposits	9.0	8.6	7.8	5.7	2.8	7.7
Bank credit	7.2	13.5	12.2	6.7	4.9	5.9

Bank group-annual growth rates (%)

Public sector banks

Aggregate deposits	6.6	6.0	4.7	3.2	6.9	11.1
Bank credit	5.2	9.2	8.7	4.7	2.1	4.4

Foreign banks

Aggregate deposits	11.7	19.2	12.0	5.8	-7.6	-1.4
Bank credit	7.7	11.1	7.7	3.9	-2.1	-8.5

Regional rural banks

Aggregate deposits	11.0	9.4	7.8	7.2	14.6	17.3
Bank credit	8.4	11.3	13.6	11.3	7.2	11.3

(Table 5.1 Continued)

(Table 5.1 Continued)

	September 2019	March 2019	September 2018	March 2018	September 2017	June 2017
Small finance banks						
Aggregate deposits	131.9	124.0	306.1	387.5	NA	NA
Bank credit	104.0	79.7	235.5	449.4	NA	NA
Private sector banks						
Aggregate deposits	16.9	15.4	18.2	17.4	14.6	19.7
Bank credit	14.4	20.2	22.8	20.9	19.0	20.3
Credit-deposit ratio (%)	**75.6**	**78.2**	**76.4**	**75.6**	**73.3**	**72.8**

Source: RBI Database in Indian Economy (dbie.rbi.org.in/DBIE).

Table 5.2 Deposits and Credit of Scheduled Commercial Banks by Bank Group, March 2018 (Figures in Brackets Indicate Share in Total)

Bank Group	Deposits (₹ Crore)			Credit (₹ Crore)	
	No. of Offices	No. of Accounts	Amount	No. of Accounts	Amount Outstanding
Public sector banks	92,362	1,433,758,420	7,646,037	88,963,657	5,543,260
	(65.1)	(75.0)	(66.9)	(45.2)	(63.2)
Foreign banks	284	4,354,049	476,533	5,632,825	367,830
	(0.2)	(0.2)	(4.2)	(2.9)	(4.2)
Regional rural banks	21,805	238,114,494	391,122	24,985,370	255,252
	(15.4)	(12.5)	(3.4)	(12.7)	(2.9)
Private sector banks	26,198	233,799,658	2,903,710	69,664,129	2,567,037
	(18.5)	(12.2)	(25.4)	(35.4)	(29.3)
Small finance banks*	1260	1,476,994	17,049	7,731,119	33,592
	(0.9)	(0.1)	(0.1)	(3.9)	(0.4)
All scheduled commercial banks	14,1909	1,911,503,615	11,434,451	196,977,100	8,766,973
	(100.0)	(100.0)	(100.0)	(100.0)	(100.0)

Source: RBI Database in Indian Economy (dbie.rbi.org.in/DBIE).

Note: *Small finance banks were created by RBI under the guidance of Government of India as public limited companies under the Companies Act, 2013, for promoting financial inclusion by extending basic banking activities to unserved and underserved sections of the population, including providing credit to small business units, small and marginal farmers, micro and small industries and unorganised entities. Small Finance Banks started operations in 2016. There were 10 small banks as of March 2018.

If the PSBs could improve their market-to-book ratio even to the level of the worst performing new private sector banks, the government would stand to gain about ₹9.1 lakh crore, which is about nine times the disinvestment target of ₹1.05 lakh crore for 2019–2020.

By and large, the PSBs have managed to achieve the targets for overall priority sector lending over the years, though there might be shortfalls in some sub-categories like agriculture or weaker sections, small and marginal farmers, etc. They are also increasingly adopting the best global banking practices in respect of asset quality management, risk management, harnessing of FinTech, building a robust cyber security architecture, financial inclusion, accounting standards, corporate governance, etc. They are also complying with Basel III standards[23] (2009) in prescribing the minimum regulatory capital requirements and in respect of buffers like the capital conservation buffer, countercyclical capital buffer and liquidity buffers (Annexure 5.3). Singed by the NPA crisis, the PSBs needed additional capital to maintain the regulatory norms, forcing the government to infuse capital into the PSBs from time to time since 2014–2015. In October 2017, the government announced a recapitalisation package of ₹2.1 lakh crore for the PSBs, of which ₹1.35 lakh crore was to have been financed through the so-called recapitalisation bonds and the rest funded through budgetary allocations and markets borrowings.[24] Out of this, during 2017–2018, ₹52,300 crore was provided to 11 PSBs that were under the Prompt Corrective Action (PCA), besides ₹35,800 to nine non-PCA PSBs. Further recapitalisation for ₹65,000 crore was planned for 2018–2019, which was subsequently enhanced to ₹1.06 lakh crore.[25]

The PCA owes its origin to the Federal Deposit Insurance Corporation Improvement Act (FDICIA) of the USA enacted in 1991, along with the introduction of risk-based deposit insurance premium. Taking a cue from the FDICIA, the RBI introduced it in December 2002 as a 'structured early intervention mechanism along the lines of the FDIC's PCA framework'. Subsequently, it was revised

---

[23] Discussed later.

[24] These bonds are not reckoned under the SLR (Statutory Liquidity ratio), nor are they tradeable.

[25] *RBI Report on Trend and Progress of Banking in India, 2017–18*, 58.

in line with the international best practices, following recommendations of the working group of the Financial Stability and Development Council (FSDC) on Resolution Regimes for Financial Institutions in India (2014) and the Financial Sector Legislative Reforms Commission (FSLRC, 2013). The latest PCA Framework, revised in April 2017, is given in Annexure 5.4. Under the PCA framework, banks with weak financial metrics are put under the RBI's watch. A bank is reckoned as risky if it slips below the norms in respect of: (a) capital adequacy ratios (CAR) (b) asset quality (NPA) and (c) profitability (ROA). The framework prescribes three risk threshold levels based on these ratios, as shown in Annexure 5.4. A bank needs to have sufficient capital at all times to continue its activities. In this regard, PCA alerts the RBI (and the depositors) if any threshold is breached, triggering a set of mandatory corrective actions depending on the particular trigger point/ threshold. It may prevent a bank from renewing or accessing costly deposits, or entering into new lines of business. Restrictions may be placed on borrowing from the interbank market, dividend distribution, branch expansion, management compensation, etc. In case a bank breaches the highest threshold, the RBI may even think of amalgamating it with another strong bank or even of winding it up. The PCA does not limit the normal lending operations of banks in any way.

In 2016–2017, 11 PSBs were put under PCA.[26] In February 2019, five of these—Bank of India, Bank of Maharashtra, Oriental Bank of Commerce, Allahabad Bank and Corporation Bank—were taken out of the PCA by the RBI after the recapitalisation money helped these banks improve their capital adequacy and other ratios. Another PSB under the PCA, Dena Bank, was merged with the Bank of Baroda with effect from April 2019. After the capital infusion announced in September 2019 as discussed earlier, the United Bank of India also came out of the PCA framework. Only four PSBs now remain under it—UCO Bank, Central Bank of India, Indian Overseas Bank and Union Bank—which are also expected to come out of PCA very soon. The Capital Adequacy Ratios of SCBs in 2017 and 2018 are shown in Table 5.3, from which it can be seen that the PSBs lag behind the private sector banks and foreign banks in this respect also.

[26] https://www.rbi.org.in/scripts/BS_SpeechesView.aspx?Id=1065#Annex_Ia, accessed 16 December 2019.

Table 5.3 Capital Adequacy of Scheduled Commercial Banks (SCBs), as on 31 March (₹ Billion)

	PSBs		Private Banks		Foreign Banks		SCBs	
	2017	2018	2017	2018	2017	2018	2017	2018
1. Capital funds	7,047	6,578	4,239	5,157	1,373	1,487	12,659	13,221
Tier 1 capital	5,480	5,270	3,643	4,470	1,292	1,407	10,414	11,147
Tier 2 capital*	1,567	1,308	596	687	81	80	2,245	2,074
2. Risk-weighted assets	58,053	5,644	27,289	31,383	7,335	7,799	92,677	95,596
3. CRAR (1 as % of 2), of which	12.1	11.7	15.5	16.4	18.7	19.1	13.7	13.8
Tier 1	9.4	9.3	13.3	14.2	17.6	18.0	11.2	11.7
Tier 2	2.7	2.3	2.2	2.2	1.1	1.0	2.4	2.2

Source: RBI, *RBI Report on Trend and Progress of Banking in India, 2017–2018*, 58.
Note: *Tier 1 capital comprises equity capital and disclosed reserves which can absorb losses as a going concern, while Tier 2 capital comprises revaluation reserves, undisclosed reserves, hybrid instruments, etc., which can be used to liquidate liabilities in the event of winding up of business.

Table 5.4 Return on Assets (RoA) and Return on Equity (RoE) of SCBs* (%)

Bank Group	RoA		RoE	
	2016–2017	*2017–2018*	*2016–2017*	*2017–2018*
PSBs	−0.1	−0.8	−2.0	−14.6
Private Sector Banks	1.3	1.1	11.9	10.1
Foreign Banks	1.6	1.3	9.1	7.2
All SCBs	0.4	−0.2	4.2	−2.8

Source: RBI, *RBI Report on Trend and Progress of Banking in India, 2017–2018*, 57.
Note: *RoA is calculated on the basis of weighted average of RoAs of individual banks in the group, weights being in the proportion of total assets of the bank as percentage of total, assets of all banks in the group. RoE = net profit/average total equity.

It is almost evident that PSBs are unable to compete with the private sector or foreign banks in terms of profitability or technology, which is obviously one reason behind their mergers to derive the economy of scale, the other reason being the possibility to exploit the existing synergies between them. In terms of profitability, PSBs are way behind the other banks, as shown in Table 5.4 and Annexure 5.5, which shows the profits earned by the SCBs during 2017–2018, a summary of which is given in Table 5.5.

During 2017–2018, except Vijaya bank, no other PSB could earn any profit or transfer a positive balance to their balance sheets. The scenario with private sector banks or foreign banks is, however, vastly different, which indicates that the banking sector as a whole is not suffering from any structural flaws, only the PSBs are. A large part of their balance sheet problems arise from their inability to handle the soaring level of NPAs, which the RBI, during the asset quality review (AQR) conducted in 2015, attributed to their aggressive lending practices, wilful default, loan frauds, corruption in some cases and also to economic slowdown. Indeed, the primary objective of recapitalisation was 'to pursue

Table 5.5 *Profits Earned by Bank Groups, 2017–2018 (₹ Crore)*

Bank Groups	Net Profit	Profit Brought Forward	Profit Available for Appropriation	Transfer to Reserves	Transfer to Proposed Dividend	Transfer to Tax on Dividend	Balance Carried Over to Balance Sheet
PSBs	−85,371	−28,730	−114,100	−11,149	188	–	−103,140
Private sector banks	41,783	105,928	147,711	18,982	8,418	246	120,065
Foreign banks	10,853	10,921	21,774	13,025	–	–	8,749
Small finance banks	297	1286	1,582	114	–	–	1,469
All SCBs	−32,438	89,405	56,967	20,972	8,606	246	27,144

Source: RBI Database in Indian Economy (dbie.rbi.org.in/DBIE).

timely resolution of NPAs'.[27] The NPAs have been at the root of their troubles and steady loss of profitability and yielding of ground to the private banks, for which the government, the unholy nexus between politicians and industrialists and a culture of crony capitalism, was far more responsible than the PSBs themselves. If they had indulged in aggressive lending, it was because they were nudged by the government and the politicians and could hardly afford not to comply, being under the command of the government. The humongous defaults in loan payments by an array of illustrious businessmen and industrialists could not have taken place without the active participation, collusion and connivance of the people who controlled the levers of the system. The likes of Vijay Mallya or Naresh Kumar Goyal hoodwinking the entire system of loan appraisal and disbursement and successfully bypassing the rigorous project appraisal standards the banks are supposed to exercise while sanctioning loans would not have been possible without the support of their friends, accomplices and beneficiaries among the political class. Today, not only the banking sector but the entire economy is paying the price of such misdemeanour; indeed, the current economic slowdown can be attributed, in a substantial measure, to the inability of the PSBs to clean up the balance sheets of their NPAs. Investment has dried up for the lack of capital in the hands of the PSBs, which are struggling to cope with the situation. The inevitable casualty has been the economic growth, which has now slumped below 5 per cent (Quarter 2, 2019–2020).

Figures 5.1 and 5.2 show the growth of NPAs for various bank groups, from which it can be readily seen that for the PSBs, there was a huge spurt in their NPAs since 2014–2015. Table 5.6 shows the gross and net NPAs of SCBs from 2005–2006 to 2016–2017, while Table 5.7 shows the gross and net NPA of individual PSBs in FY2017 and FY2018. In Table 5.8, sector-wise NPAs of SCBs are shown as on 31 March 2018, while Table 5.9 shows the bank group-wise classification of loan assets as on 31 March 2018. As per RBI guidelines,

---

[27] https://www.businesstoday.in/top-story/decoding-slowdown-despite-recapitalisation-psbs-are-high-in-npas-and-low-in-lending/story/376285.html, accessed 16 December 2019.

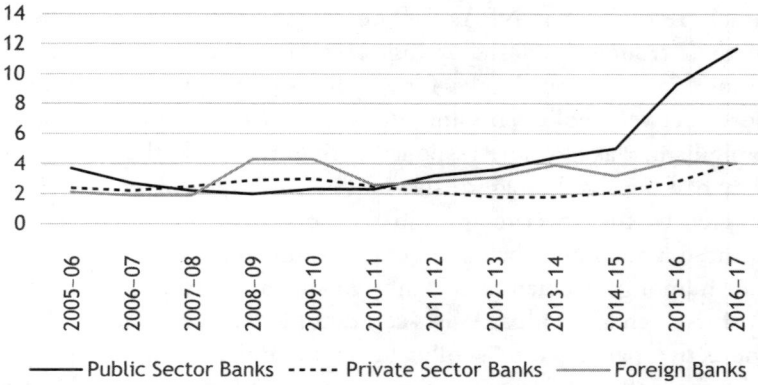

Figure 5.1 *Gross NPA as Percentage of Gross Advances*
Source: Table 5.6.

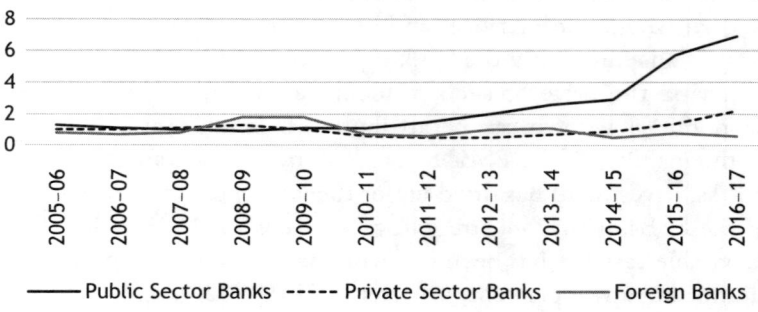

Figure 5.2 *Net NPA as Percentage of Net Advances*
Source: Table 5.6.

bank assets are classified into standard assets and non-performing assets (NPA); an NPA is a loan or advance for which the principal or interest payment has remained overdue for a period of 90 days or more. A standard asset is not an NPA and carries only the usual business risk. NPAs are further classified into 'Sub-standard', 'Doubtful' and 'Loss' assets. A sub-standard asset is one that has remained an NPA for up to 1 year; otherwise, it is a doubtful asset. Loss assets are

Table 5.6 Gross and Net NPAs of Scheduled Commercial Banks, Bank Group-wise (Amount in ₹ Billion)

Year (end March)	Advances		Non-performing Assets (NPAs)					
			Gross			Net		
				As Percentage of			As Percentage of	
	Gross	Net	Amount	Gross Advances	Total Assets	Amount	Gross Advances	Total Assets
All scheduled commercial banks								
2005–2006	15,457	15,168	518	3.3	1.9	185	1.2	0.7
2015–2016	81,711	78,965	6,116	7.5	4.7	3,498	4.4	2.7
2016–2017	84,767	81,162	7,903	9.3	5.6	4,330	5.3	3.1
Public sector banks								
2005–2006	11,347	11,063	421	3.7	2.1	146	1.3	0.7
2015–2016	58,220	55,936	5,400	9.3	5.9	3,204	5.7	3.5
2016–2017	58,664	55,572	6,847	11.7	7.0	3,831	6.9	3.9
Private sector banks								
2005–2006	4,003	3,959	114	7.0	4.0	45	3.0	2.0
2015–2016	19,727	19,393	559	2.8	1.8	267	1.4	0.8
2016–2017	22,667	22,196	919	4.1	2.6	478	2.2	1.3

(Table 5.6 Continued)

(*Table 5.6 Continued*)

Year (end March)	Advances		Non-performing Assets (NPAs)						
			Gross			Net			
				As Percentage of			As Percentage of		
	Gross	Net	Amount	Gross Advances	Total Assets	Amount	Gross Advances	Total Assets
Foreign banks in India								
2005–2006	959	976	20	2.1	1.0	8	0.8	0.4
2015–2016	3,765	3,636	158	4.2	1.9	28	0.8	0.3
2016–2017	3,436	3,323	136	4.0	1.7	21	0.6	0.3

Source: RBI Database in Indian Economy (dbie.rbi.org.in/DBIE).

Table 5.7 *Gross and Net NPA of Scheduled Commercial Banks, as on 31 March 2017 and 31 March 2018 (₹ Crore)*

Scheduled Commercial Banks	Gross NPA, 2018	Net NPA, 2018
Allahabad Bank	26,563	12,229
Andhra bank	28,124	12,637
Bank of Baroda	56,480	23,483
Bank of India	62,328	28,207
Bank of Maharashtra	18,433	9,641
Canara Bank	47,468	28,542
Central Bank of India	38,131	17,378
Corporation Bank	22,213	14,077
Dena Bank	16,361	7,839
IDBI Bank Limited	55,588	28,665
Indian Bank	11,990	5,960
Indian Overseas Bank	38,180	20,400
Oriental Bank of Commerce	26,134	14,283
Punjab and Sind Bank	7,802	4,608
Punjab National Bank	86,620	48,684
State bank of India	223,427	110,855
Syndicate Bank	25,759	13,239
UCO Bank	30,550	14,082
Union Bank of India	49,370	24,326
United Bank of India	16,552	10,316
Vijaya Bank	7,526	5,021
Public sector banks	**895,601**	**454,473**
Private sector banks	**129,335**	**64,380**
Foreign banks	**13,849**	**1,548**
Small finance banks	**893**	**436**

Source: RBI Database in Indian Economy (dbie.rbi.org.in/DBIE).

those identified by the bank as such, through its internal or external auditors or by the RBI inspectors and of which the amount has not been written off, either wholly or partially. As per an RBI circular: 'Loss asset is considered uncollectible and of such little value that its continuance as a bankable asset is not warranted, although there may be some salvage or recovery value.'[28]

From the above figures and tables, it is easy to trace the continuous slide of NPAs in respect of public sector banks. Between 2005 and 2017, the level of gross NPAs of PSBs had more than trebled, from 3.7 per cent to 11.7 per cent of their gross advances. During the same period, the gross NPAs of private sector banks had in fact decreased from 7.0 per cent to 4.1 per cent of their gross advances, while for the foreign banks, it had increased from 2.1 per cent to 4 per cent of their gross advances. At the end of 2017–2018, the Gross and the Net NPAs of PSBs stood, respectively, at ₹8.96 lakh crore and ₹4.54 lakh crore, while for the private sector banks, these stood only at ₹1.29 lakh crore and ₹64,380 crore, respectively. As we can see from Table 5.8, the major contribution to the NPAs came from the non-priority industrial sector (77.8% of total NPAs). The deterioration in the Gross NPA to Gross Advance ratio again arose mostly from larger borrowal accounts with an exposure exceeding ₹5 crore, which increased to 23.1 per cent in 2017–2018 from 18.1 per cent in 2016–2017, perhaps implying the role of crony capitalism in the whole mess.[29]

As admitted by the RBI:

> The deterioration in asset quality of Indian banks, especially PSBs, can be traced to the credit boom of 2006–2011 when bank lending grew at an average rate of over 20 per cent. Other factors that contributed to the deterioration in asset quality were lax credit appraisal and post-sanction monitoring standards; project delays and cost overruns; and absence of a strong bankruptcy regime until May 2016.[30]

However, the rise in the level of NPAs could not be arrested due to restructured advances slipping into NPAs and also because of better NPA recognition. Provisioning for the NPAs and writing them off

---

[28] https://www.rbi.org.in/Scripts/BS_ViewMasCirculardetails.aspx?id=9908#2a, accessed 17 December 2019.

[29] *RBI Report on Trend and Progress of Banking in India*, 61.

[30] Ibid, 60.

Table 5.8 Sector-wise NPAs of Banks as on 31 March 2018 (Amount in ₹ Billion)

Bank Groups	Priority Sector, of which		Agriculture		Micro and Small Enterprises		Non-priority Sector		Total NPAs	
	Amount	%*	Amount	%	Amount	%	Amount	%	Amount	%
PSBs	1,875	22.2	753	8.9	821	9.7	6,580	77.8	8,455	100
Private banks	184	18.0	78	7.6	80	7.8	840	82.0	1,024	100
Foreign banks	12	8.6	1	0.6	6	4.0	126	91.4	138	100
All SCBs	2,076	21.6	832	8.6	910	9.5	7,555	78.4	9,626	100

Source: RBI, *RBI Report on Trend and Progress of Banking in India, 2017–2018*, 63.
Note: *Share in total NPAs.

had landed the PSBs in the red. To restore them back to health, the government has to use public funds for their recapitalisation.

In a detailed, 17-page reply given to the parliamentary Estimates Committee, the former RBI Governor Raghuram Rajan had detailed the manner in which 'unscrupulous business houses were able to get a free pass from the banking system and government'. He pointed to the combination of a number of factors as being responsible for the gradual build-up of the NPA crisis, including over-optimism in the economy during 2006–2008 when a large number of bad loans had originated as banks were accepting 'higher leverage in projects, and less promoter equity' to give loans without due diligence, which was a 'historic phenomenon of irrational exuberance'. Too many loans were disbursed to 'well-connected promoters who have a history of defaulting on their loans'. Unscrupulous promoters inflated the cost of capital equipment through over-invoicing, but these were rarely checked, and a 'culture of leniency' prevailed all over. The slow growth of the economy after the global economic meltdown of 2008 after the bursting of the global credit bubble, combined with the policy paralysis that had set in at the government after the series of scams exposed political corruption during the UPA-II years, completed the cycle.[31]

Once projects got delayed, promoters lost interest, but the Bankruptcy Code was not yet enacted, and bankers could do very little against the promoters. Thus, the 'stalled projects continued as "zombie" projects, neither dead nor alive'. It was then that the real rot had started. Instead of restructuring the loans and recognising them as bad, additional loans were extended to the promoters to enable them to pay the interest and pretend that the loans were performing assets.

In reality though, because the loan was actually non-performing, bank profitability was illusory, and the size of losses on its balance sheet were ballooning because no interest was actually coming in. Unless the project miraculously recovered on its own—and with only a few exceptions, no one was seriously trying to put it back

[31] https://thewire.in/banking/raghuram-rajan-npa-parliamentary-committee-modi-government, accessed 17 December 2019.

on track—this was deceptive accounting. It postponed the day of reckoning into the future.

Malfeasance, corruption and fraud compounded the tale. 'Unscrupulous promoters who inflated the cost of capital equipment through over-invoicing were rarely checked. Public sector bankers continued financing promoters even while private sector banks were getting out, suggesting their monitoring of promoter and project health was inadequate'.[32]

For recovering the debts, debts recovery tribunals (DRTs) were set up under the Recovery of Debts Due to Banks and Financial Institutions (RDDBFI) Act, 1993 to facilitate speedy recovery of the dues without having to go through the protracted procedures of usual civil courts. The Securitization and Reconstruction of Financial Assets and Enforcement of Security Interests (SARFAESI) Act, 2002, enabled the banks and financial institutions to recover dues even without approaching the DRTs. But the amounts recovered were paltry and the process was much delayed, and the arrears kept on mounting. The inefficient recovery mechanism 'gave promoters tremendous power over lenders' as 'they could also refuse to pay unless the lender brought in more money, especially if the lender feared the loan becoming an NPA', and banks were often forced to settle the dues with low one-time settlements (OTS), absorbing the losses. It was then that the RBI created a large loan database that included all loans over ₹5 crore, which was shared with all banks to help them identify early warning signals or signs of distress.[33]

To clean up the balance sheets of banks, Rajan wanted to stop the ever-greening of projects by banks who wanted to avoid restructuring of the projects without calling them NPAs. Monitoring was strengthened and a Strategic Debt Restructuring (SDR) scheme was introduced so as to enable the banks to displace weak promoters by converting their debt to equity. All these effectively 'created a resolution system that replicated an out-of-court bankruptcy. Banks now

[32] Ibid.
[33] Ibid.

Table 5.9 *Bank Group-wise Classification of Loan Assets, as on 31 March 2018 (Amount in ₹ Billion)*

Bank Groups	Standard Assets Amount	%*	Sub-standard Assets Amount	%	Doubtful Assets Amount	%	Loss Assets Amount	%
PSBs	46,021	84.5	2,053	3.8	5,936	10.9	465	0.9
Private banks	24,506	96.0	272	1.1	700	2.7	52	0.2
Foreign banks	3,495	96.2	38	1.1	84	2.3	16	0.4
All SCBs	74,022	88.5	2,364	2.8	6,720	8.0	534	0.6

Source: RBI, *RBI Report on Trend and Progress of Banking in India, 2017–18*, 62.
Note: *Share in total NPAs.

had the power to resolve distress'. RBI completed an objective Asset Quality Review (AQR) in October 2015, which it shared with banks. Banks were simply refusing to recognise bad loans; the procedures for recognition were not uniform and varied from bank to bank. Adequate provisions were not made against the long-time NPAs, nor was anything being done to set the projects back on track. All this slowed credit growth. Until the Bankruptcy Code came, promoters did not fear losing their firms, but even after the code came, they tried to undermine the integrity of the process and thwart it through frivolous appeals. Our judicial process was thoroughly unequipped to handle the cases of each NPA through bankruptcy.[34]

Table 5.9 shows that as of March 2018, the NPAs constituted nearly 15 per cent of the assets of PSBs (aggregate of its time and demand deposits), which was much higher compared to either the private sector or the foreign banks. Doubtful assets in particular constituted the largest chunk of NPAs at nearly 11 per cent. Even the loss assets stood at nearly 1 per cent, much higher than in any other segment. The corresponding percentages in March 2017 for NPAs, Doubtful assets and Loss assets were respectively 12.5, 9.0 and 0.3. Thus, we can see that there has been a steep deterioration in the quality

[34] Ibid.

of assets of the PSBs, while neither the private banks nor the foreign banks showed such deterioration. As the RBI observed, 'on top of the elevated level of stressed assets, fresh slippages rose during 2017–2018 in respect of PSBs as against a decline in the previous year. This is largely attributable to restructured advances slipping into NPAs and a decline in standard advances'.[35]

The cleaning of balance sheets of banks is the biggest problem today facing not only the banks but the entire economy. Until this problem is settled, the economy will remain hostage to misdirected policies, crony capitalism, unwelcome controls and unholy nexuses, with collaboration or connivance by authorities and people in power. The oversight machinery of the banks also remains extremely weak and ineffective, as demonstrated by the PNB scam and ILFS fiasco.

The PNB–Nirav Modi scam of 2018 had exposed a fraud, the magnitude of which was never before seen in any PSB or PSE in India. The script looked familiar though, played out so many times by several illustrious pioneers like Vijay Mallya—use high connections to get huge loans from PSBs without any collateral, use the money for profiteering by cheating through innovative Ponzi mechanism or laundering, park the profit outside the country and keep the travel papers ready to flee to the safety of a foreign land just when the scam is about to break with cyclonic fury. Then, a familiar old pattern follows. Stock markets go into a tumble, raids are made on empty cages from where the bird has already flown away along with the feed, left out assets are attached, probes are launched, fiery speeches are made inside and outside the parliament and accusations flow thick and fast, while the bank that takes the hit meekly provides for the loss at the cost of the public exchequer. Then, everything is back to business as usual; probes lose their steam, names of the high and mighty involved in the scam are never revealed, recovery from the seized assets gets entangled in legal complications and new fraud entrepreneurs enter the field using the same old rules of the game, while the short arm of the Indian law never manages to reach the fraudsters who continue to wallow in luxury in the foreign shores, enjoying the fruits of their

---

[35] *RBI Report on Trend and Progress of Banking in India*, 61.

ill-gotten wealth. Just to reckon the cost to the public exchequer, between 2008 and 2017, the government has infused capital of ₹1.19 lakh crore into the PSBs, with another ₹2.11 lakh crore on the pipeline to recapitalise them to tide over their NPA crisis.[36]

The scam whose magnitude has now swelled to ₹14,000 crore has exposed several serious chinks in the armour of our banking and financial systems, nearly two-thirds of which are controlled by the PSBs with which most citizens trust their life's savings. It has exposed not only the absolute lack of internal control in them, but brought into question the accountability of the banking regulator RBI itself. The script of hundreds of fictitious Letters of Undertaking (LOUs)[37] issued without any security and orchestrated through the global SWIFT[38] system bypassing the Banks Core Banking System to remain undetected for 7 years only through the machinations of some middle level managers is like a phantom story, except that it is not true. We shall never find out the real-life characters hiding comfortably in the shadow of Gokuldas Shettys, now that Nirav Modi is gone, like Vijay Mallya. While RBI must share a part of the blame, so must the PNB's own Board of Directors, the Ministry of Finance, the Ministry of Financial Services, the Bank Board Bureau, the Internal and External Auditors of the Bank and CVC—all these agencies were supposed to exercise effective oversight, but none smelled a whiff of what was going on right underneath their noses for 7 long years. After the scam erupted in full force, each was busy blaming the others and scurrying for cover. The finance ministry remained blissfully clueless about the affair, and in what looked like a joke, the PNB was also given an award for excellence in vigilance by the CVC in 2017. As the Nobel Laureate Joseph E. Stiglitz had said, 'We have banks that are not only too big to fail, but too big to be held accountable'.

It is pointless to dwell on how the Nirav Modi–Mehul Choski duo had used the LOUs in a superb Ponzi scheme to defraud their naive

[36] Bhattacharjee, 'Regulate, Don't Privatise'.

[37] A Letter of undertaking (LOU) is a bank guarantee under which it allows its customer to raise funds from another bank (usually a foreign branch) as short term credit.

[38] SWIFT is a messaging network used by banks to securely transmit information and instructions through a standardised system of codes.

and trusting bankers and fooled them. Public anger is giving way to demands for the privatisation of PSBs. The demands are indeed justified as the government has no business to be in a business that it cannot manage. However, privatisation may not be the answer because the issue is regulation rather than ownership. Besides, there is absolutely no political appetite for privatisation of PSBs. An overwhelming majority of Indians still would trust their money with PSBs rather than private banks on the mistaken belief that their money is safer with the former, and no government, irrespective of the political dispensation, would dare push for privatisation and alienate such a huge chunk of voters. With the privatisation of PSBs thus being a no-brainer, all that the government can do is to offload their stakes in PSBs and merge them to achieve better economics of scale, which at last it is doing.

Banks cannot be the agents of change; they can only play a supportive role. Nationalisation could have become a game changer if it was backed up by appropriate policies and structural reforms of the sector; but, unfortunately, the government strategy remained short-sighted. Once politicians got unfettered control over the PSBs, cronyism, corruption and interference became the order of the day, when we actually needed a renewed focus on management, strengthening of regulatory institutions and assurance of public scrutiny. After liberalisation, the PSBs were made to compete with the private sector banks including foreign banks and chase quick profits that could only come from the corporate loans. However, the bank management still remained captive to the politician-bureaucratic nexus, which forced the banks to give loans to industries and people regardless of their viability. The result was the NPA crisis and ballooning of defaulting loans. The strategy went completely berserk.

PSBs in India lost at least ₹22,743 crore owing to fraudulent banking activities between 2012 and 2016, according to an IIM-Bangalore study. The government informed the parliament recently that 25,600 cases of banking fraud worth ₹1.79 billion were reported till 21 December 2017. It is not that only the PSBs were vulnerable. According to data released by the apex bank for the first 9 months of FY17, approximately 455 cases of fraud transactions—each of ₹1,00,000 or above—were detected at ICICI Bank; 429 at State Bank of India, 244 at Standard Chartered Bank and 237 at HDFC Bank. Most of these frauds were perpetrated through the collusion of bank employees themselves, indicating loose internal controls.

Banking scams have also been surfacing at an astonishing frequency since a long time, involving almost all PSBs. Side by side, bad loans have been increasing alarmingly; between 2013 and 2017, their amount has quadrupled from ₹28,417 crore to over ₹1.1 lakh crore. While some of this would be due to interest being added, the quantum of the increase is too large to be accounted by interest alone. 'Wilful default'—defaults despite the borrowers' paying capacity—has also been rising. The cumulative total of more than 50 companies or groups each with over ₹250 crore of 'wilful default' works out to about ₹48,000 crore, 80 per cent of which is due to PSBs alone. RBI data shows that between April 2013 and December 2016, all scheduled commercial banks, including private ones, lost ₹66,066 crore to 17,504 frauds, in which there were, 2,084 cases (12%) involving insiders. Still, as history has shown, a scam has nothing to do with ownership. Lehman Brothers, Royal Bank of Scotland or Merrill Lynch were not controlled by their governments, yet collapsed due to scams. The elephant in the room is the lack of a strict and effective regulatory mechanism that we have never cared to establish.

The author's case is not that PSBs should not be privatised, but that the regulatory system that covers private banks as well as PSBs in India should be made reliable, effective and unfailing, with multiple checks inserted to cover all identified risks. The existing laws and rules are more or less adequate and may only need a little re-engineering to strengthen oversight. Audit of banks is one essential instrument of this oversight.

Banks typically are subjected to four kinds of audits: statutory audit, which is basically an audit of the bank's financial statements by auditors appointed by the RBI; internal audit conducted by the bank itself; a concurrent audit of transactions by internal or external auditors; and inspection done by the RBI. Under the concurrent audit system, each bank branch is audited by not one but two teams of auditors; it is a part of the banks' early warning system to detect frauds and irregularities. None of these mechanisms, not even concurrent audits or internal audit, could detect the scam that was going on for 7 long years.

The RBI itself is audited under section 50 of the RBI Act, 1934, by auditors appointed by the central government. Though section 51 of the Act enables the government to appoint the CAG of India as auditor of the RBI, the provision has never even been invoked. The government has never allowed the CAG to audit the RBI. Even the PSBs, though they qualify as government companies with majority stake held by the government, are out of the ambit of CAG's audit, a fact that remains not mostly unknown to the general public. The CAG has the authority to audit government companies under section 19 of the CAG'S (Duties, Powers and Conditions of Service) Act, which mandates the CAG to conduct audit of government companies in accordance with the provisions of the Companies Act. Section 143 of the Companies Act, 2013 empowers the CAG to appoint the statutory auditor and direct him/her in auditing the accounts of the government company. The CAG also has the authority to conduct a supplementary audit over and above the statutory audit conducted by the statutory auditor appointed by him/her, and report the results thereof to the parliament or state legislature, as the case may be. It may be mentioned that the CAG has the power to penalise the statutory auditor if he/she fails in his/her duties as the auditor, a power which he/she exercises judiciously and regularly. The appointment of auditors is done following a robust and transparent process, and there has rarely been any complaint against the objectivity of the process. It is partly to the credit of the robustness of the CAG's oversight that even in an age when scams erupt with astonishing regularity in almost every entity under the control of the government, no major scam of the public sector companies has as yet shocked us into numbness like the way the PNB scam has.

PSBs are governed by the Banking Regulation Act, 1949 and Banking Companies (Acquisition and Transfer of Undertakings) Act, 1970. The Banking Regulation Act, 1949 gives wide powers to the RBI to control advances by banking companies and to issue directions thereon (section 21), appoint auditors or order special audit of banks if necessary (section 30), inspect banks (section 35), remove managerial and other staff, appoint additional Directors, supersede the Board of Directors and override other laws in this regard, including imposition of punishments for certain activities (section 36). Despite these statutory provisions, the RBI complains of inadequate powers. It is more likely that it has not been exercising its existing powers properly. It may draw some lessons from Mr T. N. Seshan and Mr Vinod Rai who made their institutions immensely powerful even within the existing framework of laws.

PSBs are audited by auditors appointed by the RBI under section 10 of the Banking Companies (Acquisition and Transfer of Undertakings) Act, 1970, which provides that auditors will be appointed by the central government with the approval of the RBI and will submit their report to the central government, which will be placed in the parliament. The RBI sometimes picks the auditors from the panels prepared by the CAG, but unlike the government companies, the CAG exercises no power of direction or supplementary audit of their reports, and neither does he/she review their performance or penalise those violating the auditing standards. The RBI has now delegated the powers to appoint auditors to the Board of Directors of individual banks, and the process of their appointment is shrouded in opaqueness, in which the possibility of conflict of interest in the appointment process cannot be ruled out.

Most PSBs also have a large number of branches, which is the pivot in respect of sanction of loans and their disbursement, security or collateral, documentation and recovery. Since most of these transactions are handled at the branch level, their audit naturally assumes extreme importance. There are multiple statutory auditors of a bank, and how the work gets distributed among them remains a grey area, which leads to lot of dilution and diffusion of responsibility and hence laxity in audit. The principal statutory auditors often fail to take into cognisance the poor internal controls existing within a branch.

Statutory auditors are chartered accountants, and are bound by the rules and ethical standards of the Institute of Chartered Accountants of India (ICAI), which is a self-regulatory body established by the parliament, and that, probably is its biggest flaw. ICAI includes government representatives, usually generalist bureaucrats, as part of its oversight who often lack the acumen that is required in understanding accounting and auditing to be able to exercise effective oversight; it also creates unmitigated conflicts of interest.

One argument proffered against the CAG audit of PSBs is that the CAG may not have the necessary expertise for the audit of PSBs or the RBI. But the expertise is not required under the existing regime, as these audits are kept outside the CAG's purview. Once the CAG is given the responsibility for auditing these, it is only a matter of time before the necessary expertise is acquired and inculcated by its staff. The CAG conducts three kinds of audit: compliance audit, wherein he/she checks compliance to rules, regulations and procedures; financial audit, which is basically an audit of financial statements and disclosure requirements; and performance audit, which is focused on performance, where he/she may question the rationale for giving a loan. If the government wants to protect the autonomy of the banks, the CAG may be debarred from conducting a performance audit of the banks. But he/she will still be able to see that the disclosure requirements are fully met, that rules and procedures are fully complied with and that risks have been adequately covered. PSBs will then unquestionably benefit from the CAG's expertise in appointment, regulation and supplementary audit. However, there have to be other mechanisms as well.

In the aftermath of the Enron scandal, governments realised the need for creating a non-government entity to regulate the audit profession. Before this, the audit profession was self-regulated even in the United States. This led to the creation of the Public Company Accounting Oversight Board (PCAOB), a private-sector, non-profit corporation created by the Sarbanes–Oxley Act of 2002 to oversee the audits of public companies and other issuers in order to protect the interests of investors and further the public interest in the preparation of informative, accurate and independent audit reports. The conflict of interest in self-regulatory bodies was recognised, inhibiting their ability to protect the interests of investors. All PCAOB rules and standards require approval by the US Securities and Exchange Commission (SEC). Through the PCAOB, for the first time, US public companies were subjected to external and independent oversight instead of self-regulation. PCAOB discharges four primary functions in exercising the oversight of auditors: registration, inspection, standard setting and enforcement, and is a member of the International Forum of Independent Audit Regulators (IFIAR). These actions helped strengthen the quality of auditing in the US.

We now have a National Financial Reporting Authority (NFRA) for the enforcement of accounting and auditing standards and for exercising oversight functions in respect of the work of auditors, but we still need a mechanism for IFIAR. We have a Quality Review Board (QRB) set up under section 28A of the Chartered Accountants Act, 1949, which is mandated to conduct independent audit quality reviews. QRB is not yet a member of IFIAR, for which it needs to demonstrate its independence. The IFIAR membership consists of 52 independent audit regulators from around the world, besides observers like Basel Committee on Banking Supervision, European Commission, Financial Stability Board, International Association of Insurance Supervisors, International Organization of Securities Commissions, Public Interest Oversight Board and the World Bank.

Once we align ourselves with such and other international organisations and allow the CAG access to RBI and PSB accounts, much of the malaise afflicting the banking sector can be effectively addressed. The privatisation of banks is a knee-jerk reaction, and if we privatise without strengthening their regulation, the PSBs will continue to be mired in similar scandals. Some serious reform of the banking sector is urgently called for in this regard.

Prior to 1991, the banking sector reforms revolved around application of monetary policy through adjustment of Cash Reserve Ratio (CRR), Statutory Liquidity Ratio (SLR), deregulation of interest rates and widening the scope of priority sector lending and strengthening the institutional framework through better internal control systems. Significant structural reforms were introduced in the sector only after the 1991 liberalisation, with the setting up of the first Narasimham Committee in 1991, as referred to earlier. The committee had made far-reaching recommendations, many of which were accepted by the government. Among its recommendations were reduction in the SLR and CRR rates, introduction of market-determined interest rates, structural reorganisation of the banking sector by reducing the number of banks, providing autonomy to the banking sector and removal of dual control of banks by the RBI and the government.

Another committee under Mr Narasimham, the second Narasimham Committee, also known as the Banking Sector Committee, was set up in 1998 to review the banking reforms and suggest measures for strengthening the financial system. The committee examined the issues of capital adequacy, bank mergers, bank legislation, etc., and made almost a hundred recommendations for reforming the banking sector and aligning the Indian banking practices with the global norms and best practices. Most of its technical recommendations like those dealing with income recognition norms, risk weights, capital adequacy, etc. were accepted by the government, but those that would have reduced government's control over banks and financial institutions were cold-shouldered.

The most significant recommendation of the committee which was accepted and implemented immediately afterwards and which altered the course of banking in India by bringing in a convergence with the global banking practices was the introduction of the so-called 'Prudential Norms' to ensure the safety of depositors' money, soundness of bank advances and solvency of the banks. The RBI has since issued a number of guidelines on the prudential norms from time to time to ensure that banks follow these norms.[39] The norms covered the three aspects of accounting: income recognition, asset classification and provisioning. One of the norms for income recognition mandated that interest should not to be debited to the loan accounts on an accrual basis to inflate the bank profit notionally but only on the cash basis to reflect reality. Asset classification included the introduction of sub-standard, doubtful and loss assets to be recognised as non-performing assets, as discussed earlier. Provisioning for these is necessary to make the balance sheet reflect the true state of financial affairs of the banks as it should. 'At present, there is no requirement in India for a general provision on standard assets. In the Committee's

---

[39] These guidelines are available at https://www.rbi.org.in/scripts/BS_ViewMasCirculardetails.aspx?id=5090

view a general provision, say, of 1 per cent would be appropriate and RBI should consider its introduction in a phased manner',[40] the committee had observed. In response, the RBI introduced a general provision of 0.25 per cent from 1999–2000.

Prudential norms thus imparted transparency to the operations of banks by focussing on adequacy and correctness of disclosures in accounting and financial statements of banks. A detailed discussion of the recommendations of the committee is beyond the scope of this book, but the other major recommendations of the committee included norms for capital adequacy requirements that should factor in the market risks in addition to credit risks. The committee prescribed the same risk weights on government-guaranteed advances as in the case of other advances and prescribed a minimum capital to risk (weighted) assets ratio (CRAR). It observed:

> The Committee believes that in the case of future loans, the income recognition and asset classification and provisioning norms should apply even to Government guaranteed advances in the same manner as for any other advance. For existing Government guaranteed advances, RBI, Government and banks may work out a mechanism for a phased rectification of the irregularities in these accounts.[41]

Regarding asset quality management, the committee observed, very correctly: 'No other single indicator reflects the quality of assets and their impact on banks' viability than the NPA figures in relation to advances';[42] it recommended that the ratio of non-performing assets to the total assets must be reduced. For banks with a high NPA portfolio, the committee recommended adoption of one of the two alternative approaches: transferring all doubtful and loss assets to an Asset Reconstruction Company (ARC) that would issue NPA Swap Bonds representing the realisable value of the assets transferred; alternatively, the individual banks should issue bonds, which could form

[40] Narasimham Committee Report, Para 3.36 (1998): https://rbidocs.rbi.org.in/rdocs/PublicationReport/Pdfs/24157.pdf

[41] Ibid, Para 3.37.

[42] Ibid, Para 3.19.

part of its Tier–II capital, backed by government guarantees, to help them 'bolster capital adequacy which has been eroded because of the provisioning requirements for NPAs'.[43]

Dealing with the system and methods in Banks, the committee recommended the institution of an independent loan review mechanism, especially for large borrowal accounts. On structural issues, it emphatically stated that a large bank should only be merged with other large banks and not be merged with weaker banks, which should be either transformed into profitable entities or closed down. The committee made many other recommendations covering practically all areas of functioning of the banking sector, including gradual phasing out of the Directed Credit Program 'that has a proportionately higher share in NPA portfolio of banks and has been one of the factors in erosion in the quality of bank assets',[44] technological upgradation, providing operational flexibility and sufficient autonomy to banks, financial integration with NBFCs, development of human resources, strengthening oversight, vigilance and monitoring, etc.

As it correctly emphasised: 'A strong and efficient banking system functionally diverse and geographically widespread, is critical to the attainment of the objectives of creating a market-driven, productive and competitive economy'. On leveraging information technology for promoting banking, it said:

Globally, banking and financial systems have undergone fundamental changes because of the ongoing revolution in information and communications technology. Information technology and electronic funds transfer systems have emerged as the twin pillars of modern banking development. This phenomenon has largely bypassed the Indian banking system although most technologies that could be considered suitable for India have been introduced in some diluted form. The Committee feels that requisite success in this area has not been achieved.[45]

---

[43] Ibid, Para 3.28–3.29.
[44] Ibid, Para 3.31.
[45] Ibid, Para 4.66.

The committee also spoke against the practice of 'evergreening' of loans by making fresh advances to borrowers and promoters for settling their interest dues and thereby avoiding the loans from being classified as NPAs; as we have seen, this was one reason for the NPA crisis that the PSBs are currently reeling from.

The recommendations of the two Narasimham Committees led to many significant reforms in the banking sector in India, especially in relation to the PSBs. The government has implemented many of its suggestions, including deregulation in the entry of private banks, deregulation of interest rates, introduction of capital adequacy norms, introduction of internationally accepted norms of income recognition norms, listing of PSBs in stock exchanges to subject them to market discipline, diversification of banks' operations, lowering of CRR and SLR, etc.

The second Narasimham Committee was preceded by the so-called Basel-I guidelines issued in 1988 by the Basel Committee on Banking Supervision (BCBS). The BCBS, headquartered at Basel, Switzerland, with 45 members from 28 jurisdictions, mostly the central banks and Financial Institutions (FIs) as members, sets the global standards for the prudential regulation of banks. The Basel-I guidelines focussed almost entirely on credit risk and structure of risk weights for banks introduced by the Basel Capital Accord, a capital measurement system. On the premise that for safety, a bank must have adequate capital to cover the risks of investment of such capital, it suggested a minimum capital requirement of 8 per cent of risk-weighted assets (RWA) for banks; the risk actually varies from asset to asset, which is why a weighted average needs to be taken. India formally adopted Basel-I norms in 1999, but many of the recommendations of the second Narasimham Committee complied with these norms. By the turn of the century, the entire world was connected through an intricate and interconnected global financial network, and banking operations of one country could not be dissociated from those of other countries; this demanded international cooperation. Basel norms were the outcome of this international cooperation. The consequences of such interconnectedness of financial networks and the turbulence that the collapse of the banking system in one country can cause across the world were demonstrated with devastating effect during the global economic recession of 2008. It was thus felt that to protect the safety, security and stability of the banking system, uniform standards and norms must be adopted by all nations. Three Basel norms have emerged so far as a result of international cooperation, each prescribing more stringent safeguards and standards than the one before.

Basel norms are based on three pillars: (a) minimum regulatory capital requirements based on RWAs; (b) supervisory review process involving regulatory tools and frameworks; and (c) enforcement of market discipline through transparency requiring adequate disclosures. In 2004, Basel–II guidelines were issued, which prescribed a minimum capital adequacy requirement of 8 per cent of RWAs, better risk management techniques, increased disclosure requirements and mandatory disclosure of risk exposure by individual banks to the Central Bank. After the crisis of 2008, when it was realised that banks even in many advanced economies were under-capitalised, over-leveraged and over-dependent on short-term funding and hence vulnerable to risks, Basel-III guidelines were issued in 2010. The RBIs guidelines are all Basel-compliant and some are even more stringent than the Basel norms. The Basel-III norms focussed on the four vital parameters: capital, leverage, funding and liquidity, prescribing limits for each in terms of ratios. These norms, as already stated, are forcing the government to recapitalise the PSBs at the cost of public funds; these have also indirectly nudged the government towards the merger and amalgamation of PSBs to harness their synergies and achieve the economies of scale so as to transform them into important global players.

The 14th Finance Commission recommended that a 'Financial Sector Public Enterprises Committee should be appointed to examine and recommend parameters for appropriate future fiscal support to financial sector public enterprises, recognising the regulatory needs, the multiplicity of units in each activity and the performance and functioning of the DFIs'.[46] It noted the huge capital requirement of

---

[46] Ibid, Para 16.49. Public sector financial institutions can be broadly classified as public sector banks, public sector insurance companies and the developmental finance institutions (DFIs) like NABARD, IDBI, etc.

the PSBs in the context of Basel-III guidelines (then ₹2.84 lakh crore), and observed that the fiscal costs of such recapitalisation need to be lowered 'by restricting it to select and better performing public sector banks, instead of an across-the-board policy of covering all of them, in view of the competing demands on available budgetary resources', while leaving the non-performing public sector banks 'to manage their asset portfolio and growth in tune with the available capital'. It also suggested a pruning of their numbers.[47]

Indian PSBs are today trying to adapt to the dynamic and fast-changing global financial system through various strategies. Operating in an increasingly complex and risky environment, especially in a digitally connected and hence riskier world, they are facing operational complexities like never before. Reeling under the NPA crisis, they are presently passing through rough weather. Changing their business strategies through product diversification and optimal use of technology with fool proof security, improving their internal systems and procedures, etc. are some of the ways in which they are trying to cope with the challenges facing them. The PNB and IL&FS frauds notwithstanding, the Indian banking system remains one of the safest in the world.

However, some of the important issues that still remain unaddressed include independence of the PSBs from stifling governmental control. PSBs enjoy autonomy only in name; in reality, they are under strict control by the government, which often uses them for its narrow political and electoral purposes. In this perspective, as discussed in the context of PSEs in Chapter 7 of the book, the PSBs also need to be shielded from direct governmental interference by establishing the intermediary of a Holding Company or a Banking Commission. The 14th Finance Commission, however, believed that a holding company might 'result in indirect and non-transparent fiscal obligations' for the Centre.[48] However, it is very much possible, and also desirable, to distance the PSBs from the government through a Holding Company or Banking

---

[47] Report of the fourteenth Finance Commission, Para 16.46.
[48] Ibid, Para 16.46.

Commission structure without creating additional liability for the government, as explained in Chapter 7, following a similar mechanism as suggested for the PSEs. As Raghuram Rajan had submitted to the Estimates Committee of the parliament:

> Public sector bank boards are still not adequately professionalized, and the government rather than a more independent body still decides board appointments, with the inevitable politicization. The government could follow the P J Naik Committee49 report more carefully. Eventually strong boards should be entrusted with all decisions but held responsible for them.[50]

Many of the Boards remain leaderless for long periods of time, and there is no succession plan in place. Political and patronage considerations rather than professional consideration often play a role in deciding these appointments, and all governments like pliant Boards that concur with their nominees, often by ignoring commercial compulsions. The Banks Board Bureau experiment has not been particularly successful in inducting outside talent and truly professional leaders in the PSB Boards.

Rajan identified a few important bottlenecks in the functioning of PSBs that must be addressed to make them truly competitive, such as strengthening their risk management processes and making the process of project appraisal and monitoring much more robust to lower the risk of project NPAs, putting in place 'an appropriately flexible capital structure', reinforcing the recovery process and setting of reasonable and realistic credit targets for the banks by the government including blanket loan waivers, besides ensuring that the bankruptcy process 'is effective, transparent, and not gamed by unscrupulous promoters.'[51] Even if some of these measures are implemented with earnestness and sincerity, it will not take long for the PSBs to be rejuvenated and

---

[49] P. J. Nayak Committee was set up in 2014 by the RBI to review the governance of the Boards of Banks.

[50] https://thewire.in/banking/raghuram-rajan-npa-parliamentary-committee-modi-government, accessed 17 December 2019.

[51] Ibid.

transmute into global champions, with the size and outreach that they already possess.

One of industries critical for industrial development is insurance. Businesses entail risk, and hence security against unforeseen risk that may cause loss to businesses is essential for enterprises to thrive. Thus, the growth of the insurance sector in a country captures and reflects the growth of the country's economy itself. Life insurance provides essential security to families of individuals, but for both life and non-life insurance, the commitment by policy holders is usually for a long term, and the assets of insurance companies thus represent long-term capital, a pool for investments in long-term projects like infrastructure or capital intensive projects that have long gestation periods.

Like the banks, insurance companies in India were also national-ised to protect the interests of policyholders. The state-owned Life Insurance Corporation of India (LIC) was established by an act of the parliament in 1956, and the General Insurance Corporation was created as a public sector company in 1972 for the non-life insurance business. They had a complete monopoly on insurance businesses in India until the 1991 economic liberalisation, after which the industry was opened up to the private sector, enabling them to collaborate with foreign insurance companies that had been eyeing the huge Indian market for quite some time. Thus, the number of insurance companies proliferated after 1991, needing regulation. The regula-tory body for the sector, the IRDAI, was created by the Insurance Regulatory and Development Authority Act, 1999 (IRDAA). The insurance sector has registered vibrant growth since liberalisation, which continues even now.

As of March 2019, there were 59 insurance companies in India—52 from the private sector—with 24 in life insurance and 35 in non-life insurance companies. The list of all insurance companies is shown in Annexure 5.6. Of the seven public sector companies (excluding the GIC Re, the only Indian domestic reinsurance company), LIC remains the only life insurance company in India. The performance of all of them is more or less at par with their private sector counterparts, with very high claim settlement ratios, as shown in Annexure 5.6. Except for the National Insurance Company and to some extent the United

Indian Insurance Company, the solvency ratios of the PSICs are also above the norm of 1.5 mandated by the IRDAI.[52]

All general insurance businesses in India were nationalised by the General Insurance Business (Nationalisation) Act, 1972 (GIBNA), empowering the Government of India to take over 55 insurance companies and general insurance operations of 52 other companies in India. The General Insurance Corporation of India (GIC) was incorporated in November 1972 as per section 9(1) of GIBNA for the purpose of overseeing the business of general insurance in India by transferring all the government stake in the newly created entity. After the mergers and consolidation of these 107 nationalised insurance companies, GIC was reorganised as a holding company with four fully owned subsidiary companies: National Insurance Company, New India Assurance Company, Oriental Insurance Company and United India Insurance Company.[53]

The IRDAA came into force in April 2000. It also introduced an amendment to the GIBNA, which removed the 'exclusive privilege of GIC and its subsidiaries carrying on general insurance in India', ending the monopoly of the public sector on insurance business in India and re-notifying the GIC as a reinsurer. GIC's supervisory role over its four subsidiaries ended from March 2003 after an amendment to the GIBNA when the ownership of all the five companies was vested with the Government of India. Since November 2000, GIC has been operating as the sole Indian reinsurer[54] in the domestic reinsurance market as GIC Re, providing reinsurance to all direct general insurance companies in the Indian market. The insurance sector liberalisation in 1999–2000 opened up the Indian insurance market to foreign

---

[52] https://www.investindia.gov.in/team-india-blogs/overview-insurance-industry-india, accessed 20 December 2019.

[53] https://www.gicofindia.com/en/about-us/history-in-brief, accessed 21 December 2019.

[54] Reinsurance is actually a form of insurance for insurance companies. Insurance companies purchase reinsurance policies for mitigating their risks and reducing their exposure to events that can cause severe losses. By limiting the potential loss an insurer, reinsurance protects the insurance companies from financial ruin, and thus also protects their customers' interests.

companies. There are now 10 foreign reinsurance companies operating in India. GIC Re has two foreign subsidiaries: GIC Re, South Africa and GIC Re, India, Corporate Member Ltd. in UK. It has extended operations in four overseas countries, with offices in London, Moscow, Dubai and Kuala Lumpur. The four other PSICs provide insurance services to the customers catering to almost all segments of general insurance business. With effect from 1 April 2013, Indian insurance companies were required by law to cede 5 per cent of every policy value to GIC Re, subject to some restrictions. With diversified operations, GIC Re is today emerging as a key reinsurer in Southeast Asia, the Middle East, Africa and Europe.

Life Insurance Corporation of India (LIC) was incorporated on 1 September 1956 after the amalgamation of 243 companies under the Insurance Act of 1956. It continues to remain the most significant player in the domestic life insurance market with a huge network of branches spread throughout the length and breadth of India. It also operates in many foreign markets through joint ventures, such as in Bangladesh, Sri Lanka, Nepal, Bahrain, Saudi Arabia, Kenya, etc.[55] LIC also has a wholly owned subsidiary, Life Insurance Corporation (Singapore) Pte Ltd.[56] In the 2020–2021 Union Budget presented on 1 February 2020, the Union Finance Minister outlined the government's plan to disinvest LIC to raise ₹90,000 crore for bridging the fiscal deficit, and that would require the listing of LIC in the stock exchange. LIC is the highest value public company in India, and investors would be looking forward to the issue of its shares. If managed well, the yield from it should exceed the government's expectations. The number of offices and employees of the PSICs are shown in Table 5.10.

Even though the market share of the private sector has increased over the years, in the life insurance sector, the sole public sector company, LIC, still dominates the market with a share of 66 per cent (as of January 2019), while in the non-life insurance sector, private companies enjoy a market share of 55 per cent (as of January 2019).

---

[55] LIC has 8 Zonal Offices, 113 Divisional Offices, 2,048 Branch Offices, 73 Customer Zones, 1,401 Satellite Offices and 1,240 Mini Offices (March 2018).
[56] https://financialservices.gov.in/insurance-divisions/Public-Sector-Insurance-Companies, accessed 19 December 2019.

Table 5.10 *Number of Offices and Employees of PSICs as on March 2018*

Company	No. of Offices	No. of Employees
Life Insurance Corporation of India	4,932	2,65,727*
General Insurance Corporation	8#	581
Oriental Insurance Company	1,943	13,667
National Insurance Company	1,742	13,440
New India Assurance Company	2,472	18,783$
United India Insurance Company	2,086	15,039

Source: Annual reports of the respective companies, 2017–2018.
Notes: *Besides 2,082,668 agents. #Headquarter at Mumbai; liaison offices at Kolkata, Chennai and Delhi; three overseas branch offices at London, Dubai and Kuala Lumpur; and one representative office at Moscow. $As on 31 March 2016.

In 2017–2018, the gross premiums in India reached US$94.48 billion (Life insurance: US$71.1 billion, Non-life insurance: US$23.38 billion). Despite the vibrant growth, the insurance penetration in India still remains low (only 3.69% in 2017, compared to global figures of 6.3% globally in 2016), indicating potential for future growth. The various insurance-based government initiatives like Pradhan Mantri Suraksha Bima Yojana, Pradhan Mantri Jeevan Jyoti Bima Yojana, Ayushman Bharat, etc. had also given the sector a great fillip. The National Health Protection Scheme launched in 2018 under the Ayushman Bharat programme is expected to increase penetration of health insurance from 34 per cent to 50 per cent. The increasing use of internet and easy accessibility to insurance products through internet services are also contributing to the healthy growth of the sector.[57]

Apart from the above PSICs, there are two specialised PSICs: Agriculture Insurance Company of India Limited (AIC) and ECGC Ltd. (formerly Export Credit Guarantee Corporation of India Ltd.). The AIC was incorporated in 2002 for meeting the insurance needs of

[57] https://www.investindia.gov.in/team-india-blogs/overview-insurance-industry-india, accessed 20 December 2019.

agriculture and alliance activities sector, primarily for comprehensive crop insurance. Its paid-up share capital of ₹200 crore was contributed by other PSICs and NABARD. AIC commenced operations with effect from 1 April 2003, and now covers about 2 crore farmers in the country under the National Agricultural Insurance Scheme (NAIS). With its Head Office in New Delhi, it has 17 regional offices and 3 district offices. As of March 2015, it had 274 employees.

ECGC was set up in 1957 as a wholly owned government company under the Ministry of Commerce and Industry for promoting exports by providing credit risk insurance and related services for exports, and seeks to 'improve the competitiveness of the Indian exporters by providing them with credit insurance covers'. It also offers export credit insurance covers to banks and financial institutions that provide loans to exporters, besides providing 'overseas Investment Insurance to Indian companies investing in joint ventures abroad in the form of equity or loan'.[58] With unpredictable geopolitical developments leading to political and economic instability in various parts of the world, export risks have increased manifold, and Indian exporters need such support as provided by the ECGC to remain competitive in the global scenario. As of March 2018, ECGC had 610 employees in its Head Office in Mumbai, 5 regional offices and 60 branch offices in various parts of the country. Table 5.11 shows the profitability of these specialised insurance companies.

Table 5.11 Profitability of ECGC and AIC

(₹ crore)	2016-2017	2017-2018	2015-2016	2016-2017
	ECGC Ltd		AIC	
Profit before tax	408	130	464	487
Profit after tax	282	74	307	324
Proposed dividend	73	15	NA	NA
DDT	15	3	NA	NA

Source: Annual Reports of ECGC/AIC.

[58] https://www.ecgc.in/overview/, accessed 21 December 2019.

Insurance being a complex financial area, a detailed discussion on the performance parameters or the performance of individual companies is outside the scope of this book. Hence, the discussion will be limited to analysing the aggregate results of the companies on a limited number of parameters only, as reflected in the Tables 5.12–5.17. In fact, either of the two sectors discussed in this chapter—banking and insurance—calls for a separate book to cover the important areas concerning it. From these tables, we note that in terms of profitability, in the non-life insurance sector, private sector insurers outperformed PSICs in 2018–2019; in fact, only one non-life insurance PSIC, the New India Assurance Company, could register a net profit after taxes, the rest three being

Table 5.12 *After-tax Profit of Insurance Companies (₹ Crore)*

	2017–2018	*2018–2019*
Life insurers		
LIC	2,446	2,688
Private sector	6,064	5,747
Non-life insurers		
Public sector	–2,543	–3,287
Private sector	3,798	3,584

Source: Annual Report of IRDAI, 2018–2019.

Table 5.13 *Dividend Paid by Insurance Companies (₹ Crore)*

Life insurers		
LIC	2,422	2,660
Private sector	1,770	1,781
Non-life insurers		
Public sector	309	0
Private sector	316	618
GIC Re	**1,002**	**1,184**

Source: Annual Report of IRDAI, 2018–2019.

Table 5.14 *Total Investments of Insurance Companies* (₹ *Crore*)

| | As of 31 March | |
	2017–2018	2018–2019
Life insurers		
LIC	2,526,923	2,760,658
Private sector	662,137	772,485
Non-life insurers		
Public sector	162,503	178,977
Private sector	106,426	135,354
Total		
Public sector	2,689,426	2,939,635
Private sector	768,563	907,839
Grand total	**3,457,989**	**3,847,474**

Source: Annual Report of IRDAI, 2018–2019.

Table 5.15 *Investment Income of Insurance Companies* (₹ *Crore*)

	2017–2018	2018–2019
Life insurers		
LIC	206,070	223,642
Private sector	55,754	61,158
Non-life insurers		
Public sector	15,700	15,600
Private sector	7,759	8,885

Source: Annual Report of IRDAI, 2018–2019.

in loss. The LIC paid ₹2,660 crore as dividend to the government in 2018–2019, while GIC paid ₹1,184 crore. The other four general PSICs did not pay any dividend in 2018–2019, though they had paid ₹309 crore in 2017–2018. The total investments of the PSICs amounted to ₹29.4 lakh crore in 2018–2019, up from ₹26.9 lakh crore in the previous

Table 5.16 *Break-up of Total Investments by Life Insurers (%)*

	2017–2018	2018–2019
Traditional products		
Investments in central and state govt. securities	66	67
Housing and infrastructure	8	8
Approved investments	23	21
Other investments	3	4
	100	**100**
ULIP funds		
Approved investments	94	92
Other investments	6	8

Source: Annual Report of IRDAI, 2018–2019.

Table 5.17 *Break-up of Total Investments by General Insurers (%)*

	2017–2018	2018–2019
Investments in central govt. securities	39%	42%
Investments in state govt. securities	10%	10%
Housing and infrastructure	16%	16%
Approved investments	32%	28%

Source: Annual Report of IRDAI, 2018–2019.

year, registering a healthy growth of over 9 per cent; their investment income also grew by nearly 8 per cent in 2018–2019 over the previous year. Investments of the PSICs were far above those of the private sector (₹29.4 lakh crore against ₹9.1 lakh crore in 2018–2019), indicating the far deeper market penetration by the PSICs, which they must utilise to their advantage. Most of the investments (67% for life insurers and 52% for non-life insurers in 2018–2019) were made in central and state government securities as per government dictates, the rest being in housing, infrastructure and other areas.

Regarding the PSICs, the 14th Finance Commission had stated in its report:

> In the insurance sector, substantial reforms have already been carried out through privatisation, and the public sector insurance companies are working in a market-based competitive environment. The policy of insurance companies buying substantial shares of Central public sector enterprise disinvestments at the instance of the Union Government is another issue that needs to be weighed in terms of returns on investments and the implications of simply shifting of public asset holdings from one public entity to another.[59]

Here again, the question of independence from government control comes up. The SBI and LIC both have been used time and again to bail out companies when they run into rough weather because of the government's interest. LIC, the country's largest insurer, has also been the supplier of the biggest lifeline to the government in this regard (Figure 5.3). As per current government directives, 50 per cent of funds mobilised from traditional life insurance policies must be mandatorily invested in government securities. While this may ensure safety of the funds, this also results in investment of policyholders' funds in low-return, fixed-income funds for most traditional policies, for financing the government's fiscal deficits. IRDAI perhaps needs to look into this so as to explore ways to improve the investors' returns. It is also worth considering if, in addition to the IRDAI, which appears to function independently, there also needs to be a structure to shield the decisions of the PSICs from the government's political considerations, while keeping the national economic imperatives and priorities in mind, in an objective and transparent manner.

In the past few years, the government has taken several reform initiatives and policy decisions. The Insurance Laws (Amendment) Act, 2015 allowed the enhancement of foreign investment cap in an Indian insurance company from 26 per cent to an explicitly composite limit of 49 per cent while safeguarding Indian ownership and control. Rule 9 of the Foreign Investment Rules stipulated that like the insurers, the

---

[59] Report of the Fourteenth Finance Commission, Para 16.47.

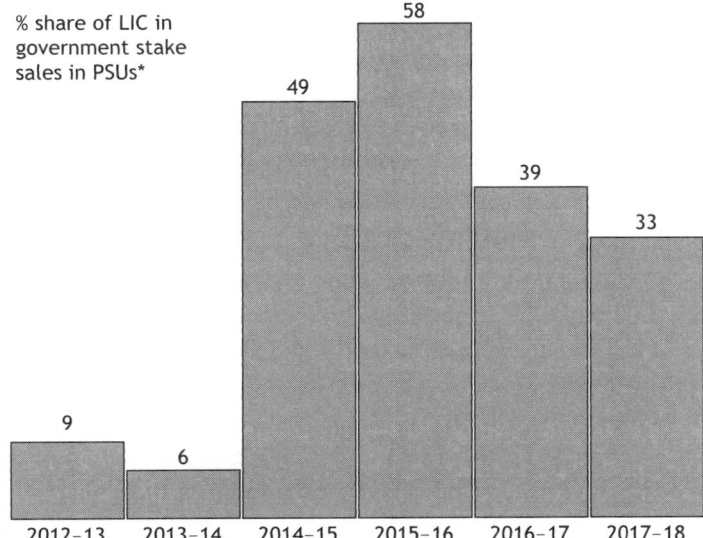

% share of LIC in government stake sales in PSUs*

*Amount invested by LIC is estimated based on the stake purchased and the stock prices of the respective PSU's

Figure 5.3 *LIC Boost to Government's Disinvestment Programme*

Source: Bhattacharya, 'Why India needs an independent fiscal council'.

FDI in insurance intermediaries would also be capped at 49 per cent.[60] However, it was felt by stakeholders that this parity was unfair since insurance intermediaries, not being custodians of the policyholders' money unlike the insurers, and who represented the IRDAI, should be allowed a higher cap. In the budget speech in July 2019, the Finance Minister enhanced the FDI limit in insurance intermediaries to 100 per cent, and accordingly, in September 2019, the Indian Insurance Companies (Foreign Investment) Amendment Rules 2019 increased this limit to 100 per cent, with some safeguards.[61]

[60] An insurance intermediary could be an individual agent or a corporate agent including banks, brokers, insurance marketing firms, etc. that serves as a bridge between consumers and insurers.

[61] https://www.lexology.com/library/detail.aspx?g=86f1f552-3fd3-458d-a7da-a3f4dc98a444, accessed 22 December 2019.

Drawing attention to the fact that India's FDI inflows in 2018–2019 had grown by 6 per cent to US$64.37 billion, the Finance minister had said: 'I propose to further consolidate the gains in order to make India more attractive FDI destination.' The government is now reported to be considering opening up the insurance sector to 74 per cent FDI under the approval route, as in the banking sector, while maintaining the current 49 per cent FDI limit through the automatic route in insurance.[62] When this happens, there is likely to be an influx of foreign capital into the sector, which will provide capital for technological upgradation to push up the current insurance penetration rate of around 3.7 per cent closer to the global average of 6.1 per cent.

The sector may see other transformational reforms in the near future too. In 2017, the New India Assurance Company and GIC Re were listed on the bourses as part of the government's plan to raise resources through disinvestment. In the 2018–2019 Budget, the government had proposed to merge the National Insurance Company with the Oriental Insurance Company and the United India Insurance Company to form a single insurance mega entity. The process could not, however, see completion due to some reasons including the poor financial health and lack of profitability of these companies. As seen earlier, two of the PSICs, the National Insurance Company and the United India Insurance Company, are struggling to maintain their solvency ratio above 1.5, and three of the four PSICs are in the red. Once they are nursed back to health, the merger is likely to take place to create a large insurance company for general insurance, like the LIC, in the line of the bank mergers announced in August 2019, after which the government may divest a part of its stake in them to raise resources for combatting the economic slowdown. Even the option of merging all the four general PSICs is reportedly being considered to create a mega insurer. They will then no longer undercut each other, and use their combined synergy to emerge into the global stage.[63] With an

[62] https://www.business-standard.com/article/economy-policy/budget-impact-fdi-cap-in-insurance-sector-may-be-raised-to-74-119070900042_1.html, accessed 22 December 2019.

[63] https://economictimes.indiatimes.com/industry/banking/finance/insure/de-merger-sale-of-3-psu-insurers-could-be-on-cards/articleshow/69911655.cms?from=mdr, accessed 22 December 2019.

expanding and increasingly prosperous middle class in India aided by the structural reforms the government seems serious about undertaking, the overall insurance industry is expected to reach US$280 billion by 2019–2020, according to the Associated Chambers of Commerce and Industry of India (ASSOCHAM). To tap this huge potential market by the PSICs, innovation and technology are the vital keys.

Annexure 5.1 *PSB Merger (Figures as on 31 March 2019)*

A	PNB	OBC	UBI	Amalgamated Bank
Total business (₹ crore)	1,182,224	404,194	208,106	1,794,524
CASA ratio (%)*	42.16	29.40	51.45	40.52
PCR (%)#	61.72	56.53	51.17	59.59
CRAR ratio (%)$	9.73	12.73	13.00	10.77
Net NPA ratio (%)§	6.55	5.93	8.67	6.61
No. of employees	65,116	21,729	13,804	100,649

B	Canara Bank	Syndicate Bank	Amalgamated Bank
Total business (₹ crore)	1,043,249	477,046	1,520,295
CASA ratio (%)	29.18	32.58	30.21
PCR (%)	41.48	48.83	44.32
CRAR ratio (%)	11.90	14.23	12.63
Net NPA ratio (%)	5.37	6.16	5.62
No. of employees	58,350	31,535	89,885

C	Union Bank	Andhra Bank	Corporation Bank	Amalgamated Bank
Total business (₹ crore)	741,307	398,511	319,616	1,459,434
CASA ratio (%)	36.10	31.39	31.59	33.82
PCR (%)	58.27	68.62	66.60	63.07
CRAR ratio (%)	11.78	13.69	12.30	12.39
Net NPA ratio (%)	6.85	5.73	5.71	6.30
No. of employees	37,262	20.346	17,776	75,384

(Annexure 5.1 Continued)

(Annexure 5.1 Continued)

D	Indian Bank	Allahabad Bank	Amalgamated Bank
Total business (₹ crore)	429,972	377,887	807,859
CASA ratio (%)	34.71	49.49	41.65
PCR (%)	49.13	74.15	66.21
CRAR ratio (%)	13.21	12.51	12.89
Net NPA ratio (%)	3.75	5.22	4.39
No. of employees	19,604	23,210	42,814

Source: The Economic Times, 'Nirmala Sitharaman announces big reforms for Public Sector Banks'.

Notes: *CASA ratio is the ratio of deposits in current and saving accounts to total deposits. A higher CASA ratio indicates lower cost of funds, as banks pay no interests on current deposits and low interests on saving deposits (3%–4%).

The provision coverage ratio (PCR) indicates the provision made against bad loans from the profit generated. Higher the PCR, lower is the unexposed part of the bad debts.

$ CRAR is also known as capital adequacy ratio (CAR), which is calculated by dividing a bank's capital by its risk-weighted assets. Under Basel-III, the international regulatory agreement to improve regulation, supervision, and risk management in the banking sector, banks must maintain a minimum capital adequacy ratio of 8 per cent, both in respect of its tier 1 capital and tier 2 capital. A higher CRAR indicates that a bank is better capitalised and hence can absorb a reasonable amount of loss. CAR is usually fixed by the Central Bank; in India, scheduled commercial banks are required to maintain a CAR of 9% while PSBs are encouraged to maintain a CAR of 12% as per RBI norms. To arrive at the CAR, the notional amount of each asset is multiplied by the risk weight assigned to it. Risk weights for different assets vary from 0% on government security to 20% on an AAA-rated foreign bank instruments.

$ Net NPA = gross NPAs − provisions. Gross NPA ratio is the ratio of total gross NPA to total advances of the bank. Net NPA ratio is the ratio of Net NPA to advances and is used to measure the overall quality of the bank's loan book.

Annexure 5.2 Branches and ATMs of Scheduled Commercial Banks (As on 30 June 2018)

S. No.	Name of the Bank	Branches					ATMs		
		Rural	Semi-urban	Urban	Metropolitan	Total	On-site	Off-site	Total
	Public sector banks	**29,201**	**25,397**	**17,677**	**18,546**	**90,821**	**83,259**	**61,839**	**145,098**
1	Allahabad Bank	1,207	763	648	625	3,243	850	262	1,112
2	Andhra Bank	745	769	669	736	2,919	3,142	792	3,934
3	Bank of Baroda	1,836	1,537	932	1,169	5,474	6,263	3,352	9,615
4	Bank of India	1,834	1,455	806	983	5,078	3,328	4,095	7,423
5	Bank of Maharashtra	615	428	329	474	1,846	1,317	557	1,874
6	Canara Bank	1,811	1,991	1,165	1,255	6,222	5,003	4,218	9,221
7	Central Bank of India	1,602	1,352	834	898	4,686	3,397	1,411	4,808
8	Corporation Bank	588	795	524	557	2,464	2,357	734	3,091
9	Dena Bank	573	433	368	418	1,792	1,326	320	1,646
10	IDBI Bank Limited	415	585	504	496	2,000	2,199	1,536	3,735
11	Indian Bank	727	785	607	631	2,750	2,731	650	3,381
12	Indian Overseas Bank	921	988	678	741	3,328	2,858	750	3,608
13	Oriental Bank of Commerce	560	627	611	601	2,399	2,337	298	2,635
14	Punjab and Sind Bank	561	278	350	325	1,514	1,114	92	1,206

(Annexure 5.2 Continued)

(Annexure 5.2 Continued)

S. No.	Name of the Bank	Branches					ATMs		
		Rural	Semi-urban	Urban	Metropolitan	Total	On-site	Off-site	Total
15	Punjab National Bank	2,579	1,698	1,199	1,105	6,581	5,298	4,142	9,440
16	**State Bank of India**	**7,764**	**6,720**	**4,178**	**4,299**	**22,961**	**26,389**	**33,209**	**59,598**
17	Syndicate Bank	1,241	1,129	816	847	4,033	3,945	400	4,345
18	UCO Bank	1,075	821	603	580	3,079	2,142	419	2,561
19	Union Bank of India	1,254	1,289	850	906	4,299	4,545	3,011	7,556
20	United Bank of India	779	408	471	360	2,018	1,040	1,098	2,138
21	Vijaya Bank	514	546	535	540	2,135	1,678	493	2,171

Source: RBI Database in Indian Economy (dbie.rbi.org.in/DBIE).

Annexure 5.3 *Basel III Guidelines*

	a. Capital requirements	
	Regulatory Capital	*As % to Risk-weighted Assets*
I	Minimum common equity tier 1 (CET 1) ratio	4.5
II	Capital conservation buffer (CCB)	2.5
III	Minimum common equity tier 1 ratio plus capital conservation buffer (I + II)	7.0
IV	Additional tier 1 capital	1.5
V	Minimum tier 1 capital ratio (I + IV)	6.0
VI	Tier 2 capital	2.0
VII	Minimum total capital ratio (MTC) (V + VI)	8.0
VIII	MTC plus CCB (II + VII)	10.5
	b. Liquidity ratios	
IX	Liquidity coverage ratio	Min. 100% by 1 January 2019
X	Net stable funding ratio	Min. 100% on ongoing basis

Source: RBI, *RBI Report on Trend and Progress of Banking in India, 2017–2018,* 25.

Annexure 5.4 PCA Matrix: Areas, Indicators and Risk Thresholds

Area	Indicator	Risk Threshold 1	Risk Threshold 2	Risk Threshold 3
Capital (breach of either CRAR or CET 1 ratio to trigger PCA)	CRAR - minimum regulatory prescription for capital to risk assets ratio + applicable capital conservation buffer (CCB)	Up to 250 bps below indicator	More than 250 bps but not exceeding 400 bps below Indicator	—
	Current minimum RBI prescription of 10.25% (9% minimum total capital plus 1.25%* of CCB as on 31 March 2017)	<10.25% but ≥7.75%	<7.75% but ≥6.25%	—
	And/Or			
	Regulatory pre-specified trigger of common equity tier 1 (CET 1 min) + applicable capital conservation buffer (CCB)	Up to 162.50 bps below indicator	More than 162.50 bps below but not exceeding 312.50 bps below indicator	In excess of 312.50 bps below Indicator
	Current minimum RBI prescription of 6.75% (5.5% plus 1.25%* of CCB as on 31 March 2017)	<6.75% but ≥5.125%	<5.125% but ≥3.625%	<3.625%
	Breach of either CRAR or CET 1 ratio to trigger PCA			

Asset quality	Net non-performing advances (NNPA) ratio	≥6.0% but <9.0%	≥9.0% but <12.0%	≥12.0%
Profitability	Return on assets (ROA)	Negative ROA for two consecutive years	Negative ROA for three consecutive years	Negative ROA for four consecutive years
Leverage	Tier 1 leverage ratio	≤4.0% but ≥3.5% (leverage is over 25 times the tier 1 capital)	<3.5% (leverage is over 28.6 times the tier 1 capital)	

Source: https://www.rbi.org.in/Scripts/NotificationUser.aspx?Id=10921&Mode=0, accessed 16 December 2019.
Note: *CCB would be 1.875% and 2.5% as on 31 March 2018 and 31 March 2019, respectively.

Annexure 5.5 Profitability of Scheduled Commercial Banks as on 31 March 2018 (₹ Crore)

Banks	Net Profit	Profit Brought Forward	Profit Available for Appropriation	Transfer to Reserves	Transfer to Proposed Dividend	Transfer to Tax on Dividend	Balance Carried Over to Balance Sheet
Allahabad Bank	-4,674	-616	-5,291	0	–	–	-5,291
Andhra Bank	-3,413	2	-3,411	52	–	–	-3,463
Bank of Baroda	-2,432	–	-2,432	-2,432	–	–	–
Bank of India	-6,044	-8,557	-14,601	362	–	–	-14,962
Bank of Maharashtra	-1,146	-1,372	-2,517	26	–	–	-2,544
Canara Bank	-4,222	–	-4,222	0	–	–	-4,222
Central Bank of India	-5,105	-5,356	-10,461	92	–	–	-10,553
Corporation Bank	-4,054	–	-4,054	-107	–	–	-3,947
Dena Bank	-1,923	–	-1,923	0	–	–	-1,923
IDBI Bank Limited	-8,238	-8,492	-16,730	434	–	–	-17,164
Indian Bank	1,259	97	1,356	1,258	–	–	98
Indian Overseas Bank	-6,299	–	-6,299	74	–	–	-6,374
Oriental Bank of Commerce	-5,872	–	-5,872	0	–	–	-5,872
Punjab and Sind Bank	-744	1,857	1,113	126	–	–	987
Punjab National Bank	-12,283	–	-12,283	-12,283	–	–	–

Bank						
State Bank of India	-6,547	-6,407	-12,955	2,124	–	–	-15,079
Syndicate Bank	-3,223	–	-3,223	62	–	–	-3,285
UCO Bank	-4,436	-1,160	-5,596	8	–	–	-5,604
Union Bank of India	-5,247	–	-5,247	159	–	–	-5,406
United Bank of India	-1,454	–	-1,454	-1,454	–	–	–
Vijaya Bank	727	1,275	2,002	350	188	–	1,463
Public sector banks	**-85,371**	**-28,730**	**-114,100**	**-11,149**	**188**	**–**	**-103,140**
AXIS Bank Limited	276	24,448	24,724	276	1,405	–	23,043
Bandhan Bank Limited	1,346	1,048	2,394	336	–	–	2,058
Catholic Syrian Bank Ltd	-97	-219	-317	0	–	–	-317
City Union Bank Limited	592	33	625	563	20	4	37
DCB Bank Limited	245	274	519	74	18	–	427
Federal Bank Ltd	879	1,451	2,330	377	175	36	1,742
HDFC Bank Ltd.	17,487	32,669	50,156	6,312	3,391	–	40,453
ICICI Bank Limited	6,777	18,745	25,522	5,561	1,457	9	18,495
IDFC First Bank Limited	859	1,647	2,506	491	305	–	1,710
IndusInd Bank Ltd	3,606	7,118	10,724	981	432	–	9,311
Jammu & Kashmir Bank Ltd	203	–	203	203	–	–	–
Karnataka Bank Ltd	326	137	463	224	113	23	102

(Annexure 5.5 Continued)

Banks	Net Profit	Profit Brought Forward	Profit Available for Appropriation	Transfer to Reserves	Transfer to Proposed Dividend	Transfer to Tax on Dividend	Balance Carried Over to Balance Sheet
Karur Vysya Bank Ltd	346	193	539	294	191	–	54
Kotak Mahindra Bank Ltd.	4,084	10,756	14,841	1,100	114	22	13,605
Lakshmi Vilas Bank Ltd	–585	62	–523	86	52	10	–671
Nainital Bank Ltd	49	–	49	32	14	3	–
RBL Bank Limited	635	88	723	526	68	14	115
South Indian Bank Ltd	335	356	691	250	72	14	354
Tamilnad Mercantile Bank Ltd	222	24	246	169	41	–	36
Dhanlaxmi Bank Ltd	–25	–837	–861	4	–	–	–865
YES Bank Ltd.	4,225	7,933	12,158	1,122	549	112	10,375
Private sector banks	**41,783**	**105,928**	**147,711**	**18,982**	**8,418**	**246**	**120,065**
AB Bank Limited	9	38	48	20	–	–	27
Abu Dhabi Commercial Bank PJSC	16	–	16	16	–	–	–
American express banking corp.	81	–357	–276	20	–	–	–296
Australia and New Zealand Banking Group Limited	58	–	58	58	–	–	–
Bank of America, National Association	734	1,768	2,502	1,184	–	–	1,318

Bank of Bahrain & Kuwait B.S.C.	12	3	15	6	—	9
Bank OF Ceylon	11	45	56	3	—	53
Bank OF Nova Scotia	57	-12	45	14	—	31
Barclays Bank PLC	319	625	944	64	—	880
BNP Paribas	386	—	386	386	—	—
Citibank N.A.	3,403	2,756	6,159	3,360	—	2,799
Cooperative Rabobank U.A.	-244	—	-244	0	—	-244
Credit Agricole Corporate and Investment Bank	-270	-168	-437	0	—	-437
Credit Suisse AG	108	—	108	108	—	—
CTBC bank co. Ltd.	2	-49	-47	0	—	-47
DBS Bank India Ltd.	-533	-241	-774	-7	—	-766
Deutsche Bank AG	910	1,713	2,623	1,831	—	792
Doha Bank Q.P.S.C	-11	—	-11	0	—	-11
Emirates NBD Bank (P.J.S.C.)	-17	—	-17	0	—	-17
First Abu Dhabi Bank PJSC	18	-5	13	4	—	8
Firstrand Bank Ltd	25	-371	-346	6	—	-352
Hongkong and Shanghai Banking Corp. Ltd.	2,313	1,729	4,042	1,703	—	2,339
Industrial and Commercial Bank of China	18	—	18	18	—	—

(Annexure 5.5 Continued)

(*Annexure 5.5 Continued*)

Banks	Net Profit	Profit Brought Forward	Profit Available for Appropriation	Transfer to Reserves	Transfer to Proposed Dividend	Transfer to Tax on Dividend	Balance Carried Over to Balance Sheet
Industrial Bank of Korea	6	7	13	1	–	–	12
JPMorgan Chase Bank National Association	1,043	708	1,751	963	–	–	788
JSC VTB Bank	–23	–6	–28	0	–	–	–28
KEB Hana Bank	21	11	32	5	–	–	27
Krung Thai Bank Public Company Limited	6	22	28	2	–	–	26
Mashreq Bank PSC	17	12	29	16	–	–	13
Mizuho Bank Ltd	197	124	321	173	–	–	148
MUFG Bank Ltd	313	399	712	477	–	–	235
National Australia Bank	10	31	41	2	–	–	38
PT Bank Maybank Indonesia TBK	–2	–45	–47	0	–	–	–47
Qatar National Bank SAQ	–2	–2	–4	0	–	–	–4
Sberbank	–15	–	–15	0	–	–	–15
SBM Bank (India) Ltd.	–105	–84	–188	0	–	–	–188
Shinhan Bank	64	–	64	64	–	–	–

Societe Generale	17	5	22	5	—	—	17
Sonali Bank	4	7	10	1	—	—	9
Standard Chartered Bank	1,911	1,815	3,727	2,293	—	—	1,433
Sumitomo Mitsui Banking Corporation	135	292	427	219	—	—	208
The Royal Bank of Scotland PLC	-181	—	-181	1	—	—	-182
United Overseas Bank Ltd	0	6	6	0	—	—	6
Westpac Banking Corporation	25	95	121	6	—	—	114
Woori Bank	6	48	54	2	—	—	52
Foreign banks	10,853	10,921	21,774	13,025	—	—	8,749
Small finance banks	297	1,286	1,582	114	—	—	1,469
All scheduled commercial banks	-32,438	89,405	56,967	20,972	8,606	246	27,144

Source: RBI Database in Indian Economy (dbie.rbi.org.in/DBIE).

Annexure 5.6 List of Insurance Companies in India (March 2019)

S. No.	Name of the Company	Claim Settlement Ratio* (%) 2017–2018	Solvency Ratio March 2019#
	Life insurance business		
1	Life Insurance Corporation of India (Public Sector)	98.04	1.60
2	AEGON Life Insurance	95.67	2.59
3	Aviva Life Insurance	94.45	2.99
4	Bajaj Allianz Life Insurance	92.04	8.04
5	Bharti AXA Life Insurance	96.85	1.71
6	Birla Sun Life Insurance	94.69	1.98
7	Canara HSBC OBC Life Insurance	95.22	3.93
8	DHFL Pramerica Life Insurance	96.62	4.60
9	Edelweiss Tokio Life Insurance	95.24	2.29
10	Exide Life Insurance	96.81	2.08
11	Future Generali India Life Insurance	93.11	1.62
12	HDFC Standard Life Insurance	97.80	1.88
13	ICICI Prudential Life Insurance	97.88	2.15
14	IDBI Federal Life Insurance	91.99	3.34
15	IndiaFirst Life Insurance Company Ltd—India First	89.83	1.74
16	Kotak Life Insurance	93.72	3.02
17	Max Life Insurance	98.26	2.42
18	PNB MetLife Insurance	91.12	1.97
19	Reliance Life Insurance	95.17	2.60
20	Sahara Life Insurance	82.74	8.44
21	SBI Life Insurance	96.76	2.13
22	Shriram Life Insurance	80.23	1.82
23	Star Union Dai-chi Life Insurance	92.26	2.53
24	Tata AIA Life Insurance	98.00	2.68

(Annexure 5.6 Continued)

(Annexure 5.6 Continued)

S. No.	Name of the Company	Claim Settlement Ratio* (%) 2017–2018	Solvency Ratio March 2019#
	Non-life insurance business		
25	New India Assurance (public sector)	85.66	2.13
26	United India Assurance (public sector)	94.38	1.52
27	National Insurance Company (public sector)	114.24	1.04
28	Oriental Insurance Company (public sector)	85.39	1.57
29	Agriculture Insurance Company (public sector, for crop insurance)	99.66 (2015–2016)	2.14
30	Export Credit Guarantee Corporation of India (public sector, for export credit insurance)	102.00 (2015–2016)	10.40
31	Acko General Insurance	NA	1.78
32	Aditya Birla General Insurance	NA	NA
33	Bajaj Allianz General Insurance	66.72	2.55
34	Bharti AXA General Insurance	82.97	1.76
35	Cholamandalam MS General Insurance	50.19	1.55
36	DHFL General Insurance	NA	2.60
37	Edelweiss General Insurance	70.00	2.40
38	Future Generali India General Insurance	75.72	1.54
39	Go Digit General Insurance	93.95	2.27
40	HDFC ERGO General Insurance	74.36	1.75
41	ICICI Lombard General Insurance	77.00	2.24
42	IFFCO Tokio General Insurance	82.39	1.66
43	Kotak Mahindra General Insurance	72.00	1.86
44	Liberty General Insurance	69.60	2.15
45	Magma HDI General Insurance	83.00	1.58
46	Raheja QBE General Insurance	76.46	3.83
47	Reliance General Insurance	84.71	1.60
48	Royal Sundaram General Insurance	80.41	1.93

(Annexure 5.6 Continued)

(Annexure 5.6 Continued)

S. No.	Name of the Company	Claim Settlement Ratio* (%) 2017–2018	Solvency Ratio March 2019#
49	SBI General Insurance	71.47	2.34
50	Shriram General Insurance	93.75	3.47
51	TATA AIG General Insurance	71.12	1.63
52	Universal Sompo General Insurance	56.30	2.24
53	Aditya Birla Health Insurance	89.00	1.62
54	Star Health and Allied Insurance	61.76	2.01
55	Apollo Munich Health Insurance	62.47	1.64
56	Max Bupa Health Insurance	50.19	1.77
57	Reliance Health Insurance	NA	1.56
58	Religare Health Insurance	51.97	1.56
59	Manipal Cigna Health Insurance	NA	2.23

Source: Annual Report of IRDAI, 2018–2019, https://www.irdai.gov.in, accessed 20 December 2019.

Notes: * The claim settlement ratio reflects the number of claims settled against the number of claims filed. It is a crucial parameter that determines the trust enjoyed by the insurer, and hence its business. Higher the ratio, better the insurer.

Solvency ratio measures the extent to which assets of insurance companies cover their commitments for future long and short-term liabilities. The ratio indicates the financial health of an insurance company by measuring the size of its capital relative to the risks it has undertaken. As per the IRDAI guidelines, all companies in India are required to maintain a solvency ratio of 1.5 (or 150%) to minimise bankruptcy risk. Liquidity ratio only takes into account the short-term liabilities whereas the solvency ratio considers all liabilities.

CHAPTER 6

Liberalisation and Privatisation

The New Social Contract

Denationalisation, deregulation, destatisation, restructuring, liberalisation, globalisation and privatisation—these were among the most favoured words used in relation to the public enterprises during the 1980s and 1990s, and ever since. As explained in the previous chapters, during these decades, most countries in the world were suffering from recession or stagflation—high inflation combined with low growth—and Keynesian prescriptions were no longer working. Welfarism was facing an acute crisis for lack of funds, and there emerged an almost universal consensus that state capitalism had been unable to deliver and was therefore passé. In the face of a severe economic crisis, most of the developed Western nations were trying to redefine the social responsibilities of the state by contracting its role.

Since the 1980s, a consensus was emerging that 'State capitalism' had by and large failed. The public sector was being equated, not always correctly, with low quality of products and services, mismanagement of resources and distribution of patronage. The prevalent thinking was that excessive government protection to them was killing competition and impeding growth and innovation, leading to flight of capital and talent. Emphasis was back on the realisation that individual freedom and free enterprise were what build the 'wealth of nations' through the 'invisible hand' of the market. Even in communist countries and socialist governments in Spain, Italy, France, Sweden, etc., governments embarked on privatising the SOEs during the 1980s and 1990s. Following Mrs Margaret Thatcher's drive in Britain, 'rolling back the frontiers of the state' became a major thrust for most governments.

In USA, Mr Ronald Reagan pledged 'to get the government off people's backs'. 'Government is not the solution to our problem', he said. 'Government is the problem'. During his Presidency (1981–1989), the USA was suffering from stagflation, forcing Regan to apply his principles, which have since become known as Reaganomics. This was essentially a combination of measures like reducing government spending and regulation, reducing federal income tax and capital gains tax and tightening money supply—in other words, limiting the role of the state. In the UK, Thatcherism was focussed on the withdrawal of state capitalism and privatisation of vital sectors of the economy, while in the stressed economies in other countries, principles of free market economy were being promoted, cutting across continents and political ideologies. Thus, the labour governments in Australia and New Zealand and socialist governments in Spain and France were equally pursuing a policy of shrinking the role of the 'Big State'.

The contagion of economic crises had spread to Asia as well—the Japanese economy had suffered a decade-long recession since the 1990s till 2002 following the collapse of the economic bubble of the 1980s, leading to what has since been known as the 'lost decade' of Japan due to economic turmoil, which was compounded by the Asian currency crisis in 1997 and the Mexican default in 1994. The economic crisis was accompanied by an acute crisis of the financial sector as financial institutions were reeling under the combined impact of falling real estate prices, plummeting stock prices and increasing bad loans, forcing the governments in these countries to cut spending. Even in Africa and Latin America, governments were forced to withdraw from state capitalism and started veering towards a free market economy. During the 1980s, about 7,000 PEs were privatised in over 100 countries. A World

Bank study undertaken in 1995 informs that massive privatisation took place in the erstwhile USSR and Eastern Bloc countries; of the 15,000 enterprises privatised worldwide during the period 1980–1992, over 11,000 took place in erstwhile East Germany only.

In 22 OECD countries in Europe and North America and in Japan, privatisation between 1990 and 2001 yielded US$554 billion, or 7.42 per cent of their combined GDPs.[1] Between 2000 and 2008, privatisation proceeds averaged US$399 million per year, across 41 developing countries in the world.[2] Overall, between 1988 and 2003, about 2,700 SOEs around the world were privatised, and by 1995, the total value of privatisation deals exceeded US$300 billion.[3] Their impact on jobs and economy was enormous.

The pace of privatisation differed from continent to continent and from country to country. In Latin America, it was driven initially by the rapid and aggressive privatisation programmes of Argentina and Mexico during the early 1990s, and by privatisation programmes in Brazil and Colombia in the late 1990s. In Africa, it began slowly with the privatisation programmes in Nigeria, Ghana, Egypt and Morocco from 1993, joined later by South Africa, Tanzania and Senegal, but the pace picked up from the early 2000s, driven by large waves of privatisation in Nigeria, Egypt, Tunisia and Algeria, and also in Ghana and Kenya. After the fall of the Berlin Wall and disintegration of the erstwhile Soviet empire, privatisation got a boost in the transition economies of the Eastern Bloc countries in Central and Eastern Europe—in fact, it became the hallmark of reform in the post-communist world. Hungary and the Czech Republic embarked on modest privatisation programmes during the mid-1990s, but privatisation gathered momentum when Russia, Poland and Slovakia joined them in the sale of state assets. After 2000, Bulgaria, Serbia and Romania would also embark on privatisation. Privatisation in Asia reached a peak

---

[1] Belke et al., 'The Different Extent of Privatization Proceeds in OECD Countries'.

[2] Breen and Doyle, 'The Determinants of Privatization'.

[3] Goulding, 'Retreating from the Commanding Heights'; Goulding, 'Privatization: Political and Economic Challenges'.

first in the early 1990s, driven by privatisation programmes in China, Indonesia, India and Malaysia. A second peak was reached in the late 1990s, shortly after the East Asian financial crisis, this time mainly from the increased sales of state assets in China and Thailand. Pakistan, Bangladesh and Sri Lanka would also join the bandwagon soon. After 2000, the income raised by asset sales in Asian countries accounted for almost half the global proceeds from privatisation.[4]

In India, too, especially after the 1991 economic reforms that ushered in globalisation and liberalisation of the hitherto closed economy, there was a realisation that the state must withdraw from business and instead facilitate the private industries to take over the businesses and industries so far monopolised by it, while restricting its role to only a few strategic sectors. The New Industrial Policy Resolution of 1991 indeed identified these sectors—only three: atomic energy, mining of atomic minerals and railways—which would continue to be reserved for the public sector.[5] All other sectors were opened for private sector participation. However, much unlike as expected, the public sector did not withdraw from the non-strategic sectors; even now, the public sector, both at the Centre and in the states, has a significant presence in most sectors—in many cases lacking much purpose, commercial or otherwise. The public sector also has a dominant presence in some sectors such as coal, crude oil and natural gas and power, even though the private sector is also significantly present in these sectors. Even when the strategic sectors, hitherto reserved for the public enterprises only, are slowly being opened to the private sector, the public sector continues to command a large market share in many of these sectors by virtue of the earlier advantages it enjoyed in a monopolistic situation with captive buyers like the armed forces, etc.

[4] Ibid.

[5] Prior to July 1991, 17 industries were reserved exclusively for the public sector, which included defence, iron and steel, heavy plant and machinery, mining, heavy electrical plant, coal and lignite, minerals oils, aircraft, air and rail transport, shipbuilding, telecommunication and power. In July 1991, except defence, atomic energy, coal and lignite, mineral oils, and railway transport, every other sector was opened to the private sector. By December 2002, the public sector's exclusive jurisdiction extended only to three sectors: atomic energy, minerals specified in schedule to Atomic Energy (Control of Production and Use) Order, 1953, and railway transport.

The UK of course was one of the biggest privatisers in the world. It had nationalised most of its core industries after the Second World War (WWII). During the post-WWII years, socialist governments in UK had embarked upon large-scale nationalisation programmes. By 1979, the share of the public sector in its economy had risen to 12 per cent, before large-scale privatisation began, which became the defining policy of the Conservative Party's 18-year-rule between 1979 and 1997, eleven of those (1979–1990) under Mrs Margaret Thatcher. Actually, by the late 1970s, the British SOEs had become a continuous drain on the exchequer. British Steel lost a billion pounds in a year, while some SOEs lost nearly £50 million a week. Privatisation was therefore almost inevitable. In the largest public offering in its history, British Telecom was privatised in 1985, followed by privatisation of many big entities like Jaguar, Britain's state-owned auto manufacturer, as well as selling of public stakes in British Sugar, Britoil, British Aerospace and British Petroleum and privatising the subsidiary operations of British Steel, British Rail and British Airways. Their impact on employment was enormous, even though some jobs shifted to the private sector. The share of the public sector in the economy reduced to a meagre 2 per cent by 1997 when Tony Blair took office, and a million jobs had by then been transferred to the private sector.

Between 1979 and 1983, 12 SOEs were completely or partly privatised in the UK, yielding £1.6 billion; during the next 4 years, almost £11 billion pounds were raised from the privatisation of 24 companies. During 1987–1991, the British Government raised £22.5 billion through the privatisation of British Steel, water supply and sewerage, regional electricity companies, etc. The succeeding government of John Major continued with the programme and divested the remaining 21.8 per cent shares of British Telecom, among others. By October 1993, almost two-thirds of the public industries and 940,000 jobs had been transferred to the private sector; these privatised industries accounted for nearly 20 per cent of the overall market capitalisation in the London stock exchange.[6] The result of all this privatisation was that industries became competitive; British Airways and British Gas turned around, and prices of gas supplied to households dropped

---

[6] Gupta, 'Privatisation in the United Kingdom', 43–45.

20 per cent after adjusting for inflation. The quality of services also improved simultaneously.

Similar privatisation also took place in France, Italy, Netherlands, Germany, Sweden, Denmark, Portugal, Turkey, Japan and South Korea. Under the socialist government of François Mitterrand (1981–1995), France had launched extensive nationalisation programmes beginning with 1981–1982, though it had nationalised its transportation, energy and finance sectors much earlier, during the post-WWII years. During 1981–1986, the total public sector represented about 21 per cent of the French production, 23 per cent of wage earners, 28 per cent of GDP, 30 per cent of exports and 49 per cent of Gross Capital Formation. Mitterrand initiated the second wave of nationalisation through a wide-reaching 1982 nationalisation law, taking control over the major industrial groups CGE, Péchiney, Rhône-Poulenc, Saint Gobain and Thomson, defence manufacturers Dassault-Bréguet and Matra, steel giants Usinor and Sacilor, computer companies Bull and ITT-France, and the pharmaceutical lab Roussel-UCLAF, along with the country's 36 biggest banks at a cost of 58 billion francs of taxpayer money.[7] The policy was reversed by the conservative governments under President Jacques Chirac (1995–2007), which resorted to massive privatisation, and the 1997–2002 period saw some of the biggest privatisations of the French public sector. A US$7.1 billion initial public offering of France Telecom was issued in October 1997, followed by a US$10.4 billion secondary offering a year later. Germany sold Deutsche Telekom. Spain sold its national flag carrier Iberia in 2001.[8]

In Japan, 'Special Public Corporations' (*tokushu hojin*), whose shares are wholly owned by the Ministry of Finance, are not subject to the corporate laws applicable to private corporations. They are instead governed by special laws subjecting them to oversight by specified ministries. In response to a national debt crisis in Japan, Prime Minister Yasuhiro Nakasone launched a major privatisation programme in the 1980s. Three major corporations were privatised: Nippon Telegraph

---

[7] https://www.dissentmagazine.org/article/lessons-from-the-nationalization-nation-state-owned-enterprises-in-france, accessed 19 October 2019.

[8] *The Economist*, 'Privatisation in Europe Coming Home to Roost'.

and Telephone Public Corporation (NTT), Japan Tobacco & Salt Public Corporation and Japan National Railways (JNR). This was followed by the privatisation of financial institutions affiliated with Japan Post, under the reformist Prime Minister Junichiro Koizumi in 2005, though the shares were offered to the public for the first time in 2015. All these privatisation initiatives were characterised by a deliberate, gradual process in which a committee outside the formal government bureaucracy was established to formulate a privatisation plan, to insulate the process from 'the vicissitudes of politics to the extent possible, so that the results were effective and the burdens of privatisation were fairly distributed'.[9] As a consequence, the post-privatisation governance has not been 'plagued by political interference or extraction of wealth from public shareholders'.[10]

Even in the emerging economies in India, Malaysia, Sri Lanka and Bangladesh, privatisation became the avowed government policy since the late 1990s. While in the developed countries privatisation was primarily driven by a renewed focus on higher growth and better efficiency, in the developing world the thrust came primarily from the budgetary constraints, in order to arrest the burgeoning fiscal deficit and debt and generate funds for social welfare programmes of the governments. Nevertheless, modernising the SOEs and making them internationally competitive by giving them access to foreign technology and capital were also important factors.

The role of state-owned enterprises in rich countries has shrunk from around 8.5 per cent of the GDP in 1984 to less than 5 per cent in 2002. The momentum of privatisation, however, slowed down in Europe after 2000. In several countries, planned privatisations of infrastructure—such as postal systems, airports and railways—were either postponed or cancelled, over concerns about the likely political fall-out from further sales. Public attitude has also undergone a notice-able shift, raising questions about whether privatisation has reached its limits. The government in the UK, instead of selling Railtrack,

---

[9] Milhaupt and Pargendler, 'Governance Challenges of Listed State-owned Enterprises Around the World', 39.
[10] Ibid.

which owned the British rail network, took it into bankruptcy and also postponed plans for privatising the financially troubled Post Office, the last big and important state-owned industry.

An estimate indicated that between 1990 and 2002, the total receipts in Europe from privatisation proceeds amounted to an impressive US$675 billion, the peak being in 1998 of US$104 billion; in sharp contrast, only US$38 billion could be collected from the public asset sales in 2001. Weak stock markets, investor scepticism and questions about what constituted true privatisation contributed to this slowdown, along with the impact of bursting of the market bubble and crashing of prices in telecom and technology shares between 2000 and 2002, especially in France and Germany. As in India, in the OECD countries, too, governments raised more than US$400 billion from asset sales since 1990, but did not really relinquish ownership control. For example, France had privatised many of its public industries in three big waves of privatisation, but the state still owned substantial stakes in many major companies—both listed and unlisted in the stock exchanges—such as France Telecom, Air France, Thales Renault, EDF, etc.[11]

China began a policy of reforming its SOEs in the 1990s, which then controlled about 75 per cent of the Chinese industry but had become bloated, debt-ridden, corrupt and inefficient. It accorded top priority to the reformation of sick enterprises by 'grasping the large and letting go the small', since small enterprises accounted for most of the losses.[12] Thousands of small enterprises were privatised, displacing large numbers of workers, while large enterprises were provided additional government support by way of tax and debt relief, substantial capital infusion, liberal import licences and greater access to domestic and international listing facilities. Between 1997 and 2003, the number of public enterprises plummeted by 37 per cent and their employment declined from 110 million to only 69 million. Many workers, especially women, were pushed into early retirement even while in their 40s, aggravating the pension shortages. However, the reforms paved the way for China's accession to the World Trade Organisation

---

[11] *The Economist*, 'Privatisation in Europe'.
[12] Mathur, 'Government's Policy of Privatization: Victim of Crony Capitalism'.

(WTO) in 2001 and the emergence of China as an export giant that could mitigate the labour market shocks to some extent. SOEs had been and remained the drivers of China's economic growth. In 2003, a holding company, the State-owned Assets Supervision and Administration Commission (SASAC), was created to manage the SOEs. The agency, which controls nearly 100 of the largest SOEs, lies 'at the heart of China's industrial deep state', as most listed SOEs have formal executive relations with the ruling Communist Party of China, and hence are subservient to the political authority, like in India, which arrangement has its inherent contradictions.[13]

Unlike the other countries, China did not go for widespread privatisation of its large SOEs, probably realising the disruption this would cause in its socio-economic fabric, given its heavy dependence on them. It preferred instead an incremental, gradualist approach to reform, whose objective was not to dilute but rather to reinforce state control more effectively and to transform the SOEs into giant international players in a socialist market economy led by them. In 2009, China Mobile and China National Petroleum Corporation together made profits of US$33 billion—more than the combined profit of China's 500 most profitable private companies. But private enterprises were also allowed to flourish, and open competition was encouraged. When China opened its economy in 1978, the Chinese public enterprises were employing almost 80 per cent of urban workers; the ratio had declined to 14.3 per cent in 2017. During the same period, their share of industrial output fell from 78 per cent to under 20 per cent, while private firms had flourished, accounting for almost all of the jobs created in 2017.[14]

Nevertheless, the performance of the SOEs as a whole also trailed way behind the performance of the private sector. While the profits of private sector enterprises rose by 18 per cent between 2011 and 2016, the profits of SOEs plunged by 33 per cent, along with increases in their NPAs. China has now embarked on a 'mixed ownership' model, allowing non-state enterprises and foreign investors to take stakes

---

[13] Holland, 'Reforming China's State-owned Enterprises'.
[14] *The Economist*, 'Are State-owned Enterprises Reformable?'

in SOEs. In 2016, 69 per cent of central SOEs and subsidiaries had adopted the 'mixed ownership' model, and more are embracing it. SOEs still play a very important role in China—they accounted for a quarter of the national assets and 14 per cent of the GDP in 2016—and dominate several strategic sectors; they are considered crucial for achieving the goals of the 'Made in China 2025' policy, which aims to build high-end manufacturing industries across all key sectors.[15]

The 2008 global financial crisis led to a global reassessment of the role of the public sector to sustain growth during an economic downturn, and the mixed model of hybrid corporations with PPPs emerged as a result, to allow private capital in state-dominated sectors. A telecommunications giant, China Unicom, had evolved by raising funds from giant private technology companies such as Alibaba and Baidu to help with digital infrastructure upgrades while retaining control for decision-making with the state. In the latest reform in China under Mr Xi Jinping, the thrust has been on consolidation within the industry verticals, which resulted in a drop in the number of the central government-owned enterprises from 113 in 2013 to 96 in 2017.

The waves of privatisation across the world should not blind us to the notion that privatisation only brings unmitigated blessings. Private sector monopoly is not necessarily better and less detrimental than state monopoly; in fact, the private sector can always beat competition by forming cartels and guilds and resorting to various other unfair practices if the regulatory environment is not adequately strong, creating greater disparities in income inequality and causing larger socio-economic havoc. Bangladesh and many other Asian countries had seen the allocation efficiency being eroded largely because of privatisation; further, the privatised sectors were delivering far below expectations and becoming dependent on the government largesse.

The new realities of rolling back the state capitalism and retreat of the state from the so-called 'commanding heights' of the economy were in a way a return to the *laissez-faire* economic liberalism and free market capitalism, albeit with a difference. The focus on economic liberalisation—of which privatisation, deregulation, free trade and

---

[15] Song, *The Past, Present and Future of SOE Reform in China.*

reduction both in government expenditure as well as in its overarching control over the economy, with a consequent upsurge in the role of the private sector were integral features—constituted a huge shift of paradigm away from the post-War Keynesian consensus, which continued till the 1980s. These constituted the essence of neo-liberalist thoughts that had emerged much earlier, during the 20th century, but resurged after the 1980s as a distinct economic philosophy and a dominant social theory, especially during the new millennium. Neo-liberalism had initially emerged as a reaction to the abject failures of the economic policies of classical liberalism, which led to the crisis of 1930s, and has since undergone many transformations. It essentially rejected the *laissez-faire* doctrine while advocating a return to the market economy but under the control of a strong state, which became known as a 'social market economy', a hybrid between classical liberalism and a socialist economy. Its chief proponents were Chicago School scholars such as Friedrich Hayek, Milton Friedman or James M. Buchanan, while some of its chief practitioners were Margaret Thatcher, Ronald Reagan and Alan Greenspan. In a pioneering 1951 essay, 'Neo-Liberalism and its Prospects', Milton Friedman laid out its principles:

> Neo-liberalism would accept the nineteenth century liberal emphasis on the fundamental importance of the individual, but it would substitute for the nineteenth century goal of *laissez faire* as a means to this end, the goal of the competitive order. It would seek to use competition among producers to protect consumers from exploitation, competition among employers to protect workers and owners of property, and competition among consumers to protect the enterprises themselves. The state would police the system, establish conditions favourable to competition and prevent monopoly, provide a stable monetary framework, and relieve acute misery and distress. The citizens would be protected against the state by the existence of a free private market; and against one another by the preservation of competition.[16]

As hoped by him, neo-liberalism has become a major current of thought in the world since the 1990s.

---

[16] Friedman, *Neo-liberalism and Its Prospects*.

Privatisation, or returning public assets to the private entrepreneur, what Friedrich Hayek called the 'spontaneous order', followed the neoliberal model of the Chicago School. It singed many and reformed others. Reformation of the public sector during the 1980s and 1990s almost universally meant privatisation. There is no denying that shifting production back to the private sector did lead to improvements in quality and reduction of cost in many cases. The exposure to intense market competition also ensured higher investments in technology and constant emphasis on quality. Although it destroyed many enterprises, especially smaller ones, this was again a natural course of evolution of economic enterprises through the process of 'creative destruction'. The process was highly disruptive, and many entities perished while some were able to survive and thrive—and even expand their footprints in the markets abroad. But its downsides were unending social turmoil caused by huge job losses and workers' miseries, to which no answer has been found. It has increased inequality in society, destroyed the social compact and diluted the architecture of the welfare state assiduously built during the post-War years.

The crisis of 2008 pushed most of the big, listed public enterprises across the world into a tailspin. Their share of global market capitalisation had shrunk from a peak of 22 per cent in 2007 to only 13 per cent in 2014, and profits nosedived. Bribery and corruption scandals erupted in many giant public enterprises across the world, like in Petrobras in Brazil in 2014. Private players started capturing the market once dominated by the state in emerging economies, like Xiaomi displacing China Mobile and private mining companies BHP Billiton and Rio Tinto eating into the market share of the state giant, Vale, in Brazil. Unlike the privatisation drives of the 1980s and 1990s when the state-controlled firms were sold outright in Europe and Latin America, under the new model, private investors were given only a subordinate role while the state retained the controlling stake and decision-making powers. Investors seemed to prefer this model, with the government standing as a guarantor and underwriter of loans should they turn bad, and invested more than US$500 billion between 2000 and 2012.[17]

---

[17] *The Economist*, 'State Capitalism in the Dock'.

State capitalism may have produced some global champions, but obviously, it had its limits. To counteract the global slowdown after 2007–2008, state-controlled banks had resorted to large-scale lending in China, India, Russia, Brazil and Vietnam. The resulting NPAs are now exacting their toil from our banking system, like in all these other countries. State companies soak up capital from the market by crowding out private borrowers and hence affecting private sector investment needs, and are not particularly efficient in using it. They are disposed towards promoting cronyism, which causes public anger and resentment. They are not only risky for the economy but also mostly underperform in comparison to private businesses by a huge margin, and are the primary drivers of 'a dangerous rise in economy-wide debt'.[18]

The pitfalls of the SOEs are well known. The SOE management style is typically bureaucratic, focussing more on processes rather than results, with diffused accountability and insensitivity to consumer needs and desires. Initiative, innovation and creativity are often found lacking, and there is considerable confusion over conflicting social, political and economic objectives. SOEs also typically suffer from overstaffing arising from political patronage, besides frequent political interference in decision-making, affecting the management's ability to take independent and efficient decisions. Assets remain underutilised and poorly maintained, while losses are easily justified on social reasons; these losses affect the government budget and contribute to fiscal deficit. Scarce resources also are misdirected for political purposes or personal gain. Centralised control of economy through SOEs often makes political democracy more fragile.[19]

The growth of public and private sectors in any economy, therefore, should be complementary so that the ill effects of one do not constrain the economy; where the demands of the public sector crowd out the private sector, the economy suffers as a whole. The

apparent trade-off between efficiency and equity suggests that growth of the public sector may be at the expense of economic

[18] *The Economist*, 'Are State-owned Enterprises Reformable?'
[19] Johnson, 'Why Privatize', 27–29.

growth. If so, growth of the public sector ultimately leads to living standards being less than they would otherwise have been if the public sector had not grown as fast or at all. Moreover, to the extent that a leviathan state exists and acts on its own (rather than the public) interest, then loss of economic potential may be exacerbated.[20]

Cutting across developmental divides, ideologies and the nature of governments, more than a hundred countries all over the world have been pursuing the policy of privatising their state assets actively since the 1990s. They encompass entities in all kinds of industries, from public utilities like power, infrastructure and transport, manufacturing, extraction of natural resources like oil and natural gas and mining, steel and electronics, hotels and food processing, cement and aerospace, to finance and insurance. In the developing world, privatisation took place in many countries goaded by international financial institutions like the World Bank and IMF, as a condition for aid packages to stressed economies in these countries. Some countries took to privatisation as a political tool, but most countries took to it to tide over the fiscal difficulties. Indeed, the fiscal and financial considerations still remain the uppermost reasons for resorting to privatisation in most developing countries, like in India. The massive privatisation programmes have yielded rich dividends to the governments all over the world but not necessarily led to increases in productivity and efficiency of all privatised entities. The change of ownership from public to private is supposed to bring the efficiency of SOEs to the level of the well-run private companies, but there are too many examples to show that the change of ownership is no guarantee for better performance in terms of higher efficiency and profitability, unless accompanied by suitable market and regulator reforms, the absence of which has led to limited gains from the privatisation drives in many countries, like in India. Reforms of the regulatory frameworks and the markets are crucial for the performance of both public and private companies, ensuring a rule-based competitive structure covering entry, exit, bankruptcy and competition among the existing companies, an area that will be explored in greater detail in the next chapter.

[20] Bailey, 'Rolling Back the Frontiers of the State', 113–114.

Evidently, there cannot be any doctrinaire one-size-fits-all model for privatisation; it has to take into account the objectives and realities in each country. Some countries resorted to 'tactical privatisation' in terms of fulfilling only short-term political objectives of attracting foreign investment and hence votes, and hence achieved little more than product differentiation, while some countries went about privatisation in a systematic manner, following a consistent, coherent and pragmatic policy. They launched privatisation when their SOEs either became too bloated or fell too far behind the times in terms of obsolescence of the technology used, making their products far more uneconomical than corresponding imported products. In many South and East Asian countries, the state had played a catalytic role to access foreign capital, technology and expertise through privatisation in order to enhance the performance of industries, and thereby exploit synergies between the economy, the state and the market. Nevertheless, without strong political support and commitment, besides careful planning and preparation, privatisation has not succeeded anywhere. Privatisation also should be treated as only a means to achieve specific objectives arising out of rational, economic and political considerations and not an end in itself.[21]

In the globally connected and flat world that we live in, national interests often merge with multinational and transnational objectives. The distinction between the public and the private is also losing significance, and globally, both are coming together in a close and mutually beneficial partnership. We are in an age when intergovernmental ventures are increasingly becoming common, like the Japanese and Chinese joint ventures in East Asian countries and even in China, which still has a significant state share in and control over the economy. The role of the state is now shifting more towards protecting the economy from the disruptive forces of new technologies rather than protecting the public sector enterprises from eternal competition, as was the case in the pre-privatisation days. As domestic economies tend to get increasingly internationalised, state regulation and control over them also tend to get relaxed, exposing them to greater risks and vulnerabilities. In this new paradigm, states' role is to protect the domestic economies from these risks.

[21] Gupta, *Towards Privatisation*, 11–14.

There are many important lessons to be learnt from the privatisation experiences of other countries. The first and perhaps the most important lesson is that privatisation conditions should be directly related to the general performance of the economy. A sustained economic growth allows for better privatisation framework and a strong financial deepening. The second lesson is that privatisation has to be complemented with a general structural transformation oriented at improving efficiency and productivity. The sector reforms have to be consistent with the general structural trend of the economy, and should be directed at achieving an improvement in competitive economic conditions specific to the sector. The liberalisation agenda has to include operational and legal reforms as well. Also, successful privatisation is never possible without adequate preparation, and the process should be honest and transparent.[22]

The adoption of the MOU mechanism to improve the performance of CPSEs in India has been discussed in Chapter 3. In fact, MOU and privatisation can be complementary to each other. South Korea used the MOU route to improve the performance and enhance the value of its enterprises before selling them. As pointed out, MOU enables the performance of PSEs to be compared across different industries, and this instils a sense of healthy competition in them to improve performance, making privatisation unnecessary. The need for privatisation should be guided by the extent to which social obligations are being discharged by the concerned enterprise; if it is high, the MOU route, rather than the privatisation route, should be adopted, while the privatisation option may be explored if it is very low.[23]

In India, the public sector was once flaunted as occupying the commanding heights of the economy. However, by the late 1980s, the landscape of the public sector has turned quite desolate, with mounting losses, lower returns on investment and shrinking market shares. 'The question today being asked is', wrote an academic, '*commanding height* of what? Red-tapism, inefficiency, absurdity, antiquity... there

---

[22] Barnes, 'Lessons from Bank Privatisation in Mexico', 277–284.
[23] Kumar, 'Non-privatizing Reforms of Public Enterprises: The Indian Case', 143–146.

is no alternative to a thorough going privatisation'.[24] But there was no consensus as yet; in fact, some found the idea of privatisation quite anachronistic: 'The idea of transferring the ownership from public sector to private sector for India is too immature, rather wrong...the state is more knowledgeable and objective and the market is imperfect and short-sighted'.[25] The reason for such polarised views was probably the contentious politics, with the idea of privatisation finding no favour with the public, the trade unions and the opposition, and hence not pursued aggressively by the government of the day, which had already unleashed a series of radical reforms in 1991, beginning the long overdue unshackling of the Indian economy. Instead of privatisation, what the Indian state did was to allow the private sector into areas hitherto reserved for the public sector, which has been termed as 'parallelisation' as opposed to 'denationalisation', and which involved selling the government's majority stake. Parallelisation was 'not the result of a premeditated, publicly articulated strategy', but a 'bureaucratic response to multiple and contradictory pressures: low returns from SOEs, lack of funds for modernisation, inability to fire workers, and demands from consumers to improve service'.[26]

By the late 1980s, the public sector in India had lost much of its reason for existence. It represented 50 per cent of the investment in manufacturing, but only 15 per cent of value added, and lagged consistently behind the private sector in terms of profitability. Excluding the petroleum sector, which enjoyed a monopolistic situation prior to 1991 (and even after that), SOEs as a whole were in the red in eight out of 10 years from 1981 to 1991 in India. However, as mentioned earlier, profitability cannot be the only benchmark for judging the performance of the public sector, whose primary reason for existence is derived from a worthwhile 'public purpose'. But as a UNIDO paper would note later, 'over the years, the policy-based division between public and private enterprise has gradually collapsed.... In the Indian

[24] Pandey, 'Economics and Politics of Privatization and India'.
[25] Pandey, 'Economics and Politics of Privatization and India' and Das, 'Improvidence in Fiscal System and Privatization', 107, quoted in Goulding, 'Retreating from the Commanding Heights', 581–612.
[26] Goulding, 'Retreating from the Commanding Heights', 582.

public sector today, there are a number of enterprises whose public purpose is hardly discernible'.[27]

In 1993, a committee headed by the former RBI Governor Dr C. Rangarajan recommended divestiture of up to 49 per cent of government equity in industries reserved for the public sector and up to 74 per cent of equity for government companies operating in the others, that is, competitive sectors. However, there were not many enthusiastic takers of the recommendation within the government, neither was there any broad national consensus on its merits. The government was loath to giving up its control, and unions were staunchly opposing any dilution of the government stake; in fact, they still do, even now. Privatisation was politically unacceptable then, and even now, there is resistance to the idea of large-scale privatisation and absence of consensus among all political parties on the issue. Manifestos of the parties carefully avoid any reference to the privatisation of the public sector: 'No political party in India...has the courage to mention privatisation as an article of faith'.[28] In the absence of any serious effort at privatisation, not much efficiency gains could be realised for the public sector.[29]

The sickness of the public sector enterprises became endemic during the 1990s. By 1995, as many as 140 central and state-owned companies were referred to the Board of Industrial and Financial Reconstruction (BIFR), which was India's corporate bankruptcy and restructuring body prior to the operationalisation of the new Companies Act of 2013. It was largely dysfunctional, with winding up orders given to only seven companies. BIFR was ineffective because companies in India were seldom allowed to go bankrupt; on the contrary, many 'sick' enterprises in the private sector had to be taken over

[27] UNIDO, *India: Towards Globalisation*, 48, quoted in ibid, 584.

[28] Singh, 'Privatization Debate and Sick Private Sector Undertakings', 19.

[29] There is a fine distinction between privatisation and disinvestment; the former entails transfer of ownership, which the latter does not. In actual terms, it translates into dilution of government stake, through sale of stock to private entities or individuals, of majority stake in case of privatisation and less than that in case of disinvestment. In disinvestment programmes where the government retains 51 per cent or more of the total equity capital of the public enterprises, the control and management of the enterprise remain with it.

by the government so as to protect their employees' interests, adding to its already heavy portfolio of troubled SOEs. Losses from such firms accounted for 22 per cent of the total SOE losses in 1992.[30]

The BIFR was set up as a quasi-judicial body in 1987 under The Sick Industrial Companies (Special Provisions) Act, 1985 (SICA), as part of the Department of Economic Affairs in the Ministry of Finance for revival and rehabilitation of potentially sick companies and closure or liquidation of non-viable and sick industrial companies. Its purpose was to examine the sickness of industrial companies and to help revive or close them as the case warranted. PSEs were brought under its purview by an amendment to SICA. SICA mandated the Board of Directors of a sick industrial company to make a reference to the BIFR, which would examine its accounts, assets and liabilities etc. In case it was convinced that the company had become sick, it would either give reasonable time to the company to make its net worth positive or it would appoint an operating agency (usually involving banks and financial institutions) to prepare a package for its revival, which might include one or more of the following: restructuring of the capital base of the company, infusion of capital, merger and amalgamation of the sick company with a healthy unit, providing soft loans, upgradation of technology and modernisation, management change, writing off the interest burden, rescheduling its loans or providing fiscal concessions like tax rebate, tax exemptions or tax reliefs, etc. If the BIFR was convinced that the sick industrial company was unlikely to recover, it could initiate proceedings with the High Court for the winding up of the company. Its decision would be binding on all the concerned parties.

Till the end of 2007, 5,471 references from the private as well the public sector were registered with the BIFR, out of which 1,337 were recommended for winding up, while 825 revival schemes were sanctioned. There were 66 sick public sector enterprises registered with the BIFR as of March 2008, of which the government had approved only 34 for revival. The performance and effectiveness of the BIFR were not particularly encouraging for many reasons. The few successful interventions of the BIFR include the recoveries of Bharat Heavy

---

[30] Goulding, 'Retreating from the Commanding Heights', 587.

Electricals Limited in the 1980s, Scooters India, Andrew Yule & Co, North Eastern Regional Agricultural Marketing Corporation and Arvind Mills in the private sector after 2000. The reasons for its ineffectiveness ranged from insufficient resources to lengthy and uncertain procedures to political unwillingness; in fact, it often became a conduit for prolonging the life of sick companies for years on end at the expense of the taxpayers' money, so much so that commentators have often described it as 'a graveyard of companies'.

With effect from 1 December 2016, SICA was repealed by the Sick Industrial Companies (Special Provisions) Repeal Act, 2003, resulting in the automatic dissolution of the BIFR and other bodies formed under the SICA. Under the new Companies Act, 2013, the National Company Law Tribunal and the National Company Law Appellate Tribunal were constituted in 2016, with jurisdiction over matters related to the management of a company as well as mergers, amalgamations and revival or rehabilitation of companies.

Under the new Companies Act, a company is defined 'sick' if its accumulated losses in any financial year equal 50 per cent or more of its average net worth during the 4 years immediately preceding the current financial year. Under SICA, companies were declared sick when their accumulated losses equalled or exceeded their net worth. Under the Companies Act, 2013 a company can be declared sick on application by secured creditors. On their disagreement for revival or to a revival package prepared by the Company Administrator of the sick company, a winding up order is passed by the NCLT.

The jurisdiction of the NCLT was further extended by the Insolvency and Bankruptcy Code, 2016 (IBC), enabling the NCLT to adjudicate the corporate insolvency processes. Thus, all proceedings pending before the BIFR and the appellate body, namely, the Appellate Authority for Industrial and Financial Reconstruction (AAIFR), stood automatically abated; however, the entity whose reference had abated could initiate fresh proceedings within 180 days of the commencement of the IBC, on 1 December 2016. The change thus consolidates the revival process for all companies under a single law, before a single tribunal, expected to make the process speedier and more efficient, subject to the NCLT getting adequate infrastructural and legal support.

Under the IBC, the corporate insolvency procedure can be initiated by any financial creditor, an operational creditor or by the company itself, by filing an application before the NCLT after complying with the prescribed procedural requirements. On admission of the application, the NCLT shall declare a moratorium period during where no legal proceedings may be instituted or continued against the debtor. Further, an 'interim resolution professional' will be appointed along with a public announcement of the initiation of the corporate insolvency process. A resolution plan may be approved by the NCLT to revive and rehabilitate the company within 180 days of the admission of the application, failing which the company is likely to be wound up as per the IBC provisions.

The New Economic Policy of 1991, while opening up hitherto prohibited sectors to the private industries, did not identify any objective of privatisation; it merely decided to disinvest 20 per cent of the equity in select CPSEs and refer the sick units to the BIFR. In the budget speech and Presidential address in 1991, it was emphasised that public sector undertakings were national wealth that should rest in the hands of citizens who had the right to own their shares, while the government would retain majority shareholding and management control over the CPSEs. No policy for privatisation was ever spelt out specifically, but the primary objectives behind privatisation were generally reckoned to include: (a) releasing the large amount of public resources locked up in non-strategic CPSEs for redeployment in social priority areas like basic health, family welfare, primary education and essential infrastructure; (b) stemming further outflow of scarce public resources for sustaining the unviable non-strategic CPSEs; (c) reducing the burgeoning public debt; (d) transferring the commercial risk exposure of public funds locked up in the public sector to the private sector if it was willing; and (e) releasing other tangible and intangible resources from the CPSEs, like the large technical manpower deployed in them and their redeployment in higher priority areas, in the social sectors that were short of such resources.[31]

Certain other benefits were also expected from privatisation, such as increasing the efficiency and self-reliance of the privatised companies

[31] Dept. of Investment & Public Asset Management (DIPAM), *Disinvestment Manual*.

by exposing them to the market discipline and competition, improving their corporate governance, ensuring a wider distribution of wealth to small investors and employees through offering shares of the privatised companies, making the capital market more efficient by imparting more depth and liquidity to it while establishing more accurate benchmarks for valuation and pricing, and facilitating the raising of funds by the privatised companies for their projects or expansion in future. Opening the SOEs to private investments was expected to increase the level of economic activities and benefit the economy, employment and government revenues in the medium to long term, besides giving consumers more choices, especially in the telecom and civil aviation sectors, by ending the state monopoly over them. The domestic industry of course had to brace for competition with cheaper, imported goods, but in the bargain, the common man was expected to get access to a whole range of quality goods at affordable prices, in the process nudging the Indian industries to become more competitive.[32]

How many of these objectives have been actually fulfilled remains highly debatable and questionable. Further, the process was also sabotaged by the unholy nexus between politicians, bureaucrats and crony capitalists who subverted the system for their own gains, which ultimately turned many of our well-performing PSUs into loss-making entities. However, the free entry of the private sector into the arena hitherto reserved for the public sector most significantly affected the CPSEs operating in sectors like telecommunication, petroleum extraction, refining and marketing, power generation and distribution and several basic goods industries like steel, aluminium, mining and transportation, etc. The policy also called for disinvestment of the government's stake while still not diluting government control over the CPSEs. Subsequent policies and reforms led to their listing in the stock exchanges with consequent changes in the accounting architecture including the disclosure norms and improvement in corporate governance. The withdrawal of budgetary support to loss-making or 'sick' enterprises warranted laying off workers to improve commercial viability, failing which they had to be closed.[33] The restructuring of the CPSEs followed as a result, with many becoming privatised.

---

[32] Ibid.
[33] Khanna, 'The Transformation of India's Public Sector'.

In this changed paradigm of free market capitalism dominated by deregulation, liberalisation and privatisation, CPSEs have been forced to submit to the market discipline and embrace open competition from domestic and international players. Protected and supported all along and unprepared for such a sudden exposure, many have perished, throwing thousands out of jobs. Both the UPA and NDA governments since the 1990s have followed this ideology manifested in increasing disinvestment and privatisation of the PSEs.

The progress of disinvestment in India has been rather slow compared to that in the other developing countries in East and South East Asia, Latin America and Central and Eastern Europe, especially in respect of infrastructure and financial services. Privatisation efforts in India so far can be divided into four distinct phases, starting with 1991–1992.[34] In December 1991, the government placed a monograph before the Parliament on the performance of CPSEs, followed by a 'Memorandum of Economic Policy for 1991–1992', which mentioned that up to 20 per cent of the government equity in selected CPSEs would be disinvested through mutual funds. The objective was to raise resources, encourage greater public participation in economic activities and promote greater accountability in the public sector.

In the landmark budget speech of July 1991 that unleashed the economic reforms in India, the Finance Minister Dr Manmohan Singh candidly admitted that the public sector had not been able to generate large investible surpluses, that 'the excessive and often indiscriminate protection provided to industry has weakened the incentive to develop a vibrant export sector' and that it had worked to the disadvantage of the country and the economy as a whole. 'At this critical juncture', he asserted:

> it has therefore become necessary to take effective measures so as to make the public sector an engine of growth rather than an absorber of national savings without adequate return. ...the portfolio of public sector investments would be reviewed so as to concentrate

---

[34] It may be mentioned that the word 'privatisation' was never mentioned in any document of the Government of India at the beginning of the process in 1991–1992. Government documents only referred to disinvestment and closure of sick public enterprises.

the future operations of the public sector in areas that are strategic for the nation, require high technology for the economy, and are essential for the infrastructure. In order to raise resources, encourage wider public participation and promote greater accountability, up to 20 per cent of government equity in selected public sector undertakings would be offered to mutual funds and investment institutions in the public sector, as also to workers in these firms.

Further, he stated:

Public enterprises which are chronically sick and which cannot be turned around, will be referred to the Board for Industrial and Financial Reconstruction, or to a similar high-powered body to be set up, for the formulation of revival or rehabilitation schemes; a social security mechanism will be created to fully protect the interests of the workers likely to be affected by the rehabilitation packages of the BIFR.

This was established in the form of a National Renewal Fund to provide a social safety net to protect the workers from the adverse consequences of the technological transformation and retrain them for an alternative productive role in the new economy. It was also assured that the public sector would be provided with autonomy in management, and corresponding accountability, through a system of MOUs between the government and public sector enterprises.

Though there was no policy statement made on privatisation, there indeed was a discernible pattern in the government's approach towards disinvestment and privatisation of the public enterprises. In a letter to the World Bank,[35] this was elucidated by Dr Manmohan Singh, which emphasised the government's intention to create no new enterprises except in sectors reserved for the public sector, no fresh nationalisation of sick industries, complete elimination of budgetary support and government loans to public enterprises within 3 years, beginning from 1992–1993, and raising of resources through partial disinvestment of public enterprises, besides referring the sick enterprises to the BIFR.

[35] Letter dated 11 November 1991, placed in Parliament on 26 February 1992; quoted in Mathur, *Public Enterprise Management*, 263.

Disinvestment and privatisation in India initially took place in different phases in a halting manner that was marred by debates, doubts and controversies. The first round of disinvestment took place from 1991 to 1993. Following the budget, in December 1991, a monograph on the performance status of public enterprises was placed before Parliament by the government. Between December 1991 and February 1992, the first tranche of 31 companies was offered for disinvestment of up to 20 per cent of government stakes held in them, determined on the basis of a complex valuation formula based on Net Asset Value (NAV) and Profit Earning Capacity Value (PECV).[36] The stakes were offered through the institutional investors who were supposed to act as buffers between the government and the stock market. The shares of these 31 CPSEs were offered in bundles, each bundle having stocks of nine CPSEs in it, and the disinvestment was done in two stages, in December 1991 and February 1992, respectively, from which ₹3,083 crore was collected. During the next financial year, in October 1992, eight CPSEs were disinvested, yielding ₹682 crore in the first round, followed by the disinvestment of shares of 12 CPSEs, yielding ₹1,184 crore. In the final round in March 1993, nine CPSEs were disinvested, yielding ₹47 crore only. The formula for valuation was changed following criticism of the previous formula,[37] inviting open tenders instead and keeping a minimum reserve price of ₹2.5 crore, which was the average of the prices recommended by three merchant bankers appointed for the purpose, IBDI, ICICI and SBI Capital Markets.[38] Details are shown in Annexure 6.1.

[36] NAV represents the value of the entity with reference to its asset base minus the attached liabilities on the valuation date. Under PECV method, the value is calculated by capitalising the average of the post-tax profits, usually for the preceding three years, at a specified capitalisation rate, which in this case was adopted as 10 per cent.

[37] A study by the Hyderabad-based IPE claimed that the government had lost ₹3,300 crore due to undervaluation, and could have realised larger values by listing all the PEs and timing the sales at more favourable market conditions. The CAG also criticised the clubbing of all the shares of different companies in a single bundle as being a reason for lowering of their values, besides lack of adequate preparation and publicity.

[38] Mathur, *Public Enterprise Management*, 263–264.

The manner in which these disinvestments were made—especially the pricing—attracted widespread criticism that put a halt to the process, with no disinvestments taking place during 1993–1994. Much of the criticism was, however, unfair, as the Finance Minister stated in the Rajya Sabha on 6 August 1993:

> It needs to be recognised that even under well-settled conditions, opinions can and do vary about the correct price of a share. Perceptions about future earning and prospects can differ significantly. This is more likely in case of public enterprises whose shares have not been traded in the past.[39]

To streamline the process, the Rangarajan Committee was appointed, which submitted its report in April 1993, as mentioned earlier. It recommended disinvesting up to 49 per cent of CPSE equity for industries explicitly reserved for the public sector[40] and over 74 per cent other industries. It also gave recommendations regarding the method of disinvestment, criteria for the valuation of shares, target clientele and other related issues. But the government did not take any decision on the Committee's recommendations.[41] The problems remained, and further processes of disinvestment met with public apathy. However, the next round of disinvestment began in October 1994, with the disinvestment of six enterprises yielding ₹2,230 crore to the government. The next sale occurred in January 1995, in which shares of five CPSEs fetched only ₹331 crore. The year 1995–1996 saw only one round of disinvestment, with four CPSES yielding only ₹168 crore, against a target of ₹7,000 crore. The tepid response resulted in a halt to further disinvestment during the next 2 years, 1996–1997 and 1997–1998. According to the Report of the World Bank (Global Development Finance), 2000, the overall earnings from privatisation till then were only US$7 billion. Till March 1999, disinvestment ranging from 2 per cent to 49 per cent had taken place in 40 undertakings; the largest

[39] Ibid, 265.
[40] Coal and Lignite; Mineral oils; Arms, Ammunition and Defence equipment; Atomic Energy, Radioactive minerals & Railway transport.
[41] https://dipam.gov.in/past-disinvestment-policy, accessed 30 September 2019.

chunk of over 40 per cent were in blue chip companies such as HPCL, VSNL, MTNL, IPCL and HOCL.

During the first 10 years, from 1990–1991 to 2000–2001, the government had managed to raise just ₹20,079 crore against the target of ₹54,300 crore from disinvestment. The annual target was achieved only in three out of these 10 years (1991–1992, 1994–1995 and 1998–1999), during which phase only minority stakes in these CPSEs were offloaded, with the government still retaining management control over all these enterprises, which was one reason it could not attract enough private interest. The lack of a clear-cut policy on disinvestment was another impediment; the government never spelt out its policies clearly or brought out any white paper on disinvestment and privatisation. The process of valuation of shares also lacked transparency; besides, the process was marred by strong opposition from trade unions, and even political will seemed to be lacking to the desired extent.[42]

The pricing of the shares of public enterprises, especially for those that were unlisted, was always problematic, while selling shares through auction also had its own problems, preventing wider public participation and the ability to tap the potential of the capital market. Timing was another important detrimental factor—shares of large CPSEs were offloaded when the markets were depressed, leading to lesser realisation from the sales. The necessary expertise in this was missing at the end of the government where babus without any such expertise presided over all important decisions on all matters, and even the CPSEs were not taken on board. Besides, the shares of only profitable PSEs like IOC, BPCL, HPCL, GAIL and VSNL could be sold to finance the fiscal deficits; many economists compared it to 'selling the family silver to pay the grocer'. The proceeds were never utilised to address the needs of the CPSEs or to expand and diversify them, neither were the problems of sick industries addressed through such disinvestment. We learnt nothing from the experiences of the other countries that had successfully negotiated their privatisation process. In the UK, privatisation was done by selling at fixed prices

---

[42] http://www.bsepsu.com/historical-disinvestment.asp, accessed 29 September 2019.

and also by tender with a fixed base price. By placing limits on indi-vidual shareholding, it was ensured that small investors also benefited from the sales. Employees who were the biggest stakeholders were given preferential terms for owning the shares of their own companies. As a result of these policies, 7 million out of a total population of 57 million owned shares of these companies in the UK. The entire process was followed by the establishment of strong public regulators in different sectors, like the Office of Telecommunications (OFTEL) in the case of British Telecommunications and the Office of Gas Supply (OFGAS)[43] in the case of British Gas. The success of British privatisation was ensured by paying meticulous attention to enlist the support and cooperation of the management and employees, with advice taken from lead managers of successful issues, merchant banks and Bank of England to decide on the pricing as well as timing of the issues while giving widespread media publicity to ensure wider public participation. All these were singularly absent in our disinvestment drives which were driven by generalist bureaucrats who were thor-oughly untrained and inexperienced in dealing with such technical and financial complexities.[44]

After the 1996 general elections, the Janata Dal-led United Front formed the government with the outside support of the Congress. In August 1996, it appointed a Disinvestment Commission, chaired by the former Planning Commission member Mr G. V. Ramakrishna; its purpose was to advice, supervise, monitor and give publicity to the disinvestment process. It was to examine carefully the withdrawal of CPSEs from the non-core and nonstrategic areas, assess its impact on the job security of employees and explore opportunities for their retraining and re-employment. The Commission was set up following the French example, which also inspired the mechanisms of Audit Board and MOUs earlier discussed in Chapter 3. The privatisation in France was implemented under the privatisation acts of 1986 and 1993 under which a Privatisation Commission was established to steer the

---

[43] OFGAS was converted to OFGEM, the Office of Gas and Electricity Markets, which is a non-ministerial government department and an independent National Regulatory Authority, in 1999.

[44] Mathur, *Public Enterprise Management*, 258–260.

process of privatisation forward.[45] The Commission was established to ensure that shares were not sold below their real value and that no preferences were made in the selection of investors. Besides, to avoid controversies of a political nature, it was essential to establish an objective and transparent process, which was also necessary to gain the confidence of the general public and investors.[46] The Privatisation Commission had independent experts from economic, financial and legal disciplines with a mandate to assess the value of shares to be offered and the choice of investors, and to determine the conditions of offer outside the regulated markets. In India, the Disinvestment Commission, however, lacked such parliamentary authority.[47]

During its extended tenure till October 2004,[48] the Disinvestment Commission had submitted recommendations on the privatisation of 41 CPSEs, proposing, instead of public offerings like in the past, strategic sales involving change in ownership and management for 29 and 8 CPSEs, respectively, while recommending for others public offerings or closure or deferment of disinvestment.[49] The strate-

---

[45] The major features of the Acts were 20 per cent foreign shareholding, 10 per cent shares earmarked for employees and compulsory authorisation of privatisation of large companies with more than 2,500 employees and a turnover of 2.5 billion francs.

[46] https://www.economie.gouv.fr/files/cptexpo2016en.pdf, accessed 18 October 2019.

[47] Mathur, *Public Enterprise Management*, 280.

[48] Subsequent to the formation of the UPA government, all the members and the Chairman of the Disinvestment Commission resigned in May 2004, and the Commission was wound up in late October 2004.

[49] Trade sale was recommended for six PSEs: ITDC, MFIL, R-0Ashok, U-Ashok, HCIL and PHL. Strategic sales were recommended for 18 PSEs: HTL, ITI, BALCO, BRPL, KIOCL, MFL, EIL, HPL, IBP, NEPA, HZL, PPCL, NFL, FACT, IPCL, HCL, SCI and HLL; in 11 cases, strategic sale has been implemented of which in two cases, privatisation has been partly implemented (19 Hotels of ITDC and 3 Hotels of HCI have been privatised). Minority share offerings were recommended for five PSEs: GAIL, CONCOR, MTNL, NOIL and NALCO; of these, the sale of MTNL shares was concluded in December 1997, while for NALCO, the disinvestment proposal was not pursued after July 2003. The closure/sale of assets was recommended for 4 PSEs: EPIL, ET&TDC, HVOC and RICL, while no disinvestment was proposed for RITES. For OIL, ONGC, NTPC, NHPC, PGCIL, SAIL and NLC, the disinvestment was deferred. (Source: https://dipam.gov.in/disinvestment-commission, accessed 9 October 2019.)

gic sale implied true privatisation with transfer of ownership and management control, though it was to be confined to non-strategic sectors. The Commission tried to address some of the issues that were left unresolved during the disinvestment made till then, such as strengthening of the profitable CPSEs to improve their profitability and competitiveness, enabling higher dividend pay-outs and hence an increase in their share prices for a better realisation of sales revenue, protection of employee interest including fair compensation through VRS, providing for employee participation in management, broad-basing the ownership, etc. For the strategic sectors,[50] it advised no disinvestment on considerations of national security. The rest of the CPSEs were classified by it into core and non-core groups, the former being engaged in industries that were capital/technology intensive, such as telecom, petroleum or power, in which it felt the presence of CPSEs was desirable in national interest and also for preventing the accumulation of economic power and capital in private hands, for which the policy prescription it suggested was retention of majority stake (51% or more) by the government. The non-core group included industries that were open to competition from the private sector and which usually included the larger number of entities for this group, the Commission suggested disinvestment up to as much as 74 per cent of the government stakes.

Most of the industries referred to the Commission were profit-making, as the sick ones were referred to the BIFR. The recommendations given by the Commission covered restructuring of the CPSEs, establishment of a disinvestment fund, delegation of greater powers, professionalising the Boards of CPSEs, etc. It also suggested guidelines on the sale process and its modalities, which included both public offerings for direct sale through a fixed price or strategic sale with or without technology transfer arrangements, joint ventures, leasing and management contract, etc. It also recommended the appointment of global financial advisers to protect employee interest and also for steering the process of disinvestment of the entities referred to it.

---

[50] As already stated, the classification of strategic areas was later revised in 2002 to include only defence, atomic energy and railway transport, treating all other undertakings as functioning in non-strategic areas.

Meanwhile, to take the programme of disinvestment and privatisation further forward, a Department of Disinvestment was created as a separate department in December 1999, which was renamed as the Ministry of Disinvestment in September 2001. From May 2004, the Department of Disinvestment became a part of the Union Ministry of Finance. By the end of 1999–2000, the institutional set-up for disinvestment included several authorities and bodies: the Disinvestment Commission, the Cabinet Committee on Disinvestment (CCD) under the direct control of the Prime Minister, the Inter-Ministerial Group, the Department of Public Enterprises and the Department of Disinvestment, besides the Core Group of Secretaries for Disinvestment, which recommended disinvestment proposals to the CCD.

It may be recalled that the period 1996–1999 was marked by huge political instability and uncertainty at the Centre. The United Front government collapsed in 1998 following withdrawal of support by the Congress, after which general elections were held in India in 1998 for the 12th Lok Sabha, which returned a hung Parliament with no party or alliance getting a clear majority. Although the Bharatiya Janata Party (BJP), under Mr Atal Bihari Vajpayee as Prime Minister, garnered support from 286 members and constituted the government, it ruled only for a few months before losing majority due to the withdrawal of support by the All India Anna Dravida Munnetra Kazhagam (AIADMK) in April 1999. In the vote-of-confidence motion in the Parliament, the government lost 272–273, that is, by a single vote, forcing a fresh general election to be held in September–October 1999, which returned the NDA government under Mr Vajpayee to power. His government was the first non-Congress government till then to last a full 5-year term, ending the period of political instability of the previous 3 years that saw three general elections. With the Vajpayee government assuming power in 1999, the disinvestment process got a boost, and the strategic sale of CPSEs by transferring ownership was launched, marking the beginning of the second phase of disinvestment of CPSEs in India.

In the budget speech of 1998–1999 earlier, it was announced that the government shareholding in CPSEs should be brought down to 26 per cent on a case-to-case basis, excluding the strategic sector CPSEs where the government would retain majority shareholding. The interest of workers was to be protected in all the cases. For this purpose, on 16 March 1999, the government had classified the CPSEs into strategic and non-strategic areas. In the budget speech of 1999–2000, it was announced that the government would continue to strengthen the strategic units and privatise the non-strategic ones through gradual disinvestment or strategic sale while devising viable rehabilitation strategies for the weak units. In a policy statement of the Union Budget for 2000–2001, the Finance Minister, Mr Yashwant Sinha, emphasised upon the restructuring and revival of potentially viable CPSEs, while closing down the non-viable ones. He also promised to bring down the government equity in all non-strategic PSUs to 26 per cent or lower, while protecting the interests of the workers. The major consideration in such lowering of government stake was to be governed by consideration of the need for the continued presence of the public sector in specific areas in public interest. The proceeds from disinvestment were to be utilised for meeting social sector expenditure, restructuring of the CPSEs and discharge of public debt.

Following this, the disinvestment process actually gathered aggressive momentum since 2000–2001. The period from 2001–2002 to 2003–2004 marked the maximum number of disinvestments, either by way of strategic sales or through public offerings of minority stake in the CPSEs. By 2004, the government's majority stakes in many profitable PSEs like Modern Food Industries Limited (MFIL), Bharat Aluminium Company Limited (BALCO), Computer Management Corporation (CMC), HTL, VSNL, Paradip Phosphates Limited (PPL), Indian Tourism Development Corporation (ITDC), Hotel Corporation of India (HCI), Hindustan Zinc Limited (HZL), Indian Petrochemicals Corporation Limited (IPCL), etc. were sold, mainly through the strategic sale route, allowing management control to pass onto monopoly industrial houses, such as BALCO and HZL to Sterlite (Vedanta group), VSNL and CMC (via TCS) to the Tatas and IPCL to Reliance, giving it command over 80 per cent of the country's petrochemical market. The realisations from these strategic sales were substantially higher than those from the minority stake sales. During this period, the government raised ₹21,164 crore from privatisation and disinvestment, even though it was less than the target of ₹38,500 crore.[51] Under both the UPA and NDA governments since then, the shares of most Navratna and Miniratna companies have been disinvested, including the shares of our most prized and profitable companies like ONGC, SAIL, NALCO, NTPC, BHEL, etc., while sick and unprofitable ones like Air India are being propped up by public funds. This is neither good economics nor good politics.

The Vajpayee-led NDA government was in fact the first government to set up a separate Ministry of Disinvestment, which was headed by Mr Arun Shouri. It privatised as many as 12 public sector companies during the tenure of NDA-1 (1999–2004), including the big and profitable enterprises like Maruti Udyog Limited (MUL). It would be interesting to assess the performance of some of the enterprises after their privatisation. Some of them were indeed case studies in how privatisation could result in remarkable improvements in performance of privatised entities. Two major public enterprises privatised in this period—HZL and BALCO—were taken over by the Vedanta group's flagship company, Vedanta Limited. HZL, which had posted a turnover of ₹1,418 crore in 2001–2002, had grown 17 times in as many years after privatisation, with its turnover exceeding ₹24,000 crore in 2017–2018. The turnover of BALCO under the same group had reached ₹9,000 crore in 2017–2018 from about ₹900 crore only in 2000–2001.[52]

In May 2002, the government approved disinvestment in MUL and sold it to the joint venture partner Suzuki Motors in two phases. In the first phase, MUL issued rights shares of ₹400 crore with the government, renouncing its rights to these shares to Suzuki, which paid ₹1,000 crore to the government as control premium to gain management control of the company. In the second phase, the government sold its existing shares through a public issue. The government completely exited MUL in 2006 with the company being renamed as Maruti Suzuki (India) Limited. Its turnover increased more than 14 times from around ₹6,000 crore in 2000–2001 to ₹88,581 during 2018–2019.

[51] http://www.bsepsu.com/historical-disinvestment.asp, accessed 29 September 2019.

[52] Dubey, 'Disinvestment Got Boost Under Vajpayee-led NDA Govt'.

The Tata Group had acquired two public sector companies CMC and VSNL. CMC Limited, involved in hardware and software systems, consultancy and networking, had increased its turnover from about ₹500 crore before getting privatised to ₹1,339 crore in 2013–2014, before being merged with TCS in 2014. VSNL was also sold to the Tata group for ₹1,439 crore and was renamed as Tata Communications; its turnover increased from almost ₹8,000 crore during 2001–2002 to around ₹17,000 crore in 2017–2018. There are unsuccessful companies among the privatised enterprises, too. Thus, MFIL was sold to Hindustan Lever (now Hindustan Unilever) in 2000; in 2006, HUL merged the company with itself, but it remained a misfit to Unilever's culture, which referred MFIL to the BIFR and subsequently sold the company to Singapore-based Everstone Capital. A comparison of receipts *vis-à-vis* targets between the NDA and UPA governments in respect of privatisation and disinvestment is shown in Table 6.1:[53]

Table 6.1 *Comparative Performance Between the NDA and UPA Governments in Respect of Privatisation/Disinvestment (₹ Crore)*

	Target	Actual Receipt	Achievement (%)
NDA-1 (Vajpayee Govt.)	63,500	29,000	47
UPA-1 & UPA-2 (Manmohan Singh Govt.)	133,000	92,724	70
NDA-2 (Modi Govt.)	309,237	280,490	91

Source: BSEPSU.com, quoted in Dubey, 'Disinvestment Got Boost Under Vajpayee-led NDA Govt'.

As far as the number of profitable enterprises was concerned, the economic reforms of 1991 did not have an immediate perceptible impact on the CPSEs. The percentage of loss-making CPSEs in fact increased from 43 in 1991–1992 to 47 in 2001–2002. The impact

[53] Ibid.

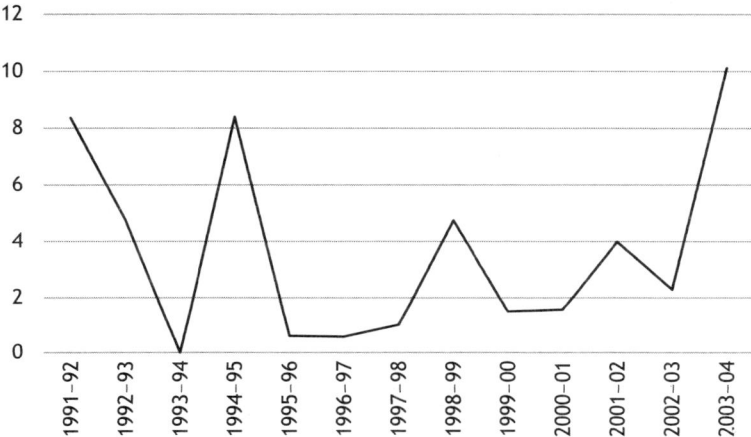

Figure 6.1 *Disinvestment Proceeds as Percentage of Fiscal Deficit*
Source: Economic Survey and Public Enterprises Survey, respective years.

would be felt only from 2009–2010, when the percentage of loss-making units declined to 27 and remained at that level ever since. Disinvestment and privatisation did finance the fiscal deficit to some extent, but its contribution varied from year to year, as can be seen from Figure 6.1, due to the inconsistent policies and inefficient implementation, often marked by the lack of transparency and also lack of coordination between the various agencies involved in the process. The privatisation experience in India does not provide any assurance about the optimal valuation methods to be applied in respect of the shares of CPSEs; it rather points to the optimality of a basket of methods to be applied depending on the specific market situation and the specific company being disinvested. Neither does the experience throw much light on the optimal route for privatisation and disinvestment among the many options available: public offering, auction, tender, negotiated sale, or some other route like liquidation, especially for unprofitable companies. Having learnt from the past mistakes when large-scale corruption had resulted in sub-optimal realisation of selling of national resources like telecom spectrum or allocation of coal blocks, the government now seems to prefer the safe route of auction for the sake of transparency and for avoiding controversy. However, it is not certain if this is the best route as far as realising the correct value is concerned. In the initial phase of disinvestment, hasty decisions without adequate planning, coupled with the inability to assess the correct timing for entering the market, had marred the process of disinvestment. These are complex issues requiring highly sophisticated technical knowledge lacking within the ministries and government departments. Unless this improves, the process of disinvestment is likely to remain inefficient with uncertain outcomes for a long time. The government can only ensure complete transparency in the process, the need for which cannot be overemphasised. Labour remains an important issue in all privatisation drives that need to be resolved amicably—many privatisations, like that of BALCO's, for example, have been delayed due to employee strikes and other related issues—and getting the employees on board remains an important consideration. There is also the issue of restructuring of CPSEs before privatising them, in order to reduce the liabilities and debts of ailing companies so as to attract the potential buyers, something that later jeopardised the privatisation of Air India. In 'defensive restructuring', any fresh investment into the enterprise is excluded in order to modernise it, which will necessarily increase its sale price and hence become counterproductive.

The third phase of disinvestment and privatisation began in May 2004 with the adoption of the National Common Minimum Programme (NCMP) by the incumbent UPA-1 government under Dr Manmohan Singh. The NCMP, supported by the Left parties, outlined the government's disinvestment policy and its intent to have a strong public sector. In a reversal of the policy of strategic sale pursued earlier, it thus promised to revive the sick and loss-making CPSEs while disinvesting only minority states in the profitable ones, and to retain management and ownership control. In January 2005, the government constituted the National Investment Fund (NIF) to channel the proceeds from the sale of minority stakes of these CPSEs. Seventy-five per cent of the annual income of NIF was to be used for selected social sector schemes in education, health, employment etc., while the remaining 25 per cent was to be used for meeting the capital investment requirements of profitable and revivable CPSEs. Instead of privatising the successful, profit-making CPSEs, the UPA government further pledged to devolve full managerial control and commercial autonomy to public companies operating in a competitive environment; these 'Navratna' companies were given the authority to raise necessary resources from the capital market. The policy also approved the listing of all unlisted but profitable CPSEs, each with a net worth exceeding ₹200 crore, through an Initial Public Offering (IPO), while retaining at least 51 per cent government stake and hence management control in these CPSEs. As a result of these policies, the disinvestment process stagnated during this period. During the 5 years from 2003–2004 to 2008–2009, the total receipts from disinvestments amounted to only ₹8,516 crore.[54]

The return of the UPA government in 2009 election boosted the stock market sentiments and initially led to a renewed thrust in disinvestment, which, as events would later unfold to prove, was driven by massive corruption. The selling of minority stakes in a number of profit-making CPSEs, both listed and unlisted, followed. In November 2009, the government approved an action plan for disinvestment in profit-making government companies that undertook to disinvest the listed profitable CPSEs, as well as to get the unlisted CPSEs with no accumulated losses and which had earned a net profit in the three preceding consecutive years, to be listed. Shares were offered to the public in respect of NHPC, OIL, NTPC, REC, NMDC, SJVN, EIL, CIL, MOIL, etc. During 2009–2010, the government collected ₹23,552 crore, though the momentum slowed down in 2010–2011, when against a target of ₹40,000 crore, only ₹14,000 crore was realised. However, in 2012–2013, the government was able to raise ₹23,857 crore against a target of ₹30,000 crore. In the following year, only ₹21,321 crore was realised against a target of ₹54,000 crore.

---

[54] Many of the loss-making PSUs earlier identified for strategic sale have been waiting for years for a buyer. There are several cases in which the disinvestment process has been going on for years without any result. The government is reluctant to use the Insolvency and Bankruptcy Code as the workers in that case may not get their dues. Between 2014 and 2019, as many as 33 loss-making PSUs were identified for closure, but closure proceedings have been initiated only in respect of a handful of firms, and the list of entities identified for strategic sale has remained static. Thus, no buyer has been found in respect of Scooters India, Pawan Hans Helicopters, Bharat Pumps & Compressors, etc.

Meanwhile, a new concept, the so-called PPP to address massive deficits in infrastructure financing—roads, ports, railways, airports etc.—is now ruling the roost, which actually shifts the state's responsibility from 'public' to 'private'. As the various CAG reports show, the terms of these partnerships are often heavily skewed in favour of private players at the cost of national revenue, confirming what many people believe the PPP to be—the 'privatisation of profits and nationalisation of losses'. A tell-tale example of what this PPP model can do to the economy has been seen in the ₹90,000 crore scam involving the Infrastructure Leasing and Financing Services (IL&FS), which has jolted our entire financial sector, sending many NBFCs and mutual funds into a tailspin, and about resolving which nobody seems to have any clue so far. The government had to step in to bail out a company that was involved in outright fraud over the last 30 years, with all its Board members escaping almost unscathed so far.

As public assets passed on to private hands, powerful conglomerates became even more powerful and economic and political power in society was redistributed and restructured. This process took away some of our best performing CPSEs, and the remaining ones were left to carve their own niches for themselves in the new scenario. Some managed the process of adjustment to the new reality with aplomb while many perished, and some are still languishing. Debates about the merits and means of privatisation the world over are far from settled. Many CPSEs have well adjusted themselves and are growing into global brands, though our state public sector enterprises continue to wallow in a very sorry state, without much hope for revival anytime soon.

The present phase of disinvestment began with the return to power of the NDA government after the 2014 general elections under Prime Minister Narendra Modi and its impressive victory in the 2019 Lok Sabha elections as well. Soon after assuming power in 2014, in one of the first major initiatives, the newly elected government disbanded the Planning Commission, the institution that was at the forefront of driving the economy through the Nehruvian philosophy of Fabian socialism, and replaced it with the NITI Aayog to act as its think tank, which, unlike the Planning Commission, did not have any power of resource allocation to the public sector or to the states. It sent a powerful signal that the public sector enterprises will have to be restructured and reformed, with the government keen on gradually withdrawing from business. Acting on the intent, however, proved rather difficult. The government's thinking was influenced by the recommendations of the NITI Aayog on the strategic sales of public sector enterprises, which, in turn, was influenced by the recommendations of the 14th Finance Commission.

The 14th Finance Commission was appointed by the UPA-2 government in January 2013, with Dr Y. V. Reddy, the former Governor of the RBI, as Chairman. Its Terms of Reference (ToR) included a specific reference to the public sector enterprises, requiring the Commission to consider 'the need for making the public sector enterprises competitive and market oriented; listing and disinvestment; and the relinquishing of non-priority enterprises', while making their recommendations. The Commission submitted its report in December 2014 for the 5-year period 2015–2020. It devoted one full chapter (Chapter 16) to the restructuring, reforms and disinvestment of the public sector enterprises. It viewed 'the need for making PSEs competitive and market oriented', 'listing and disinvestment' and 'relinquishing non-priority enterprises' as interrelated, and recognised the need for making them competitive and market-oriented, which would be necessary in order to realise higher yields from their disinvestment. Reiterating the 1998–1999 policy that government shareholding in PSEs was to be brought down to 26 per cent except in the case of the strategic sector, it preferred a 'case by case' evaluation, with a targeted investment portfolio view for each CPSE. It noted that even though there had been some progress in disinvestment in the past for raising budgetary resources, there had been no 'detailed and longer term framework' for the process. The Commission therefore highlighted the need for reassessing the role and significance of PSEs in the changed market scenario as well as for initiating a nationwide debate on their future.

Noting that most PSEs had come into existence decades ago when the realities of the market were different, with private capital being scarce and fiscal situations being tight, compared to the emerging new realities with a globally competitive private sector emerging in almost all sectors of the economy, and keeping in mind the fiscal implications and the interests of employees, the Commission observed that 'the strategic role of public enterprises in the national economy has to be considered in the context of a relatively open economy'. Therefore:

> It needs to be seen if the objectives of public sector enterprises have been achieved, and, if not, whether the original objectives have been redefined. Public enterprises were started with the objective of leveraging resources for development and there is no continued justification for public investments unless the enterprises are generating assured resources for the government.[55]

As such, strategic areas identified earlier that required the presence of the public sector in them also might have to be replaced by new strategic areas, and public sector entry might even be warranted by the imperfections of the market. It might also be advisable to explore the PPP model, to integrate 'elements of management control by the government through ownership, combined with market discipline inculcated by a measure of private ownership through listing and trading', in a dynamic way. For a comprehensive public sector enterprise policy, these new realities must be recognised along with the fiscal implications of retention or divestment of the PSEs.

The Commission recommended the 'Principles of Prioritisation' for retaining or disinvesting the government stake in the PSEs, by classifying them into enterprises in '"high priority" activities where public ownership should be predominant or in "priority" activities where a majority of public ownership would suffice' based on suitable criteria. These criteria for determining high priority or priority could be based on: (a) whether the area of operation of enterprises can be considered strategic in terms of public interest; (b) whether the enterprises have been earmarked for or assigned with 'natural resources with sovereign or quasi-sovereign functions';[56] (c) whether the enterprises are required to cater to market imperfections; (d) whether the enterprises are giving returns on investments higher than any alternative investment made by the government; and (e) whether these enterprises are public utilities, where PSEs' presence may be desirable. The rest of the enterprises

[55] Government of India, Report of the Fourteenth Finance Commission, Para 16.14.

[56] Ibid, Para 16.20.

could be categorised either as a 'low-priority' and 'non-priority' enterprises, 'based on some inter-related and non-exclusionary indicative criteria of market conditions and socio-economic considerations', including (a) whether private sector presence has been allowed and it has been functioning well in an area; (b) activities where unrestricted imports are permitted; (c) where the public enterprise is not a public utility, or is a public utility but regulated; (d) where the enterprise is not a statutory monopoly; and (e) where enterprises are loss-making and sick, unless there are other compelling reasons of broad public interest to retain them in the public sector, given the associated fiscal costs.

The Commission further suggested that in the case of non-priority enterprises, 100 per cent disinvestment would be in order, while in the cases of others, a view needs to be taken by the government about the quantum of disinvestment. In case of high priority enterprises, the disinvestment should not exceed 25 per cent, while in cases of priority industries, disinvestment should not exceed 49 per cent. In cases of enterprises categorised as low priority, disinvestment could go up to as much as 74 per cent. In case of statutory corporations, however, the Commission suggested that a more nuanced view of ownership, control and governance needs to be taken. The Commission also identified 88 CPSEs with insignificant outputs, with turnovers less than ₹100 crore and the total market share of each in its respective area being less than 1 per cent. The Commission regarded these enterprises as 'non-priority enterprises' and hence deserving of complete relinquishment of government ownership or control. Analysing the profiles of the 25 largest central public sector enterprises, it tried to categorise them into high priority, priority, low priority and non-priority enterprises. A similar exercise was undertaken for the top 10 profit and loss-making companies. Summaries of these lists, included in the Annexures 16.1 and 16.2 of the Report of the 14th Finance Commission, have been included in Annexures 6.2 and 6.3 to this chapter.[57] Such categorisation would, in the view of the Commission, '(i) facilitate co-ordinated follow-up action by policy makers and (ii) provide clarity to public enterprises themselves on their future and to

---

[57] It may be mentioned that the prioritisation made by the Commission in 2014 would be quite different from the situation prevailing now in 2019.

the financial markets about the opportunities ahead for them. The existing sick companies would all become non-priority enterprises, deserving to be divested completely. The Commission preferred sale through an open and transparent mechanism of bidding, while ensuring the interests of the workers to be protected.[58]

The Commission noted the inherent advantages of listing the CPSEs, which had significantly increased their values. As of May 2014, the total market capitalisation of 51 CPSEs amounted to ₹13.71 lakh crore. The existing policy envisaged allowing their wealth to be shared by the citizens, while the government retained management control and majority stake. The government's approach to disinvestment was guided only by fiscal considerations in making the listed profitable CPSEs resort to public offerings or issue of fresh shares, follow on public offers and permit the use of their surplus cash to buy back their own shares. The Commission noted that 'the process of disinvestment over the years has been generally *ad hoc*, based on the limited approach of short term fiscal gains to cover the budgetary revenue gaps to the extent feasible, depending on market circumstances'. It recommended that the existing policies and procedures of listing and disinvestment should be

> considered in future only within the parameters set by the approach to prioritisation for each enterprise in the entire portfolio of central public sector enterprises. We consider that the level of disinvestment should be relatable to desired level of public ownership in each category. We recommend that the level of disinvestment should be derived from the level of investment that the government decides to hold over the medium to long term in each enterprise, based on principles of prioritisation advised by us, while the process of disinvestment should take into account the market conditions and budgetary requirements, on a year to year basis.[59]

The Commission urged the government to 'identify new areas of strategic interests and sectors from the view point of enhancing the global competitiveness of the Indian industrial sector', especially in the 'fields of advanced engineering and special-capital equipment, areas of

---

[58] Ibid, Paras 16.21–16.27.
[59] Ibid, Paras 16.29–16.31.

strategic economic interests or to promote infrastructure investments for enhancing last mile access for improved services and facilities'. The fresh investment policy may consider all options, including PPPs and joint ventures with the private sector, 'to leverage the existing areas of strength, maintain the competitive edge and to cover the existing investment gaps'. The Commission also recommended the government to devise a policy in regard to the new areas of investments.[60]

As regards the utilisation of proceeds from the disinvestment that were going to the National Investment Fund (NIF), the Commission noted that NIF rules had been modified to enable their utilisation for select items of capital expenditure to obviate further borrowings from the market at higher costs, with which it agreed. However, since the NIF was a part of the Public Account of India, which was outside direct parliamentary control, the 14th Finance Commission reiterated the recommendation of its predecessor 'to maintain all disinvestment receipts in the Consolidated Fund for utilisation on capital expenditure. The National Investment Fund in the Public Account should, therefore, be wound up in consultation with Controller General of Accounts (CGA) and Comptroller & Auditor General of India (C&AG)'.[61]

The Commission very aptly observed that the competitiveness and market orientation of the CPSEs were impacted by

> the burden of implementing certain non-commercial social objectives of the government, generally in a non-transparent manner. This affects their profitability and competitiveness *vis-à-vis* the private sector. There is, therefore, a clear divergence between the government's role as a public service provider and running enterprises for profit.

The Commission recommended that they should be compensated adequately for implementing the social objectives of the government, in a timely manner and through a transparent budgetary subvention. Their monitoring and evaluation must also take into account their institutional constraints. Noting the overlap between the government's ownership

[60] Ibid, Paras 16.32–16.33.
[61] Ibid, Para 16.34.

and regulatory functions, it recommended reviewing the governance arrangement, 'especially in regard to separation of regulatory functions from ownership, role of the nominee as well as independent directors, and, above all, the framework of governance conducive to efficiency'.[62]

The Commission noted that even many profitable CPSEs were not paying dividends as per the government guidelines and that there were huge shortfalls in this, as pointed out by the CAG. While most of them were under-leveraged, being more interested in using the reserves rather than borrowing from the market to meet their capital requirements, the scope for borrowing for fresh investments remained under-explored. Reserves were also often built without specific investment plans for the future. If this process could be optimised, it would release funds for payment of dividends to the government, especially when it was faced with a tight fiscal situation. The Commission held that transfer to reserves might be permitted 'only after the entity has exhausted the options and limits for raising additional resources through debt, in terms of a defined enterprise limit on the optimum debt to equity ratio'. It recommended that the policies and procedures relating to borrowing and investment by the CPSEs, payment of dividends and transfer of excess reserves should be clearly enunciated and enforced.[63]

As regards the state public sector enterprises that have been 'historically set up by State Governments for achieving certain welfare goals or for promotional activities or as commercial enterprises', the Commission remarked that 'There are limits to the commercial viability of welfare-oriented State public sector enterprises' in areas like public distribution, cottage industries, etc. While promotional enterprises often required fiscal support, the public utility enterprises, which had a large presence in the public sector, entailed a significant fiscal burden because of government policy. The few enterprises that were earning profits, like those in land-based infrastructure and beverages trading, were able to do so because their profits arose mostly 'out of the government patronage to them rather than as a result of operational efficiency'. The poor financial performance of most of the SPSEs had

[62] Ibid, Paras 16.38–16.40.
[63] Ibid, Paras 16.43–16.44.

very seriously impacted the state finances, and the prescriptive rates of return recommended by earlier commissions could make no perceptible change on the ground. The states by and large had completely ignored the recommendations of the 13th Finance Commission to draw a roadmap for closure of their non-working companies and also a detailed operational and administrative framework for the closure/winding up of loss-making and non-working public sector enterprises, besides instituting a holding company with technical experts. As the 13th Finance Commission had observed, they remained 'a drag on the finances of State Governments'. The 14th Finance Commission reiterated its recommendations about the need for making the SPSEs financially viable, and for the relinquishment of sick and non-working public sector enterprises. Additionally, it stated that the principles of prioritisation and action based on these as suggested by it in relation to the CPSEs were also equally applicable in respect of SPSEs as well, with minor adjustments as and when necessary, and should be adopted by the state governments.[64]

The disinvestment of CPSEs had actually gathered pace since 2014, even before the 14th Finance Commission period (2015–2020), but was unaccompanied by other structural reforms necessary to revive and revitalise the public sector. The government had raised around ₹2.8 lakh crore through disinvestment during 2014–15 to 2018–19, representing over 90 per cent of the target set by itself. In 2017–18, the government was able to raise ₹100,642 crore against a target of ₹72,500 crore; in 2018–19, the amount raised from disinvestment amounted to ₹84,972 crore as against the target of ₹80,000 crore.

In August 2017, the NITI Aayog brought out a document called *India: Three Year Action Agenda, 2017–18 to 2019–20*, 'to recommend policy changes and programmes for action from 2017–18 to 2019–20, the last 3 years of the Fourteenth Finance Commission award. A second document containing the *Fifteen Year Vision and Seven Year Strategy* is currently under preparation at the NITI Aayog', as the Preface to the document declares. The document provides a comprehensive reform agenda for the union and the state governments to implement.

[64] Ibid, Paras 16.50–16.54.

The forecast for non-debt capital receipts, that is, disinvestment of public sector enterprises, in 2017–2018 was ₹84,400 crore, which was 49 per cent higher than the revised estimates for 2016–2017. The revenue forecast from disinvestment and strategic sales was kept at ₹80,000 crore in each of the two subsequent years, 2018–2019 and 2019–2020. In this document, the NITI Aayog recommended that the PSEs that did not serve any public purpose should be sold off, primarily for unlocking their full potential through private sector involvement, but the objective of revenue augmentation was also equally important.[65]

The document identified the major action areas in the near term, which included closure of sick CPSEs and strategic disinvestment of viable CPSEs. It noted that while there were 235 operational CPSEs as of 2016, 74 of these were either sick or loss-making. It recommended actions for different CPSEs including closure, revival, merger with other CPSEs, long-term lease (in the case of hotels) and transfer to state governments, besides strategic sale.[66] As the document noted: 'Any revival of a non-strategic CPSE must be based on sound commercial principles and must have an element of commercial funding, whether through equity or loan. It should not rely principally on budgetary support or sale of land'.[67] The Aayog also identified CPSEs for strategic disinvestment and submitted two lists thereof, which got the in-principle approval of the Cabinet Committee on Economic Affairs in respect of strategic disinvestment of 20 CPSEs.[68]

Subsequently, the Aayog had identified more CPSEs for strategic sale. By February 2019, five such lists were submitted by it to the DIPAM, including both profitable as well as non-profitable CPSEs and taking the total number of CPSEs identified for strategic sale to 35.

---

[65] NITI Aayog, *India: Three Year Action Agenda*, Para 3.23.

[66] The Union Cabinet had already approved the closure of six CPSEs: HMT Watches Limited, HMT Chinar Watches Limited, HMT Bearings Limited, Tungabhadra Steel Products Limited, Hindustan Cables Limited and Central Inland Water Transport Corporation, for which the concerned ministries were taking the necessary steps.

[67] NITI Aayog, *India: Three Year Action Agenda*, Paras 16.4, 16.5.

[68] Ibid, Para 16.6.

These included Air India, Air India subsidiary AIATSL, Dredging Corporation, BEML, Scooters India, Bharat Pumps Compressors and the Bhadrawati, Salem and Durgapur units of steel major SAIL. Other CPSEs for which approvals for outright strategic sale were already given included Hindustan Fluorocarbon, Hindustan Newsprint, HLL Life Care, Central Electronics, Bridge & Roof India, Nagarnar Steel plant of NMDC and units of Cement Corporation of India and ITDC, besides helicopter services provider Pawan Hans, which is a joint venture between the government and ONGC, with the government holding 51 per cent and ONGC owning 49 per cent shares.[69]

In June 2019, the Aayog identified over 50 CPSE assets for disinvestment, including non-core assets like land and industrial plants of major CPSEs such as NTPC, Cement Corporation of India, BEML, SAIL, etc. This was necessary to realise the ambitious target from disinvestment for the year, and also to generate wealth and value on equity for the shareholders, and was in addition to the 35 profitable and loss-making CPSEs previously identified by the Aayog for strategic sale, as mentioned earlier. Earlier in the year, the Union Cabinet had approved laying down an institutional framework for monetisation of identified non-core assets of the CPSEs under strategic disinvestment. Once the Ministerial panel set up for the purpose, which is headed by the Finance Minister, approves the monetisation of such assets, the process must be completed within a year.[70]

After the July 2019 budget presentation, the government identified 10 more CPSEs for disinvestment of minority stake through public offerings, taking the number of listed CPSEs to 69. In September 2019, the Aayog again submitted a list of 11 CPSEs, which included Rashtriya Ispat Nigam Limited (RINL) and Shipping Corporation of India (SCI).[71] Even though the government had set ambitious targets for strategic sale and disinvestment for 2019–2020, the recommendations of the NITI Aayog have not seen any serious implementation so

[69] https://www.thehindubusinessline.com/companies/35-cpses-lined-up-for-strategic-sale/article26166807.ece, accessed 21 October 2019.
[70] *Business Today*, 'SEBs to Dive Deeper into Debt as they Miss Uday Scheme Targets', 7 June 2019.
[71] *Times of India*, New Delhi, 14 September 2019.

far, except announcements and assurances issued by the government from time to time. The progress in terms of raising money through strategic sale has been rather limited so far during the year. Monetising non-core assets like land is also likely to pose serious challenges for many reasons, including the lack of clarity on land titles. Strategic sales of mining companies are also problematic and long drawn in view of the possible involvement of state governments concerned.

A major failure of past disinvestment was in the case of the privatisation of Air India. In March 2018, the government had decided to sell all but 24 per cent of its stake in Air India. The attempt failed not only because investors were unhappy with the government still retaining 24 per cent stake, but also because its debt of over ₹33,000 crore was bundled with the sale. Realising that investors would not be interested in inheriting such a huge liability, the government subsequently formed the Air India Assets Holding Limited (AIAHL), a Special Purpose Vehicle (SPV) to transfer a part of the airline's debt, which was not backed by any assets, or its non-core assets or non-operational assets. AIAHL subsequently raised ₹7,000 crore from the market through a bond sale to refinance its debt inherited from Air India. However, Air India's debt increased to over ₹55,000 crore in March 2018 and then to ₹58,352 crore in March 2019. In the budget it presented in July 2019 after winning its second term, the government announced its intention of offloading its entire stake in Air India, whose attractiveness to investors had increased after the collapse of Jet Airways, to meet its ambitious disinvestment target of ₹1.05 lakh crore during 2019–2020. The Finance Minister had said during her budget speech:

> Strategic disinvestment of select central public sector enterprises would continue to remain a priority of this government. In view of current macroeconomic parameters, the government would not only reinitiate the process of strategic disinvestment of Air India, but would offer more CPSEs for strategic participation by the private sector.

Realising this target of ₹1.05 lakh crore from strategic disinvestment is crucial in view of the government's decision to drastically reduce the corporate income tax rates in September 2019[72] for reviving a slowing economy, which is estimated to cause a revenue loss amounting to ₹1.45 lakh crore. As discussed earlier, Air India has been surviving on bailout packages from the government and does not have the money to pay the salaries of its staff.[73] Its market size has been shrinking continuously, from 19.4 per cent in 2013 to around 13.3 per cent in May 2017, as low cost private airlines like Indigo and SpiceJet have been claiming increasing shares of the aviation market. By March 2019, Air India's share of the market had dwindled to less than 13 per cent of the domestic market share. However, the failure of the attempts to revive Jet Airlines has somehow improved the prospects of Air India to attract fresh investors, and the government is expected to put it on the block for sale well before the end of the year.

The proposal for the outright sale of Air India was cleared by the Cabinet Committee on Economic Affairs, chaired by the Prime Minister himself, which also included the approval for the sale of five Air India subsidiaries—Air India Engineering Services, ground handling arm Air India Transport Services, Air India Charters, which operates Air India Express and Airline Allied Services, which in turn operates Alliance Air and Hotel Corporation of India, along with a joint venture between Air India Limited and Singapore Airport Terminal Services (SATS), called Air India SATS Airport Services Private Limited (AISATS), to upgrade Indian airports to world-class facilities in order to attract more airlines. Having announced its intention to sell 100 per cent stake in Air India, the government now has to take a call on the associated modalities and other related questions, including its unsustainable debt, inclusion of foreign investors in bidding and splitting of Air India's operations into domestic and

---

[72] The government slashed the corporate tax rate from 30 per cent to 22 per cent for the existing companies and from 25 per cent to 15 per cent for the new manufacturing companies. Including a surcharge and education cess, the effective tax rate for existing companies would now come down to 25.17 per cent from 34.94 per cent. This reduction is conditional to the companies foregoing any exemption or incentive which they currently enjoy.

[73] The government has already invested ₹23,993 crore out of ₹30,231 crore approved as equity infusion into Air India till 2020–2021 as part of its turnaround plan approved by the UPA-II government.

international sectors, before the actual sell-off, and whether to divest its subsidiaries simultaneously or separately, etc.

The success of the process of withdrawal from most of the business by the government will be impacted by many factors, including the present retarding phase of the economy and the slowing down of investment as a whole. However, the government has shown some consistency and sincerity in implementing the 14th Finance Commission's recommendations of prioritisation, even though the policy of such prioritisation has not been clearly spelt out as yet. However, if the proposals are backed by a strong political will, there is a distinct possibility that sometime in the foreseeable future, the strategic sales of CPSEs will succeed in attracting a sufficient number of potential buyers, and in the process, the privatised CPSEs will become more efficient and integrated with the market to become globally competitive. Studies have shown that privatisation leads to 'significantly higher profitability, higher efficiency, generally higher investment levels, higher output, higher dividends, and lower leverage post privatization'.[74] In a study undertaken in respect of pre- and post-privatisation performance of 11 CPSEs that had undergone strategic disinvestment from 1999–2000 to 2003–2004 and comparing their performance with their private sector peers using the statistical difference-in-differences (DiD) methodology,[75] the Economic Survey of the Government of India for 2019–2020 found that there were significant improvements in the performance of the CPSEs after privatisation in terms of a host of parameters like net worth, net profit, Gross Revenue, Return on assets (ROA), Return on equity (ROE), net profit margin, sales growth and Gross profit per employee due to privatisation. It found that:

> The trends confirm that the performance of the privatized CPSE and its peers is quite similar till the year of privatization. However, post privatization, the performance of the privatized entity improves significantly when compared to the change in the peers' performance over the same time period.[76]

---

[74] Government of India, *Economic Survey, 2019–20*, Vol. 1, 204.

[75] DiD estimates the effect of a specific intervention on the sample and compares the changes in their outcomes over time with a control group not subjected to the said intervention.

[76] Government of India, *Economic Survey, 2019–20*, Para 9.8, 223.

Table 6.2 *Profitable CPSEs Under Major Ministries: 2019–2020*

S. No.	Ministry of	No. of Profit-making Companies	No. of Loss-making Companies
1	Tourism	5	3
2	Textiles	4	5
3	Steel	9	4
4	Railways	17	7
5	Power	23	2
6	Petroleum and natural gas	18	4
7	Heavy industries and public enterprises	15	14
8	Defence	11	2
9	Communication	5	4
10	Commerce and industry	7	2
11	Coal	8	3
12	Civil aviation	6	4
13	Chemicals and fertilisers	12	8
	Total	**140**	**62**

Source: Government of India, *Economic Survey*, Vol. I, p. 225.

However, complete withdrawal of the government from the public sector is a no-brainer. Many of the CPSEs still remain profitable and viable. As Table 6.2 shows, out of 202 CPSEs under the 13 major ministries, each having more than 10 CPSEs under its control, as many as 140, or 69 per cent, are still profitable, though they underperform in the market.

PSEs will continue to function in many sectors, both strategic and non-strategic, but perhaps with a much broader set of goals than commercial, which is consistent with their founding principles. It is therefore necessary to formulate policies and incorporate the global best practices to transform the remaining CPSEs into truly national and international brands and champions, which is the subject of the next and the last chapter of this book.

Annexure 6.1 Disinvestment of the CPSEs: 1991–1992 to 2010–2011 (₹ Crore)

Year	Target Receipts	Actual Receipts	Methodology Adopted
1991–1992	2,500	3,038	Minority shares sold through auction in bundles for very good, good and average companies.
1992–1993	2,500	1,913	Share sold separately for each company.
1993–1994	3,000	–	Equity of seven companies sold by open auction, but proceeds received in 1994–1995.
1994–1995	4,000	4,843	Sale through auction.
1995–1996	7,000	362	Equity of four companies auctioned.
1996–1997	5,000	380	GDR (VSNL) in international market.
1997–1998	4,800	902	GDR (MTNL) in international market.
1998–1999	5,000	5,371	GDR-VSNL; domestic offerings of CONCOR and GAIL; cross purchase by three oil sector companies, that is, GAIL, ONGC and IOC.
1999–2000	10,000	1,860	GDR-GAIL; domestic offering of VSNL; capital reduction and dividend from BALCO; strategic sale of MFIL.
2000–2001	10,000	1,871	Sale of KRL, CPCL and BRPL to CPSEs; strategic sale of BALCO and LJMC.
2001–2002	12,000	5,632	Strategic sale of CMC, HTL, VSNL, IBP, PPL, hotel properties of ITDC and HCI, slump sale of Hotel Centaur, Juhu Beach, Mumbai, and leasing of The LaLit Ashok, Bangalore; special dividend from VSNL, STC and MMTC; sale of shares to VSNL employees.
2002–2003	12,000	3,348	Strategic sale of HZL, IPCL, hotel properties of ITDC, slump sale of Centaur Hotel, Mumbai Airport, Mumbai; premium for renunciation of rights issue in favour of SMC; put option of MFIL; sale of shares to employees of HZL and CMC.

Year	Target	Achievement	Details
2003–2004	14,500	15,547	Strategic sale of JCL; call option of HZL; offer for sale of MUL, IBP, IPCL, CMC, DCI, GAIL and ONGC; sale of shares of ICI Ltd.
2004–2005	4,000	2,765	Offer for sale of NTPC and spill over of ONGC; sale of shares to IPCL employees.
2005–2006	–	1,589	Sale of MUL shares to Indian public sector financial institutions andbanks as well as employees
2006–2007	–	–	–
2007–2008	–	4,181	Sale of MUL (₹2,366.94 cr) shares to public sector financial institutions, public sector banks and Indian mutual funds and sale of PGCIL (₹994.82 cr) and REC (₹819.63 cr) shares through offer for sale.
2008–2009	–	–	
2009–2010	–	23,552	₹2,012.85 cr NHPC, ₹2,247.05 cr OIL, ₹8,480.098 cr NTPC, ₹882.52 cr REC, ₹9,930.42 cr NMDC
2010–2011	40,000	22,763	₹1,062.74 cr SJVN, ₹959.65 cr EIL, ₹Cr 15,199.44 cr CIL, ₹3,721.17 cr PGCIL, ₹618.75 cr MOIL, ₹582.45 cr SCI
2011–2012	40,000	13,894	₹1,144.55 cr PFC, ₹12,749.5 cr ONGC
2012–2013	30,000	23,957	₹124.97 cr NBCC, ₹807.03 cr HCL, ₹5,973.27 cr NMDC, ₹3,141.51 cr OIL, ₹11,457.54 cr NTPC, ₹310.15 cr RCF, ₹627.84 cr NALCO, ₹1,514.50 cr SAIL
2013–2014	40,000	15,819	₹571.71 cr MMTC, ₹259.56 cr HCL, ₹101.08 cr NFL, ₹30.17 cr ITDC, ₹4.54 cr STC, ₹358.21 cr NLC, ₹2,131.28 cr NHPC, ₹1,637.32 cr PGCIL, ₹497.32 cr EIL, ₹1,886.78 cr BHEL, ₹5,341.49 cr IOCL, ₹3,000 cr CPSE-ETF, ₹0.0040 cr employee OFS of NMDC
2014–2015	43,425	24,349	Employee OFS: ₹3.60 cr of NFL, ₹48.16 cr NTPC, ₹1,719.54 cr SAIL, ₹22,557.63 cr CIL, ₹4.16 cr MMTC, ₹3.17 cr HCL, ₹12.45 cr NALCO

(Annexure 6.1 Continued)

(Annexure 6.1 Continued)

Year	Target Receipts	Actual Receipts	Methodology Adopted
2015–2016	69,500	23,997	₹1,608.00 cr REC, ₹1,671.00 cr PFC, ₹53.33 cr DCIL, ₹9,369 cr IOC, ₹642.5 cr EIL, ₹5,014.55 cr NTPC, ₹1,155.20 cr CONCOR, ₹198.85 cr BDL buyback, ₹4,284.37 cr HAL buyback
2016–2017	56,500	46,247	₹2,716.55 cr NHPC, ₹262.49 cr IOCL & ₹203.78 cr NTPC Employee OFFERS, ₹2,831.71 cr NALCO buyback, ₹399.93 cr HCL, ₹7,519.15 cr NMDC & ₹793.87 cr MOIL buyback, ₹2,201.14 cr NBCC, ₹1,802.60 cr BEL buyback, ₹31.38 cr EIL Employee OFFERS, ₹2,638.24 cr CIL buyback, ₹2,096.35 cr SUUTI, ₹21.27 cr NHPC & ₹0.93 cr DCIL Employee OFFERS, ₹9.34 cr CONCOR Employee OFFERS, ₹5,999.99 cr CPSE-ETF, ₹2,000 cr remittance from SUUTI, ₹484.95 cr MOIL, ₹6,682.32 cr disinvestment of SUUTI Holdings in ITC, ₹1,672.66 BEL, ₹1,948.52 cr NHPC buyback, ₹1,429.38 cr NLC buyback, ₹2,499.99 cr CPSE-ETF (FFO 2)
2017–2018	72,500	100,057	₹3.73 cr HCL Employee OFFERS, ₹1,191.73 cr NALCO OFFERS, ₹1,207.35 cr HUDCO IPO, ₹1,135.26 cr OIL buyback, ₹205.15 cr RCF, ₹4,153.65 cr strategic disinvestment, ₹530.72 cr NFL OFFERS, ₹404.71 cr HCL OFFERS, ₹470.01 cr CSL (IPO-Piggy Back), ₹657.81 cr EIL buyback, ₹9,117.92 NTPC OFFERS, ₹79.51 cr BEL Employee OFFERS, ₹151.14 cr NTPC Employee OFFERS, ₹450.53 cr BDL buyback, ₹9,704.16 cr C IPO Piggy Back, ₹722.29 cr NLC OFFERS, ₹0.36 cr HCL Employee OFFERS, ₹7,653.32 cr NIA IPO Piggy Back, ₹14,500 cr Bharat 22—ETF NFO, ₹50.51 cr NALCO Employee OFFERS, ₹253.48 cr MDL buyback, ₹190.59 cr IRCON buyback, ₹921.50 cr HAL buyback, ₹77.62 cr GRS E buyback, ₹49.55 cr HSCC (India) Ltd. buyback, ₹455 cr SPMCIL buyback, ₹1,223.13 cr NMDC OFFERS, ₹36,915.00 cr HPCL–ONGC Deal (off market) ₹29.96 cr NBCC (India) Ltd. Employee OFFERS, ₹238.92 cr Antrix Corp. Ltd. buyback, ₹558.68 cr SJVN Ltd. buyback, ₹1,400.00 cr Income from management of SUUTI's investment, ₹217.76 cr BEL buyback, ₹130.85 cr MOIL buyback, ₹950.35 cr BDL IPO, ₹4,054.66 cr HAL IPO.

Year			
2018–2019	80,000	84,972	₹434.14 cr MIDHANI IPO, ₹8,325.26 cr Bharat 22—ETF, ₹460.51 cr RITES IPO, ₹466.00 cr IRCON IPO, ₹342.90 cr GRS E IPO, ₹5,218.30 cr CIL OFFERS, ₹205.34 cr KIOCL Ltd. Buyback, ₹285.00 cr HSCC (India) Ltd. Strategic Disinvestment, ₹17,000.00 cr CPSE-ETF FFO 3, ₹260.41 cr NALCO Ltd. Buyback, ₹989.86 cr NLC Buyback, ₹17.33 cr CIL Employee OFFERS, ₹137.30 cr CSL Buyback, ₹992.41 cr BHEL Buyback, ₹397.90 cr NHPC Ltd. Buyback, ₹10,404.59 cr Bharat 22 ETF-FFO 2, ₹2,647.00 cr IOCL Buyback, ₹5378.66 cr SUUTI Sale of Axis Banks Shares, ₹2,510.51 cr ONGC Ltd. Buyback, ₹9,350.07 cr CPSE-ETF FFO 4, ₹1,039.71 cr CIL Buyback, ₹768.77 cr NMDC Ltd. buyback, ₹1049.17 cr DCIL strategic disinvestment, ₹14,499.99 cr PFC-REC deal strategic disinvestment, ₹720.80 cr Oil India Ltd. buyback, ₹210.60 cr MSTC Ltd. IPO, ₹79.80 cr NTCC Ltd., ₹779.02 cr sale of shares under the custody of CEPI
2019–2020	105,000	12,357	₹475.89 cr RVNL IPO, ₹1,881.21 cr enemy shares sale, ₹10,000.39 cr CPSE-ETF FFO-V
Grand total	**568,225**	**433,209**	

Source: https://dipam.gov.in/disinvestment-till-now/2502, accessed 28 August 2019.

Annexure 6.2 Illustrative Categorisation of Top 25 CPSEs in Terms of Net Turnover/Revenue for the Year 2012–2013 (₹ Crore)

S. No.	CPSE Name	Turnover	Profit/Loss	Govt. Holding (%)	Return on Equity (%)	Market Capitalisation as on 31 September 2014	Illustrative Categorisation
1	IOC	470,651	5,005	78.92	18.19	87,989	High priority
2	BPCL	250,649	2,643	54.93	15.89	47,391	Priority
3	HPCL	215,877	905	51.05	6.59	16,327	Priority
4	FCI	120,844	−4	100	−0.20	Unlisted	Priority
5	ONGC	83,309	20,926	69.23	16.81	349,535	High priority
6	MRPL (ONGC subsidiary)	68,838	−757	71.62	−11.7	10,787	Priority
7	NTPC	66,200	12,619	84.5	15.70	114,694	High priority/priority
8	BHEL	50,963	6,615	67.72	26.07	49,062	Priority/low priority
9	SAIL	49,987	2,170	79.99	5.29	28,748	Low priority
10	GAIL	48,195	4,022	57.35	16.60	57,012	Priority
11	CPCL (IOC subsidiary)	46,859	−1,767	51.88			
12	MMTC	28,599	−71	99.33	−5.27	6,355	High priority/priority
13	BSNL	25,655	−7,884	100	−12.39	Unlisted	Priority

14	SECL (CIL subsidiary)	21,408	4,299	100	49.84	Unlisted	High priority
15	STCL	19,042	18	91.02	3.04	1,197.60	Non-priority
16	OVL (ONGC subsidiary)	17,558	3,929	100			
17	PFC	17,260	4,420	89.78	18.37	30,968	Priority
18	AI	16,078	−5,199	100	33.24[1]	Unlisted	Priority/low priority
19	HAL	14,329	2,997	100	22.40	Unlisted	Priority
20	RINL	13,565	353	100	2.83	Unlisted	Low priority
21	RECL	13,519	3,818	66.80	21.87	24,682	priority
22	PGCIL	12,758	4,235	69.42	16.07	62,617	High priority
23	PECL	12,183	97	100	26.78	Unlisted	Non-priority
24	MCL (CIL subsidiary)	10,784	4,212	100	47.12	Unlisted	High priority
25	NMDC	10,713	6,342	90	23.05	65,576	High priority

Source: Annexure 16.1, report of the Fourteenth Finance Commission, Government of India.
Note: In case of subsidiary company, the holding indicated is by the parent company.
[1] Both shareholders' funds and profits are negative.

Annexure 6.3 Assessment of CPSEs Falling in the Category of Top Ten Profit/Loss-Making Companies, Which Do Not Fall in the Category of Top 25 Companies on Turnover Basis (₹ Crore)

S. No.	CPSE Name	Turnover	Profit/ Loss	Govt. Holding (%)	Return on Equity (%)	Market Capitalisation as on 31 September 2014	Illustrative Categorisation
Profit making							
1	CIL	279	9,794	89.65	47.74	215,609	High priority
Loss making							
2	MTNL	3,429	-5,321	56.25	–	1,877	Non-priority
3	HPFMCL	4	-1,561	51.00	–	NA	Non-priority
4	HCL	0.07	-885	99.60	–	NA	Non-priority
5	BPRL (BPCL subsidiary)	0	-383	100 (held by BPCL)	–	Unlisted	Non-priority
6	HFCL	–	-381	100	–	Unlisted	Non-priority
7	FC(T)L	2,364	-354	97.38	–	1,922	Non-priority
8					–		Non-priority
9					–		Non-priority
10					–		Non-priority

Source: Annexure 16.2, report of the Fourteenth Finance Commission, Government of India.

CHAPTER 7

Reform and Reform Roadmap of PSEs

The *Istituto per la Ricostruzione Industriale* (IRI), or Institute for Industrial Reconstruction, was established in Italy in 1933 as a temporary body to tackle the financial crisis that had been building up for quite some time. Italy had emerged from the First World War devastated in every respect. It had spent more on the war than its total expenditure during the previous 50 years and lost about a million of its youth who were either dead or rendered incapacitated through injuries in the war. The war debt and food shortages led to spiralling inflation and threw the economy into a prolonged depression. By 1922, when the fascists under Benito Mussolini had come to power, its economy was already teetering on the brink of a collapse. Then, it was the turn of the Great Depression to hit Italy with full force during the early 1930s. Industries started failing, triggering a corresponding crisis in the banks that were interlocked with the failing industries and had lent money that could not be repaid by them. Three major Italian banks, the *Banco di Milano*, the *Credito Italiano* and the *Banca Commerciale Italiana*, went bankrupt in May 1931. As the financial crisis deepened, the meltdown spread in both the financial and industrial sectors, and unemployment rose sharply. The government was forced to act finally, and it created the IRI in January 1933 to take over *Banca Commerciale Italiana*, *Credito Italiano* and *Banco di Roma*, the three major banks with 'large problem portfolios of industrial shareholdings', giving Italy the largest industrial sector in Europe through government-linked companies (GLCs).[1] In a speech to the Chamber of Deputies on 26 May 1934, Mussolini boasted: 'Three-fourth of the Italian economy, industrial and agricultural, is in the hands of the state'.[2] Eventually, the IRI 'became the owner not only of the three most important Italian banks, which were clearly too big to fail, but also of the lion's share of the Italian industries'.[3] It would eventually become one of the biggest holding companies of the world.

After World War II, IRI was instrumental in financing Italy's reconstruction through the big infrastructure projects by building roads and telephone networks and investing in the steel and engineering sectors. It became Italy's largest public sector employer and remained so for a long time. It owned stakes in a number of companies from Alitalia, Italy's national airline, to a company that even made Christmas cakes. As its outreach got extended, politicians became increasingly involved, dictating where investments should go, and IRI became a tool of state planning. 'The effect of giving the public sector businesses objectives that were not aimed at profit was like that of a Trojan horse,' rued Piero Gnudi, its chairman. 'It let the political parties in'.[4] As *The Economist* commented: 'IRI and its subsidiaries became part of the political spoils system. Appointments were fought over by party bosses'.[5] When profit and professionalism are replaced by spoils and patronage, losses occur and 'IRI's losses rose from 670 billion lire ($540m) in 1991 to a staggering 10.2 trillion lire, equivalent to 12 per cent of the public sector's entire current deficit in 1993'.

Its consolidated debt reached 72 trillion lire in 1992. By then, the whole Italian economy was in crisis: the lira had collapsed, and

[1] Government-Linked Company or GLC means corporate entities, either private or public, that is listed in stick exchanges, in which the government owns a stake using a holding company. Government may own majority (controlling stakes) or minority stakes in the GLCs. Malaysia also uses this model for managing its SOEs.

[2] Toniolo, *The Oxford Handbook of the Italian Economy Since Unification*, 59.

[3] Russo, 'Bank Nationalizations of the 1930s in Italy', 407–408.

[4] *The Economist*, 'End of an IRI'.

[5] Ibid.

the government had exhausted its ability to borrow. In July 1992, IRI was incorporated. That meant it had to abide by civil-code law—and thus could not run up further debt without recapitalising.[6]

This was followed by extensive divestiture of its 'motley bunch of assets', which included its ice cream, olive oil and canned vegetables businesses, followed by privatisation of *Credito Italiano, Banca Commerciale Italiana*, steel, catering, supermarkets and Telecom Italia between 1992 and 1997, raising 90.8 trillion lire. In June 2000, IRI finally was liquidated, by transferring to the Treasury Ministry, its sole shareholder, IRI's residual shareholdings, including a controlling stake in Alitalia, and almost the whole of the *RAI—Radiotelevisione italiana*, the national public broadcasting company of Italy. In June 2000, just before liquidation, it completed a public offering of its shares in Finmeccanica, an aerospace and defence subsidiary whose name is not unknown in India, an offering that raised €5 billion ($4.8 billion), as also the sale of its controlling interest in *Aeroporti di Roma*, the Italian capital's airport company, for €1.3 billion. In December 1999, IRI raised €6.7 billion by selling its controlling stake in *Autostrade*, Italy's toll-motorway network. Thus, the clock had turned full circle, and IRI gave back to the market what it had taken from it.[7]

In a way, the rise and fall of IRI are symptomatic of what can happen to the public sector if politicians are allowed to meddle with business decisions of SOEs; guided by their electoral considerations rather than any economic rationale for investments and other commercial decisions, they manage to suck them dry. Making PSEs open to manoeuvring and manipulation by bureaucrats and politicians ends up in crony capitalism or incestuous corporate relationships, as we have seen in India so many times in the past; it has also happened across the globe. Hyundai had raised US$1 billion to bail out the Halla Group when it collapsed in Korea in 1997; it was later found that the founder of the Halla Group was the younger brother of Hyundai's head. In Thailand, two senior managers of the Bangkok Bank of Commerce, which was already facing serious financial trouble with bad debt

---

[6] Ibid.
[7] Ibid.

amounting to US$3 billion, had lent funds to themselves and some senior politicians, but instead of letting it collapse, Thailand's central bank had to spend a large amount of public money to bail it out.[8] These are examples of weak corporate governance and can be fixed by strengthening corporate governance standards.

The public sector has to maintain a delicate and dynamic balance between its social and commercial objectives so that it is able to discharge its social obligations while remaining commercially viable. IRI is only one example; many PSEs have gone their way and ended up bankrupt. What happened to IRI closely resembles the state of affairs in many of our own PSEs, with the government bureaucracy and the politicians ruling the roost. Air India, BSNL and MTNL are the latest in a long series of PSEs gone bust because of crony capitalism and government interference. The primary purpose of any meaningful reform would be to shield them from such unwelcome interference from the government, bureaucracy and parliament. Many countries have learnt this lesson the hard way.

International experiences show that contradictions and economic risks arising from a large public sector can be mitigated by two mechanisms: either by complete state sell-outs or by establishing robust mechanisms to keep SOEs at an arm's length from the government and assiduously barring government bureaucrats and politicians from exercising any control. Only a few countries have succeeded in this. They depoliticised their enterprises, professionalised their management and gave substantial autonomy by freeing them from bureaucratic interference, with the Government's role being limited to issuing broad directives on policy issues, while leaving all strategic, tactical and operational issues exclusively at the hands of the SOE management.

The ways in which ownership of SOEs can be exercised by the State through the centralised or decentralised models have already been discussed earlier in Chapter 2 (p. 69–70). An example of a well-managed centralised agency is Temasek Holdings of Singapore. After its independence in 1965, Singapore had pursued economic growth by

---

[8] Anwar and Sam, 'Singaporean Style of Public Sector Corporate Governance', 41–68.

taking stakes in many companies, including start-ups. Temasek was established in 1974 to take over the government's stakes in 35 companies held by the Ministry of Finance. Its initial portfolio included several important firms of Singapore, including its shipyard and its famous Jurong Bird Park managed by the Wildlife Reserves Singapore. Today, it holds stakes in a wide range of areas including telecommunications, financial services, energy, natural resources, transport, healthcare, etc. Temasek's charter mandates it to increase the value of its holdings over the long term. Since its inception, Temasek's portfolio has multiplied manifold—it is now worth S$313 billion[9] or US$ 230 billion, as of March 2019, up S$183 billion over the last decade. Only 26 per cent of its holdings remain in Singapore itself in GLCs like Singapore Airlines, of which it owns 56 per cent, and SingTel, a telecom company of which Temasek owns 52 per cent of the stakes. Forty per cent of its holdings are spread over the rest of Asia (26 % in China alone), while the remaining 34 per cent of holdings are in the other continents, including 10 per cent in Europe, 15 per cent in North America and 6 per cent in Australia and New Zealand.[10] Besides providing clarity of objectives, the Temasek model also allows the state to distance itself from the management of its enterprises without relinquishing control and ownership. Temasek avoids interfering in the day-to-day running of the Government-Linked Companies (GLCs) in its portfolio, which are free to hire professional managers at market rates. It does not directly appoint board members either, as a matter of rule.

Temasek has evolved as a successful and active global investor; it is in fact what is called a Sovereign Wealth Fund.[11] Some of the companies held by it have established themselves as global brands, like DBS Bank, Keppel Corporation and Singapore Airlines; and some others have grown into 'national Champions' like SingTel, Singapore Power,

---

[9] Singaporean Dollars.

[10] https://www.temasekreview.com.sg/overview/performance-overview.html, accessed 2 November 2019.

[11] A sovereign wealth fund is owned by the state and comprises financial assets such as stocks, bonds, other financial instruments or properties. A sovereign wealth fund manages these assets through investments and disinvestments in financial or other assets.

etc. It has also made many successful foreign acquisitions. Studies show that Singaporean GLCs enjoy a higher market value relative to the book values of their assets than comparable private firms do. They also generate higher average returns on their assets compared to their private sector counterparts.[12]

For better corporate governance of PSUs, a clear separation between the Government's policy, regulatory and shareholder functions is a *sine qua non*. The Temasek model effectively meets this end. As a shareholder, Temasek professionally manages its subsidiary companies by appointing qualified managers and technical experts in their Boards. It procures or sells the assets of the group through global investment and disinvestment. The government only manages the policy and stands at an arm's length from the holding company. Regulatory function is exercised through a statutory body called Accounting and Corporate Regulatory Authority (ACRA), something like our Registrar of Companies but with much wider powers and scope.

A similar model was proposed in India in 2011 by the government-appointed Panel of Experts on Reforms headed by Mr S. K. Roongta, the former CMD of SAIL, which proposed a single holding structure (SHS) for CPSUs, in the form of a holding company, which would manage investments and disinvestments and appoint the Boards of its subsidiaries, much like the Temasek model. However, neither the UPA nor its succeeding NDA government took any action on its recommendations, which, *inter alia*, included enhanced functional autonomy, a stable 3-year tenure for the chairman and managing directors and freedom from the clutches of administrative ministries, etc. We shall discuss the Roongta Panel recommendations later in greater detail.

The public sector has been an indispensable part of the Indian economy and industry, and it can be predicted safely at this point of time that it shall continue be so in the foreseeable future despite the spate of disinvestments the government has launched on the advice of the NITI Aayog. As we have seen, over the last few decades, the

---

[12] *The Economist*, 'Reforming China's State-owned Firms, From SOE to GLC'.

profile and importance of the public sector have undergone radical transformation, and today, the orientation has been shifted from the primacy of its social welfare objectives towards commercial viability, operational profitability, competitiveness and innovation. In the strategic areas, especially in defence and national security, its presence and contribution have not only remained undiminished, but are perhaps more important now than ever before. New models have emerged, like public-private partnerships and citizen ownership and participation, along with adoption of global standards of corporate governance. The MOU system has transformed and improved the public sector's competitiveness. Gradually, the overarching government control of the earlier era has also been reduced through Ratna and other mechanisms by giving the PSEs ever more delegation of powers and greater autonomy. But still, the government remains the owner, regulator, controller and final arbiter in all matters concerning the PSEs, and its role often overshadows the autonomy given to them. So far, the government has reserved for itself the authority to exercise powers in respect of key areas like appointment of chairmen and the boards of directors, determination of their wages and employment policies, decisions on merger, acquisition or disinvestment, or major capital expenditure decisions. Ministers and bureaucrats keep on interfering with the PSEs in a routine manner, much beyond and in direct violation of the scope of any formal arm's-length relationship.

It is indeed of utmost importance to determine the optimal level and character of interactions between the government and PSEs. Too much control will reduce them to a government department, with all the associated disadvantages for the functioning of a commercial enterprise on commercial lines, while too little may spell trouble for the government if and when any enterprise accumulates huge losses or gets involved in a scam. Besides, as explained earlier, the public sector has to have a social orientation and remain citizen-centric rather than profit-centric; in times of economic or financial emergency, disaster or national calamities, PSEs are the ones to rely upon to mitigate the sufferings of the citizens. They are also needed to protect the citizens against the monopolistic behaviour of the private sector, to ensure that utilities, goods and services are always available to the citizens at affordable rates. Their role and importance in building and maintaining essential infrastructure cannot be compromised except at great social and economic risks. At the same time, they need to be operationally independent, financially self-reliant and commercially competitive, and for this, it is essential that there has to be a formal, institutionalised separation between the government and the public sector.

Many attempts were made to distance the SOEs from the government by giving enhanced autonomy to the SOEs and by optimising their performance by making their management responsible for performance. One such method was the introduction of the MOU system discussed in Chapter 3, which was based on a set of agreed performance indicators between the government, the owner, and the entity. The concept was developed and experimented in France and South Korea before it was introduced in India. The government's ownership role also introduces several contradictions, often by blurring the distinction between the owner and the manager. By interfering with the decision-making process of the SOEs, the government often assumes the role of the manager, which obstructs professional management practices without any accountability. The failure of the government can be, and is often, passed off as the failure of the SOE, of which we have plenty of examples in India—Air India, BNSL and MTNL being the latest ones.

The government owns the SOEs, but there are various models under which the ownership functions can be exercised and managed. Creating the buffer of a holding company is one such method. Then, there are management contracts, under which SOEs are given to private parties for management. Sri Lanka experimented with this model with its textile mills and tea plantations. A very common practice is the Joint Sector, in which public companies are jointly owned by the state and a private entity, with the government retaining management control by holding majority stakes, or the government holding minority stake and transferring management control to the private entity. However, more than the ownership issues, what is important is the way the owner functions and its relations to the entity owned. Among the public sector, there are also departmentally run commercial enterprises like the Railways, Ordnance Factories or the Department of Posts and Telecommunications. These can be corporatised to improve their efficiency and to shield them from government or parliamentary interference in their day-to-day affairs, by turning them into independent corporate entities separate from the government.

As we have seen earlier, in the developed capitalist countries, public sector reform has followed the familiar course involving decentralisation, deregulation, privatisation and marketisation, confinement of the government to the role of providing a conducive environment for the free interaction of market forces in the economy, along with shrinking the size and role of the state in business. The residual public sector enterprises remaining with the state were supposed to be driven by a 'state-backed capitalism' rather than 'state capitalism'. However, despite privatisation and disinvestment of the public sector, some countries refused to decentralise and dismantle their 'state capitalism'. China and India are examples of this, even though both these countries moved closer to the so-called 'Washington Consensus', which is actually a set of free-market economic policies supported by international financial institutions like the IMF and the World Bank, and also the US Treasury. The term 'Washington Consensus' was coined by the British Economist John Williamson in 1989, who identified the 10 commandments of the model that span fiscal discipline (low borrowing, reducing subsidies to increase spending on health, education, etc.), trade liberalisation, openness to direct foreign investments, tax reform, market reform (market-determined interest and exchange rates and open competition through removal of tariff barriers), privatisation of state enterprises and individual property rights.

It would be instructive to go through the reform experiences of other countries, especially of SOEs in China, which share a lot of similarities with Indian SOEs and followed similar reform trajectories, at least in the initial phases. In both China and India, the public sector was recognised as the major driver of the engine of growth, which dominated the commanding heights of the economy and still remain dominant in the strategic sectors. In many important sectors including the strategic sectors, large companies and groups had developed in both the countries, for example, Shenhua and Coal India in the coal sector, Chinese National Petroleum Corporation (CNPC) and

ONGC in the oil sector, State Grid Corporation (SGC) and NTPC in the power sector, Baosteel and SAIL in the steel sector and Bank of China and SDBI in the banking sector, respectively.[13] Even the slogans of the two countries for development and reform are becoming similar—'Small government, large society' in China, 'Minimum government, maximum governance' in India—though the slogans remained what they are—only empty slogans.

China started reforming its public sector enterprises by distancing the government from them, initially through management contracts, and as discussed in the previous chapter, resorted to massive privatisation of small, public-owned entities during the 1980s.[14] It was followed by the 'modern enterprise system' in order to separate the state as owner from the day-to-day management of the SOEs. Reforms were aimed at giving 'greater autonomy to management, to impose financial discipline, to encourage firms to merge and restructure themselves, and to expose them to competition'.[15] Later, China found the holding company concept useful—superior to both management contracts and privatisation. In November 2013, the Development Research Centre (DRC), a government think-tank, came out with an ambitious plan for overhauling the SOEs, and cited Singapore's holding company, Temasek, as a potential model.[16]

Given China's size and complexity, it would be incorrect to take a simplistic view of the developments in its public sector by reducing it to a one-size-fits-all model for the entire country. In fact, there were public entities owned not only by the central and the provincial governments, but there were SOEs owned by town or village enterprises as well, and each developed and followed its own path and style of reforms. There were more than 100,000 medium- and large-sized state enterprises alone, which were owned by the State

[13] Yi-Chong, *The Political Economy of State-owned Enterprises in China and India*, 2.

[14] Jun and China Hainan Institute of Research and Development, 'Reforms of Public Enterprises in China', 5–15.

[15] *The Economist*, 'The Long March to Capitalism'.

[16] *The Economist*, 'Reforming China's State-owned Firms, From SOE to GLC'.

in the mid-1990s. By 1992, non-state industries accounted for more than half the gross industrial output of China, their share reaching 60–70 per cent in some coastal provinces; for example, in Liaoning province, which was the old industrial base of China, the share of the non-state sector in 1993 was as much as 89 per cent of the industrial output. It may be mentioned that most economic activities, as well as most of the population of China, are still concentrated in the narrow coastal zone on the Eastern part of China that is fed by its three major rivers, the Yangtze, the Yellow River (Huang He) and the Pearl River (Zhujiang), and most of the rest of China is too arid and inhospitable to support a large population and hence large-scale economic activities that need a large labour force.

To be able to compete with the non-state sector, SOEs needed to develop efficiency, achieve the economics of scale and reinforce the division of labour based on specialisation while increasing and enforcing the levels of accountability. Most SOEs suffered on account of scale; they were small, their material consumption and hence production cost were high, and the scale and output too low to make them profitable. Faced with the challenge of competition, they had to either go out of business or reinvent themselves through a merger/coalition and reorganise themselves into a larger group to strengthen competitive ability in order to be able to compete globally.

There were various constraints due to the peculiarities of the Chinese political system on account of the 'unchangeable-ness' of ownership, jurisdiction and fiscal channel for taxation. Due to extensive government control on all economic activities, no proper corporate structure or culture could evolve in China; especially at the provincial and local levels, officials distributed patronage and money through the SOEs. Corruption was endemic, like in PetroChina, where more than 100 high-ranking officials came under corruption investigations between 2013 and 2015. SOEs also shouldered a huge debt burden due to the heavy social responsibility and employment of a redundant workforce they were obliged to employ, and by the end of 1994, their combined budget deficits rose to 41.4 per cent, with many of them being in dire straits financially. The returns on assets for most of them were close to zero or negative. Instead of carrying out reforms at the level of the entities, that is, micro-economically, China concentrated instead on reforming the macro-economic structure itself, by totally transforming the state asset ownership and control system to create an ecosystem in which entities would be forced to reform themselves.

There were many constraints and contradictions that had to be resolved—the SOEs designed to operate in a traditional economic structure had to operate and compete in a free market for which they were unprepared, not unlike in India after 1991, without much fundamental reforms having been undertaken in respect of their traditional administrative and managerial systems. In the first phase of the reforms, when the SOEs were coming out of the centralised planning system, the bureaucratic accountability became diffused, which led to state asset depletion, a steep rise in the debt–asset ratio and an increase in NPAs, affecting their profitability. 'By the mid-1990s, China's SOEs looked like an economic disaster waiting to happen, with potential to trigger political and social instability', observed an academic, following which 'There came the second phase of SOE reform where the SOE policy was changed from 'reform without losers' to 'reform with losers'.[17] Company law was enacted in 1994 to impart legal status to the SOEs, and in 1995, the government adopted the policy known as '*zhua da fang xiao*' (manage the large and let go the small). Between 1995 and 2001, the number of SOEs fell by two-thirds, from 1.2 million to only 468,000.[18] The share of SOEs in industrial enterprises fell from 40 per cent to 2.6 per cent, and between 1998 and 2003, 40 per cent of their employees were laid off. This *Gaizhi*, or 'restructuring' had, like in India, also bred a variety of private-public hybrids, besides the giant SOEs in strategic sectors, and by 2010, 123 of these were controlled by the government, with 23 being defined as 'national champions' or 'backbone companies', including all the companies or groups named earlier. In fact, all these companies were in the Fortune 500 list, with their global rankings ranging from 5 for CNPC and 7 for SGC to 293 for

---

[17] Yi-Chong, 'The Political Economy of SOEs in China and India', 5.
[18] *The Economist*, 'Bamboo Capitalism'.

Shenhua.[19] The growth of these giants had close parallels in India. As *The Economist* commented:

> When people think of state capitalism, China springs to mind, with its giant and opaque government-controlled firms. But India, more cuddly and less competent, is not too dissimilar. Some 40 percent of the profits of the profits of its 100 biggest listed firms come from state controlled ones. In finance, energy and natural resources, they control at least two-thirds of the production.[20]

The reforms initially paid rich dividends; the SOEs' return on assets improved significantly from a near-zero level in 1998 to almost 7 per cent a decade later, though short of the private-sector average, after which their fortunes ebbed. As private firms grew, the profitability of SOEs fell, and their RoAs fell to about 5 per cent, almost half of the RoAs of their private peers.[21] By 2017, there were more than 150,000 operative SOEs, two-thirds of these being owned by local governments and the rest by the central government. Private firms proved to be much more productive, while a disproportionate share of resources was invested in the public firms, with about half of all bank loans going to these entities. The share of investments in SOEs' assets had declined from nearly 60 per cent in 2004 to almost half of that in 2015, after which it has been growing faster than private-sector investment and accounted for over 35 per cent by 2017. As economic growth in China has started slowing now, China is relying increasingly on its SOEs to spend more to stimulate the economy, even though such spending pushes up their debt to dangerous levels; in 2015, the debt : equity ratio of the SOEs had exceeded 1.6, compared to less than 1.2 for the non-state firms. However, their presence in the global market has become ever more pronounced, especially in the industries of banking, steel, coal, automobile, gold, mining, aerospace, defence, etc. China's 200 biggest SOEs now account for 9 per cent of global

---

[19] Yi-Chong, 'The Political Economy of SOEs in China and India', 6.

[20] *The Economist*, 'Adventures in Capitalism, Special Report on Business in India'.

[21] *The Economist*, 'Fixing China Inc'.

revenues in coal mining, 6 per cent in automobile manufacturing and 5 per cent in construction. [22]

The big-bang privatisation actually never happened in China, and SOEs, instead of shrinking, in fact became bigger, at the cost of thousands of smaller ones. Like in its economy, in respect of SOEs also, China has followed the path of 'gradualism'. Reforms like allowing employees to own shares in their companies have been launched gradually in SOEs. In the Shanghai International Port Group (SIPG), a city-owned firm, 80 per cent of the 22,000 employees hold a stake and are more focussed on the company's growth. The mixed ownership model has entered and entrenched itself in a big way, allowing SOEs to sell stakes to private investors, as in the case of Yunnan Baiyao. However, at the national level, the results have been less encouraging, with accusations of 'privatisation of assets and nationalisation of losses' flying in thick and fast, just like in India. Selling of majority stakes, though allowed, has been rather uncommon. The dominant philosophy still remains that the SOEs should continue to play a dominant role in the economy, but should be run in a better manner, with focus on the market.[23]

China stared the Holding Company experiment with its aviation, metallurgical and petrochemical industries. Like India, China also identified the sectors important for state monopoly or control as public utilities, telecommunications, aviation, railways, banks, energy and important raw materials industries. The SASAC was established in 2003 to oversee China's biggest SOEs through the consolidation of various other industry-specific ministries after the large-scale privatisation of the SOEs. SASAC was made responsible for managing the remaining SOEs; it appointed their top executives, approved mergers and disinvestments and decided on all other strategic measures. SASAC had accumulated assets worth 23.4 trillion yuan (US\$3.6 trillion) by 2017. Its companies had combined assets of 161 trillion yuan (US\$26 trillion), and revenue of more than 23.4 trillion yuan

---

[22] *The Economist*, 'Reform of China's Ailing State-owned Firms is Emboldening Them'.

[23] Ibid.

(US$3.6 trillion), making it the largest economic entity in the world. SASAC today oversees most SOEs and is pushing for the creation of bigger 'national champions' under its control. The two biggest railway equipment makers and the two biggest shipping groups of China have been combined by it, and more such mergers are in the offing, including even the medium-sized companies in chemicals, property, ports, cement and more, to harness the advantages of scale. Practically, all companies overseen by SASAC are structured as corporations and are legally separate from the government, with their own boards of directors that are allowed to function independently.

The average SOE in China today has about 13 times more assets than the average private-sector firm, according to World Bank estimates, and in many industries, the only competition that an SOE faces is from another SOE. As *The Economist* points out, the rationale for the mergers is to prevent SOEs from competing against each other as they explore the foreign markets, as had happened with railway equipment makers in the past. China is consciously trying to 'create conglomerates that can dominate domestic and international markets through sheer size'.[24] Unlike in the past, Chinese SOEs from construction to steel to railways today are increasingly focussing on foreign rather than domestic markets in which they are already well-entrenched. China's economic dominance was led by the private manufacturers, but the SOEs still dominate the commanding heights of economy in China in all vital and strategic sectors essential for growth. The state accounts for more than 80 per cent of market capitalisation in sectors such as energy, industry and utilities, like in India. Through the 'State Capital Investment and Operation' companies (SCIOs),[25] China is trying to manage the existing assets of the state and invest in new ones. Funded by the state, these SCIOs are used to break into new high-tech sectors, and into the so-called 'strategic emerging industries', which include new energy, biotechnology and IT companies, among others. With cheap capital from the state, these SCIOs are in a position to extend the reach of the state to the private sector.

[24] Ibid.
[25] Ibid.

As of 2019, China is home to 109 corporations listed on the Fortune Global 500 list, of which as many as 93 are state-owned. Hitherto driven by manufacturing and export, both of which are slowing due to the ongoing global recession, the Chinese economy is now transitioning from an investment- and export-driven economy to an innovation-driven economy dependent on domestic consumption. SOEs have always been the vehicle for all economic reforms in China, and they are supposed to be in the driver's seat again in this transition. But saddled with huge debts compared to their equity and with poor returns on their assets, they are increasingly looking like lacking a coherent strategy. China's private sector is now poised to emerge as the main driver of its economy; it contributes 60 per cent of China's GDP and is responsible for 70 per cent of innovation and 80 per cent of urban employment; it also accounts for 90 per cent of the new jobs created. Private wealth accounts for 70 per cent of China's investment and 90 per cent of its exports.[26] Through its Belt and Road Initiative (BRI), China is getting for its SOEs huge infrastructure projects to be executed in many countries, but the possible consequences of such projects for those countries in terms of making them heavily indebted and hence dependent on China are attracting huge global opprobrium. Many of these contracts have already been rescinded by a number of countries. Another global concern in respect of its private companies is security—Huawei is a leader in the global 5G revolution and is eager to spread its network globally, but because of the irrevocable nexus between China's private companies and the Communist Party apparatus, other countries are weary of allowing Huawei to enter the 5G market in their own countries for fear of their security getting compromised.[27]

China is following a unique policy—to make the SOEs big, efficient and globally competitive without relinquishing much control—by further consolidating the state control while simultaneously allowing the market to be the ultimate resource allocator, and reserving its option to intervene if and when needed. However, given

[26] https://www.weforum.org/agenda/2019/05/why-chinas-state-owned-companies-still-have-a-key-role-to-play/, accessed 31 October 2019.
[27] Ibid.

the market penetration of its SOEs globally, restoration of global trust and addressing global security concerns are essential, coupled with liberal market reforms to provide the necessary impetus to the private sector. Given the slowing growth, China must continue with its market-oriented reforms, but that might raise the demands for democratic political freedom within China that its leaders are loath to give to its people.

Mixed ownerships or joint ventures, also called public-private partnerships, have been tried in many countries including in India; the results are also mixed. One of the first experiments with this model in India pertained to the automaker Maruti Udyog Limited. Maruti's story is instructive in many ways. Maruti began its corporate journey in 1981, and became a joint venture (JV) company in 1982 with 26 per cent stake held by Suzuki Motor Corporation of Japan. Even then, it satisfied all definitions of a public sector enterprise and was indeed one. But by virtue of the joint venture, it had access to much advanced Japanese technology, skill and management. The JV agreement provided that for certain types of decisions, like capital investment, employment or selling of capital goods, prior concurrence of Suzuki would be needed. Thus, surplus labour could not be engaged even when political dispensation wanted it like in the case of other PSEs. It also prevented the surplus resources generated by it internally to be diverted to other CPSEs, as the Planning Commission was wont to do. Suzuki's stake was increased to 40 per cent in 1987, and after the economic liberalisation, in 1992, it was further increased to 50 per cent. Thus, Maruti and Suzuki both came to own 50 per cent equity, and Maruti ceased to be a government company, the government having less than 51 per cent. Government rules, regulations, CAG's audit, CVC's superintendence or Parliamentary oversight did not apply to the company any longer. However, till then, it had been operating in a non-competitive, almost monopolistic market; now, it was exposed to competition in which many PSEs would eventually perish. Maruti survived and flourished partly because of the support it received from its JV partner, itself a successful automaker with global exposure.[28]

---

[28] Bhargava, 'State Ownership to Joint Sector', 117–128.

Becoming a non-PSE enabled Maruti Suzuki India to abandon the management practices of PSEs, especially in managing the human resources. It abolished the multiple grades and scales of pay and time scale promotions, and replaced them with productivity-linked incentives and bonus schemes. Department-wise budgeting was introduced, and managers were made responsible for achieving their respective budgetary targets, with suitable delegation of the power to take necessary decisions. Training was imparted to the staff and managers to learn to abandon the old way of doing things and adapt to the practices needed for a new, competitive environment. Trade union was not allowed to have any political affiliation. Decentralisation, reorganisation of activities, a flatter organisational structure instead of a multi-layered hierarchy, unlike in a typical PSE, and innovation were encouraged and rewarded. Suzuki further increased its stake in the company to 56.21 per cent in 2013.

Maruti Suzuki India suffered a serious setback in 2012 when its Manesar plant in Haryana was hit by unprecedented violence over wage disputes by the production workers, who attacked supervisors and started a fire that killed the company's General Manager of Human Resources and injured 100 other managers, including two Japanese expatriates. This led to a prolonged closure of the plant for more than a month, dismissal of a large number of workers, huge losses for the company amounting to almost ₹100 crore a day and plunging of its share price in the stock market. However, Maruti seemed to have recovered and, as of July 2018, commanded a share of 53 per cent of the Indian passenger car market. Maruti's story teaches that once free from governmental rules, regulations and control, a company can reengineer its processes and systems to reinvent itself and become a champion. Even the state governments can, with the right mix of vision, pragmatism and financial foresight, achieve this end for its PSEs.

Tamil Nadu Industrial Development Corporation (TIDCO) was established in 1965 to promote the industrial development of the state, and between 1965 and 1995, it promoted as many as 98 companies—10 in the public sector (51% or more equity holding by the government through TIDCO), 45 in the joint sector (maximum 26% equity holding by the TIDCO), 43 in the associate sector (11%

equity holding by the TIDCO) and what is called the escort sector (1% equity holding by the TIDCO), the idea behind the last two being to ensure the government's involvement and speedy clearances of the necessary approvals. Since liberalisation, the government had divested its equity in 20 companies, including 12 in the joint sector and eight in the public sector. The joint sector brought in new technology, and one of these companies was Titan Watches—a joint venture between the Tata Group and the Government of Tamil Nadu—which was started in 1984 and in which TIDCO held 26 per cent equity. TIDCO still has 26 per cent stake in Titan, which is a market leader in watches in India.[29] Titan had since diversified into many areas, from jewellery to eyewear to fragrance to helmets, and is today the Tata Group's largest consumer company. In 2011, it acquired the famous Swiss watch company Favre-Leuba to enter the European market.

Even re-engineering the existing structure to ensure greater involvement of the larger society in decision-making can transform the work culture to improve performance. South Korea introduced a system of 'Management Responsibility' to manage and reform its public enterprises, under which government intervention and control were gradually reduced, while granting them autonomy and flexibility and putting emphasis on the evaluation of final performance. A Parliamentary Act of 1983, the 'Government Invested Enterprises Management Act', changed the way the enterprises were hitherto being managed, repealing the earlier laws and creating an institutional structure through which the new philosophy was to be implemented. The new structure comprised a ministerial level Public Enterprise Management Evaluation Council (PEMEC), which also included outside experts with specialised knowledge, in the Ministry of Finance and Economy (MOFE), to evaluate their final results and to decide on the privatisation and establishment of new public enterprises. The Act provided for clear separation of policy decision-making from the executive functions and the introduction of an incentive system. The evaluation was done through Performance Evaluation Task Forces having 30–40 members, which included professors, researchers, public accountants

---

[29] Narayanan, 'The Joint Sector Concept', 102–111.

and others, thus creating universal interest and involvement from all the strata of society in the state enterprises. Boards of enterprises were also similarly diversified to include members from different walks of life. In effect, the entire society was thus involved actively in the management as important stakeholders.[30] South Korea did privatise some of its public enterprises, but the 1983 Act restructured and streamlined the functioning of its public enterprises and made them more profitable and competitive. It proved that privatisation was not the only way to make the enterprises profitable.

From the privatisation experiences across different countries, we have learnt that for successful privatisation, efficiency enhancement should be made the primary goal, that transparency should never be compromised and that the market should be allowed to determine the value of the enterprise. Further, the sale proceeds should be utilised for retirement of debt and for addressing the deficiencies, whether related to new capital or new technology, of the concerned entities. If privatisation is not done in the right way to maximise the financial and economic gains by weighing the costs and benefits of various options and adopting the correct mix at the correct time, the effects of such privatisation might be opposite to what was intended. Privatisation is also important to free up the assets locked in sick or unproductive enterprises for productive use elsewhere in the economy.[31]

OECD emphasises three things: clarity of objectives of PSUs—both commercial and non-commercial—establishment of appropriate governance structures and ownership functions designed to serve these objectives, with sufficient transparency and disclosure.[32] It is also important to shield PSUs from political control by preventing the appointment of politicians or serving bureaucrats to their Boards. Many countries have insulated their ailing PSUs from politicians and bureaucrats. SOEs in Sweden are required to have a majority of

---

[30] Sbin Il, 'The Management Responsibility System in Korean Public Enterprises', 205–210.

[31] Kikeri, 'A Framework of the Methods of Privatisation', 237–246.

[32] http://www.oecd.org/corporate/ca/corporategovernanceofstate-owneden-terprises/44215438.pdf, accessed 2 November 2019.

independent directors in the Board. Norway bars active politicians including MPs and Ministers, State Secretaries and civil servants from the Boards of SOEs. Many countries like Finland place restrictions or limits upon civil servants being appointed as Board members. Similar rules are there in Germany and New Zealand also.[33] Many countries have created a directors' pool from where all the Board members, including the chairman and managing directors, are appointed. The reforms have turned most of their SOEs into profitable entities, and many of them have grown to become global brands. Strengthening the appointment procedures through such objective institutional processes and empowering the management to act autonomously, while making them accountable to the government/parliament for the achievement of commercial and non-commercial targets have worked wonders for these countries. In OECD countries, studies point out a direct correlation between lesser governmental control and better performance of enterprises between 1998 and 2013; most OECD countries in fact had reduced direct government control over businesses. Some have established a centralised asset management system under a single coordinating authority, through appropriate legal frameworks like corporate governance legislations.

The success of any reforms of the PSEs would obviously also depend upon the effectiveness in achieving non-commercial goals, besides fiscal and financial considerations. The non-economic objectives make the process of reform of PSEs a little more complex, because such objectives often impact their commercial performance. The non-commercial objectives are often tied up with sectoral policies; hence, PSE reforms often impinge on reforms of other policy areas. However, it has been the experience from across the world again that any attempt to reform, whether through privatisation, disinvestment, restructuring or redesigning the PSEs' systems, etc., would not be effective unless accompanied by appropriate reforms of the market or specific sectors and in the overall regulatory framework in which the SOEs operate. A well-functioning market with a strong regulatory framework is a prerequisite for success, with rules and institutions governing entry,

[33] OECD, *Corporate Governance Boards of Directors of State-owned Enterprises*, 52.

exit, bankruptcy, and the strengthening of competition. For successful reforms of PSEs, a combination of measures is generally required, from changes in the legal framework and corporate governance structures of SOEs to addressing the sector- and company-specific circumstances, but for effecting successful reforms, some common elements are essential. These include measures like establishing a single decision-making line through the organisation of ownership functions, ensuring a clear separation between ownership and other state functions in relation to the PSE, changing the governance structure and reporting modalities if necessary, establishing transparency in setting commercial and non-commercial objectives and disclosing their costs and sustainability, empowering the management, strengthening appointment procedures, etc.[34]

It is not necessary that the processes will always be smooth. Many scandals have surfaced in many countries, posing serious governance challenges for reforming the public sector, especially where mixed ownership structures have been involved. State ownership creates its own agency problems that explode into scandals from time to time. The agency problems may arise between managers and shareholders or between majority and minority shareholders; the problem becomes intensified when the state is the largest shareholder, creating multiple conflicts of interests and stoking rent-seeking behaviour by the politicians. One example of such scandals is the Brazilian oil giant Petrobras, a state-controlled firm whose shares are listed both domestically and on the New York Stock Exchange. It was once cited as an international model of solid corporate governance and performance. The government used Petrobras as a tool for its macroeconomic policy to keep inflation under control by keeping the domestic oil prices significantly below the international market price, resulting in major losses to the company and a reduction in its investment capability. Petrobras was also at the centre of the massive and still ongoing (as of September 2019) Lava Jato ('Carwash') investigation that plunged Brazil into its largest corruption scandal, highlighting crony capitalism at its worst, where politicians from the ruling dispensation appointed many of

---

[34] European Commission, *State-owned Enterprises in the EU.*

Petrobras's most important executives who orchestrated a massive bid-rigging scheme to generate a campaign slush fund for the politicians while providing lavish pay-outs to corrupt officials. The amount that had to be written off as a fallout of this scandal amounted to more than US$2.5 billion estimated in 2015, but the total losses are likely to be much more.[35]

In order to restore the confidence of investors and society in the listed SOEs, Brazil is trying to strengthen the corporate governance in them. In 2015, an 'SOE Governance Program' was launched, which was specifically tailored to the listed SOEs, without legislative or regulatory change, but requiring stricter adherence to the corporate governance rules, on a voluntary basis. The program, requiring the fulfilment of 25 requirements, is based on four pillars: (a) disclosure and transparency, (b) internal control structures and practices, (c) composition of boards and management and (d) protection of inside information. Based on fulfilment of these requirements, the companies are certified by an agency. In 2016, Brazil enacted a statute providing for a special legal regime for SOEs and mixed enterprises and imposing a number of new governance rules on them, some of which were overlapping with the requirements of the earlier SOE Governance Program. Institution of independent internal audit and a permanent audit committee, establishment of a risk and compliance unit, prescription of minimum qualifications for and restrictions on the appointment of directors and requirement of a minimum of 25 per cent of the Board to be comprised of independent directors were some of the important features of this statute. While the relevant line ministries still continue to play important roles in the SOEs' governance and management, Brazil has strengthened and streamlined the institutional arrangement for their overall monitoring and governance.[36]

Countries in different parts of the world have responded to the governance challenges facing the PSEs in myriads of ways, but changing the ownership structure has found favour with most. To separate

---

[35] Milhaupt and Pargendler, 'Governance Challenges of Listed State-owned Enterprises Around the World', 2–3.
[36] Ibid, 31–33.

its roles as the owner and the regulator in respect of the SOEs, France created its holding Agency *Agence de participation de l'État* (APE) for its numerous companies where the government held whole or partial ownership, though not all government equity stakes are held through APE.[37] APE considers the financial interests of the state in exercising its role as the owner, and functions in consultation with the concerned ministries. In contrast to the role of Temasek, APE's role is not limited to managing its portfolio companies under strictly commercial terms, but also includes 'managing its investments from an industrial perspective, and on establishing a clear, long-term industrial and economic development strategy for the companies concerned' in order to 'optimize the value of its assets and the specific business and social aims of each of the companies concerned', especially in strategic sectors such as defence, energy, and automobile. In 2014, the government outlined its new policy for intervening as the owner, comprising the four key objectives of

> i) ensuring that the government has sufficient control over compa-
> nies of strategic public interest operating in areas key to France's
> sovereignty; (ii) guaranteeing the existence of resilient companies
> able to fulfil the country's basic requirements; (iii) supporting
> corporate growth and consolidation, particularly in sectors and
> industries that are key to French and European economic concerns;
> and (iv) subject to EU regulations, helping corporate bail-outs on
> an *ad hoc* basis in systemic risk cases.[38]

In the United States, the 20th century saw the emergence of quite a few of the so-called Government-Sponsored Enterprises (GSEs), especially after the financial crisis of 2008 when the US government was forced to acquire equity stakes in various private firms in the bailout programme that followed in the immediate aftermath of the

---

[37] For example, while the government accounts for over 85 per cent equity of AREVA, APE holds only 29 per cent of its shares, the major shareholder being CEA, France's Alternative Energies and Atomic Energy Commission.

[38] Milhaupt and Pargendler, 'Governance Challenges of Listed State-owned Enterprises', 10–12.

crisis. Earlier, during the 18th and the 19th centuries, the US federal and state governments had shareholdings in many banks, railroads, canal companies, etc., which posed a clear conflict of interest due to the states' role also as regulator. Hybrid enterprises emerged when the US government participated in the First Bank of the United States of 1791, though the conflict of interest ceased to be a major impediment for their functioning. However, following the Great Depression of the 1930s, the Congress had enacted the Government Corporation Control Act (GCCA) of 1945, seeking to restrain the formation of government corporations and enhance their accountability. Still, a number of GSEs emerged; however, they function on a model of state support without ownership. While imbued with a public mission, they still continued to be owned and controlled by private shareholders, the government's role being limited to the appointment of minority directors. Two of the most prominent GSEs thus created were the Federal National Mortgage Association (Fannie Mae) and Federal Home Loan Mortgage Corporation (Freddie Mac), both of which were listed in the New York Stock Exchange in 1968 and 1989, respectively. Their mission was to promote access to housing by supporting the secondary market for residential mortgages, and later to facilitate financing to low- and middle-income borrowers. Even though their federal charters explicitly disclaimed any liability or guarantee from the government for their loans, the market believed that the guarantee was implicit and that the government would underwrite the liabilities in the event of any default—the 2008 crisis would prove this assumption right.[39]

The government, however, tried to distance itself from these companies even prior to the crisis, and in 2004, President George W. Bush had forgone his prerogative to appoint government directors to their boards, allowing the private shareholders instead to elect all the directors. In the aftermath of the crisis, the US government was forced to acquire equity stakes in the distressed financial institutions as a 'reluctant shareholder' as a temporary measure, with lower equity stakes and control rights. The acquisitions did not follow a single, coherent model, but happened through various financial and non-financial

[39] Ibid., 13–15.

arrangements. Thus, while in General Motors the federal government acquired a majority stake by exchanging its existing debt for equity, in the case of AIG, it acquired almost 80 per cent stake but surrendered direct control by transferring its shares to a trust. Government intervention was the highest in Fannie Mae and Freddie Mac, which were taken into conservatorship in 2008, with the government acquiring control and suspending the voting rights of shareholders. Four years later, through another controversial arrangement, their future profits were transferred to the government at the expense of private shareholders, once again highlighting the conflict of interest between the state's role as owner and regulator. Except Fannie Mae and Freddie Mac, the government has since sold all its stake acquired during the financial crisis, returning the firms entirely to the private ownerships. By and large, the government refrained from exercising direct influence in the management and governance of SOEs, and curbed the spectre of political intervention by transferring ownership to a trust. The preferred mode of exercising control was also not by acquiring equity but by supporting the SOEs through loans and grants and ensuring a strong presence of independent directors.[40]

In India, reforms so far have involved outright privatisation of CPSUs, unaccompanied by the necessary reforms in the overall regulatory framework in which they operate. The boundary between the government's roles as the owner and the regulator also remains blurred. Privatisation, corporatisation or unbundling of activities, as we have seen in the power sector in India especially, have been driven primarily by public finance constraints. Funds raised through disinvestment have been used to reduce fiscal deficits and public debt. Change of ownership from public to private is supposed to raise the efficiency of PSUs to the level of well-run private companies, but there are too many examples to show that change of ownership is no guarantee for better performance in terms of higher efficiency and profitability, unless accompanied by suitable market and regulator reforms, which are yet to be effected. The wave of privatisation in the United Kingdom during the 1980s and 1990s was followed by the creation

[40] Ibid., 16–19.

of several regulatory bodies such as the Office of Rail and Road, the Office of Gas and Electricity Markets (OFGEM), the Office of Communications, the Water Services Regulation Authority and the Financial Conduct Authority.[41] Malaysia had created a watchdog body, Minority Shareholders Watching Group—a think tank sans politicians to monitor breaches and to ensure better corporate governance. As already emphasised, reforms of the regulatory frameworks and the markets are crucial for the performance of both PSUs and private companies, ensuring a rule-based competitive structure covering entry, exit, bankruptcy and competition among existing companies.

One thing is clear, however, that in any reform, setting the goals and objectives is much more important than following the rules and procedures that dominate the governmental control systems everywhere. As argued by David Osborne and Ted Gaebler in their 1993 book, *Reinventing Government*, the essence of public sector reforms is the introduction of market mechanisms within the government and leveraging change through the market. The objectives thus would be transforming rule-based organisations into result-oriented organisations, shifting emphasis in funding from inputs to outcomes, moving from 'hierarchy to participation and teamwork, and community owned government, empowering rather than serving'.[42] Countries that have implemented successful reforms also followed a common route—identifying core areas and withdrawing from the rest, separating the responsibilities for policy and delivery, empowering SOEs through autonomy and providing them the required flexibility to face competition from the private sector, implementing objective systems of performance enhancement and evaluation coupled with instituting an appropriate and fair incentive and reward system, changing ownership and control structure to professionalise the entities and establishing robust institutional architecture to shield them from political or bureaucratic influences, while simultaneously carrying out reforms in the market and the regulatory environment.

---

[41] http://www.oecd.org/corporate/ca/corporategovernanceofstate-owneden-terprises/44215438.pdf, accessed 2 November 2019.

[42] Lane, 'Public Sector Reform', 4–6.

A plethora of committees and study groups has been appointed from time to time to address the problems of the PSEs in India. Some of these committees have been referred to at the appropriate places in the earlier chapters. The COPU, in its 49th Report (1981–1982) and the Economic Administration and Reforms Commission (1983–1984) had recommended more autonomy for PSEs. The Krishnamurthy Committee (1991) and the Rangarajan Committee (1992) were constituted for suggesting modalities for disinvestment. Various models and metrics have been suggested by experts from time to time in respect of privatisation, performance assessment and disinvestment of the PSEs. Several Committees, such as the Administrative Reforms Commission (1967–1968), the Arjun Sengupta Committee (1986) and the L K Jha Committee (1987), had pointed out that unwelcome interferences by the government had jeopardised the independent functioning of the PSEs and affected their profitability. The Estimates Committee (1962–1963), the COPU (1987–1988) and other experts had also highlighted the need for establishing a commission like the UPSC for selecting personnel for the top posts. All these recommendations have mostly been ignored by the government. The Board vacancies in most CPSEs had remained unfilled for prolonged periods, and most Boards had more than one government nominees.

As discussed earlier in Chapter 4, the Seventh Finance Commission had highlighted the need for the SPSEs to earn a rate of return for the first time, and the subsequent Finance Commissions also focussed on this aspect. The recommendations of the Finance Commissions have been discussed in Chapter 4. The erstwhile Planning Commission had set up a Study Group on Reforms in State PSEs in India in 1999 under the chairmanship of Dr N. J. Kurian, whose recommendations have also been briefly discussed in Chapter 4. Needless to say, for protecting the vested interests of the politicians and bureaucrats in these enterprises which offered a cushy parking place to them with all attendant privileges even at the cost of strained state exchequers, these recommendations were mostly glossed over by the state governments. Nevertheless, it is important to reflect upon a few specific recommendations relevant to reforms of the SPSEs.

One of the most significant recommendations of the Study Group on Reforms in State Public Sector Undertakings was the setting up of a statutory and independent Disinvestment Commission by every state, comprising economists, engineers, lawyers, accountants, public enterprise managers and labour experts.[43] SPSUs were classified into six categories, as discussed earlier; the report suggested that in each category, the best, average and low performers should be identified. The enterprises in the average and low categories should devise strategies to rise to the level of the best performing enterprises, failing which they should be disinvested. As the Study Group noted:

> in the post-reform era the State is expected to promote growth by acting as a catalyst and a facilitator and not get directly involved in provision of goods and services. Each public sector enterprise could be ranked as high or low on three parameters in a matrix format viz., public purpose, profitability and mobilisation of financial resources. In case the enterprise is high on all the three parameters (HHH), it could be retained in the public enterprise portfolio. If the public enterprise is low on all the three parameters (LLL), then it could be divested from such portfolio. The enterprises falling in the remaining categories could be restructured (eg. HLL, HLH, LLH).[44]

By and large, states should withdraw from the manufacturing, trading and services sectors, while other enterprises may be retained or restructured suitably to meet the demands of social obligations of the states for 'public purposes'. For 'deciding whether to retain, restructure or privatize the State PSUs, the States may keep in view the criterion followed by the Disinvestment Commission i.e. the public purpose served by the PSUs'.[45]

Another important recommendation is the introduction of the MOU system in the SPSUs in the line of that existing in the CPSEs,

---

[43] Government of India, *Report of the Study Group on Reforms of State Public Sector Enterprises*, Para 7.3.

[44] Ibid, Para 7.2.

[45] Ibid, Para 7.2.

which, as we have seen in Chapter 3, has contributed significantly to the improvement of their performance by redefining the 'relationship between the State Governments and State PSUs'. As the report noted, MOU could be a useful instrument in bringing about this strategic and important reform by giving them independence and more functional autonomy and to stop the interference of the state governments in their day-to-day functioning, which is a chronic bottleneck constraining their performance.[46] Odisha introduced MOU in respect of one of its PSUs, the Odisha Mining Corporation, which happens to be the largest mining enterprise among all SPSUs. It also incorporated a few more suggestions emanating from the Study Group report, like the institution of a renewal fund (Odisha State Renewal Fund Society), a VRS scheme and strengthening of corporate governance systems within the organisation. A few other states, like Assam, have also attempted to introduce an MOU system in their PSEs, without much appreciable result because of various structural and capacity constraints. Tamil Nadu has also introduced it, but the MOU system is yet to be implemented in seriousness in its PSEs. The DPE has prescribed a model MOU for the SPSUs.[47]

Another structural reform necessary to streamline the working of the SPSEs, according to the Study Group, was the establishment of a state level nodal agency to coordinate the work of SPSUs. At the central level, there is the DPE, but very few states have such a nodal agency. Professionalisation of the managers and fixed tenures of their CMDs is another vital reform necessary to enable them to make a break with their past and be forward-looking, confident and competitive.[48] Strengthening of corporate governance within them is a *sine qua non* for improving their overall performance. The states also have an obligation to compensate their own PSUs through explicit budgetary provisions for the cost of meeting social obligations

[46] Ibid, Paras 7.13, 7.16.

[47] https://dpemou.nic.in/MOUFiles/MOUModel.pdf, accessed 8 November 2019.

[48] Government of India, *Report of the Study Group on Reforms of State Public Sector Enterprises*, Paras 7.13, 7.15.

as dictated by the states' policies, which often run counter to their commercial viability.[49]

The implementation of all these recommendations is important for effecting any meaningful reform of the state enterprises. As many as 1,136 SPSEs are too huge a number to be managed efficiently and this number must be drastically reduced by carefully choosing the specific strategic sectors and entities the states must have a presence in, and selling, closing and disbanding the rest by appropriate mechanisms, which is the first requirement. Instead, the states still are continuing to create a few enterprises every year, even as more of their PSEs are falling sick and becoming dysfunctional with each passing year. The focus should rather be on strengthening the well-performing ones and listing them in the stock exchanges. As long as they remain unlisted, their shares are not traded in the market, and the discipline that the market imposes will continue to be evaded, disabling them to grow and become competitive.

The Fourteenth Finance Commission's recommendations in relation to the CPSEs and SPSEs have been discussed in detail in the relevant chapters. Most of these recommendations are yet to be implemented by the government. While suggesting the protection of the basic interests of existing workers of CPSEs at a 'reasonable fiscal cost', the Fourteenth Finance Commission had recommended that employment objectives should be considered also in terms of creating new employment opportunities. It recommended the categorisation of enterprises into 'high priority', 'priority', 'low priority' and 'non-priority' areas for coordinated follow-up action and, more importantly, to provide clarity to PSEs themselves 'on their future and to the financial markets about the opportunities ahead for them'. The unlisted and sick enterprises in the non-priority areas should be divested from the portfolio of CPSEs only through transparent auctions. It further recommended that the level of disinvestment should be determined from the level of investment in them that the government decides to hold, over the medium to long term, based on the above principles of

[49] Ibid, Para 7.22.

prioritisation, while market conditions and budgetary requirements should guide the disinvestment process. The Commission recommended that the central government should share a small part of the proceeds from disinvestment with the states, depending on distribution of their units among the states and the location of the divested units.[50] Nothing like this has happened so far.

The Commission recognised the institutional constraints within which their managements operate, and urged these to be reckoned while evaluating their performance. If they are required to implement the social objectives of the government, which may affect their commercial objectives, they should be adequately compensated in a timely manner through 'a transparent budgetary subvention', including for losses on account of administered price mechanisms.[51] It also wanted the government to fix the policies and procedures relating to borrowing by the CPSEs, as well as for payment of dividends and transfer of excess reserves, and also for investments by them.[52]

As regards the SPSEs, it has urged the SPSEs, like the CPSEs, to reckon the new realities of the market emphasised upon the need to be commercially viable and financially sustainable, and made it clear that its recommendations regarding the CPSEs related to prioritisation, disinvestment and relinquishment are equally applicable to the SPSEs as well. States, therefore, have an obligation to rethink their current practices and policies regarding their ailing PSEs, and act with a sense of utmost urgency to restructure their own finances by withdrawing from most SPSEs and restructuring and reforming the rest.

In the budget speech for the Fiscal Year 2016–2017, the Union Finance Minister had stated:

A new policy for management of Government investment in Public Sector Enterprises, including disinvestment and strategic sale, has been approved. We have to leverage the assets of CPSEs for generation of resources for investment in new projects. We will encourage

[50] Ibid, Para 16.36.
[51] Ibid, Para 16.39.
[52] Ibid, Para 16.43.

CPSEs to divest individual assets like land, manufacturing units, etc. to release their asset value for making investment in new projects. The NITI Aayog will identify the CPSEs for strategic sale. We will adopt a comprehensive approach for efficient management of Government investment in CPSEs by addressing issues such as capital restructuring, dividend, bonus shares, etc. The Department of Disinvestment is being re-named as the 'Department of Investment and Public Asset Management (DIPAM)'.

In accordance with this, in May 2016, DIPAM issued guidelines for capital restructuring of the CPSEs, including payment of dividends, splitting of shares, issuing bonus shares and buyback of shares. However, most other recommendations of the Commission, whether with regard to the CPSEs or the SPSEs, still remain unaddressed.

One of the most significant recommendations of the Fourteenth Finance Commission was that the governance arrangements, especially the separation of its regulatory functions from ownership functions, the role of the government nominee as well as independent directors 'and, above all, the framework of governance conducive to efficiency', should be reviewed.[53] While recommending this, the Commission cited the report of the Panel of Experts on Reforms in Central Public Sector Enterprises, which had highlighted that for good corporate governance within the CPSEs, the composition and functioning of the Board of directors is vital, along with the strengthening of vigilance, a suitable manpower planning strategy, succession planning and the listing of every CPSE to make them conform to the discipline enforced by the market.

The aforesaid 'Panel of Experts on Reforms in Central Public Sector Enterprises' was constituted by the Planning Commission in August 2010. It was headed by Mr S. K. Roongta, a former chairman of the Steel Authority of India Ltd., and was tasked with examining a range of issues concerning the CPSEs. These included issues related to human resource management, corporate governance, re-examining the MOU system, exploring effective partnerships with the private sector,

[53] Ibid, Para 16.40.

diversification, mergers and consolidation, leveraging technology, etc., and to suggest a road map to them. The Panel submitted its report in November 2011. The report made several important recommendations, as discussed below, which, if implemented, would transform the landscape of our public sector enterprises.

Regarding the corporate governance issues in CPSEs, the Panel recommended the mandatory constitution of a few committees by each CPSE, namely, (a) Strategy and Business Development Committee of the Board, (b) Audit Committee, (c) Human Resources Committee and (d) Nomination and Remuneration Committee. It suggested that the CPSE Board should 'have a strategy offsite once a year to set direction for the company towards diversification, acquisition, joint ventures, new business entry and review of organisational structure etc.'[54] Regarding the role of the government directors in the Board, the Panel recommended on issues 'where the Government has no specific views, the role of the Government Directors should be akin to those of the Independent Directors'.[55]

As regards the appointment of independent directors to the Boards of CPSEs, the panel recommended that independent directors may be appointed out of a list of approved names by the DPE/PSEB and that this list should be updated every 6 months after identifying the knowledge gaps existing in the Boards of the concerned CPSEs. There should be a Search Committee to identify such names, and their recommendations should be sent directly to the DOPT, while keeping the concerned administrative ministry in the loop.[56] There is also an urgent need to streamline the process of appointment of CMDs and other full-time members of CPSE boards, by expediting the process of vigilance clearance by the CVC and removing other impediments.[57] For selection of CMDs/CEOs of CPSEs of the Maharatna and Navratna companies that are critical to the national economy, a separate specialised body may be constituted within the PSEB exclusively for this purpose. The

[54] Report of Panel of Experts on Reforms in Central Public Sector Enterprises (CPSEs), Summary of Recommendations, Para 1.1.

[55] Ibid, Para 1.4.

[56] Ibid, Para 1.5.

[57] Ibid, Para 1.6.

criteria for selection should have greater emphasis on the leadership qualities, strategic thinking, capabilities to manage external environment, etc., apart from the domain/sectoral expertise'.[58] For the sake of maintaining transparency on this important aspect, 'an update should be provided in every session of Parliament on the vacant positions of CMDs of CPSEs'. They should have a minimum tenure of 3 years, irrespective of their age at the time of first appointment.[59]

Regarding vigilance management in CPSEs, the Panel recommended that: 'A vigilance frame-work that recognises that vigilance as a function is to be primarily performed by the management, needs to be evolved in consultation with CVC'. This was necessary to overcome the 'growing culture of indecision and attitude of playing safe, flowing from an environment of suspicion and easy presumption of guilt'.[60]

The Panel advocated the adoption of an appropriate manpower planning strategy by every CPSE to identify the key skills and talent requirements across all levels within them, from the medium as well as the long term perspectives, and formulate a strategy to fill in the gaps.[61] It recognised the 'pressing need to provide autonomy to CPSEs to devise their own recruitment policies for all positions below the Board level'.[62] This, as observed earlier, has been a crucial aspect of the reforms of SOEs across the world—to shield them from undue political or bureaucratic influence in the matter of appointments, which often gave way to crony capitalism and usurped the professional decision-making role in these organisations. The Panel recommend that: 'The CPSE should create multiple access points for induction, to meet their talent requirements' including engagement of specialists as may be required.[63] Further, the CPSEs should also be empowered to frame their own compensation policies.[64]

---

[58] Ibid, Para 1.7.
[59] Ibid, Para 1.8.
[60] Ibid, Para 1.9.
[61] Ibid, Para 2.1.
[62] Ibid, Para 2.4.
[63] Ibid, Para 2.4.
[64] Ibid, Para 2.5.

The Panel studied the current system of MOUs prevalent in the CPSEs, which was 'conceptualised when CPSEs were operating in a regulated environment'. It suggested some basic changes in the current MOU system to increase their effectiveness 'not only for evaluation of the business performance of CPSEs but also to give direction to their businesses', by relating them to the organisation's plan for 'diversification, acquisition, formation of JVs, new/strategic businesses, usage of ICT, R&D initiatives, HR development and organizational changes, etc.'.[65] Physical performance parameters in MOUs should be benchmarked with industry parameters including the private sector, with international benchmarking for specific sectors, in order to encourage the CPSEs to emulate these benchmarks, within a specified time frame, to increase their international competitiveness.[66] Greater autonomy should also be given to CPSE Boards for the selection of consultants, vendors with proprietary technologies, technology partners, joint venture partners and companies for acquisition.[67]

For managing the identified surplus land in the possession of the loss-making CPSEs, the Panel recommended the establishment of a 'Public Sector Land Development Authority (PSLDA), on the lines of the Rail Land Development Authority, for the purpose of developing such lands and unlocking their real value', through commercial bidding to generate resources that could be ploughed back to the sick enterprises for their revival.[68]

The Panel made a number of recommendations on technology and institutional collaboration, which included for every CPSE a technology policy, an IT plan, a technology committee as part of the R&D organisation within the CPSE, scaling up of its R&D budget, especially within the Maharatna and Navratna CPSEs, supplementing internal research with joint research and collaborations by forging partnerships with other institutions like the CSIR, IITs and other national laboratories.[69] It also recommended the setting up of a 'Centre

---

[65] Ibid, Para 3.1.
[66] Ibid, Para 3.2.
[67] Ibid, Para 4.1.
[68] Ibid, Para 4.7.
[69] Ibid, Paras 5.1–5.5.

for Innovation to assist CPSEs in developing and implementing strategies to strengthen their technology base'.[70]

One of the questions that has remained problematic since the Constitution came into existence relates to the constitutional status of PSEs. Article 12 of the Indian Constitution defines the term 'State'. As per this, the term State includes 'the Government and Parliament of India and the Government and the Legislature of each of the States and all local or other authorities within the territory of India or under the control of the Government of India'. While there are no disputes regarding government, legislature or local authorities, it is the phrase 'other authorities' which has not been defined in the Constitution, making it open to judicial interpretations. The matter was also examined in detail by the Law Commission, upon being referred to it by the Bureau of Public Enterprises. The results of its examination were submitted to the government in its 145th Report on 'Article 12 of the Constitution and Public Sector Undertakings' in 1992.

The definition of 'State' in Article 12 is only for the purpose of application of the provisions contained in Part III of the Constitution dealing with fundamental rights requiring a high degree of commitment from the State, which is obliged to protect these rights of citizens, and hence the question of what is included in the definition of State becomes important for the purpose of determining the responsibility for enforcing and protecting these rights of citizens. If the PSE qualifies as State, then there are additional obligations for it to discharge these responsibilities, which might interfere with its independent functioning as a viable commercial entity. For example, Article 38 of the Constitution enjoins the state to promote the welfare of the people by securing and protecting effectively a social order in which justice, social, economic and political, shall underpin all the institutions of the state. As stated in the 145th Report of the Law Commission:

> The State is further directed to strive to minimise inequalities in income, and endeavour to eliminate inequalities in status, facilities and opportunities, not only among individuals, but also amongst groups of people residing in different areas or engaged in different

---

[70] Ibid, Para 5.6.

vocations. This Article, and other Articles e.g. 39, 39A, 41, 42 and 46, lay down fundamental policies, which the State is required to follow in making laws with a view to securing a welfare State.[71]

Directive principles may not be not justifiable, but nevertheless must guide the various organs of the state. Since the PSEs function under the control and direction of the government, they, therefore, are obliged to function in a manner expected from 'State', even while carrying out purely commercial activities. This also makes any commercial or administrative decision taken by the PSE management subject to judicial review under Articles 32 and 226 of the Constitution.

The term 'State' has been interpreted in different contexts at different times by judicial pronouncements, but in general, they favour the PSEs to be included under the definition of the 'State'. Using the principle of *ejusdem generis,* that is, of the like nature, the Madras High Court, in the case of University of Madras v/s Santa Bai (AIR 1954 Mad 67, (1953) IIMLJ 287), said that those authorities were covered under the expression 'other authorities' which performed governmental or sovereign functions. However, in Ujjain Bai v/s State of U.P. (AIR 1962 SC 1621), the Supreme Court rejected the principle of *ejusdem generis*, observing that there was no common genus between the authorities mentioned in Article 12.[72]

In respect of authorities performing commercial activities or activities promoting educational or economic interests, the Supreme Court[73] said that in order to be a state, it was not necessary for the authority to perform governmental or sovereign functions. Instead, it laid down the criteria for the purpose of recognising an authority as a state, which are wide enough to include all bodies created by a statute on which powers are conferred to carry out governmental or quasi-governmental functions. They should be created by the Constitution of India with the power to make laws. This automatically made all PSEs qualify as State.

[71] 145th Report of the Law Commission, Para 3.2.

[72] http://www.legalserviceindia.com/article/l271-Article-12.html, accessed 19 November 2019.

[73] Rajasthan State Electricity Board v. Mohal Lal (AIR 1967 SC 1857).

In the case of R. D. Shetty v/s International Airport Authority (1979 SCR (3)1014), the Supreme Court had laid down five tests for a corporation to qualify as 'other authority': (a) whether the entire share capital of the corporation is owned or managed by State; (b) whether it enjoys a monopoly status; (c) whether the extent of state control over the corporation is 'deep and pervasive'; (d) whether the functions of the corporation are of public importance and closely related to governmental functions; and (e) whether what belonged to a government department formerly was transferred to the corporation.[74] The Court further observed that there were several factors to be considered in determining whether a corporation was an 'agency or instrumentality of Government', like

> whether there is any financial assistance given by the State, and if so, what is the magnitude of such assistance; whether there is any other form of assistance given by the State, and if so, whether it is of the usual kind or it is extra ordinary; whether there is any control of the management and policies of the corporation by the State and what is the nature and extent of such control; whether the corporation enjoys any State conferred or State protected monopoly status and whether the functions carried out by the corporation are pubic functions closely related to governmental functions.

It mentioned that these factors were not exhaustive and that it was not possible to make an exhaustive enumeration of the tests to convincingly answer the question of whether a corporation was governmental instrumentality or agency.[75]

In U.P. Warehousing Corporation v/s Vijai Narain, ((1987) 3 SCC 395), it was held that the U.P. Warehousing Corporation,

---

[74] 145th Report of the Law Commission, Para 2.3.

[75] 'whether there is any financial assistance given by the State, and if so, what is the magnitude of such assistance; whether there is any other form of assistance given by the State, and if so, whether it is of the usual kind or it is extra ordinary; whether there is any control of the management and policies of the corporation by the State and what is the nature and extent of such control; whether the corporation enjoys any State conferred or State protected monopoly status and whether the functions carried out by the corporation are pubic functions closely related to governmental functions'—Pages 1641–1642 of AIR 1979 S C 1628.

which was constituted under a statute and owned and controlled by the government, was an agency or instrumentality of the government and therefore 'the State' within the meaning of Article 12. In Som Prakash v/s Union of India, (AIR 1981 SC 212 11) also, the Supreme Court held that a government company (Bharat Petroleum Corporation Ltd) fell within the meaning of the expression 'the State' used in Article 12.[76]

In Sukhdev Singh v/s Bhagat Ram (AIR 1975 SC 1331 at 1363), LIC, ONGC and IFC were held to be State for performing functions very close to governmental or sovereign functions. The corporations are State when they enjoy the power to make regulations that have the force of law in addition to clearance of the above five tests.[77] The Court observed in the case, 'A finding of state financial support plus an unusual degree of control over the management and policies might lead one to characterise an operation as state action'. In the Central Inland Water Transport Corporation Limited v/s Brojo Natlz, (AIR 1986 SC 1571) also, the Supreme Court ruled that any agency or instrumentality of the government will be covered by the expression 'other authorities'.

From the above discussion, it would seem that the preponderant considerations for pronouncing an entity as the state should be the source of its funding and whether its functional character is governmental in essence. If its primary control lies with the government by virtue of the above, it would qualify to be an agency or instrumentality of the state within the meaning of Article 12. The expression 'other authorities' will therefore automatically include all constitutional or statutory authorities, statutory corporations or government companies. This interpretation led to many problems, making the decisions taken by the PSEs open to judicial reviews.

First, regarding service matters, it was becoming virtually impossible to terminate the service of any employee even if the rules allowed such termination on 3 months' notice—the employees had practically acquired a permanent employment status. Second, regarding award

[76] Academike, *Other Authorities Under Article 12 of Constitution*.
[77] http://www.legalserviceindia.com/article/l271-Article-12.html, accessed 19 November 2019.

of contracts, even where the PSE management knew for certain the bad credentials of a firm, it couldn't refuse to deal with that firm by virtue of Article 14 (Equality before law), without following the elaborate formalities stressed upon in the judicial pronouncements on the matter. Third, courts were routinely granting injunctions and interim orders on the PSEs, affecting their independent functioning, leading to 'mounting litigation' over 'trivial matters'.

The Law Commission examined in detail the arguments in favour of and against amending Article 12 to take the PSEs out of its ambit in view of the 'difficulties that may be experienced by public sector undertakings in the matter of award of contracts, rejection of tenders, service matters and the like arising out of the present applicability of Article 12 to such undertakings', and finally concluded that: 'Such an amendment would not be a proper or necessary measure'.[78] It further went on to say, 'Having regard to the Preamble and total philosophy of the Constitution, even if such an amendment is made, some of the problems experienced by the public sector undertakings would still survive under the ordinary law'.[79] Besides, the Commission expressed the doubt that even if such an amendment was passed, there were chances that 'in the light of the theory of non-amenability of the basic features of the Constitution as at present recognised, such an amendment will pass muster on the Constitution level'.[80]

In April 2005, The Group of Experts on Empowerment of CPSEs (the Arjun Sen Gupta Committee) had also considered this question and observed that the mandatory legal implications of Article 12 inhibited the functioning of CPSEs as commercial entities, unlike their private sector competitors, and recommended that this issue needs to be revisited. The Roongta Panel also examined this matter and observed that the matter had again acquired added importance, especially 'on the account of RTI (2005) being used by rivals and disgruntled vendors/contractors to elicit information of confidential nature'. It finally concluded: 'Considering the impact of CPSEs as

[78] 145th Report of the Law Commission, Para 5.22.
[79] Ibid.
[80] Ibid.

deemed to be covered under "State" on the entire functioning of these Enterprises, the Panel feels that it is an appropriate time to revisit the issue in its entirety'.[81] The government is yet to take a call on this matter, like all other recommendations of the panel.

In the last chapter of their report, the Roongta Panel provided a new conceptual paradigm for the PSEs, though there was a lack of unanimity about this paradigm among the Panel members. Nevertheless, the model suggested by the Panel merits serious consideration, as these suggestions also converge with the ideas that emerge from this study in respect of reforming and restructuring our PSEs. The model suggested by the Roongta Panel is 'a mix of a sovereign wealth fund, a single holding structure and the Government acting as a venture capitalist'. The Panel clearly stated:

> There is need to create a single holding structure (SHS) for all future CPSEs. It could also be considered to transfer the ownership of Maharatna companies to this structure, to begin with. This SHS would be in the nature of a holding company owning different stakes in different CPSEs, to be decided by its Board.[82]

As we have seen, this was the model followed by almost all countries that have successfully transformed their SOEs into profitable companies with global outreach that created immense wealth for them and their countries. This model would automatically shield our PSEs from vested interests in our political and administrative apparatuses subverting their commercial objectives and provide real autonomy to the management of these companies to run their operations. The Panel suggested that the SHS should have an independent Board with an equal number of members drawn from within and outside the government, with the Board chairman being appointed by the Prime Minister. The Panel suggested 12 members for this Board. The SHS itself may be managed by a small team, like a mutual fund, and would be responsible for managing its own portfolio, with the objective to optimise the returns for the government in line with the directions of its Board, either by

[81] Roongta Panel Report, Para 2.25.
[82] Ibid, Para 7.3.

way of dividends or through divestitures of its stake as decided by it. It would also be responsible for taking all decisions regarding investments on the basis of the strategic intent of the government and managing the investments. It would independently decide on the extent of holding and timing of divestment or exit and take all decisions regarding its subsidiary entities including the selection and appointment of their chairmen and directors. The companies themselves will be kept outside the purview of any ministry and will function as Board-run companies, but they will not report to the CEO of the SHS entity.

> The CEO would only manage the Government's stake in the different companies and provide a year-end report on the financial performance of each of the invested entities for its Board. In special circumstances, the Chairman of the SHS could ask for the CEO of an invested company to be replaced—very much like a big shareholders today can put pressure on the Board to change a CEO. The performance of SHS entity could be monitored by say an Empowered Group of Ministers (EGOM) to whom it would be accountable.[83]

The elements for determining a workable model for SHS would comprise:

1. A legal structure of the SHS defining the structure of the CPSEs and their classification within it;
2. Criteria defining entry into new sectors, the manner of such entry, the extent of holding, etc.;
3. Criteria for listing the CPSEs in stock exchanges and related issues;
4. Constraints in ownership—foreign, strategic partners, retail investors or employee ownership—and the stake the government should retain—majority or minority;
5. Exit policy and procedure;
6. Structure of an effective institutional oversight mechanism, including criteria and method for performance assessment, etc.[84]

[83] Ibid.
[84] Ibid, Para 7.4.

An important issue flagged by the Panel was that the 'governing policies in respect of the units could be framed by the Board in keeping with the industry sector under which the unit fell'.[85] Thus, the compensation, assessment, HR and other policies of a CPSE belonging to a particular sector should be aligned with the corresponding industry benchmarks and not with any other CPSE. The Board of an individual CPSE should have the complete autonomy to decide on all issues pertaining to that particular entity like compensation, procurement, entering into partnerships or joint ventures, etc. This would make them truly independent commercial entities, enabling them to compete with the private sector on a level playing field. Lastly, while creating the SHS, the anomalies that arise from operating the Article 12 of the Constitution on the CPSEs should be removed by taking them outside its purview of State, through a suitable constitutional amendment and other arrangements.[86]

As would be clear from the above discussion taking into account the reform experiences of different countries, a clear separation of the government's roles as owner and majority shareholder of PSEs, as well as their regulator, enforcer of the regulations and policymaker is a must for empowering them with real autonomy and decision-making power on strategic matters. The Temasek model or the SHS model suggested by the Roognta panel will effectively serve this end. The government and the PSEs must be kept at an arm's length from each other in order to ensure that the former's policymaking prerogative does not constrain the commercial operation of the latter. Side by side, the regulatory environment must be strengthened by creating an independent regulatory body and bringing into it expertise from different fields. The body must be given adequate independence, and it should also discharge the role of an arbiter between the government and the SHS. The PSE ecosystem not only involves the relationship between the government and the PSE, but it also involves citizens who are its owners and customers as well. For the PSEs' transparent and efficient operations, every stakeholder must be actively involved in it with a sense of owning, belonging and contributing to it. There

[85] Ibid, Para 7.5.
[86] Ibid.

have to be transparent mechanisms for evaluation and monitoring of the performance and quality assurance of the PSEs and for informing the citizens on these through an institutional analysis and reporting system. The PSE ecosystem must be underpinned by an ownership structure to prevent governmental and bureaucratic interference in any manner, a robust legislative and regulatory framework, strong and transparent corporate governance and operational efficiency with accountability, which would be the essential pillars of PSE reforms.

In addition to the above, we need to reduce the size of our CPSEs drastically and professionalise their management. Given the strong predisposition of our politico-administrative system to interfere and subvert any state institution for their own narrow and vested interests, it is essential to institute appropriate legal and administrative checks to shield them from any political or bureaucratic interference. To this end, the entry of any active politician or serving bureaucrat into the Board of any CPSE should be debarred by law. The government can have its say in their affairs only through the Board of the SHS, where it can appoint the government directors and chairman, but the majority of the Board should be constituted by independent directors drawn from among the experts in various fields. The CPSEs will remain accountable to the Parliament/government only through the SHS, and there should not be any direct interface between the government and the individual CPSEs. The interests of the government in terms of policy and financial returns expected from the companies must be decided at the beginning of the year, on a fair and reasonable basis, through MOUs or other mechanisms, which shall be mediated by the SHS; the CPSEs will individually remain accountable to the SHS for their performance and for meeting those expectations. For performing the social objectives and welfare programmes at the cost of commercial objectives, the government must adequately compensate the PSEs.

To professionalise the management of the CPSEs, the recruitment of their chairmen, managing directors and Board members should be made from a permanent panel drawn up for the purpose, renewable, say, every 3 years, without any interference by the government. The present system of recruitment through the PESB, which is functioning under a ministry, is unsatisfactory, being susceptible to political and other extraneous influences. There should be an autonomous body like the UPSC having members also drawn from outside the government to do the necessary selection for this purpose. As regards recruitments of professionals for the managerial and technical posts in these companies, the present system is relatively unbiased and can be continued with. The companies must be made to conform to the highest standards of corporate governance and accountability, in line with global practices. If they aspire to be globally competitive, they must adopt and adapt to the global standards and benchmarks.

It is absolutely an undeserving and impractical idea for the state to withdraw from business altogether. For a country that is emerging as the third largest economy in the world aspiring to become a $5 trillion within a few years, it cannot ignore the sectors vital for its economic and social development and leave them at the caprices of the profit-driven private sector. While there is no alternative to the commercial viability of CPSEs, their social and welfare orientations have to be assimilated into their commercial objectives in an optimal way. Strategic sectors may be opened to the private sector, but the public sector will always remain an important player in these sectors. As we have seen, even in some of the sectors that were opened to private investment long back, the PSEs still continue to command market shares larger than their private counterparts even now. However, urgent withdrawal from a large number of non-core sector is crucial—after all, 444 is too unwieldy a number for the CPSEs to be managed efficiently by any government. The government must decide the sectors critical for the PSEs to remain and withdraw from all the rest after ensuring appropriate returns from their disinvestments. For this, their prioritisation and listing at the stock exchanges are necessary. Listing itself will improve the efficiency and hence the worth of the CPSEs by forcing them to submit to the market discipline and competition, for which they may need some additional investments and support to upgrade their technology, which the government may provide. Our goal should be to transform the remaining entities, especially each of our Ratna companies, into strong global brands, to compete successfully with the best companies in the world, and become not only Indian winners but global champions. Without reforming the ownership structure and reducing outside interference in their functioning, this would never happen.

As mentioned earlier, there are 1,136 SPSEs as well, and while some meaningful reforms have been undertaken in respect of the CPSEs, by and large, the SPSEs have continued to languish helplessly in an environment of rent-seeking and favour-dispensing political gamesmanship. The public sector reform would not carry much meaning without the corresponding reforms of the SPSEs. While renewing the public sector can be the principal theme for reforming the CPSES, for the SPSEs, it should be dismantling the existing structure of SPSEs before any meaningful reform can be carried out. As seen in Chapter 4, there is a tendency on the part of the states to proliferate their numbers for accommodating politicians and bureaucrats as their heads, so the primary task is to stop this practice. This will not happen in isolation; for this, all states have to arrive at a consensus through an institutional mechanism using the spirit of cooperative federalism. Creation of an institutional mechanism and empowering it to discuss and decide on all public sector enterprises in the country, whether in the states or at the Centre, may be the first step in such consensus building. Such an institution, working on the spirit of cooperative federalism like the GST Council can then decide the sectors the government must withdraw from, and to identify and establish a fast-track mechanism for that. Once the number of SPSEs has been drastically reduced, it will be possible to revamp the structure and management of the remaining SPSEs, using a similar methodology as suggested for the CPSEs. Wherever feasible and where synergies exist, central PSUs may be persuaded to manage the SPSEs. The essential prerequisite is to depoliticise them, professionalise their management by appointing experienced managers and shield them from politicians or bureaucrats.

Many of our states—even the advanced ones—by and large still remain mired in the ethos of the old economic, social and political orders even though these orders have collapsed everywhere irrevocably. This mind-set prevents a systematic movement towards consolidation of the benefits of economic reforms as reflected in destatisation, privatisation and marketisation of the SPSEs. Such a movement would have facilitated the modernisation and revitalisation of the SPSEs, leading to the possibility of their adaptation to the new realities that the Fourteenth Finance Commission had talked about. After cleansing the states of entities that serve no purpose other than providing a parking space for the politicians and bureaucrats, those that remain should be professionally nurtured by depoliticising and de-bureaucratising them, changing their ownership structure, providing them with independence, autonomy, flexibility and support, strengthening their corporate governance systems and introducing mandatory MOUs and listing at stock exchanges while benchmarking them against the industries in respect of their performance, compensation and competitiveness.

For any transformational reform, political will, determination and statesmanship on the part of the leaders are essential. Unfortunately, these attributes have not yet been demonstrated in the context of PSEs in India, and political expediency has always got the better of genuine institutional reforms. Privatisation in our country has been made synonymous with public sector reforms, which, as we have seen, is not necessarily the case. The public sector, managed properly with resolve and vision, can again become a driver for change and prosperity for the entire country, as it was once upon a time, and can be revived and rejuvenated once again to serve the nation and its citizens.

References

Academike. *Other Authorities Under Article 12 of Constitution.* Articles on Legal Issues [ISSN: 2349–9796], 15 January 2015, https://www.lawctopus.com/academike/authorities-article-12-constitution/, accessed 19 November 2019.

Agarwal, Sanjay K. *Corporate Social Responsibility in India.* New Delhi: SAGE Publications, 2008.

Abramova, Alexander, et al. 'State-owned enterprises in the Russian market: Ownership structure and their role in the economy', *Russian Journal of Economics*, 3, no. 1 (March 2017): 1–23, https://doi.org/10.1016/j.ruje.2017.02.001, accessed 14 June 2019.

Anwar, Sajid, and Choon-Yin Sam. 'Singaporean Style of Public Sector Corporate Governance: Can Private Sector Corporations Emulate Public Sector Practices?' *New Zealand Journal of Asian Studies* 8, no. 1 (June, 2006): 41–68.

Atlee, Clement. *The Labour Party in Perspective.* London: Left Book Club, 1937.

Bailey, S. J. 'Rolling Back the Frontiers of the State'. In *Public Sector Economics*, 113–114. Macmillan Texts in Economics. London: Palgrave, 1995.

Balassa, Bela. *Public Enterprise in Developing Countries.* Development Research Department, Washington DC: World Bank, 1987.

Barnes, Guillermo. 'Lessons from Bank Privatisation in Mexico'. In *Public Enterprises, Restructuring and Privatization,* 277–284. World Bank, Washington DC, 1992.

Belke, Ansgar, Frank Baumgärtner, Friedrich Schneider, and Ralph Setzer. 'The Different Extent of Privatization Proceeds in OECD Countries: A Preliminary Explanation Using a Public-Choice Approach'. *Public Finance Analysis* 63, no. 2 (June 2007): 211–243, https://www.jstor.org/stable/40913147, accessed 23 September 2019.

Bella, Gabriel Di, Oksana Dynnikova, and Slavi Slavov. 'The Russian State's size and its footprint: Have they increased'. IMF Working paper, 26 March 2019.

Bhargava, R. C. 'State Ownership to Joint Sector'. In *Reforming State-owned Enterprises,* edited by S. L. Rao, 117–128. New Delhi: NCAER, 1996.

Bhattacharjee, Govind. 'Coalgate Revisited'. *The Statesman,* 29 March 2015. https://www.thestatesman.com/opinion/coalgate-revisited-54701.html

Bhattacharjee, Govind. 'Regulate, Don't Privatise'. *The Statesman,* 13 and 14 April 2018. https://www.thestatesman.com/opinion/regulate-dont-privatisei-1502621418.html; https://www.thestatesman.com/opinion/regulate-dont-privatiseii-1502621939.html

Bhattacharya, Pramit. 'Why India Needs an Independent Fiscal Council'. *Livemint*, 10 February 2019. https://www.livemint.com/budget/news/why-india-needs-an-independent-fiscal-council-1549814189020.html

Bottomore, Tom. *Marxist Sociology.* London: Macmillan Press Limited, 1975.

Breen, Michael, and David Doyle. 'The Determinants of Privatization: A Comparative Analysis of Developing Countries'. *Journal of Comparative Policy Analysis: Research and Practice* 15, no. 1 (2013): 1–20, doi:10.1080/1387698 8.2013.741439, accessed 24 September 2019.

Buck, Trevor, Steve Thompson, and Mike Wright. *Post-Communist Privatisation and the British Experience*, in *Public Enterprise*, International Centre for Public Enterprises in Developing Countries, Ljubljana, Vol. 11, Nos. 2–3, June–Sept, 1991, 185–200.

Büge, Max, Matias Egeland, Przemyslaw Kowalski, and Monika Sztajerowska. *State-owned Enterprises in the Global Economy.* https://www.weforum.org/agenda/2013/05/state-owned-enterprises-in-the-global-economy/, accessed 14 December 2018.

Burns, Emile. *An Introduction to Marxism.* London: Lawrence & Wishart Ltd., 1952.

Business Today. 'SEBs to Dive Deeper into Debt as they Miss Uday Scheme Targets'. *Business Today*, 6 May 2019, https://www.businesstoday.in/top-story/sebs-to-dive-deeper-into-debt-as-they-miss-uday-scheme-targets/story/343900.html, accessed 18 August 2019.

Carrol, Archie B. 'The Pyramid of Corporate Social Responsibility'. In *The Corporate Social Responsibility Reader,* edited by John Burchell. New York: Routledge, 2008.

Chatterjee, Anupam. 'UDAY Scheme: DISCOMS Cut Losses, But Their Dues to GENCOS Mount'. *Financial Express*, New Delhi, 11 June 2018, https://www.financialexpress.com/economy/uday-scheme-Discoms-cut-losses-but-their-dues-to-gencos-mount/1200937/, accessed 18 August 2019.

Cowe, R., and M. Hopkins. 'Corporate Social Responsibility: Is There a Business Case?' In *The Corporate Social Responsibility Reader,* 107–109. Routledge, London, 2008.

Crick, Bernard. *Socialism.* New Delhi: World View Publication, 1998 (Indian Reprint).

Cunningham, Frank. *Democratic Theory and Socialism.* Cambridge: CUP, 1987.

Das, Kumar. 'Improvidence in Fiscal System and Privatization'. In *Privatization: Bane or Panacea*, edited by Ruddar Datt. New Delhi: Pragati Publications, 1993.

Das, Ashish Kumar, and Padmalaya Mohapatra. *Corporate Governance, Principles and Practices.* New Delhi: Saroop Book Publishers, 2015.

Department of Investment & Public Asset Management (DIPAM). *Disinvestment Manual,* February 2003, https://dipam.gov.in/sites/default/files/Disinvestment%20Manual%20-%20February%202003_0_0.pdf, accessed 25 September 2019.

Department of Public Enterprises. *Classification and Categorisation of CPSEs.* https://dpe.gov.in/sites/default/files/Chapter_5_Classification_Final_0.pdf, accessed 2 July 2019.

Department of Public Enterprises. *Empowering Public Sector Enterprises in India.* New Delhi: DPE, MoHE&PE, GoI, Shipra, 2008.

Department of Public Enterprises. 'Public Sector in India: Overview and Profile'. Government of India. Chapter 1, https://dpe.gov.in/sites/default/files/Chapter-1-Overview%20%26%20Profile_Final_0.pdf, accessed 2 July 2019.

Department of Public Enterprises. *Public Enterprises Survey 2017–2018.* Government of India, 182. https://dpe.gov.in/public-enterprises-survey-2017-18

Department of Public Enterprises. *Public Enterprise Survey 2018–2019.* 7–18 Vol 1, Annexure Statement 1, S1–8.

Dhameja, Nand, and Pranab Banerji, eds. *Public Enterprises Management: Issues and Challenges.* New Delhi: Indian Institute of Public Administration, 2011.

Dubey, Jyotindra. 'Disinvestment Got Boost Under Vajpayee-led NDA Govt'. *India Today*, 16 July 2019. https://www.indiatoday.in/diu/story/disinvest-ment-got-boost-under-vajpayee-led-nda-govt-here-s-how-public-sector-companies-fared-post-privatisation-1563694-2019-07-06

Ebeling, Richard M. 'Karl Marx and the Presumption of a 'Right Side' to History', Part II. *Capitalism Magazine*, 12 June 2017, https://www.capitalismmagazine.com/2017/12/, accessed 9 June 2019.

Elkington, John. *Cannibals with Forks: The Triple Bottom Line of 21st Century Business.* Oxford: Capstone, 1999.

Engels, Friedrich. *Anti-Duhring*, https://www.marxists.org/archive/marx/works/1877/anti-duhring/introduction.htm, accessed 7 June 2019.

Engels, Frederick. *Origins of the Family*, Chapter IX, https://www.marxists.org/archive/marx/works/1884/origin-family/ch09.htm, accessed 8 June 2019.

European Commission. *State-owned Enterprises in the EU: Lessons Learnt and Ways Forward in a Post-crisis Context*, 2016, https://ec.europa.eu/info/sites/info/files/file_import/ip031_en_2.pd, accessed 5 November 2019.

Financial Statements of the Companies and Public Enterprises Survey, Vol. 2, 2017–2018. https://dpe.gov.in/public-enterprises-survey-2017-18.

Floyd, Robert H., Clive S. Gray, and R. P. Short. *Public Enterprise in Mixed Economies: Some Macroeconomic Aspects*, 41. Washington: IMF, 1984.

Friedman, Milton. 'The Social Responsibility of Business is to Increase Its Profits'. In *The Corporate Social Responsibility Reader,* edited by John Burchell. Routledge, 2008.

Friedman, Milton. *Neo-liberalism and Its Prospects.* https://miltonfriedman.hoover.org/friedman_images/Collections/2016c21/Farmand_02_17_1951.pdf, accessed 24 September 2019.

Friedmann, W. *The Public Corporation: A Comparative Symposium*, 576. London: Steven & Sons, 1954.

Ganesh, Gopal. *Privatisation and Labour.* New Delhi: Academic Foundation, 2008.

Ganesh, Gopal. *State Level Public Enterprises in India: Performance and Prospects.* New Delhi: Bookwell, 2010.

Gangadhar, V., and S. Kavitha Devi, *Disinvestment of Central Public Sector Enterprises, An Appraisal.* Ambala: The Associated Publishers, 2007.

Goulding, A. J. 'Retreating from the Commanding Heights: Privatization in an Indian Context'. *Journal of International Affairs* 50, no. 2 (1997): 581–612.

Goulding, A. J. 'Privatization: Political and Economic Challenges'. *Journal of International Affairs* 50, no. 2 (Winter 1997): 338–692.

Government of India. *Annual Report (2001–2002) on the Working of State Electricity Boards & Electricity Departments*, xvii. New Delhi: Planning Commission (Power & Energy Division), May 2002.

Government of India. *Economic Survey, 2019–2020*, Vol. 1. Govt of India, New Delhi, February 2020.

Government of India. *Report of the Fourteenth Finance Commission*, Govt of India, New Delhi, December 2014. Para 16.14.

Government of India. *Report of the Study Group on Reforms of State Public Sector Enterprises* (Planning Commission). Planning Commission, Govt of India, New Delhi, August 2002.

Goyal, Malini. What India Can Learn from Singapore & China's Successful PSU Models. *The Economic Times*, June 8, 2014. https://economictimes.indiatimes.com/news/economy/indicators/what-india-can-learn-from-singapore-chinas-successful-psu-models/articleshow/36215704.cms?from=mdr

Gupta, Asha. 'Privatisation in the United Kingdom'. In *Towards Privatisation*, 43–45. Delhi: BR Publishing Corporation, 1999.

Haralambos, Michael. *Sociology, Themes and Perspectives.* Oxford: OUP, 1980.

Harari, Yuval Noah. *Sapiens, A Brief History of Humankind.* London: Random House, 2015.

Haywood, Andrew. *Political Ideologies: An Introduction*, 6th ed. London: Palgrave Macmillan, 2017.

Holland, William. 'Reforming China's State-owned Enterprises'. *Asia Times*, 30 July 2018, http://www.atimes.com/reforming-chinas-state-owned-enterprises/

Indian Express. 'ONGC Cash Reserves at Record Low, Spend on Exploration Dips'. New Delhi, 22 November 2019. https://indianexpress.com/article/business/companies/ongc-cash-reserves-oil-production-record-low-6131084/

Jahan, Sarwat, Ahmed Saber Mahmud, and Chris Papageorgiou. 'What is Keynesian Economics?' *Finance & Development* 51, no. 3 (September 2014), 53–54. https://www.imf.org/external/pubs/ft/fandd/2014/09/pdf/basics.pdf

Johnson, Gordon. 'Why Privatize'. In *Public Enterprises, Restructuring and Privatization*, edited by Jack L. Upper and George B. Baldwin, 27–29. Washington: International Law Institute, 1995.

Jun, Wang, China Hainan Institute of Research and Development. 'Reforms of Public Enterprises in China'. In *Reforming State-owned Enterprises*, edited by S. L. Rao, 5–15. New Delhi: NCAER, 1996.

Katzarov, Konstantin. *The Theory of Nationalisation*, 13. The Hague: Martinus Nijhoff. 1964.

Kaur, Amandeep, and Lekha Chakraborty. 'UDAY Scheme's Progress Shows Few Hits, Many Misses (a research study)'. *Livemint*, 6 December 2018.

https://www.livemint.com/Home-Page/GBWI6DOjxN3e0m4np47o0I/UDAY-schemes-progress-shows-few-hits-many-misses.html

Khanna, Sushil. 'The Transformation of India's Public Sector: Political Economy of Growth and Change'. *Economic and Political Weekly* 50, no. 5 (31 January 2015): 47–60.

Kikeri, Sunita. 'A Framework of the Methods of Privatisation'. In *Reforming State-owned Enterprises*, edited by S. L. Rao, 237–246. New Delhi: NCAER, 1996.

Kumar, Suresh. 'Non-privatizing Reforms of Public Enterprises: The Indian Case'. In *Public Enterprises, Restructuring and Privatization,* edited by Jack L. Upper and George B. Baldwin, 143–146. Washington: International Law Institute, 1995.

Lane, Jan-Erik. 'Public Sector Reform: Only Deregulation, Privatisation and Marketization'. In *Public Sector Reform: Rationale, Trends and Problems,* edited by Jan-Erik Lane, 4–6. SAGE Publications, 1997.

Lee, Barbara W., and John Nellis. *Enterprise Reform and Privatisation in Socialist Economies*, 101–118. Washington: World Bank, 1990.

Mandal, Tarun. *Public Sector Enterprises in India.* New Delhi: Serials Publications, 2012.

Mandal, Tarun. *Recent Trends Towards Disinvestment in India: An Empirical Study on Selected Dimensions.* New Delhi: Abhijeet Publications, 2013.

Mathew, George. 'Banks Staring at Huge Stressed Loans of Private Power Companies'. *Indian Express*, Mumbai, 25 October 2012. http://archive.indianexpress.com/news/banks-staring-at-huge-stressed-loans-of-private-power-companeis/1021659/

Mathur, B. P. *Public Enterprise Management*, 2nd ed. New Delhi: Macmillan, 1999.

Mathur, B. P. 'Government's Policy of Privatization: Victim of Crony Capitalism'. *The Journal of Governance* Volume 8, January 2014: 72–87.

Marx, Karl. *Preface to A Contribution to the Critique of Political Economy*, 1859, https://www.marxists.org/archive/marx/works/1859/critique-pol-economy/preface.htm, accessed 7 June 2019.

Marx, Karl. *Critique of the Gotha Program*, Part 1, 1875. https://www.marxists.org/archive/marx/works/download/Marx_Critque_of_the_Gotha_Programme.pdf

Marx, Karl. 'Das Capital'. In *Wage Labour and Capital*, Chapter 5, https://www.marxists.org/archive/marx/works/1847/wage-labour/ch05.htm, accessed 7 June 2019.

Marx, Karl, and Friedrich Engels. *The Communist Manifesto*, Chapter 1, Footnote 1, 50. Signet Classic, 1998.

Mehta, Pradeep S. 'Achilles Heel of the Power Sector'. *The Hindu Business Line*, 15 October 2015. https://www.thehindubusinessline.com/opinion/columns/achilles-heel-of-the-power-sector/article7766479.ece

Mejstrik, Michal. *Privatisation in Czechoslovakia*, In *Public Enterprise*, International Centre for Public Enterprises in Developing Countries, Ljubljana, Vol. 11, Nos. 2–3, June–Sept, 1991, 151–162.

Milhaupt, J., and Mariana Pargendler. 'Governance Challenges of Listed State-owned Enterprises Around the World: National Experiences and a Framework for Reform'. ECGI Working Paper Series in Law, April 2017, Cornell International Law Journal, Vol. 50, No. 3 (2017), New York, 39.

Minhas, B. S. *Planning and the Poor*, vii. New Delhi: S Chand, 1974.

Mishra, R. K., Anupama Dubey, and V. Srikanth, eds. *Management and Social Science Research: An Institutional Experience.* New Delhi: Academic Foundation, 2019.

Mishra, R. K., Laksmi Kumari, and J. Kiranmai. *Reforming Pubic Enterprises.* Delhi: Kalpaz Publications, 2008.

Ministry of Disinvestment. *Disinvestment in States.* Government of India, June 2002.

Mitra, Ashoke. 'A Note on the Mahalanobis Model'. *Economic Weekly*, Vol. 9, Issue No. 11, 16 Mar, 1957: 372–374. https://www.epw.in/journal/1957/11/special-articles/note-mahalanobis-model.html

Mohapatra, Ranjan. 'Road Ahead for the MoU System'. *Financial Express*, 12 June 2018. https://www.financialexpress.com/archive/road-ahead-for-the-mou-system/963203/, accessed 10 July 2019.

Moore Jr, Barrington. *Authority and Inequality Under Capitalism and Socialism: USA, USSR and China.* London: Clarendon Press, 1987.

Moreno de Acevedo Sánchez, Enrique. 'State-owned Enterprise Management Advantages of Centralized Models'. Inter-American Development Bank Discussion Paper No. IDB-DP-454, Washington DC: June 2016.

Narayanan, N. 'The Joint Sector Concept'. In *Reforming State-owned Enterprises*, edited by S. L. Rao, 102–111. New Delhi: NCAER, 1996.

Newman, Michael. *Socialism: A Very Short Introduction*, 118–120. Oxford: Oxford University Press, 2005.

NITI Aayog. *India: Three Year Action Agenda, 2017–18 to 2019–20*, New Delhi: 2017. http://niti.gov.in/writereaddata/files/coop/IndiaActionPlan.pdf

OECD. *Corporate Governance Boards of Directors of State-owned Enterprises: An Overview of National Practices.* Paris: OECD, 2013.

Ownership and Governance of State-Owned Enterprises: A Compendium of National Practices, OECD, 2018, 23–34. http://www.oecd.org/corporate/Ownership-and-Governance-of-State-Owned-Enterprises-A-Compendium-of-National-Practices.pdf

Pandey, Shridhar. 'Economics and Politics of Privatization and India'. In *Public Enterprises, Restructuring and Privatization*, edited by Ruddar Datt, p. 178 *Bane or Panacea*, New Delhi: Pragati Publications, 1993.

PriceWaterhouseCoopers. 'State-owned Enterprises: Catalysts for Public Value Creation?' A Report by PriceWaterhouseCoopers, 2015, 8. https://www.pwc.com/gx/en/psrc/publications/assets/pwc-state-owned-enterprise-psrc.pdf, accessed 14 June 2019.

Proudhon, Pierre-Joseph. *The General Idea of the Revolution*, Cosimo Classics, New York, 2007: 1851.

Public Enterprise. *International Centre for Public Enterprises in Developing Countries* 11, nos. 2–3 (June–September 1991).

Purkayastha, Prabir. 'The Crisis of the Power Sector Reforms—Part I'. 25 November 2016. https://www.newsclick.in/crisis-power-sector-reforms-part-i, accessed 18 August 2019.

Purkayastha, Prabir. 'The Crisis of the Power Sector Reforms—Part II'. *Peoples Democracy* XL, no. 49 (4 December 2016). https://www.peoplesdemocracy. in/2016/1204_pd/crisis-power-sector-reforms-—-part-ii, accessed 18 August 2019.

Rajan, Raghuram G., and Luigi Zingales. *Saving Capitalism from the Capitalists.* London: Random House, 2003.

Ranade, Ajit. 'Role of 'Fintech' in Financial Inclusion and New Business Models'. *Economic & Political Weekly* 52, no. 12 (25 March 2017): 125–127.

Rao, S. L., ed. *Reforming State-owned Enterprises.* New Delhi: NCAER, 1996.

Ray, Subhasis, ed. *Corporate Social Responsibility Cases.* Hyderabad: The ICFAI University Press, 2004.

RBI. *RBI Report on Trend and Progress of Banking in India, 2017–18,* 58. https://rbidocs.rbi.org.in/rdocs/Publications/PDFs/0RTP2018_ FE9E97E7AF7024A4B94321734CD76DD4F.PDF

Reddy, S., ed. *Corporate Citizenship: The Social Aspects.* Hyderabad: The ICFAI University Press, 2005.

Rondinelli, Dennis A. 'Can Public Enterprises Contribute to Development? A Critical Assessment and Alternatives for Management Improvement'. In *Public Enterprises: Unresolved Challenges and New Opportunities*, 35–36. New York: United Nations, 2005.

Russo, Costanza A. 'Bank Nationalizations of the 1930s in Italy: The IRI Formula'. *Theoretical Inquiries in Law* 13, no. 2 (2012): 407–428.

Savas, E. S. *Privatization and Public–Private Partnerships.* New Delhi: Affiliated East West Press, 2001.

Sbin Il, Kang. 'The Management Responsibility System in Korean Public Enterprises'. In *Reforming State-owned Enterprises*, edited by S. L. Rao, 205–210. New Delhi: NCAER, 1996.

Sharma, Seema G. 'Corporate Social Responsibility in India: An Overview'. *The International Lawyer* 43, no. 4 (2009): 1515–1533. www.jstor.org/ stable/40708084

Singh, S. K. 'Privatization Debate and Sick Private Sector Undertakings'. In Ruddar Datt, ed. *Bane or Panacea*, Pragati Publications, New Delhi, 1993, p 178.

Song, Ligang. *The Past, Present and Future of SOE Reform in China*, 25 October 2018, http://www.eastasiaforum.org/2018/10/25/the-past-present- and-future-of-soe-reform-in-china/

Soros, George. *The Crisis of Global Capitalism.* London: Little, Brown & Company, 1998.

Spreckley, Freer. *Social Audit: A Management Tool for Co-operative Working.* Sully, Penarth CF64 5SE, United Kingdom: Beechwood College, 1981.

Srinivasa Raghavan, T. C. A. *Dialogue of the Deaf.* New Delhi: Westland Publications, 2017.

Sree Ram, R. 'States will need to walk the talk for discom revival plan success', *Livemint*, 9 November 2015.

The Economic Times. 'Nirmala Sitharaman Announces Big Reforms for Public Sector Banks: Key Highlights'. New Delhi, 30 August 2019. https://economictimes. indiatimes.com/news/economy/policy/nirmala-sitharaman-announces-fresh-reforms-special-agencies-to-monitor-loans-above-rs-250-crore-to-avert-another-nirav-modi-like-situation/articleshow/70909169.cms

The Economist. 'The Long March to Capitalism'. 11 September 1997. https:// www.economist.com/special/1997/09/11/the-long-march-to-capitalism

The Economist. 'End of an IRI'. 22 June 2000. https://www.economist.com/ business/2000/06/22/end-of-an-iri

The Economist. 'Privatisation in Europe Coming Home to Roost'. 27 June 2002. https://www.economist.com/special-report/2002/06/27/coming-home-to-roost

The Economist. 'Bamboo Capitalism'. 3 March 2011. https://www.economist.com/ leaders/2011/03/10/bamboo-capitalism

The Economist. 'Adventures in Capitalism, Special Report on Business in India'. 22 October 2011. https://www.economist.com/special-report/2011/10/22/ adventures-in-capitalism

The Economist. 'Reforming China's State-owned Firms, From SOE to GLC'. 23 November 2013. https://www.economist.com/finance-and-economics/ 2013/11/23/from-soe-to-glc

The Economist. 'Fixing China Inc'. 30 August 2014. https://www.economist.com/ china/2014/08/30/fixing-china-inc

The Economist. 'State Capitalism in the Dock'. 20 November 2014. https://www. economist.com/business/2014/11/20/state-capitalism-in-the-dock

The Economist. 'Reform of China's Ailing State-owned Firms is Emboldening Them'. 22 July 2017. https://www.economist.com/finance-and-economics/2017/07/22/ reform-of-chinas-ailing-state-owned-firms-is-emboldening-them

The Economist. 'Are State-owned Enterprises Reformable?' 18 December 2018. https://www.economist.com/business/2018/03/01/are-chinas-state-giants-reformable

The Times of India. 'PSB Mergers: Technology, HR Synergy, Key Challenges'. New Delhi, 31 August 2019. https://timesofindia.indiatimes.com/busi-ness/india-business/psb-mergers-tech-hr-synergy-key-challenges/article-show/70917156.cms

Toniolo, Gianni, ed. *The Oxford Handbook of the Italian Economy Since Unification.* Oxford: Oxford University Press, 2013.

Trivedi, Prajapati. *A Critique of Public Enterprise Policy.* New Delhi: International Management Publishers, 1992.

UNIDO. *India: Towards Globalisation.* London: UNIDO, Economic Intelligence Unit, 1995.

Warrier, M. G. *India's Decade of Reforms: Reserve Bank of India at Central Stage.* Mumbai: Notion Press, 2014.

World Bank. *Bureaucrats in Business Database*, 1997, 268–71. http://www.worldbank.org/html/prdfp/bib/bibdata.htm, accessed 26 June 2019.

World Bank. *Corporate Governance of Central Public Sector Enterprises*, 19. http://siteresources.worldbank.org/FINANCIALSECTOR/Resources/India_CG_Public_Sector_Enterprises.pdf, accessed 30 July 2019.

Yi-Chong, Xu., ed. *The Political Economy of State-owned Enterprises in China and India.* London: Palgrave Macmillan, 2012.

About the Author

Govind Bhattacharjee is a former civil service officer who retired as Director General from the Office of the Comptroller and Auditor General of India, New Delhi, in 2018. During his long service career spanning more than three decades, he has served in various capacities in India and abroad and completed many important assignments, national and international, including a 4-year tenure as tax adviser to a foreign government. He is currently a Professor of Applied Economics at the Indian Institute of Public Administration, New Delhi.

Dr Bhattacharjee is a prolific writer and columnist with versatile interests in diverse areas ranging from public finance to photography and popular science. He has so far published nine books and numerous research articles in academic journals and national newspapers. He is also a regular contributor to science journals. His latest published books include *Special Category States of India* (a seminal work on the subject) and *GST and Its Aftermath: Is Consumer Really the King*, co-authored by Dr Debasish Bhattacharya (SAGE Publications). He is also the author of an acclaimed trilogy on evolution, *Story of Universe, Story of Evolution* and *Story of Consciousness*.

Index